Mind: An Essay on Human Feeling

Mind: An Essay on Human Feeling

Abridged Edition

Susanne K. Langer

**Abridged by
Gary Van Den Heuvel**

**The Johns Hopkins University Press
Baltimore and London**

© 1988 The Johns Hopkins University Press
All rights reserved
Printed in the United States of America

Original volumes © 1967, 1972, 1982 The Johns Hopkins University Press

The Johns Hopkins University Press
701 West 40th Street
Baltimore, Maryland 21211
The Johns Hopkins Press Ltd., London

The paper used in this publication meets the minimum requirements of American National Standard for Information Sciences—Permanence of Paper for Printed Library Materials, ANSI Z39.48-1984.

Library of Congress Cataloging-in-Publication Data

Langer, Susanne Katherina Knauth, 1895–1985
  Mind : an essay on human feeling.

  Includes index.
    1. Mind and body. 2. Emotions. 3. Psychology—Philosophy. 4. Human evolution—Psychological aspects. 5. Psychology, Comparative. 6. Ethnopsychology. I. Van Den Heuvel, Gary. II. Title.
BF161.L28   1988   128'.2   88-45414
ISBN 0-8018-3705-7 (alk. paper)
ISBN 0-8018-3706-5 (pbk. : alk. paper)

Foreword

When, in the great Sixth Meditation, Descartes undertakes to rethink philosophically how we relate to our bodies, he offers the stunning observation that we are not *in* our bodies the way a pilot is in a ship. Rather, in a sense his official philosophy had not prepared us for, the mind (or "soul") of man is "so tightly bound up and united with [the body] that it forms with it what is almost a single entity." Descartes goes on to say that "feelings of hunger, thirst, pain, and so on are nothing else but confused modes of thinking." Thinking is our essence as human beings, Descartes famously proposed, but when thought is embodied it acquires modes and dimensions it would never have had in its pure state. Imagination, for example, is a bodily intrusion on thought, and feelings in particular are muddled modes of thinking—muddled by the peremptory and distracting demands of our incessantly needful physiological selves.

Susanne Langer's thesis is the exact inverse of this: for her, perhaps because we are never not embodied, feeling is our essence as human beings, and rational thought but one of its more perspicuous modes. The shift of feeling to center stage in our mental life must in her case be explained by the shifting of art to center stage in what she supposed was a philosophy of the human spirit more adequate than her predecessors—with the exception perhaps of Schopenhauer, whom she greatly resembles as a thinker—had thought to give. Art was not given much philosophical weight in Descartes' time, and when he thought about painting at all, Descartes' view was very little advanced beyond Plato's, for whom painting, and art in general, is an occasion of illusion and false belief. It would not have occurred to him that art is a mode of cognition, as Langer argued that it was in her powerful *Philosophy in a New Key,* or that art, as she concludes in *Feeling and Form,* is "the creation of form symbolic of human feelings." The feelings symbolically expressed in the highest achievements of humanity must be considerably more, if her thesis is correct, than "hunger, thirst, pain and so on"; and it was inevitable, given the will-to-system of every original philosopher, that the feelings would become the subject of a specific philosophical investigation. It was no less inevitable, given the immensity of the domain of feeling, as Langer construed it, that the investigation would become a life-work and its result the substance of a vast book.

"I am using the word 'feeling' not in the arbitrarily limited sense of 'pleasure or displeasure,' to which psychologists have often restricted it, but on the contrary in its widest possible sense, i.e., to designate anything that may be felt. In this sense it includes both sensation and emotion—the felt responses of our sense organs to the environment, of our proprioceptive mechanisms to internal changes, and of the organism as a whole to its situation as a whole." So she wrote in an important essay before she embarked on the present work, in which the master thought is that "feeling . . . is the mark of mentality." Mind *is* feeling, and its study "leads down into biological structure and process until its estimation becomes (for the time) impossible, and upward to the purely human sphere known as 'culture.'"

Her sense of philosophical responsibility required Susanne Langer, as she undertook to chart the entire domain bounded by the human body and by human culture, to master all the relevant science over this immense territory. This resulted in an unwieldy book and one, moreover, in hostage to its empirical materials, which in the nature of scientific advance went out of date without her thought going out of date with it. So the supporting material obscures the philosophical architecture, like a dense scaffolding, and renders inaccessible to philosophical scrutiny one of the most audacious philosophical visions of recent times. Whether as architecture it will stand on its own can hardly be answered until it is made available to criticism by philosophers understandably impatient with so intimidating a text. It was an inspiration to undertake an abridged version of a work inadequate in its original execution to the vision it sought symbolically to express.

Arthur C. Danto

A Note on the Abridgment

Any abridgment has its unhappy compromises. To reduce a lengthy original work, one must either jettison much of the detail supporting the main lines of reasoning, as well as the tangential lines that enhance the overall argument, or else eliminate some of the main lines altogether in favor of more fully supporting those that remain. The problems inherent in these choices seem particularly acute in the case of Susanne Langer's essay on mind. Pioneering an interdisciplinary approach in her study of mental phenomena, Langer constructed her argument in literally meant scientific terms. She elaborated upon, and generalized from, an astonishing range of disciplines, fashioning a conceptual structure by which explorations into biological, psychological, social, and ethical domains might "proceed as so many developments of our most exact systematic knowledge."

The cumulative effect of innumerable detailed cuts might be to make the abridgment look more a priori than the original. The robustness of the argument might suffer, too, and some of the life in Langer's work, which to a degree derives from her mooting a variety of opposing ideas, might be lost. But these consequences would be far less regrettable than leaving the impression that Langer failed to adhere to rigorous scientific and scholarly procedures, which she attempted faithfully to follow throughout the treatise.

Despite the shortcomings associated with attenuated detail, eliminating major portions of the original in order to preserve something of the argument's density was not a viable choice. Langer develops her thesis through an internal dialectic that evolves in much the same way as the evolution of mind itself in the natural history she traces. Gaps in the dialectic would destroy the coherence of the whole.

The interdisciplinary range of the essay challenges an abridger to consider carefully specialized versus nonspecialized levels of knowledge. Ideally the argument should maintain the balance achieved in the original between subtlety sufficient to engage the specialist and overviews general enough to keep the nonspecialist from becoming enmired. Langer was that rare scholar with the erudition and creativity to accomplish such a feat. In the original she took ample time to become conversant with specialists' concerns in fields as far apart as aesthetics, ethnology, biochemistry, and mathematics, yet she remained comprehensible to a larger audience. I hope that this balance has not been upset in this edition.

Particularly in Part II of the essay, "The Import of Art," Langer faced a similar dilemma: either to repeat seminal ideas developed in her previous works or to rely on the reader's familiarity with them. In the end she felt that treating her book *Feeling and Form* "as though it were a previous volume of the present book" seemed "the least onerous in a necessary choice of evils." But for that reason the task of abridging Part II proved especially troublesome. Moreover, because Langer generalized from her earlier work on the principles of artistic creation and expression and applied the results to a study of the rise and development of mind, the abridgment of Part II focuses predominantly on cognitive issues. It concentrates on the intuitive processes of the artist in the execution of his or her "Idea."

The prospect of confronting the complete three-volume work must seem daunting to many potential readers, and this abridgment was undertaken with the aim of introducing Langer to a wider audience, with the conviction that her magnum opus deserves a broader readership than it has achieved. Readers who find profit and interest here are urged to turn to the original edition.

Gary Van Den Heuvel

Contents

Foreword   *Arthur C. Danto*   v

A Note on the Abridgment   *Gary Van Den Heuvel*   vii

Introduction   xi

I / *Problems and Principles*

1: Feeling   3
2: Idols of the Laboratory   15
3: Prescientific Knowledge   23

II / *The Import of Art*

4: The Projection of Feeling in Art   35
5: The Artist's Idea   49
6: A Chapter on Abstraction   68
7: On Living Form in Art and Nature   80

III / *Natura Naturans*

  8: The Act Concept and Its Principal Derivatives   103
  9: On Individuation and Involvement   118
10: The Evolution of Acts   134
11: The Growth of Acts   154

IV / *The Great Shift*

12: On Repertoire and Instinct   169
13: Animal Acts and Ambients   183
14: On Animal Values   201
15: Interpretations   214
16: The Specialization of Man   237
17: Symbols and the Evolution of Mind   256
18: Symbols and the Human World   282

V / *The Moral Structure*

19: The Spirit-World   301
20: The Dream of Power   318
21: Dream's Ending: The Tragic Vision   339
22: The Ethnic Balance   354
23: The Breaking   370

VI / *Mathematics and the Reign of Science*

  Foreword   389
24: The Open Ambient   391

  References   401

  Index   407

Introduction

The central problem of the present essay is the nature and origin of the veritable gulf that divides human from animal mentality, in a perfectly continuous course of development of life on earth that has no breaks. For animals have mental functions, but only man has a mind, and a mental life. Some animals are intelligent, but only man can be intellectual. The thesis I am about to develop here is that his departure from the normal pattern of animal mentality is a vast and special evolution of feeling in the hominid stock. This deviation from the general balance of functions usually maintained in the complex advances of life is so rich and so intricately detailed that it affects every aspect of our existence, and adds up to the total qualitative difference which sets human nature apart from the rest of the animal kingdom as a mode of being that is typified by language, culture, morality, and consciousness of life and death.

The main task entailed by the undertaking of a new attack on the problem of mind in the context of natural history, without resort to metaphysical assumptions of non-zoological factors for the explanation of man's peculiar estate, is to keep the biological concept adequate to the greatness of the reality it is supposed to make comprehensible. It is relatively easy to carry a biological principle, discovered in protozoan or even the lowest metazoan forms of life, through to higher and higher levels; but in the course of that advance the principle usually becomes ever less important until its manifestations, though still discoverable, are trivial. The simple taxes, such as phototaxis, which are major principles of behavioral control in lowly organisms, still have some effects in most mammalian species, but generally very little significance. What is interesting at the higher levels is to find the principles which eclipse the ones that are paramount in the little flagellate and still important in the earthworm. Such scientific advances are not quickly made, and our real understanding of life consequently cannot be reached by the hasty generalization of a few biological findings to constitute a doctrinal or methodological "ism." Yet I think the philosopher who gives up hope of constructing adequate interpretive concepts in the face of mere difficulty, slowness and occasional frustration is shirking the assignment automatically given to him by the advance of science.

The assumption of some non-physical ingredient in human life, or even in all life, has a different kind of inadequacy. It does not tend to trivialize the phenomena of mind, but by treating all vital phenomena (and finally, as a rule, non-vital ones as well) as so many appearances of one Essence, it never takes one beyond those appearances to any details of their relations to each other or to the Essence, which is covered by a single word—Mind, Soul, *Lebensgeist*—and is unanalyzable. Oddly, people who find this kind of view "deeper" than a scientific view have no means of delving below the surface manifestations. To understand life means to discover the differences (which are sometimes not sharp, and may even be only statistically appreciable) between organic and inorganic nature, and neither reduce the former to the latter nor, contrariwise, treat the symbolically rich appearances of winds, waters, mountains and heavens as vital phenomena.

The things or events in nature to which vitality is erroneously ascribed are not instances of life, but symbolic images of it. Religious thought, whether savage or civilized, operates primarily with images, by the long-sanctioned "principle of analogy." That this approach to the problems of life and mind does not lead to any exact knowledge need hardly be argued today. Yet there is a value in images quite apart from religious or emotional purposes: they, and they only, originally made us aware of the wholeness and over-all form of entities, acts and facts in the world; and little though we may know it, only an image can hold us to a conception of a total phenomenon, against which we can measure the adequacy of the scientific terms wherewith we describe it. We are actually suffering today from the lack of suitable images of the phenomena that are currently receiving our most ardent scientific attention, the objects of biology and psychology. This lack is blocking the progress of scientifically oriented thought toward systematic insight into the nature of life and especially of mind: the lack of any image of the phenomenon under investigation, whereby to measure the adequacy of theories made on the basis of physical models. In borrowing models from physics, one is apt to borrow its image of reality as well; and that image derives from inorganic nature. It is becoming more and more obvious that it does not fit the forms of life very far above the level of their organic chemistry.

It was the discovery that works of art are images of the forms of feeling, and that their expressiveness can rise to the presentation of all aspects of mind and human personality, which led me to the present undertaking of constructing a biological theory of feeling that should logically lead to an adequate concept of mind, with all that the possession of mind implies. The fact that expressive form is always organic or "living" form made the biological foundation of feeling probable. In the artist's projection, feeling is a heightened form of life; so any work expressing felt tensions, rhythms and activities expresses their unfelt substructure of vital processes, which is the whole of life. If vitality and feeling are conceived in this way there is no sharp break, let alone metaphysical gap, between physical and mental realities, yet there are thresholds where mentality begins, and especially where human mentality transcends the animal level, and mind, *sensu stricto*, emerges.

An image is different from a model, and serves a different purpose. Briefly stated, an image shows how something appears; a model shows how something works. The art symbol, therefore, sets forth in symbolic projection how vital and emotional and intellectual tensions appear, i.e., how they feel. It is this image that gets lost in our psychological laboratories, where models from non-biological sciences and especially from intriguing machinery have taken the field, and permit us to analyze and understand many processes, yet lead us to lose sight of what phenomena we are trying to analyze and understand.

Here the image of feeling created by artists, in every kind of art—plastic, musical, poetic, balletic—serves to hold the reality itself for our labile and volatile memory, as a touchstone to test the scope of our intellectual constructions. And once a measure of adequacy is set up for theories, models of biological processes may be taken from anywhere—billiard balls, crystal formations, hydraulics, or small-current engineering. A philosophy of life guided by the vital image created by artists (all true artists, not only the great and celebrated ones) does not lead one to deprecate physical mechanisms, but to seek more and more of them as the subtlety of the phenomenon increases. The better one knows the forms of feeling the more there is to account for in the literal, sober terms of biological thinking, and the bolder such thinking tends to become.

It is not usual in any intellectual field to give long or strenuous thought to the elements that enter into pure semblances. The techniques of art are different from those of science, and studio thought is not that of the laboratory. This means, of course, that to make art illuminate a field of science one has to be intellectually at home in both realms. Art is just as comprehensible as science, but in its own terms; that is, one can always ask, and usually can determine, how the artistic semblance of life is made and in what it consists. This sort of analysis I undertook in *Feeling and Form*, and have subjected to some generalization in the present book, to make the significant traits of that semblance available as a measure of what we are seeking to describe in the systematic concepts and direct language of science. The great value of a permanent image is that one can resort to it to recover an elusive idea, and reorient one's intellectual progress, when enticing simplifications and reductions have turned it away from its long course into shorter alleys that do not really lead to the same goal. Under the aegis of a holistic symbol, the concept of life builds up even in entirely scientific terms very much like the vital image in art, with no break between somatic and mental events, no "addition" of feeling or consciousness to physical machinery, and especially, no difference of attitude, point of view, working notions, or "logical language" dividing physics and chemistry from biology, or physiology from psychology. No matter how far apart the beginnings of research in various fields may be, their later developments converge, and in advanced stages tend to dovetail, and close like the perfect sutures of our skull, which become well-nigh invisible in ripe old age.

The relationship between the making of the vital image and its use in discovering the significant problems of psychology, morality and related contexts is demonstrated by the fact that Part II of the present essay, dealing wholly with artistic issues, leads directly into Part III, which is biological in matter and method. Similarly, Part IV, concerned with the development of mentality and the "great shift" to human mental life, epitomized in the concept of "mind," rests squarely on the three foundational parts; just as the social theory (Part V) is implicit in Part IV, to which the epistemological ideas of the final part also go back.

The serious philosophical need of our day is a conceptual structure that may be expanded simply by modification (not metaphorical extension) of definitions in literally meant scientific terms, to cover wider fields than physics and chemistry proper, so that the exploration of those problematical domains—biology, with its special areas of genetics, evolution theory, neurology, etc., psychology, already departmentalized into animal and human, normal and abnormal, educational, social, and so on, the complex disciplines, mainly economic, that deal with values, and whatever other fields claim to be future "ologies"—may proceed as so many developments of our most exact systematic knowledge. To construct such concepts is, I believe, the task of professional philosophers; it is too large to be done by other intellectual workers on a basis of incidental insights reflected on in leisure hours. It requires familiarity with philosophical ideas, both general and technical readings in many fields, and logical training to the point of a liberated logical imagination; competences which may be demanded of philosophers, but hardly of anyone else.

Most scientifically minded philosophers, e.g., logical positivists and some phenomenologists, will probably approve these methodological ruminations as a rejection of metaphysics, and many existentialists will condemn them on the same grounds. But I do not reject or deprecate metaphysics; only it seems to me to be the natural end, not the beginning, of philosophical work. A.N. Whitehead once defined metaphysical statements as "the most general statements we can make about reality." Such statements, to be valid, must be built up by processes of generalization of systematic knowledge, not made on a basis of preconceived generality; and being attained stepwise, they are not likely to be ultimate, but only to be our present furthest reaches of thought. Whether this essay attains to any such synoptic view—or even to glimpses of truly metaphysical value—will have to be judged at its conclusion.

One word more: I am making no attempt to prove the sole rightness of my approach to the central problem mooted in the following pages, the problem of conceiving mind as a natural phenomenon, a "natural wonder," and to us the greatest of all such wonders of nature. To convince the contrary-minded is a hopeless task and an arrogant undertaking; they have their reasons for thinking as they do, as I have mine for my way. The foundations of a theory cannot be factually proven right or wrong; they are the terms in which facts are expressed, essentially ways of saying things, that make for special ways of seeing things. The value of a philosophical outlook does not rest on its sole possibility, but on its serviceability, which can only prove itself in the long run, by its multifarious turns, its amenability to mathematical or logical development, its scope and its applicability to factual findings. So, all I am seeking to do is to explain why I hold the views presented in the following pages, and to contribute to the work of more or less likeminded thinkers, dealing with the paradoxes of experience that always harbor the seeds of new conceptions.

S. K. L.
Summer, 1966

I / Problems and Principles

1 / *Feeling*

> **Gefühl ist der mütterliche Ursprung der übrigen Erlebnisarten und ihrer aller ergiebigster Nährboden.**
>
> **Felix Krueger**

Feeling, in the broad sense of whatever is felt in any way, as sensory stimulus or inward tension, pain, emotion or intent, is the mark of mentality. In its most primitive forms it is the forerunner of the phenomena that constitute the subject matter of psychology. Organic activity is not "psychological" unless it terminates, however remotely or indirectly, in something felt. Physiology is different from psychology, not because it deals with different events—the overlapping of the two fields is patent—but because it is not oriented toward the aspects of sensibility, awareness, excitement, gratification or suffering which belong to those events.

The vexing question in the philosophy of the biological sciences is how something called "feelings" enters into the physical (essentially electrochemical) events that compose an animal organism. The presence of such intangible entities, produced by physical (especially nervous) activities, but themselves not physical, not occupying space, though (according to most theorists) they do have temporal character, is hard to negotiate in the systematic frame of anatomy, physiology or the more circumscribed, physiological study of nervous process, neurology. Feelings, considered as entities or items, are anomalies among the scientifically acceptable contents of the skin. Yet they are universally conceived in this paradoxical fashion, and either accepted or rejected as scientific data of just such anomalous character; whether they are to be admitted or not seems to depend on whether one cares more about empirical evidence or about theoretical conceivability.

The fact that we feel the effects of changes in the world about us, and apparently of changes in ourselves, too, and that all such changes are physically describable, but our feeling them is not, presents a genuine philosophical challenge. The oldest line of attack was to treat "the psychical" as a sort of shadow, produced by physical events, but running parallel to them without further systematic value, as an "epiphenomenon." Our apparent reactions to such psychical data as pain could be conceived as induced not by the pain itself, but by its physical counterparts. This theory really amounted to little more than saying that psychical entities lay outside the realm of physiological psychology, which was aspiring to the status of a science. The epiphenomenalists, who found it impossible to imagine a psychical entity pushing a physical one around, still did not question how physical events could have effects of an admittedly non-physical kind, that is, effects categorically incompatible with their causes—and, indeed, with any elements of the system that was supposed to engender them.

But the next generation did question this mystery, and one important and flourishing school, at least, capitalized on the answer, which was that the alleged causes and effects could not possibly belong to the same system, and consequently could not be what they were supposed to be with respect to each other. They must belong to different systems; these systems might bear some relation to each other. At this point, the new semantic orientation which philosophical thinking received from Cassirer, Russell, Whitehead, and most forcibly from Ludwig Wittgenstein's *Tractatus Logico-Philosophicus*, published in 1922, presented a happy hypothesis: the two systems contain equivalent statements of the same natural facts, but in different "logical languages." The system couched in physical terms is greater than that which can be constructed in psychical terms, but the latter is equivalent to a subset of the former.

This interpretation is based on the analogy of alternative systems of mathematics, equally descriptive of physical space, but starting with different "primitive concepts" and "primitive propositions," and therefore taking incommensurable forms. But the analogy is not really sound; for mathematical statements in the most diverse systematic terms are still all equally mathematical, and work with elements of the same metaphysical category, namely, mathematical elements; whereas nerves undergoing electrochemical changes, and contents of consciousness—emotions, sensations, ideas—as elements of different systems, are not of one metaphysical category. This is attested by the fact that they cannot be handled by comparable operations. Their incommensurability is not of the kind that can result from differences of logical formulation, but springs from two different concepts of reality: reality as "primary substance," or "matter," and reality as the "datum," or "immediate experience." Ever since Locke, in the epoch-making *Essay*, set up the latter without abandoning the former, we have had a double standard in psychology. The empiricist concept of mind, modeled on that of the material world, made for two orders of basic elements instead of one, and defied the attempt to relate them causally; for the elements of a model and the corresponding items in the object it represents cannot be causally connected. They are two possible "loci" for one formal pattern, not one "locus" for two different-looking but logically equivalent patterns; the alleged semantic shift from one symbolism to another is really a metaphysical shift from one interpretation of the same abstract system to another. But two interpretations, or "loci," of one form cannot be causally linked in a larger pattern.

On the whole, the relation of mental events—i.e., felt impingements and activities—to the rest of nature is the subject matter of psychology, which demands studies in neurology, genetics, and also careful introspection and clinical protocol analysis for its systematic understanding. If we are indeed speaking two "logical languages" and always tending to mix them, as recent immigrants in a new country mix its spoken language with their native tongue, we must settle on one or the other.

It soon becomes apparent, however, that it is not a choice of language that confronts us. If "psychophysical entities" occur in nature, the vocabulary of natural science must be able to designate them, and to accommodate itself to discourse about them; if this is not possible, it is not our language that is inadequate, but our basic assumptions.

Physicalism and its opposite, the assumption of an immaterial "psychic factor" in living structures, are attempts to define the subject matter of psychology, in the belief that if we knew exactly what we are dealing with we could apply scientific methods to this material and thus find the basic laws which govern it, as physicists have done in their proper realm.

But it may be questioned whether this is really a profitable approach. The precise definition of the matter and scope of a science is more likely to become accessible in the course of intimate study, as more and more becomes known about it, than to be its first step. Physics did not begin with a clear concept of "matter"—that concept is still changing rapidly with the advance of knowledge—but with the working notions of space, time and mass, in terms of which the observed facts of the material world could be formulated. What we need for a science of mind is not so much a definitive concept of mind, as a conceptual frame in which to lodge our observations of mental phenomena. The field of inquiry should then define itself in various ways, by stages; but at every stage it should articulate with the rest of our scientific thinking, and especially with those fields which lie adjacent to it, biology on the one hand and ethnology on the other. It is our working vocabulary that has to be coherent and adequate. So far, it has never met one of these requirements without sacrificing the other.

This dilemma is clearly illustrated by the fact that people who handle psychological problems not under the conditions of the laboratory, where problems may be (and are) cut down to fit the capacity of the apparatus and the sanctioned procedures, but under the pressure of necessity—psychiatrists, neurologists, therapists of all schools, who deal with human behavior in crisis—can neither use the notions of non-material "psychical factors" among material ones, acts occupying a zero length of time, or "functions" which are not processes, nor can they abide by the prohibitions and dictates of behaviorism. They cannot forgo the use of introspective data, fantasies, dreams and alleged memories which cannot be empirically checked; above all, they have to deal with feeling, no matter how the admission of its existence confuses their philosophical notions.

One thing every psychiatrist and clinical neurologist knows is that neither the principle of causal connection which we find in physical nature, nor the phenomena properly called "mental"—feeling, thought, sensation, dream, etc.—can be ruled out of his domain. Our so-called "objective" set of data—the elements of physics, relatively concrete or abstract, molar, molecular or atomic, according to the level of the physicist's problem—seems to fall naturally into a logical system of almost inexhaustible complexity without more than passing and minor loss of coherence. But "subjective" data do not. Whichever way you arrange such items, they do not compose a universe of discourse in which they can be operationally connected with each other, and still less a class of non-physical events to be intercalated among physical ones. So, presumably, our treatment of "subjective" data as elements categorically distinct from physical elements, but to be related to the latter, is untenable. Something is profoundly wrong with our conception of "the psychical"; some very fundamental notions need to be reformulated to give us more acceptable meanings, negotiable and illuminating, for the moot words "psychical," "conscious," "thought," "feeling" and others of the same shady character that fall under the present taboo in respectable laboratory parlance.

The basic misconception is, I think, the assumption of feelings (sensations, emotions, etc.) as items or entities of *any* kind, whether produced by physiological processes, or independent of them, non-physical "genuine functions" of a "life" or "soul" casually "making use of" bodily mechanisms. This is a genuine metaphysical fallacy; yet those theorists who have tried to treat it as semantic had an essentially right idea, for the conception of such psychical "factors," which is expressed in the question of how something called "feeling" can enter into physical processes, probably is essentially of linguistic origin. The fact that we call something by a name, such as "feeling," makes it seem like a kind of thing, an ingredient in nature or a product. But "feel" is a verb, and to say that what is felt is "a feeling" may be one of those deceptive common-sense suppositions inherent in the structure of language which semanticists are constantly bringing to our attention. "Feeling" is a verbal noun—a noun made out of a verb, that psychologically makes an entity out of a process. To feel is to do something, not to have something; but to "have" a feeling, a sensation, a fear or an idea, seems a perfectly equivalent way of conceiving the fact expressed by the verb. The supposed equivalence is given in the syntax that governs our intellectual processes. It is, perhaps, not as purely a product of language as current doctrines make it appear; there is a deeper reason, of course, why language (despite considerable variations among different tongues in this respect) tends to hypostatize acts as entities. That reason should become apparent in a later chapter. Just now the effect, not the source, of the reifying tendency of our grammar presents the philosophical challenge. It is the concept of feeling—the modulus of psychological conception—that I propose to reconstruct.

In the first place, the phenomenon usually described as "a feeling" is really that an organism feels something, i.e., something is felt. What is felt is a process, perhaps a large complex of processes, within the organism. Some vital activities of great complexity and high intensity, usually (perhaps always) involving nervous tissue, are felt; being felt is a phase of the process itself. A phase is a mode of appearance, and not an added factor. Ordinarily we know things in different phases as "the same"—ice, water and steam, for instance—but sometimes a very distinctive phase seems like a product. When iron is heated to a critical degree it becomes red; yet its redness is not a new entity which must have gone somewhere else when it is no longer in the iron. It was a phase of the iron itself, at high temperature. Heat is not a thing, but an agitation, measurable in degrees, not amounts, and when the iron is no longer hot there will be comparable degrees of heat, or of some equivalent process or sum total of processes, outside the iron. But the redness simply disappears; it was a phase of heated iron.

A striking demonstration of how constituents of one kind, brought together in a special combination, may seem to produce a new ingredient which is, however, a phase of their own occurrence, is given by Rutherford Boyd in the design shown (Fig. 1-1).

Unlike many other aspects of vital processes, which are propagated outward with the processes themselves beyond the organism as effects on its surroundings, the phase of being felt is strictly intraorganic, wherever any activities of life attain it. It is an appearance which organic functions have only for the organism in which they occur, if they have it at all. Millions of processes—the whole dynamic rounds of metabo-

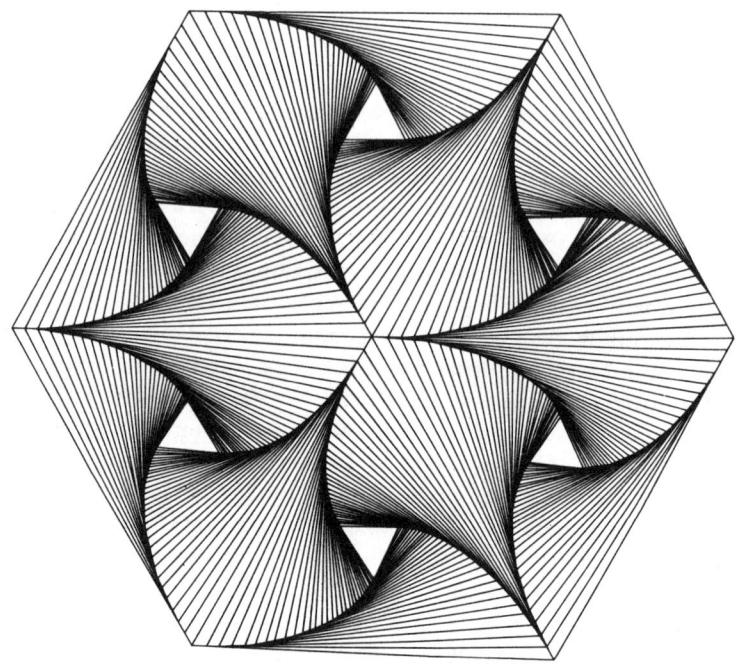

Figure 1–1. Mystery of the Vanishing Triangle. (Design by Rutherford Boyd, "Mathematical Ideas in Design," *Scripta Mathematica* 14 [1948]. Reprinted with permission of Yeshiva University.)

lism, digestion, circulation and endocrine action—are normally not felt. One may say that some activities, especially nervous ones, above a certain (probably fluctuating) limen of intensity, enter into "psychical phase." This is the phase of being felt. It may develop suddenly, with great distinctness of quality, location and value-character, as in response to a painful stimulus; or, only with less precise location in the organism, like a shock of terror; or a deeply engendered process may go gradually, perhaps barely, into a psychical phase of vague awareness—come and gone—a sense of weariness or a fleeting emotive moment. The normal substrate of "feeling tone," from which the more acute tensions build up into specific experiences, is probably a dynamic pattern of nervous activities playing freely across the limen of sentience.

It is this transiency and general lability of the psychical phase that accounts for the importance of preconscious processes in the construction of such elaborate phenomena as ideas, intentions, images and fantasies, and makes it not only reasonable but obvious that they are rooted in the fabric of totally unfelt activities which Freud reified with the substantive term, "the Unconscious." There may be a describable system of functions that terminate in felt events, i.e., something that could fairly be called "the unconscious system"; but so far I do not think we have found more than a few lines of functional development, which may or may not belong to a single system. In this respect the theoretical basis of classical psychoanalysis is overassumptive. But the inconceivability with which it has often been charged stems from a philosophical error that is remediable—the belief that desires, ideas or emotions cannot be psychologically engendered and psychologically modified if they are essentially physiological processes, so that physiological psychology and "dynamic" psychology are rival sciences. As soon as feeling is regarded as a phase of a physiological process instead of a product (perhaps a by-product) of it, a new entity metaphysically different from it, the paradox of the physical and psychical disappears; for the thesis I hope to substantiate here is that the entire psychological field—including human conception, responsible action, rationality, knowledge—is a vast and branching development of feeling. This does not mean that all reasoning is "really" rationalization, all judgment "really" emotional, all moral intentions specious, and so on. There is not some primitive form of feeling which is its "real" form, any more than a bird is "really" an egg or water is "really" a vapor. Emotion as we know it is not even a primitive form of feeling; it is not a rudimentary nervous process, such as fairly simple organisms might exhibit, in a psychical phase. Human emotion is phylogenetically a high development from simpler processes, and reason is another one; human mentality is an unsurveyably complex dynamism of their interactions with each other, and with several further specialized forms of cerebral activity, implicating the whole organic substructure. Our knowledge of neural functions is as yet very scrappy and tentative, but I think research has reached the point at which the understanding of these specializations becomes a scientific target rather than a piece of science fiction.

As there are many distinct nervous processes, some originating at the periphery of the central nervous system, others within it, especially in its core which is the brain, so there are many ways in which activities may be felt. The most important distinction within the realm of feeling is between what is *felt as impact* and what is *felt as autogenic action*, or to alternately state the latter, *felt as action*. The existence of these two fundamental modes of feeling rests on the nature of vitality itself. The pattern of stimulus and response, the guiding principle of most psychological techniques, especially in the laboratory of the animal psychologist, is a simplified schema derived from that natural division.

There will be much more to say about this; for the present we may consider the two modes of feeling as given typically with the fundamental relation of living systems to the surrounding world. A closer look at that relation may serve to explain the difference between these two chief ways of feeling organic processes. Just now, however, we are concerned with the general and patent fact that an animal organism is always under the influence of the world around it, and in its turn always affects at least its immediate neighborhood, if only by using up oxygen, exhaling carbon dioxide, radiating warmth, even when it is not eating anything or excreting its waste.

One trait of that interchange, however, is rarely if ever explicitly stated, perhaps because it is so familiar that it seems self-evident to every biologist: it is the asymmetrical character of the interaction. The exchange is not strictly speaking a relation between two systems, for the environment is not a system in the same sense as the organism is. It is not so much "a complex of activating agencies" as a conglomerate of them, some in short supply, some unlimited, but not systematically organized among themselves, nor meted out with any respect for the organism's uses. There may be barely enough food, and a thousand times more than enough air, water and light; and the surrounding space will usually take up excretions and exudations to any degree. The exchange of matter is, therefore, not really a mutual transaction, but one in which the inanimate world has the gross control, while the fine control rests with the organism. This asymmetry of the two factors in the many-sided, continuous pattern of exchanges makes the organism a center of activity. The environment may also enfold other organisms, but to the organism in point they are parts, though perhaps rather special parts, of the surrounding world. In extreme cases the whole relevant environment may be another organism, e.g., for parasites living in the bodies of other creatures. All divisions we can make are somewhat fluid, and nearly all general rules have exceptions.

An organism is a continuous dynamism, a pattern of activity, basically electrochemical, but capable also of large, concerted forms of action with further principles of organization. Its round of functions is continuous, and every constituent action in it, every chemical transformation, osmotic exchange, contraction of muscle, discharge from glands, etc., is more or less finely adjusted to the immediate situation created by the environment. Many of these activities are internal to the organism, so the direct environment of the tissues engaged in them is composed of other parts and products of the same system. Environment is, in fact, a relative concept. The active structures in any metazoic organism are incredibly detailed, and its activities are usually composed of smaller and smaller complete cycles of action, in subordinate but functionally distinct structures. Each active unit, be it a single cell or an integral complex, has its direct environment as long as it exists, i.e., performs. All vital action, whether of the organism as a whole in its surroundings or of an organ internal to it, is interaction, transaction, in which the functioning unit has the fine control, and the medium in which it maintains itself has the gross control; that is, the latter determines what is given, the former what is taken.

The provision, usually not precisely measured for the needs of the agent, comes as impact, and has to be dealt with; as it makes action possible it also makes it compelling. The organism, *in toto* and in every one of its parts, has to "keep going." Every act of a living unit transforms its situation and necessitates action under the impact of that new development as well as of any fortuitous changes coinciding with it. This is what Whitehead called the "creative advance" of nature. It is certainly the pattern of life.

The structure of every entire organism reflects this basic functional law: whether it be a vertebrate covered with skin or a unicellular creature with a semi-permeable cell wall one or two molecules thick, its periphery is adapted to the exigencies of contact with the plenum of external events. The organism may or may not react with far-reaching effects upon its surroundings, but in any case it presents some mechanism which filters the impinging influences, letting only some substances or some propagated vibratory patterns (temperature, light rays, etc.) go through it for the rest of the body to meet. The periphery is specialized to handle emergencies. Its activities are normally of an improvisational character, adaptable, quickly responsive. If they rise to the level of being felt they are generally felt as impact; that is, without preliminaries, presenting themselves almost instantly, and with the semblance of coming inward from outside. This last aspect has generally not been recognized. Theories of perception which assume that feeling occurs only at the inner terminus of nervous activity, and in doing so does not express transitional dynamic pattern, have therefore to meet the problem of how percepts are "projected" into an outer world instead of seeming to be inside us, like thoughts.

Sensations are a class of felt activities. The special organs of sense that develop as permanent structures in all but the lowest animal forms are peripheral areas highly elaborated to deal with impingements which the rest of the body covering filters out entirely, or admits in a general way that creates no elaborate pattern, and which often activate no organic processes which have any special psychical phase. Our sense organs are "processing" mechanisms, and also peripheral outposts protecting the active deeper parts which are less capable of improvising responses. The high and varied elaboration of those receptor organs causes their activities to be felt not only as impact, but as qualitatively different kinds of impact, the incommensurable deliverances of sight, hearing, smell, taste and the various tactile senses, respectively. Sensations arise from within the body, too, but more typically the sources of sensations are peripheral; and they always carry, however vaguely, some indication of an impingement met and dealt with. Taken together they constitute a major department of feeling, sensibility.

The counterpart to this essentially centripetal action springs from the constant functioning of the central nervous system itself (or whatever precedes it in the lower forms of life). An act engendered predominantly from within, such as the "firing" of an assembly of neurons as a result of organic processes without specific external stimulation, if it is felt, is differently felt from a response to environmental impact. Its psychic phase begins gradually, rising from a background of general body feeling and a texture of emotive tensions so closely woven that the separate strands of process in it are not distinct, but compose a "mental state," which includes the body feeling as a constant somatic factor, usually very near the threshold of the psychical phase, playing across it. Against this background, more specifically articulated acts are felt as envisagements, intentions, cogitations, insights, decisions, etc. They are felt to arise without the attack of a sensory impact, and to proceed from within us toward their termination in expression, which may be muscular motion, or the forming of an image apparent in the space between our eyes and their focus point, or an act of tonal imagination proceeding still more vaguely toward the outside world. Their neural paths are probably centrifugal from areas of most intense activity in the higher parts of the brain, stimulated from other cortical centers and from deeper centers, but not directly from the peripheral organs of perception. Since they are not acts of coping with constantly and ineluctably impinging forces, their structure is organic, developmental, rather than reactive and improvisational. Perhaps that is why they are felt more intimately as our own actions. Their rhythm is recognizable as vital rhythm. They are felt as autogenous action springing from the central parts of the organism, rooted in its emotivity; while perceptions are largely felt as impact, starting from the organism's peripheral organs as external forces play on its gamut of sensibility.

If one conceives the phenomenon of being felt as a phase of vital processes, in which the living tissue (probably the nerve or a neuronal assembly) feels its activity, the problem of how nerve impulse can be "converted" into thought and thought into nerve impulse becomes a different sort of problem. The question is not of how a physical process can be transformed into something non-physical in a physical system, but how the phase of being felt is attained, and how the process may pass into unfelt phases again, and furthermore how an organic process in "psychical phase" may induce others which are unfelt. Such problems, even if far from solved, are at least coherent with the rest of biological inquiry and logically capable of solution.

Conditions of consciousness are certainly plausible enough if we view the mental phenomenon not as a product of neural impulses, but as an aspect of their occurrence. We might compare the phenomenon of being felt to a less problematical one in everybody's experience. When a tree leans over a quiet surface of water, its visible form is reflected by the surface under normal conditions of daylight. The tree's being reflected is an aspect of the whole natural situation; a complex situation, but of frequent occurrence. There is no ontologically real but non-physical "inverted tree" produced by the physical interaction of the upright tree and the water. With many objects and mirrors we can produce reflections at will, and place ourselves to see or not see them at will. We can turn the rear-view mirror in a car to abolish the reflection of lights following us, or shift our own position so as not to receive it. Also, in using the mirror for backing up, we learn that right and left in kinetic space are represented by their opposites in the peculiar visible phase of the mirror surface caused by the situation; but there are no "mirror things" intercalated among the objects we negotiate as we back into a space. Yet the reflection is a genuine occurrence, a phase of the mirror, and, indeed, the only phase that makes the mirror important to us.

The changed concept of feeling, which calls almost at once for the distinction between a sense of autogenic action and a sense of impact, roughly establishing the realms of emotivity and sensibility, suggests a corresponding conceptual change with regard to the terms "subjective" and "objective." These terms are derived, of course, from the traditional dichotomy of subject and object, perceiver and perceived. In the context of organic activities here assumed, that dichotomy is not simply given, and whether it can and should be theoretically constructed remains to be seen. Yet "subject" and "object" do mean something, whether their usual intention is acceptable or not; they are important words, especially in such derivative forms as "subjective" and "objective," "subjectified" and "objectified." Sometimes, in making a systematic framework, it is more profitable to define terms in a special form than to start with the grammatically normal; and it is the adjectival form that will be defined here. By "subjective" I mean whatever is felt as action, and by "objective" whatever is felt as impact. Cognate meanings will be logically derived as they become relevant.

The first consequence of these definitions is that one does not find a class of objective things, with which the scientist is concerned in his laboratory, and another class of subjective things which are scientifically embarrassing. Any felt process may be subjective at one time and objective at another, and contain shifting elements of both kinds all the time. "Subjective" and "objective" denote functional properties. Since organic functions have dynamic forms, which they build up and melt down again constantly, their identifiable properties are transient. The properties in question are two possible modes of feeling, i.e., of psychical phases of activity.

Feeling stands, in fact, in the midst of that vast biological field which lies between the lowliest organic activities and the rise of mind. It is not an adjunct to natural events, but a turning point in them. There must have been several such turning points in the evolution of our world: the rise of life on earth, perhaps the beginning of irreversible speciation, the first true animal form, the first shadows of a "psychical phase" in some very active animal, and the first genuinely symbolic utterances, speech, which marked the advent of man. It is with the dawn of feeling that the domain of biology yields the less extensive, but still inestimably great domain of psychology.

That is why I make feeling the starting-point of a philosophy of mind. The study of feeling—its sources, its forms, its complexities—leads one down into biological structure and process until its estimation becomes (for the time) impossible, and upward to the purely human sphere known as "culture." It is still what we feel, and everything that can be felt, that is important. The same concept that raises problems of natural science takes one just as surely into humanistic ones; the differences between them are obvious, but not problematical. Society, law and institutions create their own issues to be appropriately resolved. An adequate concept of "psychical" should serve all psychological purposes.

2 / Idols of the Laboratory

> When half-gods go, The Gods arrive.
>
> R. W. Emerson

The social sciences, originally projected by Auguste Comte in his sanguine vision of a world reformed and rationally guided by science, have finally come into recognized existence in the twentieth century. They have had a different history from the natural sciences which had a free and unsupervised beginning; and the most productive thinkers of those maverick days ventured on some wild flights of fancy. Not so the founders of the "young sciences" today. They began their work under the tutelage of physics, and—like young ones emulating their elders—they have striven first and hardest for the signs of sophistication; technical language, the laboratory atmosphere, apparatus, graphs, charts and statistical averages.

This ambition has had some unfortunate effects on a discipline for which the procedures of classical physics, for instance, the experimental techniques of Galileo, may not be suitable at all. For decades, therefore, the literature of those new disciplines, especially of psychology, has dealt in large measure with so-called "approaches," not to some baffling and challenging facts, but to all the facts at once, the science itself. Every theoretical thinker in the field set out to define and circumscribe this science and propose a strict proper method for its pursuit, until a rotating program committee seems to have had the lion's share in the whole venture.

In proportion to the effort spent on all these "approaches," the harvest of interesting facts and systematic ideas remains meager (which, of course, is not to say that there are none). By comparison with other biological sciences, both the method and the findings of laboratory psychology look extremely simple. Their essential simplicity is sometimes masked by a technical vocabulary, and even an algorithmic-looking form of statement; but when we come to the interpretation of the "variables," their values prove to be such elements as "somebody," "some fact," "some object," without any formal distinction between a person, a fact and an object, which would make it logically not possible to interchange them, as it would have to be to assure the formula any sense.

To speak of "hominid individuals" instead of "persons" and of "verbal behavior" instead of "speech," of a clinical interview as a "stimulus to verbal behavior," and so on, is to translate ordinary thinking into a jargon for literary presentation. Jargon is language which is more technical than the ideas it serves to express. Genuine scientific language grows up with the increasing abstractness or extraordinary precision of concepts used in a special field of work, and is therefore always just adequate to express those concepts. It is not deliberately fixed (with the exception of Latin nomenclature in taxonomy), but may become completely technical if scientific thought moves very far away from ordinary thought. Jargon, on the other hand, is a special vocabulary for common-sense ideation. It is an Idol of the Laboratory, and its worship is inimical to genuine abstractive thinking. A sociologist or psychologist who will spend his time translating familiar facts into professionally approved language must surely have more academic conscience than curiosity about strange or obscure phenomena. We are often told that such exercises are necessary because the behavioral sciences are young, and must establish their formal rules, vocabularies and procedures. Not long ago chemistry was young, too; its modern history only began with Lavoisier, who died in the Reign of Terror. But did any chemist ever write an article to show how a recipe for fudge could be stated in proper chemical form, i.e., without any household words?

Another source of idolatry is the cultivation of a prescriptive methodology, which lays down in advance the general lines of procedure—and therewith the lines of thought—to be followed. According to its canons all laboratory procedures must be isolated, controllable, repeatable and above all "objective." The first three requirements only restrict experimentation to simple responses, more significant in animal psychology than in human contexts; but the fourth is a demon. The Idol of Objectivity requires its servitors to distort the data of human psychology into an animal image in order to handle them by the methods that fit speechless mentality. It requires the omission of all activities of central origin, which are felt as such, and are normally accessible to research in human psychology through the powerful instrument of language. The result is a laboratory exhibit of "behavior" that is much more artificial than any instrumentally deformed object, because its deformation is not calculated and discounted as the effect of an instrument. Language, in such a situation, does not belong entirely to the behavioral exhibit; the act of using it is a part of the psychological material, which may or may not be relevant to the intended observation, and so are the subjective phenomena to which it refers; but the semantic function of the words is part of the perceptual medium, the instrument of observation. The speaker, who is the experimental subject, automatically participates in the work; both he and the experimenter handle the semantic instrument. If his observation or power to report is inadequate the instrument is crude. Many vitally important data have to be treated as insecure because the experimental conditions did not permit a definitive view. This is as true of protocol statements as it is of one-way screens, tachistoscopes and galvanometers.

The relativity of the subject-object division, which lets that division come now at the eye, now at the lens of the microscope, or—in psychological observation—now between the experimenter and the experimental subject, now between the latter's report and its matter of reference, is one of the serious instrumental problems for scientific psychology. But it is more than that; it is one of the most interesting phenomena characterizing human material itself. Its extraordinary interest and its exact significance will become apparent later, in connection with the theory of symbolic activity in general. The fact that I wish to point out here is that to make a fetish of "objectivity" means to assume, in the first place, that some phenomena are intrinsically objective and others intrinsically subjective so that they can be accepted or rejected accordingly; it is one of the tacit assumptions which have frustrating metaphysical implications, and lead some great biologists and pathologists to accept strange philosophical doctrines as the only possible supports for those assumptions. In the second place it means that problems of the relationships between subjective and objective factors in mental activity are removed from the psychologist's proper sphere of investigation. These relationships, and the terms that develop in conjunction with them—symbols, concepts, fantasy, religion, speculation, selfhood and morality—really present the most exciting and important topics of the science of mind, the researches toward which all animal studies are oriented as indirect or auxiliary moves. To exclude such relationships for the sake of sure and safe laboratory methods is to stifle human psychology in embryo.

The emulation of physical science naturally leads to premature attempts at mathematical expression of known or presumed regularities in behavior. In the interest of the quickest possible mathematization the observed facts may be pared down to a few overt actions in situations which elicit the simplest and most invariable movements. An almost paradigmatic instance of this practice is the treating of stimulus and response in a psychological organism as a direct parallel to input and output in a machine and investigating that output without reference to intervening mechanisms within the organism. But engineers do, in fact, understand the intervening machine, and their correlations of input and output would have no scientific value—though, perhaps, some limited practical use—if they did not. The "direct parallel" presupposes, furthermore, that input and output are known, and that organisms are linear systems—that is, that each stimulus element will keep its identity through its transformation from input to output, so that the total response will be the arithmetical sum of those transformed stimuli. Unfortunately, however, this does not seem to be the case.

There are many scholars in the programmatic sciences, sociologists as well as psychologists, whose immediate objective is to "mathematicize" their findings as fast as they are found and even faster, evidently feeling that the dress of mathematics bestows scientific dignity no matter how or where it is worn. The most obvious and therefore most popular means to this end is the use of statistics, often based on as few as a score of cases, if not fewer. Another, more imaginative, practice is to apply the terminology of higher mathematics—relativity, quantum theory, topology, doctrine of aggregates—to vaguely conceived behavioral items, which seem thereby to be quantified and established.

In a sober but trenchant critical article (1944), I. D. London has shown even so influential and important a venture as Kurt Lewin's "field theory" to be only verbally modeled on the field theory of relativity physics, since Lewin's key concept, force, has no analogue in real topology, and his psychological "field" conforms to no known geometry. The result is that Lewin can use none of the powerful principles of substitution that make topology reveal new facts in physical science.

Here, I think, we have the central and fatal failing of all the projected sciences of mind and conduct: the actual machinery that their sponsors and pioneers have rented does not work when their "conceptualized phenomena" are fed into it. It cannot process the interpretations that are supposed to be legitimate proxies for its abstract elements. Lewin, for instance, designates chewing and swallowing as "regions." But can such terms be generalized so that it is entirely a matter of formal manipulation to prove that they are or are not identical, that they can or cannot be simultaneous, or what is the product of either of them if combined with sneezing?

In many cases, the mathematization of behavior is the work (or better, the dream) of non-mathematicians to whom single expressions or propositions encountered in an alien field look analogous to some conceptual constructs of their own. The analogy would soon break down if they could carry their interpretation through all the algorithmic possibilities of a formal system. There are exceptions to this general rule but the applications in every case require such simplifications of the facts that the approximation of the instance to the form is very tenuous.

So the intellectual results are disappointing. Such a powerful machinery should make the behavioral sciences rocket to success. Instead of that, it has so far left psychology, sociology, anthropology, and ethical theories just where they were before. The reason for the failure of even well-equipped expeditions into the mathematical realm is that abstract concepts borrowed from physics, such as units of matter—even with the adjective "living" to qualify them—and their motions, do not lend themselves readily to the expression of psychologically important problems. The aim of the work is to make mathematics applicable to a given material. In genuinely scientific research the aim is to explain events (their prediction is primarily a check on the validity of the explanatory hypothesis), and mathematics is not employed unless it is needed; but it is quickly needed, because the terms in which natural processes are conceived were originally abstracted from the exemplifying concrete system by observation of those processes themselves, and may therefore be elaborated and manipulated to any extent without danger of absurdity or of only trivial meaning. They are not descriptive categories under which things and their accidents are ranged, but abstract concepts which must be manipulated in order to describe anything at all. Newton's famous apple would not have revealed any astronomical relations if he had only relegated its falling to a general category of "descending" (John Dewey would have had him say "descendings"), and treated its fall from a tree to earth as a special case of "descending," to be subsequently differentiated from that of a cat's jumping voluntarily off a wall, etc. The relation of two masses, i.e., of apple and earth, respectively, as masses, in terms of which Newton described the fall, was not a visible relationship at all; for neither the quantitative proportion nor the mutual attraction of the two objects was a sensible aspect of the event he witnessed. Were it not for the concepts of mass and gravitation, which do not themselves denote any natural objects or events, but are purely conceptual terms, there would be no similarity at all between the fall of an apple to the ground and the motion of the moon round the earth—let alone the swing of the tides under the influence of moon and sun.

The terms of the behavioral sciences, on the other hand, are not abstractions, but concrete elements about which general statements are made. There is no justification for "postulate sets," "theorems," or other systematic forms unless one operates with abstract concepts in terms of which rats, food, boxes, lights, shocks and all other relevant factors may be described and distinguished, treated as members of classes established by systematically derived defining functions, and related one to another (or to others) purely as such. But for this sort of systematization the basic concepts are lacking. The "systems," consequently, are very simple codifications of informally conceived facts, some of which have measurable features: repetitious phases, changing tempo, concomitantly controllable factors. Even the more ambitious "factoring" of human behavior is as yet only a taxonomic approach to that immense subject, with somewhat sharpened and refined common-sense principles of classification, which may lead analysis further than ordinary observation. But all such treatments are far from any mathematically exact science.

The deceptiveness of simple achievements as models for highly complex ventures becomes apparent when one follows rather closely the processes of generalizing, extending, or otherwise transferring the "laws" found in the animal laboratory to human life. That liberalization is not effected by generalization, but by metaphorical use. Generalization widens the denotation of a term without changing its connotation, as a trade name denoting a specific manufacturer's product sometimes becomes the common name for this sort of product after the registration lapses; but metaphorical use changes the connotation of terms in an unspecified though often extreme fashion, and consequently makes their denotation indefinite. The moot problem of what verbal element is paralleled by what empirical datum is, however, not the most serious result of the metaphorical practice; even more serious is the fact that the liberalized concepts cannot be related in the same ways as the literally designated ones nor, indeed, in any systematic ways. Analogies are essential to thought, but they cannot be automatically used to pass from known to unknown domains of nature.

It is interesting to find that some excellent experimenting psychologists are aware of this and other fallacies in the many advocated "approaches" to their projected science, including the danger that too much programmatic steering of research may be detrimental to its actual progress. They seem, in fact, to be recognizing the Idols of the Laboratory one by one—Physicalism, Methodology, Jargon, Objectivity, Mathematization—and taking leave of them, sometimes with declarations that they never worshiped them anyway, sometimes with apparent regret and apology.

We are faced with the real fiasco to which the programmatic sciences have come—that in worshipping their picture of Science they have rarely come to grips with anything important in their own domains. One notable exception is the quiet work done in the fields of sensory psychology. Another exception is the progressive research going on in psychoneurology. But psychology proper, under the rubric of "the science of behavior," instead of slowly extending such work to its limits and letting it rest, for the present, at those points, has by-passed it and imitated more finished masterpieces instead of chipping away at its own.

All these insights and changed attitudes are entirely to the good, yet in themselves they are not enough to launch an intellectual enterprise. The basic need is for powerful and freely negotiable concepts in terms of which to handle the central subject matter, which is human mentality—properly, and not foolishly, called "mind." But such concepts are still missing, or at least unrecognized; and as long as they are missing there will always be some primitive, scientifically useless entity—soul, entelechy, metaphysical Subject or vital essence—ready to slide into the vacant place to work havoc with the incipient science. This ever-present danger creates a constant desire on the part of psychologists to fill that empty place somehow with borrowed concepts, or at worst to shut it off with a verbal screen such as the "physicalist" vocabulary of behaviorism. Meanwhile, however, our understanding of mental phenomena does not progress except by inches. We have reached a point at which a sounder substructure is required, and the philosophical work of construing the facts in logically negotiable, intellectually fertile ways is imperative.

If a philosophical theory of mind can serve the mental and social sciences at all, its effects in those fields of research are likely to be radical. It is not a matter of giving new definitions to old terms and going on with former lines of thought and experimentation. It means going back to the beginnings of thought about mental phenomena and starting with different ideas, different expectations, without concern for experiments or statistics or formalized language; if the concept of mind is philosophically sound it should serve to define mental processes in ways that make one suspect connections and derivations, and should lead from odd facts to bold hypotheses to verification by any possible means. The experiments should suggest themselves automatically, and techniques and language grow up apace. But this might take a generation, and meanwhile we would have no science of mind, only notions to work with.

The state of having turbulent notions about things that seem to belong together, although in some unknown way, is a prescientific state, a sort of intellectual gestation period. This state the "behavioral sciences" have sought to skip, hoping to learn its lessons by the way, from their elders. The result is that they have modeled themselves on physics, which is not a suitable model. Any science is likely to merge ultimately with physics, as chemistry has done, but only in a mature stage; its early phases have to be its own, and the earliest is that of philosophical imagination and adventure.

It is even conceivable that the study of mental and social phenomena will never be "natural science" in the familiar sense at all, but will always be more akin to history, which is a highly developed discipline, but not an abstractly codified one. There may be a slowly accruing core of scientific fact which is relevant to understanding mind, and which will ultimately anchor psychology quite firmly in biology without ever making its advanced problems laboratory affairs. Sociology might be destined to develop to a high technical degree, but more in the manner of jurisprudence than in that of chemistry or physics. Were that, perchance, the case, then the commitment to "scientific method" could be seriously inimical to any advance of knowledge in such important but essentially humanistic pursuits.

Whatever the future, let us not jeopardize it any further by denying to our researches the free play which belongs to brain children as well as to animal and human infants. The philosophical phase we have missed lies at the very inception of research; if we would build a sounder frame of psychological, ethical and social theory, it is to that incunabular stage that we must return.

3 / *Prescientific Knowledge*

> **Nelle cose confuse l'ingenio si desta à nove inventioni.**
>
> **Leonardo da Vinci**

To start the study of mind with an inquiry into the nature of feeling is to start *in medias res*. Feeling includes the sensibility of very low animals and the whole realm of human awareness and thought, the sense of absurdity, the sense of justice, the perception of meaning, as well as emotion and sensation. The advantage of starting from an intermediate point is that the scope of one's inquiry may expand in both directions. There is no need of assuming that all organic responses are felt; there is some evidence that even fairly high human cerebral functions, guiding behavior and influencing conscious mental activities, may take place without entering into a psychical phase themselves. A reasonable judgment about what animals feel or do not feel is not based only on analogy between their behavior and our own, but also on the phylogenetic relationship between their activities and those human ones which rise to feeling (this is a point the humanizers of "mechanical brains" and cybernetic models ignore). The substructure of psychology is part and parcel of its subject matter, though it may be pure chemistry. In the opposite direction lie complexities of perception and conception, emotional sensitivity and selectivity, logical and semantic intuition, abstraction, communication, and cognition—the phenomena we ultimately want to describe, understand, and relate systematically.

We all have direct knowledge of feeling—"knowledge by acquaintance," as Bertrand Russell has called it—but very little of what he termed "knowledge by description," or knowledge *about* feeling. Science is essentially "knowledge about." What is more, a science does not arise directly from pure experience: such experience is a backward check on ideas that have long become general, and in their generality fairly exact. That is to say, every science arises from prescientific knowledge about its subject matter, empirical and haphazard, but developed by practice to considerable detail and precision. A great deal of correct and applicable mechanics was known before any physics had been developed. Prescientific empirical knowledge of chemistry came from cooking, preserving, tanning, embalming, and medicine which all too often gave cause for embalming. And in astronomy, the use of instruments and charts was developed and practiced expertly by navigators, who had no theory, but had to keep exact bearings.

Builders may know the basics of mechanics, cooks find out chemical properties, and sailors map the sky; but who has any such naive yet expert knowledge of psychical phenomena? Who knows the essentials of feeling? The real patterns of feeling—how a small fright, or "startle," terminates, how the tensions of boredom increase or give way to self-entertainment, how daydreaming weaves in and out of realistic thought, how the feeling of a place, a time of day, an ordinary situation is built up—these felt events, which compose the fabric of mental life, usually pass unobserved, unrecorded and therefore essentially unknown to the average person.

It may seem strange that the most immediate experiences in our lives should be the least recognized, but there is a reason for this apparent paradox, and the reason is precisely their immediacy. They pass unrecorded because they are known without any symbolic mediation, and therefore without conceptual form. We usually have no objectifying images of such experiences to recall and recognize, and we do not often try to convey them in more detail than would be likely to elicit sympathy from other people. For that general communication we have words: sad, happy, curious, nauseated, nervous, etc. But each of these words fits a large class of actual events, with practically no detail. An adjective never presents the complexities of the intraorganic processes from which overt behavior arises, whereas feeling really begins far below the issue of such processes in visible or audible action. Words are intrinsically public, and refer to the public aspects of life; and to understand someone else's words we need not follow their implications very far into his private ways of feeling. In understanding the sense of the word, however, we usually do not imagine what the speaker feels like, but simply note his attitude, in expectation of his subsequent behavior, and take our attitude toward him accordingly. Our own is what we feel, and he does not.

For most practical purposes, the nature of feeling does not need to be known conceptually beyond the point to which language, voice, physiognomy and gesture will express it. But for the study of mind such conceptual knowledge is needed, because the dynamic forms of felt experiences are a major exhibit of the rhythms and integrations, and ultimately the sources, of mental activity. Feeling is the constant, systematic, but private display of what is going on in our own system, the index of much that goes on below the limen of sentience, and ultimately of the whole organic process, or life, that feeds and uses the sensory and cerebral system.

Unfortunately, direct observation without any conceptual frame is impossible; some schema is bound to impose itself on the findings in the very process of seeking them, and the data reflect the expectation of the observer to whom they are supposed to be purely "given." To turn "knowledge by acquaintance" into "knowledge by description" is not a simple procedure of reporting private experience, because the formal possibilities of language are not great enough to reflect the fluid structure of cerebral acts in psychical phase, by which the substructure below the threshold of sentience is suggested, guiding physical research on the highest of vital phenomena. The earliest introspectionists were, in fact, the most influenced by theory, because they worked uncritically with the epistemological model provided by British empiricism—the supposed mosaic of pure sense data linked by a sort of magnetic process, association, into compound entities that were stored away as memories, and could somehow be retrieved from storage for later use. Most of the modern "classical" psychologists were more anxious to simplify their findings so they could be systematized than they were to examine them patiently and empirically. Before we had any clear image of the phenomenon we call "mind" we committed ourselves to a model, the system of physical laws, whereby the material was automatically cut down to what the model could represent, and the very subject matter of psychology—the psychical phase of vital functions—was eliminated altogether, leaving only its overt record, behavior.

I said, "Before we had any clear image...." An image is not a model. It is a rendering of the appearance of its object in one perspective out of many possible ones. It sets forth what the object looks or seems like, and according to its own style it emphasizes separations or continuities, contrasts or gradations, details, complexities or simple masses. A model, on the contrary, always illustrates a principle of construction or operation; it is a symbolic projection of its object which need not resemble it in appearance at all, but must permit one to match the factors of the model with respective factors of the object, according to some convention. The convention governs the selectiveness of the model; to all items in the selected class the model is equally true, to the limit of its accuracy, that is, to the limit of formal simplification imposed by the symbolic translation.

It is different with images. An image does not exemplify the same principles of construction as the object it symbolizes but abstracts its phenomenal character, its immediate effect on our sensibility or the way it presents itself as something of importance, magnitude, strength or fragility, permanence or transience, etc. It organizes and enhances the impression directly received. And as most of our awareness of the world is a continual play of impressions, our primitive intellectual equipment is largely a fund of images, not necessarily visual, but often gestic, kinesthetic, verbal or what I can only call "situational." The materials of imagination which I crudely designate here as "images" will be discussed at length in later parts of the book. Suffice it now to point out that we apprehend everything which comes to us as impact from the world by imposing some image on it that stresses its salient features and shapes it for recognition and memory.

The high intellectual value of images lies in the fact that they usually, and perhaps always, fit more than one actual experience. We not only produce them by every act of memory (and perhaps by other acts), but we impose them on new perceptions, constantly, without intent or effort, as the normal process of formulating our sensory impressions and apprehended facts. Consequently we tend to see the form of one thing in another, which is the most essential factor in making the maelstrom of events and things pressing upon our sense organs a single world (Fig. 3–1). In this way all the things which one image roughly fits are gathered together as instances of one conception. The image is not, I think, made of an accumulation of specific impressions, as many specific photographs, superimposed, constitute a composite photograph. The original image may have been derived in roundabout and irrecoverable ways. But it fits many impressions, even if somewhat imperfectly, nearly enough to permit their treatment as things of one kind; which is to say, it permits their interpretation in terms of the conception which the image expresses.

As one image, in the broad sense of envisagement, gestalt, may have many exemplifications, so one object may also exemplify various gestalten. Ordinarily, in the kind of thinking which civilized adults today call "common sense," every familiar physical object has a stable dominant gestalt according to which it is publicly classified, i.e., named; and how it is named largely determines the way we experience it even privately. The standard designation expresses what is considered the object's "real" nature; if it is called anything else, which brings it under a different rubric, this is regarded as a metaphorical designation.

In our semantic studies we generally assume that there is a clear distinction between the literal meaning of a word or a statement and its

 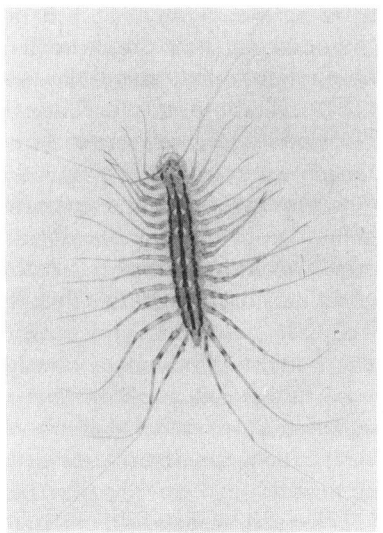

Figure 3–1. (*Left*) carvings of Bark Beetle (probably *Scolytus*); (*right*) house centipede, *Scutigera forceps*. (Left photo by Henry F. Dunbar; right photo by Louis Darling.)

metaphorical extensions. This assumption, which is almost a premise of common sense to civilized human beings, may nonetheless be unsafe in reconstructing the part language has played in the articulation not only of ideas, but of perception, the making of the world out of the fragmentary findings which prompt our overt actions and covert felt responses. The primitive use of words may have been much less bound to specifiable objects than its present use, much richer in connotation and therefore more elastic in denotation, so that literal and metaphorical meanings were not distinguishable, but the same word simply meant a variety of things which could all symbolize each other. The anthropological doctrine that primitive men knew the physical world before they were aware of mental activity, and borrowed words with physical meanings to refer metaphorically to mental states and functions, is open to doubt. On grounds of more general phylogenetic patterns it is at least as reasonable to suppose that the light of the sun and the light of reason or of joy were named by the same word because they were charged with the same feeling, and consequently taken as the same thing, and that their distinct characters only showed up in language in the course of its logical development. The physical meaning became the "literal" one because it was the most public and therefore socially the most negotiable one. Physical light is a permanent, ever-available symbol for everything that "light" may have meant in its earliest uses, which were probably quite spontaneous applications to a large vague class of things similarly felt.

Knowledge begins, then, with the formulation of experience in many haphazard ways, by the imposition of available images on new experiences as fast as they arise; it is a process of imagining not fictitious things, but reality, the making of reality out of impressions which would otherwise pass without record. The depth and reach of the imaginative functions in the making of human mentality will be discussed in a later part of this essay, but their very early occurrence is important here. The imposition of imagery on all materials that present themselves for perception, whether peripheral or intraorganic, enters into the most naive experience, and into the making of our "empirical" world. It is more primitive than the adoption of any "model." The use of a model belongs to a higher level of conception, the level of discursive thought and deliberate analogical reasoning. But the process of seeing things as exemplifications of subjectively created images gives us the original, objective phenomena that theoretical reasoning seeks to understand in causal terms, often with the help of highly abstract working models.

To return, at long last, to the unanswered question: who has a naive but intimate and expert knowledge of feeling? Who knows what feeling is like? Above all, probably, the people who make its image—artists, whose entire work is the making of forms which express the nature of feeling. Feeling is *like* the dynamic and rhythmic structures created by artists; artistic form is always the form of felt life, whether of impression, emotion, overt action, thought, dream or even obscure organic process rising to a high level and going into psychical phase, perhaps acutely, perhaps barely and vaguely. It is the way acts and impacts feel that makes them important in art.

In the course of projecting the forms of feeling into visible, audible or poetic material, an artist cannot escape an exact and intimate knowledge of those passages of sentience which he succeeds in expressing. He is not a psychologist, interested in human motivation and behavior; he simply creates an image of that phase of events which only the organism wherein they occur ever knows. This image, however, serves two purposes in human culture, one individual, one social: it articulates our own life of feeling so that we become conscious of its elements and its intricate and subtle fabric, and it reveals the fact that the basic forms of feeling are common to most people at least within a culture, and often far beyond it, since a great many works do seem expressive and important to almost everyone who judges them by artistic standards. Art is the surest affidavit that feeling, despite its absolute privacy, repeats itself in each individual life. It is not surprising that this is so, for the organic events which culminate in being felt are largely the same in all of us, at least in their biologically known aspects, below the level of sentience. Yet in the highest development—the psychical phase of activities hard to observe even in ourselves, except through some focusing and arresting device—individual differences may be extreme. One cannot safely argue from uniformity at one level of vital processes to uniformity at another, that is, from physiological directly to psychological similarities among creatures of a species, especially the most highly individuated species, Man. That is why psychology is not a "branch" of physiology: there is no way in which physiology can put forth such a branch. But if we can find systematic access to the intricate and multifarious ways of feeling which build up the whole pattern of the mind in the course of human life, we may hope to trace them to their sources below the psychological level, and perhaps conjoin two sciences in a single system of facts, once we really have two sciences.

The direct perception of artistic import, however, is not systematic and cannot be manipulated according to any rule. It is intuitive, immediate, and its deliverances are ineffable. That is why no amount of artistic perceptiveness ever leads to scientific knowledge of the reality expressed, which is the life of feeling. What it gives us is always and only an image. But without this or some other image we cannot ask questions about the empirical data with which knowledge begins, because the image enters into the objectification of the data themselves. Unless they are objectively seen and intimately known we cannot formulate scientific questions and hypotheses about them.

Feeling is a dynamic pattern of tremendous complexity. Its whole relation to life, the fact that all sorts of processes may culminate in feeling with or without direct regard to each other, and that vital activity goes on at all levels continuously, make mental phenomena the most protean subject matter in the world. Our best identification of such phenomena is through images that hold and present them for our contemplation; and their images are works of art.

What makes a work important is not the category of its expressed feeling, which may be obvious or, on the contrary, impossible to name, but the articulation of the experiential form. In actual felt activity the form is elusive, for it collapses into a condensed and foreshortened memory almost as fast as the experience passes; to hold and contemplate it requires an image which can be held for contemplation. But there is no simple image of our inner dynamisms as there is of visually perceived forms and colors and of sound patterns. A symbol capable of articulating the forms of feeling is, therefore, necessarily presented in some sort of projection as an extraorganic structure that conveys the movement of emotive and perceptive processes. Such a projection is a work of art. It presents the semblance of feeling so directly to logical intuition that we seem to perceive feeling itself in the work; but of course the work does not contain feeling, any more than a proposition about the mortality of Socrates contains a philosopher. It only presents a form which is subtly but entirely congruent with forms of mentality and vital experience, which we recognize intuitively as something very much like feeling; and this abstract likeness to feeling teaches one, without effort or explicit awareness, what feeling is like.

The image of feeling, however, does not provide us with any scientific concept such as psychological research requires. That is the function of a model. An image may be—and usually is—built up on entirely other principles than the phenomenal character of its object, and its own construction may be utterly different, while the created semblance confronts us like the phenomenon itself. A model, on the other hand, need not share any phenomenal traits with its object, but symbolizes its structure or function and is true to the original in every proportion and represented connection, to a stipulated limit of accuracy. A model is usually based on a single systematic abstraction which can ultimately be expressed in mathematical terms. Consequently it is a model, not an image, that one works with in science. At an advanced stage of scientific research resort to images revealing the original data becomes unnecessary; the macroscopic facts are sufficiently well known to be used as a check against the elaborate speculations to which the powerful abstract concepts lend themselves, and which are often illustrated by highly ingenious models. A play of imagery at that level only hampers invention, because it limits logical conception to the imaginable. But problems of this sort arise only with the full development of systematic knowledge in completely mathematicized fields.

Few people realize how excellent a presentation of psychological data is to be found in the arts. A few scholars have become aware of it—Köhler, Husserl, Fauré-Fremiet, Bertalanffy, Portmann and undoubtedly some others also. But no one, as yet, has pursued the revelation to the point of finding problematical facts never presented before, or recognizing vital patterns in pure art which may be keys to essential relations in the life of feeling. There is a wealth of such material presented indirectly in the technical problems artists have to solve to attain and sustain expressiveness, which is the same as to create a work of art.

In solving such problems, an artist rarely thinks about feeling, at least in the way which we usually call "thinking about" something. He thinks about his work, about what is wrong, what seems right, where the "dead spot" really is, what can put "life" into it; he judges what is expressive and what is inexpressive, but very seldom formulates in verbal thought the idea to be expressed. He will know it when he succeeds in embodying it. Discourse tends to arrest it; if the embodiment is not perfect the work will be somehow out of kilter and make new technical demands. The essentially intuitive process of artistic construction is as intriguing a psychological problem as the process of artistic apprehension. Neither is understood as yet.

To learn the facts of feeling from art, the best general practice is to follow the evolution of a work from one technical problem to another. A student of art would presumably be interested above all in the solutions; a student of actual sentience, however, in the reasons for their necessity. Gradually, but not systematically, the image of living form builds up from the exigencies of its creation. The principles of such image-making are entirely different from those of biological growth and function; the image projects nothing but the empirical datum, but this it presents with a degree of precision and detail beyond anything that direct introspection is apt to reveal. In the arts, and especially in their technical triumphs, lies the store of prescientific knowledge from which a science of psychology may draw its first inspiration.

II / *The Import of Art*

4 / *The Projection of Feeling in Art*

The theory of art from which this whole philosophy of mind arose is the theme of a previous book, *Feeling and Form*, wherein it has been developed chiefly with reference to the distinct basic abstractions and created dimensions giving rise to the respective great orders of art—plastic, musical, poetic, etc. The theory itself is systematically set forth there, and the chief implications of its tenets discussed in some detail, which is necessary if it is to be judged on its actual credentials, rather than accepted or rejected on a basis of a few catchwords whereby it can be relegated to an "ism," and thus quickly evaluated as current or obsolete. To reiterate that whole exposition here would involve us in chapters of discussion which would, after all, be largely repetitious; in presenting new studies built on former work one cannot possibly start from the beginning of the entire story every time. Some acquaintance on the reader's part with the foundations of the new ideas has to be presupposed. Instead of repeating myself, therefore, I shall make frequent reference to *Feeling and Form*, even as though it were a previous volume of the present book, because this practice seems the least onerous in a necessary choice of evils.

In some respects the treatment of art itself in this book transcends the compass of *Feeling and Form*. There my main concern was with the principles of creation and expression as they appear, often quite particularly, in each of the great orders of art, and with the equally particular problems and techniques which consequently arise in the different arts. The ultimate unity of art, which most philosophers seek by resolutely ignoring or denying any differences between music and painting, painting and literature, and so on, I expected to find precisely by tracing those differences as far as possible, to their vanishing point, where no more traits can be found that belong to some arts but not to all. That there are some fundamental principles by virtue of which we subsume so many distinct pursuits under the single word "art" is experientially hard to doubt, and in the last part of *Feeling and Form* those principles do come to light.

The questions dealt with in this book pertain equally to all the creative arts. What is a projection? How does an artist project an idea of feeling by means of his work? How does the idea become perceptible? And finally: what new empirical knowledge of the morphology of feeling can we derive from its image in works of art, and what light can this knowledge throw on the unfelt processes of life and the emergence of feeling, animal mentality, human experience and mind? These are far-reaching issues that invade many fields of special study. The amount of significant work that has been done becomes more impressive as the ramifications of the philosophical issue—the construction of a biological concept of mind adequate to the phenomenon itself—become explicit, and the consideration of them ineluctable.

To start, then, with the most elementary question: what does it mean to speak of "projecting" an idea? What is a projection?

Literally, of course, a projection is something that extends in one direction beyond the generally smooth contours of a mass. A bracket projects from a wall, or horns from an animal's head. In so doing, the projecting item stands out noticeably and presents itself most readily to perception. This is, I think, the circumstance that gives the concept of "projection" its metaphorical value. All uses seem to go back to the enhanced perceptibility of a projecting object or feature; and I think it is safe to say that, in all metaphorical senses, a projection is a principle of presentation. The operation of such a principle may be intentional, as in a cartographer's work, or purely spontaneous, unintended, as in the outward reference of sights and sounds, or even unadmitted—perhaps vehemently denied, as in the case of paranoid projection of a patient's attitudes and motives. Graphic renderings, ordinary sense data, and the paranoiac's alleged observations all appear to be presented to us as impinging "data."

"Projection" is really a word-of-all-work; sometimes it is used to denote a principle, as I just used it above in saying that a projection is a principle of presentation. Sometimes it is applied to the act of making the presentation, i.e., setting up the symbol; the paranoiac's projection of his own feelings into someone else, who serves him as a symbol of himself, is held to be an act, and indeed a mistake on his part. And finally, perhaps most often, we call the symbol itself a projection of what it symbolizes. In this sense, art may be said to be a projection of the artist's idea into some perceptible form; the expressive object he creates is called a projection of the life, mood, emotion or whatever he makes it express. Ordinarily the sense in which the word is used is easily gathered from the context, so it would be pedantry to specify it by a modifier every time; but it should never be forgotten that "projection" is really an ambiguous term, which may have to be explicitly defined in analytic or speculative discourse where precision is all-important.

During the twentieth century logicians and epistemologists have developed the concept of logical form, and discovered its relevance to the long-baffling problems of symbolic expression and communication. Evidently the process of projection rests on the recognition of one and the same logical form in different exemplifications, which are, therefore, different expressions of it. Very frequently one of the examples is much easier to perceive and hold in view than the other; then that negotiable one is used as a symbol, to make the obscure or elusive one conceivable, especially if the latter is the more important to conceive.

When we take, say, a thermometer reading, the stand of the mercury column is an indicative sign of the temperature actually prevailing. That physical covariance is what makes the thermometer a meter, an instrument, but even without its instrumental character it has an intellectual value which it retains though the bulb break and the tube be emptied; for besides being a device to determine actual temperatures, it is a symbol of the conceptual order in which all possible temperatures may be arranged so that any particular one may be unequivocally designated and any two may be distinguished and compared. All possible temperatures together form a one-dimensional continuum, which can be symbolically projected as a spatial one-dimensional continuum, i.e., a line; this visible line can be measured against a series of equal lengths marked off and numbered, a scale; so the continuum of possible temperatures appears in spatial projection as a series of degrees of heat. The glass tube in which the mercury rises and falls exemplifies the line, and is a visual representation of the conceivable range of temperatures (physically our thermometers are limited to part of the entire range, but theoretically, of course, they have no upper limit, and the lower is absolute zero); the mercury column in it is a device whereby the actual temperature at the moment may be found in terms of the symbolically established degrees.

This is one of the simpler examples of symbolic projection, in which the basis of isomorphy, i.e., sameness of logical form in the visible phenomenon and the more elusive one it represents, is obvious. It is adduced here as a stock example, to typify the conceptual process, which is an essentially symbolic process pervading all human mental activity—perception, appreciation, selfhood, emotion, as well as thought and dream. To understand its origin and offices is the chief purpose of human psychology, the study of mind. But the general semantic theory of projection, symbolic presentation and conceptual formulation has to be taken for granted here, where we are concerned with one of its special and very complicated applications—the analysis of artistic expression, or presentation of what artists call "the Idea" in their works.

Naturally enough, people who reflected long and seriously on the nature and import of art were the first to realize that here was a sort of significance that differed from the definable meaning of words, and a logic that was not like the logic of discourse, yet was a form of reasonableness. Here was something like a symbol but not a conventional symbol, and something that was more than a symbol—a form that contained its sense as a being contains its life.

In logic every symbol stands proxy for one defined or initially accepted idea; the symbols may be assigned and reassigned simply by fiat—"let x equal this, y equal that"—and nothing but the definition of "this" and of "that" enters into the current meanings of the respective terms. Logical symbolism is the extreme of literal expression, and a logician's (or mathematician's) intention is to allow no leeway at all for alternative or additional meanings. In ordinary language, the precise connotation and denotation of a word usually represents only a core of its meaning in discourse. Words are our most powerful symbols; their use is universal, constant, as natural to man as walking on only two limbs; nothing can hold him to an unchanging standard of verbal expression, as long as he finds that he can, in fact, use words in highly unusual ways and still be understood. So even the strict dictionary meanings change with time, and the senses admitted as "figurative" in one age are regarded as literal in another, and usages which no lexicographer would list as correct at all force themselves into public acceptance by dint of popular tendencies to error that the psychology of language so far has not fathomed.

At the opposite extreme from mathematical expression stands the great phenomenon of artistic expression, the symbolization of vital and emotional experience for which verbal discourse is peculiarly unsuited. Epistemologically this sort of symbolic presentation has hardly been touched. The philosophers of science and mathematics have drawn a great black line between propositional language used to state facts as unequivocally and literally as possible, and all other kinds of expression and their various purposes, which are lumped together under one caption, "emotive." This category embraces self-expression, the symbolization of wishes and fears in dream or fantasy, myth and other religious beliefs, and all artistic expression, which positivistic thinkers generally regard as an exhibition of the artist's own emotions, either in lyrical sighs and confessions, or by representation of things which evoke his emotive responses.

Like most sweeping and simple classifications, the treatment of all non-propositional symbols together as one kind with one function has thoroughly confused the study of human mentality as a whole, and especially of the crucial humanizing activity, symbolic projection. No crasser oversimplification could possibly be made than the assumption that symbolic processes are either concerned with receiving, handling and storing information, or with externalizing and working off emotions. The effect of symbolic expression is primarily the formulation of perceptual experience, and the constant reformulation of the conceptual frames which the cumulative symbolizing techniques—conscious or unconscious, but rarely altogether absent—establish, one upon another, one in another, one by negation of another.

The dependence of different modes of thought on respectively different symbolic forms has been treated at length, with admirable scholarship and awareness of its implication, by Cassirer in *The Philosophy of Symbolic Forms*. Since the publication of that pioneer work, a number of books and articles have appeared which reiterate and apply its basic ideas, but none, so far as I know, has gone on to develop the differences among the forms beyond those which Cassirer indicated. The whole progressive genesis of conceivability, the evolution of human thinking in all its complexity, lies in the divergences of those forms. The objection has sometimes been brought against the doctrine of distinct symbolic forms that it places all orders of thought—the most fanciful and the most scientific—on a par as far as truth is concerned. I do not think this criticism is valid, though the emphasis Cassirer gives to the intellectual value of mythical conception invites it, if we gauge the intellect by a direct relation to truth. But intellect (perhaps unlike animal intelligence) has many indirect relations, too, with that ideal attainment; there are many steps in the processes of concept formation before the measure of factual cognition becomes paramount, and the "truth value" of mythical formulations belongs to this preparatory stage.

Not so the truth value of art. Artistic conception, for all its similarities to mythical ideation and even dream, is not a transitional phase of mental evolution, but a final symbolic form making revelation of truths about actual life. Like discursive reason, it seems to have unlimited potentialities. The facts which it makes conceivable are precisely those which literal statement distorts. Having once symbolized and perceived them, we may talk about them; but only artistic perception can find them and judge them real in the first place.

What the many researches on symbolism published in the English-speaking world today all tend to skip is the nature of the symbolic projection itself. They are generally occupied with its effects; that is why they stand so ruggedly apart, with no clue to the reason why the most diverse sorts of elements may be called "symbols" (for instance, "symbols" in chemistry and in psychoanalysis). But the differences in the ultimate appearances of symbolic projections lie in their many ways and means; and the sphere where diverse means and very subtle ways of projecting ideas force themselves on one's attention is the sphere of art. The reason is not hard to find: for art has no ready-made symbols or rules of their combination, it is not a symbolism, but forever problematical, every work being a new and, normally, entire expressive form.

A work of art is a single symbol, not a system of significant elements which may be variously compounded. Its elements have no symbolic values in isolation. They take their expressive character from their functions in the perceptual whole. Art has a logic of its own (and by "a logic" I mean a relational structure), which is very complex; it is largely by virtue of its complexity that it can present us with images of our even more complex subjective activity.

The artist's eye sees in nature, and even in human nature betraying itself in action, an inexhaustible wealth of tensions, rhythms, continuities and contrasts which can be rendered in line and color; and those are the "internal forms" which the "external forms"—paintings, musical or poetic compositions or any other works of art—express for us. The connection with the natural world is close, and easy to understand; for the essential function of art has the dual character of almost all life functions, which are usually dialectical. Art is the objectification of feeling; and in developing our intuition, teaching eye and ear to perceive expressive form, it makes form expressive for us wherever we confront it, in actuality as well as in art. Natural forms become articulate and seem like projections of the "inner forms" of feeling, as people influenced (whether consciously or not) by all the art that surrounds them develop something of the artist's vision. Art is the objectification of feeling, and the subjectification of nature.

The rationale of the ancient and almost ubiquitous practice of representation in painting and sculpture lies in this dialectical aspect of the arts. Our present cultivation of non-representational art, for all its importance, is episodic in history. It is a purification of vision that has become necessary, partly because people's conception of portrayal had degenerated to a point of complete misconception, and partly because, at just that same time, an entirely new demand on formulative, intuitive vision arose from the social stresses and disconcertments of a new age. A new mentality was crying for recognition and projection. The power of abstraction became a central need, and the elimination of referential meanings threw the whole task of organizing the work on the artist's imagination of sheer perceptual values. The great "abstract" painters and constructivist sculptors are clearing the way to a new vision; and when they have found and completely mastered the principle of its presentation, they presumably will turn to nature again for the same purpose as always before. And it will look different to their eyes. This view is corroborated by Pierre Francastel (1948, 1951, 1952), who has dealt with artistic organization of space and its influence on our perception of actuality and, consequently, with the dialectical exchange of imagination and perception on what appears "realistic" in art. He advances the thesis that the spatial conception of the Renaissance painters was not the discovery, made once and for all, of visual space "as it really is," but was a re-imagination of space necessitated by changes in practical and scientific conception, and was a gradual achievement.

The intuition of artistic import is a high human function which so far both psychology and epistemology have completely by-passed. Yet its roots lie at the same depth as those of discursive reason, and are, indeed, largely the same. Probably the chief reason why it has never been recognized as a characteristic mental act is that the treatment of art as emotional self-expression and social communication is so much more familiar to common sense that it is axiomatically accepted, and once accepted, obscures the subtler phenomena of metaphorical presentation and insight.

But why should common sense find the concept of art as a direct expression of actual emotions easier to accept than the concept of the art symbol? It is because the latter idea requires a distinction which is not always easy to make and maintain. It takes some analytic effort to distinguish between an emotion directly felt and one that is contemplated and imaginatively grasped. In the case of outward events and objects, it is usually not hard to judge whether we are confronted with them here and now, or remember them, or have read or heard of them, or whether they are products of our own imagination. Emotions are felt as actions originating within us. An emotion, mood or disposition actually felt is as subjective as any thought about it; so the conception of feeling, and the contemplation of it as a part of the larger inward activity that characterizes human life, is not automatically distinguished from the actual occurrence called "having" that feeling. No wonder, then, that when an artist is said (by himself or someone else) to be engaged in expressing an emotion he is *ipso facto* supposed to have it and to be giving vent to it, as he might by shouting or gesticulating, and to be causing the same emotion in each person who sees or hears his self-expressive display. This assumption is made even more seductive by the fact that creative work always produces an actual excitement, which is colored by the feeling to be projected, and is sometimes more massive than the intended import. It is, I believe, this intellectual excitement, the feeling of heightened sensibility and mental capacity which goes with acts of insight and intuitive judgment, that the artist feels as he works, and afterwards evokes in those people who appreciate his creation. But this is not the import of art; what the created form expresses is the nature of feelings conceived, imaginatively realized, and rendered by a labor of formulation and abstractive vision. Their envisagement may be spontaneous and easy or very arduous and slow; the result need not show the way it was achieved.

There is, however, no basic vocabulary of lines and colors, or elementary tonal structures, or poetic phrases, with conventional emotive meanings, from which complex expressive forms, i.e., works of art, can be composed by rules of manipulation. It is easy enough to produce standard cadences, manufacture hymn tunes according to familiar models and some experiential knowledge of standard alternative resolutions, etc.; but such products are at best mediocre, and their import too slight to show any articulation of feeling. The analysis of spirited, noble or moving work is always retrospective; and, furthermore, it is never definitive, nor exhaustive.

Now, that is certainly an odd enough logical characteristic to make any logician question the possibility of such a structure. I have pondered that question myself for many years, yet always with the conviction that the structure exists and has to be explained. The explanation of its peculiar resistance to systematic treatment lies in the nature of the symbolic projection effected in art.

The fact that different modes of thought derive from different principles of presentation, which is to say, that they operate with different projections of their subject matter, has long been recognized. At the beginning of our century, Jean Philippe published a very interesting book entitled *L'image mentale (évolution et dissolution)*. The importance of Philippe's analysis of imagination for the study of art as a special symbolic projection lies in two fundamental tenets advanced and substantiated in *L'image mentale*: that the primary function of images is representation (which is to say that they are essentially and originally symbolic), and that their formation is a living process, and therefore as complex as all living processes are. The first of these two guiding propositions provides a key to the art projection: for the work of art is a constructed image, and should reflect the basic structure of the primitive and spontaneous image; if that structure is determined by the elementary function of representation, it must express first and always the natural laws of representation.

The laws of representation which govern image-making are not laws of optics, but of visual interpretation, which begins with the act of looking. What Philippe says of the bodiless mental image rings true when it is applied to the plastic image, and corroborates that the work of art is not a "copy" of a physical object at all, but the plastic "realization" of a mental image. Therefore the laws of imagination, which describe the forming and elaboration of imagery, are reflected in the laws of plastic expression whereby the art symbol takes its perceptible form. These perceptible forms are built up by means of visual conceptions, such as figure and ground, direction and change of direction, opposition, proportion; differentiation of color, and interaction of colors within a field of general coloration; volume, and visual changes of volume with torsion.

The principal difference in the effects of calculated and imagined spatial forms, respectively, is that the former seem "dead," "empty," "unfelt." Something about systematically executed models is so radically different from products of imagination that one is led to look for a basic difference in the whole symbolic projection. The art image has an irresistible appearance of livingness and feeling, though it may not represent anything living. A hat on a table, a pile of rocks, may have as much life as a dancing faun, and far more life than an "action photograph" of a dancer. It is this sort of vitality and feeling that constitutes the import of the work; it is conveyed entirely by artistic techniques, not by what is represented. Representation of objects is a device, though such a natural one that plastic expression has grown up on the principles of representation, which reflect the processes of visual imagination, the subjective envisagement of things and the increasing conceptual differentiation of their spatial properties. Those spatial properties, however, which are abstracted in the interest of artistic expressiveness are not essentially the geometric ones; they are noted and formulated chiefly with an eye to their dynamic, cohesive and other non-geometric aspects, because the space they are to organize is not actual space (the space of our actions, which is abstracted and refined by scientific thought), but virtual space.

Based on such abstractions and having such a purpose, the process of creating an art symbol is entirely different from that of making a model of an object. It is guided by imagination, and imagination is fed by perception; there lies the reason for all drawing from nature, as for all Aristotle's poetic "imitation." The process itself is a labor of sustained imagination, which exemplifies the laws of imagination, not of optics, acoustics, phonetics or whatever scientific study pertains to the material employed. The material is, in fact, never entirely circumscribed, as it is in the sciences. Sound, for instance, is not an object of study in geology (though it might be used as an indicator), but it can be a true element in architecture; great bells in a tower bring the edifice to life, and their tolling belongs to the architect's conception of the tower.

The techniques of art are intricate, subtle and manifold beyond any prevision or accounting. And this brings us back to Jean Philippe's work, to his second thesis: that the forming of a mental image is an act, a vital process, as ramified and complex as all functions of living things are. The product of that act, i.e., the image itself, which presents with something like the objectivity of a percept, still bears the stamp of the thing it really is—part of the cerebral process itself, a quintessence of the very act that produces it, with its deeper reaches into the rest of the life in which it occurs. In the actual event this involvement with the whole vital substructure is simply given by the feeling of activities interplaying with the moments of envisagement. But works of art are not natural occurrences with the stamp of life upon them. They are constructed symbols, made in the mode of imagination, because imagination reflects the forms of feeling from which it springs, and the principles of representation by which human sensibility records itself. If a piece of art is to express the pulse of life that underlies and pervades every passage of feeling, some semblance of that vital pulse has to be created by artistic means. But of this, more afterward.

The great complexity of the imaginal processes which scientific psychologists are all too apt to miss is implicitly if not explicitly known to all intuitive artists, whose work is guided by an artistic idea, and not by a discursive one such as a program or prescriptive theory of art. So it is not surprising that Philippe's study of mental imagery received a further development at the hands of a psychologist who had spent part of his life as a musical performer. I do not know whether Philippe Fauré-Fremiet received a stimulus from his precursor, or found the same approach independently. It is, actually, not quite the same; for in his first book, *Pensée et re-création*, he starts from his artistic experience, assuming that it will reveal the ways, if not laws, by which images are formed, and traces their operation through more casual and fragmentary mental activities, the endless, varied improvisations of ordinary life in which imagination is more or less constantly engaged. This is, essentially, the path I am taking here, though with a further premise by which not only the processes but also the products of art become starting points for the understanding of mind, and, indeed, for fundamental inquiries into its entire evolution from primitive biological traits and tendencies. That premise (which was not a premise but a conclusion in *Feeling and Form*) is that works of art exhibit the morphology of feeling.

What he means by the word "re-creation," which figures in the titles of his two books that are relevant here, is the symbolic projection of experience, whereby it is, as he says, "realized." All conscious experience is symbolically conceived experience; otherwise it passes "unrealized." But this symbolic conception can be practically instantaneous. In a work of art, the idea has to be embodied in a perceptible creation, worked out coherently as an organic form.

His later book is less concerned with art and more with life than *Pensée et re-création*, but it is in *La re-création du réel et l'équivoque* that he furnishes a key to many problems of the art symbol, namely, in the peculiarity of its logical projection, which makes it untranslatable and indivisible, but also makes it "organic," "living" and "emotive," though no emotion or even living creature capable of emotion be represented in it. The peculiarity he notes belongs to all imaginative construction: that its elements need not lie all in one and the same symbolic projection. Their respective transformations may be made on different principles. In the ordinary, spontaneous envisagements involved in our consciousness of actual experience and of its precipitate in memory, different projections alternate as we "realize" fragmentary facts mixed with a more or less inchoate current of discursive thought, spoken or tacit. Images arise and fulfill their purpose, conjoining their functions in our thinking without any mutual adjustments of visual scale, clearness, degree of schematization or directness of reference. We shift from one momentary vision to another without any sense of their incongruity because as a rule they are used only instrumentally, so as visual experiences *per se* they are simply not compared. Only their deliverances are compared.

It is different in art. Here the same multiplicity of logical projections prevails, but since a work of art is a single symbolic form presented to perception, it has to encompass all its elements without losing its unity of semblance and sense. That difficulty seems formidable enough to make one ask: why not limit the technique of art to one ruling principle of presentation? The answer is that the artist's idea cannot be expressed by such simple means. Herein precisely lies the incapacity of verbal statement to form and convey conceptions of feeling. What can be stated has to be logically projectable in the discursive mode, divisible into conceptual elements which are capable of forming larger conceptual units by combinations somehow analogous to the concatenations of words in language. The principles of verbal concatenation are few enough to be formally known as rules of syntax and grammar; the combinable units are known, too; and though the meanings of those elementary symbols do have some range, only Humpty Dumpty can ignore their conventional sense entirely. Word meanings change, but only with time.

The most salient characteristic of discourse is that its symbolization of concepts is held to one dominant projection, which enables users of words to "run through" elaborate combinations of them, building up meanings by accretion. Other expressive devices may find their way into the pattern of discourse, but they are contingent to the basic pattern, and their sense is very aptly said to be "between the lines." The "lines" of discourse are propositional constructions; other accepted forms, which are not strictly propositional—interrogative, imperative, vocative—are auxiliary forms developed in use. The essence of language is statement.

The single pre-eminent projection of language is both its power and its limitation. It makes language not only a means of symbolization, but a symbolism; in fact, it is the paradigm of symbolisms, so that every discursive form is usually, and rightly enough, called a language. The fundamental principle of such organization, which imposes itself on our tacit conceptual processes as well, is "logic" in its traditional sense, reflected in the various grammatical systems of particular languages.

The enormous power of language, whereby we are enabled to form abstract concepts, concatenate them in propositions, apply these to the world of perception and action, making it a world of "facts," and then manipulate its facts by the process of reasoning, springs from the singleness of the discursive projection. A symbolism to be currently manipulated as a tool in practical life must have a single set of rules; and the units deployed by those rules, the words of the language, must be as unequivocal as possible. We all know that unequivocal verbal meanings are hard to secure and even harder to maintain; the necessity of scientific languages for very precise and abstract discourse testifies to that. But we do have ways of bringing words with unduly many meanings back to a "strict sense" by agreement, if only in a given context.

The same characteristics, however—its atomistic structure and singleness of projection—set limits to the expressive power of language. It is clumsy and all but useless for rendering the forms of awareness that are not essentially recognition of facts, though facts may have some connection with them. They are perceptions of our own sensitive reactions to things inside and outside of ourselves, and of the fabric of tensions which constitutes the so-called "inner life" of a conscious being. The constellations of such events are largely non-linear, for where sequences occur they normally occur simultaneously with others, and every tension between two poles affects (evokes, modifies, cancels or precludes *ab initio*) many concomitant ones having other poles. The tensions of living constitute an organic pattern, and those which rise to a psychical phase—that is to say, felt tensions—can be coherently apprehended only in so far as their whole non-psychical organic background is implied by their appearance. That is why every work of art has to seem "organic" and "living" to be expressive of feeling. Its elements, like the dynamic elements in nature, have no existence apart from the situations in which they arise; but where they exist they tend to figure in many relationships at once.

This multiplicity of functions is reflected in any symbolic form that can express the morphology of feeling—a fact which makes discursive expression a poor candidate for that office. But another product of human mentation, the spontaneous image, has exactly this character, which psychologists designate as a tendency to be "overdetermined" in significance.

The only adequate symbolic projection of our insights into feeling (including the feeling of rational thought, which the discursive record of rational order has to omit) is artistic expression; and the material for this is furnished by the natural resources of imagination. But artistic expression has an enormous range; for what we usually call a mental image—a visual fantasy—is only one kind of figment produced by our brain, prodigally, in sleep as well as waking, apparently without effort. Forms of sound and of bodily movement and even envisagements of purposeful action are similarly engendered, and have the same sort of plasticity and the same tendency to take on symbolic functions as visual forms. With these diverse materials, variously endowed people create works of art in the several great orders—music, drama, painting, dance, and so on. The potentialities of the imaginative mode seem to be endless.

As literal language owes its great intellectualizing power and its usefulness for communication to the relative simplicity of its logical structure, which also sets its limits of expressiveness, so the non-discursive structure of artistic presentation prevents art from ever being a symbolism which can be manipulated by general rules to make significant compositions, but at the same time is the secret of its great potentiality. Its elements are all created appearances which reflect the patterns of our organic and emotional tensions. The illusion of tensions is the stuff of art.

The creative processes which build up an artist's image of subjective acts are numberless, because they can work in combination by many projective techniques at once, mingling several principles of presentation. A work of art is like a metaphor, to be understood without translation or comparison of ideas; it exhibits its form, and the import is immediately perceived in it. One might well call it a metaphorical symbol.

Every symbolic projection is a transformation. There are projections which are merely transpositions, such as the projection of a picture from a slide to a screen, but they are not symbolic. The function of a symbol is not only to convey a form, but in the first place to abstract it; and this requires transformation, because it is the sameness of logical structure in experientially different loci that makes it apparent. In most people's thinking, as well as in our written records, numbers appear as numerals. Yet we may translate our numerals into those of a different system, for instance, Arabic into Roman, "7" into "VII." Then the number seven—a purely mathematical concept—appears as "VII," at least after a little habituation. A still more radical symbolic transformation, psychologically speaking, takes place when we watch changes of a perceptually inaccessible sort by means of a device, e.g., the passage of time by the advance of the hands in a clock, or the fluctuation of prices on the stock market by the progressive action of the ticker tape. Ordinarily, in such contexts, we disregard the symbol and consider ourselves in direct touch with the reality it conveys; yet we know, upon very little reflection, that a symbol intervenes, and that its physical character is merely so irrelevant to its meaning that we ignore it. Its elementary meanings are assigned by convention and could be changed by agreement.

The art symbol, however, does not rest on convention. There are conventions in art, and they do change, but they govern only the ways of creating the symbol, and not its semantic function. When they change, it is not by any agreement but by individual departure from them. The import of art inheres in the symbol, which has no dispensable or changeable physical character at all, because it is an image, not an index; its substance is virtual, and the reality it conveys has been transformed by a purely natural process into the only perceptual form it can take. Feeling is projected in art as quality.

What I call "quality" here is, of course, not what the British empiricists meant by that word when they distinguished primary and secondary qualities, and spoke of simple qualities and their compounds—mixed colors, for instance, or mingled odors. There is a kind of quality that different colors, or even a tonal form and a visual one, may have in common; even events may have the same quality, say of mystery, of portentousness, of breeziness; and a word like "breeziness" bespeaks the qualitative similarity of some moods and some weathers. Homer refers to "the wine-dark sea," although Greek wine is red, and the Mediterranean is as blue as any other sea water. But the translucent blue in the curve of a wave and the glowing red in a cup of wine have a common quality.

It is quality, above all, that pervades a work of art, and is the resultant of all its virtual tensions and resolutions, its motion or stillness, its format, its palette, or in music, its pace, and every other created element. This quality is the projected feeling; artists refer to it as the "feeling" of the work as often as they call it "quality." The image of feeling is inseparable from its import; therefore, in contemplating how the image is constructed, we should gain at least a first insight into the life of feeling it projects.

5 / *The Artist's Idea*

> **Bei jedem Kunstwerk, gross oder klein, bis ins kleinste, kommt alles auf die Konzeption an.**
>
> **Goethe**

Aesthetics, as its unhappy name bespeaks, started as an analysis of sensibility, though it was aimed from the beginning at making some systematic description of the pleasures of the higher senses, vision and hearing. These pleasures were soon found to be easily destroyed or at least eclipsed by most people's proclivity for using their eyes and ears only to identify things and receive information about them, to orient themselves and steer their own courses of action. To enjoy the deliverances of sense as such appeared to be, at least in our practical-minded society, an unusual indulgence; and so the aesthetic attitude became the first requirement for the experience of aesthetic pleasure, and sometimes seemed even to be the active source of it.

Gradually the concept of art as a formed image revealing the life of feeling has been worked out by many thinkers, especially a fair number of articulate and keen-minded artists. Most of those theorizing artists began with the assumption that their work was a direct outward expression or "objectification" of emotions they were actually undergoing as they composed it, and ended with the realization that they were expressing their knowledge of subjectivity rather than their momentary moods or passions; that this knowledge of "felt life" stems from a person's own experience, but always from the whole of it, so that even if raw emotional upheaval may have furnished a maelstrom of new feeling and exerted a strong pressure to formulate and transmute it, yet that feeling is not all that feeds the work; an artist's long-developed background of emotional conception, his individual sensibility, his own ways of articulating and projecting assimilate the feeling to his entire art before it finds expression. What he holds in mind as he works on a new expressive form is not an upheaval, but an idea.

One of our foremost artist-critics, T. S. Eliot (whose theoretical work, I now think, was not duly appreciated in *Feeling and Form*), wrote quite early in his life: "The more perfect the artist, the more completely separate in him will be the man who suffers and the mind which creates; the more perfectly will the mind digest and transmute the passions which are its material" (1920, p. 48). Neither did he, even in his youth, ever regard the music of words as a purely sensuous beauty to please the listening ear. Sound and structure, imagery and statement all go into the making of a vehicle for the poet's idea, the developed feeling he means to present. With Eliot, the conception of art as the impersonal expression of feeling (he always spoke of it as "emotion," but I think he meant, as I do, whatever can be felt) was not only entertained, but avowed, discussed and singlemindedly adopted.

At once its wide implicative power becomes apparent, and offers solutions of some of the "chestnut problems" of older philosophies of art: how a work can express more than its maker knew, why it may be read differently, even in logically incompatible ways, yet correctly by different people without therefore being only a mirror of their own subjective states, how it can be "original" although materials, techniques and any number of stylistic conventions which have gone into it are familiar and the artist was not afraid to follow a tradition or repeat a theme; such problems come crowding as soon as their solutions are in the offing.

Eliot has put into words some of those emergent explanations; for instance, that the art symbol (i.e., the work) may present more than the artist was aware of, because in the process of manipulating its elements all sorts of possibilities of form appear that he recognizes as organically motivated, inherent in the style of the piece or dictated by what he has already done, as its natural continuation; the artist is the first person to see a new quality arise, which he develops as best he can, capturing a new feeling which he could not have conceived before. Just as we may, in discourse, state a fact of which we are aware and then find that we have stated, by implication, further facts of which we were not aware until we analyzed our assertion, so an artist may find that he has articulated ideas he had not conceived before his work presented them to him. He may even continue to construe the expression he has created, and see new significance, just as any other beholder of the work may. And because of the "over-determined" character of art, he may see more, or less, or simply a different import from what someone else just as truly sees.

The essential function of art is not communication; for in communication the first requisite is always that the meaning which the recipient finds in the mediating symbol is the meaning its user intended. Naturally the artist intended to convey an idea, and if his work is good, his idea is expressed in it; but since the perception of import is intuitive, and there is no such machinery as language commands—paraphrastic restatement, logical demonstration and what not—to induce an unready intuition, some other import, incidentally presented, may eclipse the intended one for a differently predisposed mind. And the incidentally articulated reality may even be the greater and more vital one. It may stem from the limbo of the artist's unavowed knowledge, and may some day confront him in its objective presentation, too, when he revisits his own work. Such discoveries cause a moment of self-estrangement: "Did I compose that?—I wonder whether I could do that now." Most artists have experienced such impacts.

The prime function of art is to make the felt tensions of life, from the diffused somatic tonus of vital sense to the highest intensities of mental and emotional experience, "stand still to be looked at," as Bernard Bosanquet said, "and, in principle, to be looked at by everybody" (1915, p. 6). That brings us face to face with the problem of objectification.

This issue, too, Eliot has attacked, and his attack on it has become famous. "The only way of expressing emotion in the form of art," he said in one of his most frequently quoted passages, "is by finding an 'objective correlative'; in other words, a set of objects, a situation, a chain of events which shall be the formula of that *particular* emotion; such that when the external facts, which must terminate in sensory experience, are given, the emotion is immediately evoked" (1932, pp. 124–25). Yet I think there is an error in this prescription—an error which rests on a confusion, subtle (or its author could not have fallen into it), yet crucial: the mistaking of a principle of poetic construction for a principle of art (this confusion is treated more fully in *Problems of Art*, Lecture 8, "Principles of Art and Creative Devices"). The making of the art symbol, which is the work itself, is very complex, and in it other types of projection are involved, which have to be distinguished from the expression of the import of the whole. One of these other types is the "objective correlative." It is, as he said, a formula which the poet finds for the rendering of a particular emotion; but it is for an emotion presented in the work, not by the work. The feeling of the work itself appears as a perceptible quality, and there is no formula for the creation of that effect, which is not a correlative of feeling, but its transformed appearance. Where and how that transformation is made remains the problem in hand.

But first, a word about Eliot's finding, to explain why I do not regard it as a principle of art as such: the "objective correlative" is a general device for depicting emotion occurring within the virtual world of the story told or dramatized. It is a principle of representation, creating the emotions of the fictive persons by putting the concrete image of their motivating objective conditions before us; but the emotion is "evoked" in those persons, not in us. It was, indeed, in his criticism of Shakespeare's practice in *Hamlet* that Eliot's recognition of that basic dramatic technique was formulated, and all the examples he consequently adduces illustrate this same technical purpose; as soon, however, as it is extended to the situation as it looks to a *persona dramatis*, and then even further to the author's situation in relation to his material, both the emotion and the correlative shift their meanings, so that the concept of objectification becomes blurred. Consider, first, the purely structural use of the principle set forth in the instances on which the theory seems to have been initially based, given in this passage:

"If you examine any of Shakespeare's more successful tragedies, you will find this exact equivalence; you will find that the state of mind of Lady Macbeth walking in her sleep has been communicated to you by a skillful accumulation of imagined sensory impressions; the words of Macbeth on hearing of his wife's death strike us as if, given the sequence of events, these words were automatically released by the last event in the series. The artistic 'inevitability' lies in this complete adequacy of the external to the emotion; and this is precisely what is deficient in *Hamlet*. Hamlet (the man) is dominated by an emotion which is inexpressible, because it is in *excess* of the facts as they appear" (ibid., p. 125).

"Hamlet (the man)"; so far, our tacit supplementations to the somewhat ambiguous terms "inexpressible" and "as they appear" may keep sense quite clear: Hamlet's emotions are inexpressible to the audience, being in excess of the "facts" as they appear to the audience. To motivate Hamlet's actions we must impute to him emotions which are not created for us with the actions. The formula, in this case, should serve to make visible to the audience the feelings of a person in the play, and such feelings are as virtual as the situations and overt acts of that person himself. The "objective correlative" here is a principle of dramatic presentation.

With the next step, however, the dramatic principle is changed to a psychological one, and applied, within the play, to Hamlet's inability to understand his own feeling because "he cannot objectify it, and it therefore remains to poison life and obstruct action" (ibid.). This is certainly a different issue. The protagonist's inability to understand himself must rest on the dramatic condition that the facts as they appear to him do not let him explain his emotions to himself. This condition might, however, be quite clear to the audience, as it is in *King Lear*, where the king's actions have created a situation which motivates the defection and hypocrisy of his daughters for us, but not for him, because he does not see his own part in it. If Hamlet (the man) fails to understand his emotions for want of an objectifying symbol, this virtual situation may be analogous to our actual want of a symbol in *Hamlet* (the play) to convey them to us, but the two failures occur on entirely different semantic levels, and cannot involve the same function of an "objective correlative."

Finally, at another remove, the principle is applied to the play itself, and the critic tells us that "the supposed identity of Hamlet with his author is genuine to this point, that Hamlet's bafflement at the absence of objective equivalent to his feelings is a prolongation of the bafflement of his creator in the face of his artistic problem" (ibid.). This last issue, the artistic problem, is really an entirely different matter; to treat the feeling conceived, the import of the play itself, as something in need of an "objective correlative" to represent it seems to me to bespeak a misconception of the artist's task. The expressive form, the work, is a symbol created, not found and used. One finds motifs and devices, and represents characters and their emotions, but the poetic import of the composition is not represented—it is presented, as the perceptible quality of the created image.

So we are back to the problem that I broached above and left suspended: how does the artist transform his idea of feeling—which must be vague, elusive, amorphous before it appears in any projection—into the objective datum, the perceptible quality of a poem, a musical piece, a painting or whatever else he gives us? How does he envisage that quality before he or anyone else has seen it? The answer is, I think, that he has seen it; it is this apparition that he tries to re-create. His idea is initiated by experiences, or perhaps even one isolated experience, of actuality colored by his own way of feeling (rather than by some emotion of the moment), and the image he creates is of the way things appear to his imagination under the influence of his highly developed emotional life.

What any true artist—painter or poet, it does not matter—tries to "re-create" is not a yellow chair, a hay wain or a morally perplexed prince, as "a symbol of his emotion," but that quality which he has once known, the emotional "value" that events, situations, sounds or sights in their passing have had for him. He need not represent those same items of his experience, though psychologically it is a natural thing to do if they were outstanding forms; the rhythm they let him see and feel may be projected in other sensible forms, perhaps even more purely. When he finds a theme that excites him it is because he thinks that in his rendering of it he can endow it with some such quality, which is really a way of feeling. That process is the abstractive process of art. It is true that, as one aesthetician after another has declared and stressed, an artist at his work does not think abstractly; but he thinks abstractively. He does not use the ready-made general concepts of ordinary discourse to reason verbally about his work—which is what they mean by "thinking abstractly"—to any great extent; but he is entirely absorbed in making a new abstraction, without the aid of that spontaneous, progressive generalization which is the normal machinery of intellectual abstract conception.

Yet a person engaged in painting or composing, building up a novel or a scenario, a dance, or a monument—whatever may be his art—is not consciously making an abstraction, either. He is working toward the quality he wants this particular piece of his to have. If he is young, he is apt to have seen it in someone else's art rather than in other domains of life; that is, to have seen it created, where the more obvious techniques encourage him to make a start, with some confidence that his own individual vision will develop before he is through, and give his work a new value. But, young or old, great talent or small, to make any work of art the maker must have an idea to realize.

The ways of getting and holding an artistic idea are extremely various and unpredictable. Some artists begin with emotion, pure and simple; some with a concrete symbol or even a sober fact, and a phrase or poetically perfect line to say about it. A line which rings true is usually the embryo of a poem. But how that line arose in the poet's mind cannot be generally described. All that the stimulus has to do is to bring back vividly a feeling the artist has once known that imposed itself on things about him like a special light, and gave them the quality he wants to impart to the image he is making.

Yet this is only one type of creative experience. Many an artist's guide is not memory at all, but a conviction that the quality he cannot clearly envisage yet will emerge, and that he will know its pure expression when he sees it. There is enough of it in the first formal conception to beget a sense of congruence or incongruence in most of his further moves (sometimes it takes some trial and error). There is some analogy to this in our discursive, speculative thought, in that a thinker often sees a promise of new ideas, a potential use, in a general proposition he has not analyzed and deductively exploited or even safely established yet.

The achievement of artistic quality is the first, last and only aim of the artist's work. That achievement is expression of "the Idea"—an idea of human emotion and sentience, of which the work is a projection. There is no compromising with standards of beauty such as regularity, balance, decorative color, etc.—many eminent aestheticians to the contrary notwithstanding. If regularity does not serve to create the emotive quality, it is tiresome. If balance does not spring from the rhythm of feeling, such balance looks frozen. Color does not seem decorative if it does not enhance the appearance of livingness; and if it does it is expressive.

Here, I regret to say, I cannot share the view of Sir Herbert Read, with whom I do agree on some fundamental views he has expressed in the past. The opposition he professes to find between "vitality" and "beauty" seems to me to bespeak an unduly limited sense of the latter term, making it equivalent to what Bosanquet called "easy beauty," as against the "difficult beauty" of less canonical art. To argue that paleolithic art is not beautiful because the painters did not consciously aim at making it so (which we cannot know), and did not compose their representations into abstractly conceived designs (Read 1955, p. 29), equates "beauty" with regularity and symmetry of form. In these confines, indeed, no great range of feeling can come to expression.

The dichotomy between beautiful art and expressive art is a firmly established principle of modern criticism; Nietzsche's contrast of Apollonian and Dionysian, Curt Sachs' "ethos" versus "pathos" art, Read's conflict between beauty and vitality, all denote the same fundamental duality, so one can hardly deny that such a duality exists.

Yet a genuine phenomenon may be misinterpreted, and its structure misconceived accordingly. The two tendencies in art, formalization and expression, are generally taken to serve two different aims, the one to please the "higher senses," the other to relieve emotional pressures; and the ideal artistic attainment, consequently, is supposed to be a perfect compromise between these two aims, doing the highest possible justice to each, as Sir Herbert proposed.

I think it far more likely that every artist has only one artistic aim, whatever non-artistic interests he may also find opportunity to satisfy by his work. The sole artistic intent is to present his idea of some mode of feeling in the nameless but sensible quality which shall pervade his nascent creation. There may be many reasons why he wants to realize and present this particular import; it may preoccupy him, torture him, so he has to objectify and face it; it may merely intrigue him, because he has but partly known it, and thinks his own work would complete the revelation; or—very often, perhaps normally in working on commission or by command—the material and the stipulations themselves suggest a form congenial to the artist's "habit of emotion," which is the tenor of his artistic imagination. Such reasons have little to do with the seriousness of his intent once the work is undertaken, the motif accepted, the general feeling adumbrated in the first structural conception.

The developed rhythms of life appear in our traditional artistic rhythms, visual, musical or poetic, which are intrinsically "ornamental"—that is, sensuously organizing any material on which they are imposed, assuming its spontaneous transformation into a virtual field in which forms arise for pure perception. The first effect of formal design is to animate a surface; if the surface is curved, design lends its curves continuity by expressing their directions as flowing lines; if it is angled, borders or symmetrical forms emphasize the angles as conjunctions of areas, like meetings of segments in complex organisms, which individuate the parts and at the same time establish their mutual limitations. Even the visible expansion of an unbroken plane is peculiarly enhanced and brought to account by evenly deployed forms, which may be the simplest geometric figures or very intricate, just so long as they occur in rhythmic repetition. The second great function of design, which may be the more important, at least if we measure its importance by its influence on the further potentialities of art, is the establishment of symmetry, or correlation of counterparts, which creates the axis as a structural element. At once we have right and left of a median; the projection of body feeling into symmetrical forms meeting along a straight line is such an elementary act of visual intuition that the forms are actually seen to "balance" the moment that line is upright. Our sense of space is gravitational as much as visual; the similar and opposed figures seem to exert the same pull on the axis so that the apparent tension is resolved only when the axis is erect in our field of vision. Balance establishes the vertical, and implies the ground line, the horizontal. Here is the simplest principle of monumental as well as pictorial organization; but what gives a symmetrical deployment of figures this formalizing power is that it expresses our deepest vital feeling, equilibrium, the resting tonus of the whole organism. Its import is simple, but immediately received; the safest device to achieve living form is symmetrical composition. Sir Herbert aptly designates such balance as "the still center"; but it is the still center of life, not of geometric figure, which *qua* geometric is no more still at the center than anywhere else. To oppose the basic equilibrium of vital form to "vitality" itself, and to regard the latter as an interest on the part of the artist different from that of achieving "that ideal category of representation which we call *beauty*" (Read 1955, pp. 32–33)—so that he is forever compromising his ideal, trying to eat his cake and yet keep it—makes the appreciation of art a constant juggling of two standards, and critical judgment an equally constant weighing of excuses.

If one conceives art to be a projection of feeling by means of a transformation of subjective, intraorganic realities into objective, though virtual, forms of directly perceptible quality, the problem of artistic import loses some of its mysterious (not to say mystical) aspect. At least it breaks up into more manageable, distinct issues, which are of general epistemological interest and even motivate some psychological queries. Of the latter sort is the whole complex problem of immediate sensory experience, on which some work has long been in progress: how, and to what extent, do we detect qualities not correlated with some known function of a specific sense organ? What do we really receive, at various stages of life and under its various conditions, in the mode of direct sensory impact? But the other sort of inquiry it engenders, the epistemological, centers on the meaning of "intuition"; and as this is of prime importance to the whole theory of "presentational" or "metaphorical" symbolism, it has to be at least briefly introduced here, although it is slated for more thorough treatment in connection with a later issue, the emergence of "mind" from animal mentality.

Intuition is the basic intellectual function. The word has been popularly used to denote some alleged possession of information without any demonstrable source—foreknowledge of rationally unpredictable events, factual knowledge without any access to the facts, etc.; it is also used as a synonym for instinct, which it certainly is not. I am using it here in the strict sense which it was given by Locke in his *Essay*. In that sense, "intuition" is direct logical or semantic perception; the perception of (1) relations, (2) forms, (3) instances, or exemplifications of forms, and (4) meaning (Locke 1690, Bk. IV, chap. ix, sec. 3). Locke, who had reason to be wary of the word because the arch-opponents of his empiricism, the churchmen, rested their moral and theological beliefs on "intuition," often used the term "natural light" in its stead.

The development of intuition, if not its very beginning, appears in the evolutionary theater as a hominid specialty; wherever else its roots may reach and show some budding life, it is in the human stock that it has had a steady growth, and made a radical difference in the entire design of that species, shifting its operational basis from directly stimulated instinctive action to more or less planned activity. By virtue of a symbolic envisagement of the world, human action has its symbolic rendering or conceptual form, too, which fits into the envisaged world (usually narrowed down to a situation) as a dynamic element, a potential change anticipated in imagination, so its performance or non-performance becomes a true option. This is, of course, the most obvious and momentous effect of the ability to use symbols, i.e., of logical and semantic intuition. But it is not the only one—not even the only one of first magnitude. Perhaps the deepest change which the dawn of "natural light" has made in man is the vast expansion of his emotional capacity, under the more or less constant stimulation provided by the play of significant imagery and spontaneous ideation that have become his nature. Sheer conceptions evoke emotions, emotions focus and intensify attention, attention eventuates in symbolic expression that formulates more conceptions and sustains or reshapes emotion; so the conceptual frame in which we feel our own activity and the impingements of outward events grows larger as long as the emotive and intellectual processes keep pace with each other in a dialectical advance, rhythmically self-sustaining like all major organic functions.

Intuition lies at the base of all specifically human mental functions, and even deeply modifies those which we still share with other creatures, so that most of our truly instinctive acts appear vestigial beside the complexity and adaptedness of theirs. The ordinary intuitive acts, such as the recognition of similar formal structures in sensuously dissimilar things, the reception of one as symbolic of the other, the spontaneous production of new perceptible entities—from private images to publicly objectified things or events—to present all sorts of abstracted forms *in concreto*, are as natural to us as the motions of our limbs, uncoordinated at first, but patterned and integrated in the normal course of maturation, and later developed selectively to various degrees by employment. We need not undertake such acts deliberately: symbolic projection and interpretation are spontaneous responses which we may become aware of and cultivate, or always perform at the unremarked level of what Coleridge called "primary imagination."

This brings us back to paleolithic art, and the opinion of several important critics that it is not beautiful because its makers had no notion of beauty, that it is not expressive because they were not seeking expression, and even that it is not art because they had no artistic intention. The appreciation of expressive form seems to be primitive and immediate in man, and long before things natural and supernatural, real and imaginary, physical and ideal could have been sorted out for him as so many categories of experience, they appear to have served as opportunities for creating symbols of his intuitive realizations. It is a prevalent fashion today to say that ancient art was produced without interest in any but utilitarian values. That opinion rests on a modern distinction between efficacy and aesthetic appeal which does not occur to the unsophisticated mind. It is reflected also in the frequent misconception of magic as a prosaic activity performed just as one would perform a necessary chore. Magic is always mysterious power, and is viewed with awe as a special gift granted more freely to some persons than to others. Its employment is "practical" in the same sense as prayer; it is often built into purposive action; but its essential function is the ritualistic expression, or "realization," of the act of mind as a power among the symbolically conceived powers of nature. It is always mystical, fervent and, in its more advanced stages, religious; and although its exercise may be coupled with efficacious methods, their success becomes a demonstration of its power—not simply a result of the rite, but its consummation. The same consideration applies to the modern anthropological tenet that primeval human societies must have been entirely practical, as animals appear to be, and had no artistic interests.

As it happens, the magic intent of the ancient animal paintings seems highly probable, but this does not rule out the artistic motive, nor even make it a secondary, extraneous, super-added interest. The projection of human feeling into visible forms may be a completely unconscious process, not only at the beginning but even throughout the work, yet gather momentum steadily with the growth of the form and guide the consciously intended act of pictorial representation. It is not as mammoth or reindeer that the deep inward rhythms of life are objectified, but as the flowing unity of lines and the distribution of accents, the tensions inherent in the strokes and virtual volumes, not in the repre-

Figure 5–1. Reindeer, Font-de-Gaume Cave, Dordogne, France.

sented animal's anatomy (Fig. 5–1). And I believe this kind of expression is elementary, prepared in the early phases of human vision. Ontogenetically it has been observed by psychologists who call it the "physiognomic" stage of perception, in which over-all qualities of fearfulness, friendliness, serenity, etc., seem to characterize objects more naturally than their physical constitution. Whether this ontogenetic phase of our mental development has a phylogenetic counterpart is, of course, problematical, but there is some support for the hypothesis that human mentality as a whole passed through a period of much more active physiognomic seeing than it exhibits in most of the world today. Expressive form, or beauty of design, need not have been a deliberate concern added to representational intention, to vindicate the theory that representation was the only conscious intention and aimed at magical power. If those early painters saw essentially in the physiognomic way, they would inevitably paint physiognomic images to render what things looked like, and would be filled with awe at the emotional expression. They could not paint inexpressive forms first and then decide to make them artistic.

Expression of conceived feeling seems to me the real criterion of art; and if such expression is intuitive, then artistic activity may occur without any verbalized intention, without preconceived standards and under any circumstances which induce people to produce objects, rites or utterances of distinctive form, no matter for what purpose. By all other measures which have been set up—emotional self-expression, recording of personal attitudes, a conscious purpose to create beauty, to intensify sensory experience or to realize standards of perfection which nature only approximates (i.e., to satisfy the canons of composition, such as unity in diversity), symmetry, the relation of separate forms to each other, etc.—some things which competent people generally accept as examples of art are ruled out of the sacred precinct; and my own response to the juried exhibit which remains usually is: "This, too, is art."

Yet the measure I would apply—the measure of created form with vital import—sets its limits, too. One has already been remarked; where there is no evidence of any intuitive use of the material for the embodiment of feeling, we are not dealing with art, good or bad. There also are products which present artistic problems, but rarely emerge, at their completion, as total works of art: dress designs, too stringently governed by "the whirligig of taste" to realize their maker's true ideas (though traditional costumes, scarves, kimonos often do so, and then are genuine art works), or discursive writings, which are full of literary challenges, but produce, in the end, no literary image of mental experience, no illusory process of growing thought, but only the literal report or discursive argument itself, to be analyzed, judged and, if it is philosophical, eagerly refuted. History, essays, even scientific expositions can be true literature, but that achievement, which consists in a complete use of the undistorted actual discourse as a motif for artistic composition, is so rare that its instances are always masterpieces.

Perhaps the most controversial limitation, however, which the concept of "art" as a symbolic projection of feeling puts upon the extension (denotation) of the term is that it excludes so-called "animal art." The symbolic transformation and objective presentation of ideas is characteristic of human thought, being an intellectual process that involves the spontaneous, abstractive perception of forms and formal identities, and correspondingly of exemplification and significance; all of which are acts of intuition probably peculiar to man. Intuition is the basis of intellect. Animals often show intelligence, but not intellect. It is the intuitively grounded, symbolic activity—spontaneous and prodigal in man, and very rare if not quite absent in animals—that makes the difference between intelligent response to signals from the actual environment, and the intellectual functions that characterize a mind.

A great many people, faced with some of the more extraordinary courtship displays of animals, such as the bower-bird's preparation of his domain, or with the mimicry of heard sounds by some birds, especially in captivity, which really pose baffling psychological problems, are not content to leave the problems open for a long and complicated course of reasoning. Such reasoning would have to include weighing the implications of explanatory theories as well as the evidence supporting them, for an easy and obvious explanation of biological phenomena may cause havoc in the rest of our systematic thinking about life and mind.

Scientists and especially philosophers have to square their aesthetics with their psychology and both with their biological concepts, evolutionary, Aristotelian, idealistic or whatever their persuasion. If animals are to be admitted as artists, then either they must be thought to share, to some degree, our mental powers of symbolic expression, or art must be conceived as an activity not requiring symbolic expression—as emotional demonstration, or as pure pleasurable sensory stimulation.

Both hypotheses seem to me untenable; the former because if animals were capable of ritual acts, practiced ceremonials or had standards of respectability, they would have the rudiments of culture, so their groups would be clans, not flocks or herds. The latter assumption, which would make animal artistry quite plausible, is inadequate to the human phenomenon.

In human life, art may arise from almost any activity, and once it does so, it is launched on a long road of exploration, invention, freedom to the limits of extravagance, interference to the point of frustration, finally discipline, controlling constant change and growth. Among animals there are no schools of art, no primitive, classical and decadent periods. Human primitive art is intimately allied with religion, magic and all public activities, so it ranges from the carved doorway of the Men's House to the songs and drums of war. It is the spearhead of culture; before men have clothing, before they can count, their dances may be grotesquely splendid, their bodies adorned with lines that enhance their motions and postures. In this they suggest the nuptial displays of bower-birds and the communal excitement of caribou. But in man, the first formalized gesture, the first stone shaped to fit the hand and seeming magic by virtue of its form, initiates a new era of mental life. That is because the gesture not only may be a movement of complicated and perfect form, but—however simple or imperfect—is made in order to realize the form. The shaped stone, treated as primitive implements usually are—with concentration on appearance—is not only a tool, it also presents itself at once, through tactual satisfaction and by its visible shape, as an intaglio image of the grasp; this semblance is a translation of touch into sight, bringing the feeling of the human hand to visual expression. Here is "expression" in the conceptual sense, a projection of the feeling, whereby it is conceived, not actually felt, through the appearance of the stone. It was thus gradually conceived as the maker of the tool worked with hand and eye. It is darkly but more steadily seen, by him and other people, now that it is embodied in an object, "objectified."

The visible and audible forms, usually repeated to the point of intimate familiarity, become significant for an imaginative mind; the fact that all our perception has a "physiognomic" element in it, which may be heightened so that it dominates vision or lowered until it becomes negligible, makes it possible for the artist to see actuality as an expressive image, endowed with a "quality of feeling," which serves to hold his idea and let it haunt him before he has formulated any projection of it. This, I presume, is why representation is so common a practice that one cannot regard it as artistically unimportant, and even as an irrelevant, historical accident, as some aestheticians do who have found that it is not indispensable. The represented thing—be it a prehistoric game animal, or the dancing Siva, the perfect cone of Fujiyama, the Mother of God—is the natural "motif," the source of the artist's excitement which literally "motivates" his work; it was the first organizing form for his idea, that gave him his start. In sculpture and pictorial art the boldest innovations and advances, which required the most intensive conception, have, as a matter of historical fact, almost always been achieved in works with an arresting and organizing subject matter.

To us, every distinct form that is recognized as unsubstantial seems imaginal. Even a non-representational picture is an image—not of physical objects, but of those inward tensions that compose our life of feeling; almost as quickly as we construe a pure appearance confronting us, we interpret it, which is to say, we have an immediate intuition of meaning, and "realize" that intuition—to use Fauré-Fremiet's term—by giving the form a locus in our universe.

That is an entirely different function from self-display, release of actual emotion or the aesthetic pleasure birds may be taking in their own calls or apes in their deployments of color. It is an intellectual function which involves no reasoning. That sounds paradoxical, if not absurd; yet there is no contradiction in it. "Reasoning" is the process of building up insight into relations which are too complex to be grasped by direct inspection of the highly elaborate exhibit or statement, in which many terms are implicitly connected with others in several directions at once, and perhaps are even determined in their nature by such relations—that is, are functions of other terms. Reasoning is the use of logic to make implicitly given conditions explicit; and logic is a fundamentally simple yet powerful machinery for getting from one intuition to another, systematically, successively, without losing any member of the series. The sort and degree of complex relational pattern which can be understood directly, without discursive analysis and technical process of reasoning, varies widely from one individual to another. There are, for instance, persons to whom numerical relations are immediately apparent which other people have to deduce by a long train of concatenated intuitive judgments. Both procedures are equally intellectual.

The perception of the formal aspects of concrete realities makes logical projection, or rendering of such realities in symbolic terms, possible and their recognition in those terms intuitive. Intuitive processes are not always immediate, and they may be selectively evoked, blocked or modified. The understanding of language is of this sort. It dawns at some time within the first two or three years of one's life under conditions of hearing speech, although the meaning of every phrase or word has to be conventionally determined. We have no intuition of what this or that word means; our intuition is, rather, of the fact that the articulated utterances of man are not chirps and cries, but speech—that is, we have an intuition of significance as such. Where this semantic perception is missing, there may be high animal mentality, but human mentality—mind—cannot reach a normal development.

Neither can it where feeling is a formless welter. If emotional reaction is sporadic and indistinct, though perhaps violent when it occurs, sensibility is likely to be crude, and its interpretive element limited to the practically essential minimum.

A highly developed mind grows up on the fine articulation of generally strong and ready feeling, both subjective—that is, autogenous—and objective, aroused by peripheral impacts. Where the process of interpretation is constantly elicited both by sensory impacts and by an active central production of images, inward verbalizing and variable emotional tone, that process becomes sure and flexible, and tends to enter into detail; for a mind so endowed, the semblances of most situations are complex, but complexity can rise to a high degree without becoming confused. And, furthermore, situations are not necessarily of the moment or of the outside world; symbolic activity begets its own data for constant interpretation and reinterpretation, and its characteristic feelings, especially of strain and expectation, vagueness and clearness, ease and frustration, and the very interesting "sense of rightness" that closes a finished thought process, as it guarantees any distinct intuition.

What makes this "sense of rightness" and the correlative "sense of wrongness" interesting for theory of mind is that these feelings are really the ultimate criteria whereby we judge the validity of logical relations. Once we see that a given proposition, A, implies another proposition, B, it is impossible to deny the validity of "$A \supset B$"; the sense of its rightness is absolute. Only a change of interpretation affecting the meaning of A or B could remove our immediate sense of conviction. Logical conviction is such a pin-pointed feeling that it has, in itself, none of the widespread and involved character of emotion; it seems the very opposite of emotion, although all sorts of highly cathected ideas may gather around it, and make it a tiny firm center in a maelstrom of fantasies. This intensive and exclusive focus on a distinct, discursively rendered concept, such as a proposition, is a structural characteristic of the feeling known as "logical conviction"; it makes that feeling easy to isolate from the matrix of sense and emotion in which most of our mental acts are deeply embedded. And, furthermore, it leads to the peculiar social circumstance that it is relatively easy to confront different individuals with the same challenge to feeling, unimpaired by the usual modifications due to personal context. This makes for a unanimity in logical convictions that has few if any parallels in the realm of human feeling, and gives to logical perception an air of "objectivity," i.e., of coming as impact upon us, not because we receive it with our peripheral sense organs, but because it is the same for all normally constituted people, to an even greater extent than any sense datum.

As a result of this formal peculiarity, logical conviction seems so different from other autogenous felt actions that it and they have traditionally been regarded as deriving from radically different respective sources, and meeting as antagonistic powers in the human mind, which is their battleground throughout life. Reason and feeling, logic and emotion, intellect and passion or however we name the incompatible pair, are most commonly treated as two opposed principles of motivation which can be reconciled only by striking a balance between them, sacrificing much passion, sympathy and gratification of desire to reason, and a little rational judgment to the admitted "natural affections." The alternative to this classical view is the prevalent modern one of rationality as a superficial process of "rationalization," not really determining action, which can be traced entirely to passional motives, but hiding those motives under a veneer of alleged "higher" aims and pseudo-logical plans.

The weakness of both doctrines is, I think, the same: they both treat reason as something intrinsically different from other mental functions, something not subject to spontaneous excitation, like fantasy or vivid memory, which are apt to be activated by emotion, but rather a constant, standard competence available for use by the organism, like an instrument. The concept of the brain (simplified by being stripped of all its interpretive and emotive functions) as a computer reinforces that view.

The principles of logic are exhibited both by the "mechanical brains" of systems engineering and by human thought. George Boole, who formulated the so-called "algebra of logic," called his famous treatise *The Laws of Thought*. But there is much more to rational thinking than the highly general form which may be projected in written symbols or in the functional design of a machine. Thinking employs almost every intuitive process, semantic and formal (logical), and passes from insight to insight not only by the recognized processes, but as often as not by short cuts and personal, incommunicable means. The measure of its validity is the possibility of arriving at the same results by the orthodox methods of demonstrating formal connections. But a measure of validity is not a ground of validity. Logic is one thing, and thinking is another; thought may be logical, but logic itself is not a way of thinking—logic is an abstract conceptual form, exemplified less perfectly in our cerebral acts than in the working of computers which can outdo the best brains a thousandfold in speed, with unshakable accuracy.

There are many indications that rational thinking is a highly specialized phase of that constant symbolization and symbol concatenation which seems to be a spontaneous activity of the human brain, brought into close contact with the outward senses, and under their influence, by virtue of a cardinal intuitive function, the recognition of instances, or specific contents for conceived forms. The truly intellectual phase of symbol using, or "thinking" in a strict sense, is a late development concomitant with a fully articulate use of language. It was probably preceded in all societies by a period of riotous imagination, stemming from a chronic overload of emotional responsiveness.

These are all hypothetical propositions to be argued in a later part of the present essay (Part IV, "The Great Shift," on human mentality). The reason for adducing them, tentatively, at this point is to suggest that the wide discrepancy between reason and feeling may be unreal; it is not improbable that intellect is a high form of feeling—a specialized, intensive feeling about intuitions. There are corroborations of this idea in the psychological literature, which frequently notes, at least, the similarity of form between intellectual processes and emotive ones. But my reason for entertaining the hypothesis of the derivation of all forms of human experience—self-awareness, *Weltanschauung*, mental suffering and joy, social consciousness or what you would name—from primeval feeling is the image of feeling created by art throughout its long, ramified history; that image seems to be capable of encompassing the whole mind of man, including its highest rational activities. It presents the world in the light of a heightened perception, and knowledge of the world as intellectual experience. Rationality, in this projection, is not epitomized in the discursive form that serves our thinking, but is a vision of that thinking itself, of a vital movement outstripping the sure, deep rhythms of physical life, so its tensions against those rhythms are felt as keen and precarious moments within the very limits of supportable strain; the sense of rationality appears as brilliance, perfection of form, a semblance of the tersest economy (which may be achieved with or without an actual restriction of means), or of great daring in the certainty of equally great competence (where the daring may be purely virtual, the competence that of a machine; there are beautiful designs in our contemporary art which depend for their feeling quality on their milled precision of form, and yet—without deluding anyone—create an impression of consummate skill).

Between all different levels and modalities of feeling, however, there are no breaks, as there have always seemed to be between the traditionally assumed realms of sense, emotion and intellect. There are graduated changes, and sudden shifts of rhythm; proliferations of detail, and sweeping simplifications; but the import of art is one vast phenomenon of "felt life," stretching from the elementary tonus of vital existence to the furthest reaches of mind. All psychical phases of human nature may furnish the "ideas" of art.

The expression of such ideas, however, reveals the nature of what is expressed, in a direction that is not open to actual experience: the unfelt activity underlying every event that enters the state of feeling. The work of transforming and projecting our concepts of psychical data forces their characteristic form on our notice, because a symbolic projection made for immediate intuitive apprehension has to be highly articulated; and, as a matter of long experience, we know that every form which seems to be charged with feeling also appears "organic," and makes the impression of "livingness," though it may not even remotely suggest any sort of living creature. This semblance of organism is implicit in the artist's "Idea." He probably thinks and does nothing explicit to attain it, because he thinks beyond it: but as soon as it is lacking and the work is "dead," it is emotionally inexpressive too.

It is this circumstance which really led me to think of feeling as a phase of vital process itself under special conditions, instead of as a new substantive element produced by such a process; as the incandescence of a heated wire, under better-known circumstances, is a condition of the wire itself and not an added entity. This led in turn to more and more intimate studies of the artistic projection, the ways of abstracting and organizing, individuating and deepening or etherealizing the virtual form. Those ways are legion, and constitute the artist's technique. The aims they serve are equally rich and diverse, and are, of course, the more significant aspect of his work, but they are not directly accessible. The readiest way to find them is to give attention to the means of their realization, i.e., to study the devices by which the expressive image is constructed and developed, and continually ponder what is the purpose of any problematical move. And here the power of the symbol really comes to light; for the great examples of any art exhibit—not in their physical structure, but in their virtuality, their perceptible form—an image of life that suggests some new basic concepts for biology and psychology. The aspects of vital functions that appear when one views them from their highest points, where felt impulses and conscious activities largely prevail, emphasize general characteristics of animate nature which are usually disregarded at lower levels of life, but are the very traits that make its generic continuity apparent. The necessity of "living form" for any rendering of psychical events rests simply on the fact that such events are the very concentration of life, acts in which the deeper rhythms of the organism, mainly unfelt, are implicated so that the dynamic structure of the individual is reflected in the forms of feeling as it is in the form of every voluntary movement of the body.

But in the development of cerebral activity to the human level, some characteristics inherent in all such activity become highly specialized and finally transformed so they have no close analogues in the mentalities of other creatures: imagination, intuition and the whole gamut of new powers these engender, primarily of course speech and reasoning. These characteristics become paramount in forming the emotional patterns of man and even his perceptions, which are shot through and through with conceptual elements, so human experience is a dialectic of symbolic objectification and interpretive subjectification. But that is an anticipation at this point.

What is in order here, however, is the fact that an image of mind is that of a living process, and therefore entails the projection of "living form" in a symbolic transformation. The basic transformation in art is from felt activity to perceptible quality; so it is a "quality of life" that is meant by "livingness" in art. This vital appearance is exhibited, of course, by living forms in nature, which—as that great morphologist D'Arcy Thompson has observed—are almost all records of growth, i.e., of biological activity; yet the most convincing images of such forms have often resulted in art where no natural model furnished the motif, and the shape seems to have sprung directly from the symbolic intuition of the artist. The principles of life are reflected in the principles of art, but the principles of creation in art are not those of generation and development in nature; the "quality of life" in a work of art is a virtual quality which may be achieved in innumerable ways. Yet it is in noting the differences between biological exemplifications of living form and the ways of creating its semblance in art that one finds the abstractions of art which emphasize the obscure, problematical aspects of life that are destined to develop into or to underlie higher activities, felt as emotion or sensation or the spontaneous ideation that is the intellectual matrix of human nature, the mind.

6 / A Chapter on Abstraction

The problems of abstraction in art have never been philosophically surveyed and analyzed. They arise in practice, and people who meet them there solve them practically, piecemeal, often without even putting them consciously into any category. They occur as questions of what to do next, how to handle a disturbing or commonplace passage, how to concentrate or unify an impression. Those artists who have reflected more generally on abstraction either decry it, or praise it as the aim and acme of their art. In the first case, of course, they mean the kind of abstraction made in literal discourse, in the second some sort of nondiscursive appeal to intuition. But what sorts of the latter there may be is not the creative artist's concern. He will find the ones he needs. It is the philosopher's business to recognize their variety and reflect on their functions, their relations to each other and their implications for the concept of mind.

Scientific concepts are abstracted from concretely described facts by a sequence of widening generalizations; progressive generalization systematically pursued can yield all the powerful and rarified abstractions of physics, mathematics and logic. The process of establishing them may, therefore, be designated as "generalizing abstraction."

The sort of abstraction, however, which artists mean when they use the word approvingly is of a different sort, and its procedures have never yet received any systematic study. Pointing out that they are not based on generalization and are not carried on by discursive thought tells us only what they are not, but provides no notion of what they are. Artistic abstraction is, in fact, of many kinds; some of these are peculiar to art, or at least unimportant in other contexts, and some are common to many mental activities and occur even in the ordinary use of language for social communication. Semantic intuition plays such a great role in human life that it is not surprising to find it elicited by many means, and as abstraction is involved in all symbolic functions, it also might be expected to occur in various ways and have several different forms.

The several different forms involved in the arts, however, are so different that one cannot arrange them in any order with respect to each other. They seem to have no such respect. The recognition of each one opens a new beginning in the analysis of whatever work of art one happens to find it in, and when one's analysis in terms of the given kind of abstraction has gone as far as it can go, it has not yielded the secret of how the artist's "Idea" is brought to expression. Some other abstractive principle seems to be at work, something stemming from an entirely different source. There are, in fact, at least four or five independent sources of abstractive techniques, and the interplay of logical projections which they engender creates the semblance of irrationality and indefinability which is the delight of artists and the despair of aestheticians.

The impatient or even angry tone in which most artists speak of abstraction when they mean the product of generalization springs from a perfectly sound conviction that the kind of thinking to which generalizing abstraction belongs is not only foreign to art, but inimical as well. The limitations inherent in verbal conception and discursive forms of thought are the very *raison d'être* of artistic expression; to surpass those limitations requires the abandonment of the activity which entails them, and which tends to interfere with the more precarious process of implementing formal intuitions of another kind than those usually called "logical": the process of perceiving and rendering the forms of feeling which are not amenable to generalizing abstraction. Because our verbal forms of thought are supported by conventions, they are incomparably easier to hold and to organize than the crowding, chaotic materials which sensuous or poetic imagination provides without any accompanying directions for use. Discursive thinking, once started, runs on in its own loosely syllogistic pattern from one proposition to another, actually or only potentially worded, but with prepared forms of conception always at hand. Where it seizes on any material—sensations, memories, fantasies, reflections—it puts its seal of fixity, categorical divisions, oppositions, exclusions, on every emerging idea, and automatically makes entities out of any elements that will take the stamp of denotative words. By virtue of its habitual exercise, it has an easy victory over any other process of conception and expression that competes with it; and similarly its mode of abstraction overrides the subtler abstractive techniques of art.

So far, the sort of abstraction that underlies artistic expression has not been given a name to distinguish it from generalizing abstraction. It is the reason for the difference in approach, rather than the type of approach itself, that must furnish the defining function of a whole class of abstractions not attainable by way of generalization. Such are all the abstractions which can be made only by presentational symbols; and perhaps the term "presentational abstraction" will serve most readily as the counterpart of "generalizing abstraction" to mark the main distinction here in question.

Presentational abstraction is harder to achieve and a great deal harder to analyze than the generalizing form familiar to scientists and recognized by epistemologists. It has no technical formula which carries the entire pattern from one level of abstractness to another, as progressive generalization of propositions does when it is exercised simultaneously on all the terms or all the constituent relations of a given order in a system. It has, in fact, no series of successive levels of abstractness to be reached by all elements in the complex of a symbolic projection at the same time. If we look at art as a whole, through the ages, and at all its kinds in all cultures, it seems to be capable of expressing the entire range and complexity of human experience as I have just pictured it in the foregoing chapter; and it is not hard to see why that projection should demand such a multiplicity of means, and why presentational abstraction should have so many forms.

The artist's most elementary problem is the symbolic transformation of subjectively known realities into objective semblances that are immediately recognized as their expression in sensory appearances. Such a basic transformation is made at the outset by the establishment of the primary illusion, the initial projection of an appearance as such, which creates the main substance (in the sense of *substantia*, not of matter) of every piece; it makes the most direct sort of presentational abstraction. The further development of the vital image, however, to the degree where its internal rhythmic relations appear more than just organic, more like the free play of thought, its immediate qualities like the warmth of emotion, its newness like an advancing awareness of its own, requires indirect and subtle orders of abstraction: isolating, metaphorical, secondary, transcending and perhaps others for which one could invent suggestive names. Let us begin with the most recognized and essential.

When competent artists or critics speak of the ultimate values they find in finished works, they speak of quality, feeling, expressiveness, significance and (if they are old-fashioned, or if they dare) of beauty, apparently meaning essentially the same thing by all these words. But when they talk about works in progress, or about completed ones analytically, they talk in different terms; then they are likely to speak of tensions and resolutions, and all their language shifts to dynamic metaphors: forces in balance or imbalance, thrusts and counterthrusts, attraction and repulsion, checks and oppositions. Different arts favor different metaphors, but tension and resolution are the basic conceptions in all of them.

The most fundamental elements seem to be tensions; and upon closer inspection, tensions show some peculiarly interesting traits. By their very occurrence they immediately engender a structure. They act on each other in a great variety of ways—they can be handled so as to intersect without losing their identity, or contrariwise, so that they fuse and compose entirely new elements. They can be intensified or muted, resolved either by being spent or by being counterbalanced, modified by a touch, and all the while they make for structure. This appears to be true in all the great orders of art; in every one of them, a general range of tensions is set up by the first element—line, gesture or tone—which the artist establishes. In performed works this immediate effect of a single, first-presented element is often apparent to the audience as well as to the author. The rise of a curtain in the theater, even on an empty stage, is a perfect example. In Martha Graham's *Primitive Mysteries* the curtain is lifted on black darkness; the whole tensive frame of the piece is given in that moment. In the plastic arts the creation of the decisive tensions unfolds in such an obvious way only for the artist, but to him it is none the less clear. Such tensions arise from any operation on the blank ground, for instance, the introduction of a line or a spot, or spots, of color.

The existence of a tension pattern in music requires no demonstration to anyone who can hear sound as music at all, and to the few who cannot it is undemonstrable. In western music it is most obvious in the resolution or withholding of resolution of dissonant chords, but in purely melodic successions the movement toward their natural conclusions is no less resolvent. What is actually done with tensions in the making of a symbolic form is most readily analyzed in musical composition, where their presence is so obvious that not only artists in other fields but even the "gestalt" psychologists resort to the vocabulary of music all the time to describe virtual or actual dynamic patterns.

From a great number of statements by artists and theorists in all the arts, it is fairly patent that the establishment and organization of tensions is the basic technique in projecting the image of feeling, the artist's idea, in any medium. They are the essential structural elements whereby the "primary illusion" of the incipient work is established, its scope and potentialities given and its development begun.

The pattern of tensions inherent in a work of art reflects feeling predominantly as subjective, originating within us, like the felt activity of muscles and the stirring of emotions. To regard the projection of this pattern as the whole being of the work leads to a "subjectivist" theory of art, which steers close to the concepts of direct emotional expression all too commonly applied to music and lyric poetry. The isomorphy of actual organic tensions and virtual, perceptually created tensions is so close that if the creation of the latter constituted the whole art process, our reception of art might really be simply empathetic or even sympathetic. But a true work of art—certainly any great work—is often above sympathy, and the role of empathy in our understanding of it is trivial. Art is an image of human experience, which means an objective presentation.

The need of its objectification has traditionally been met by a different principle of abstraction, a principle naturally inherent in perception itself, which organizes the impinging sensations spontaneously into large units: the tendency to closure of form, to simplification, known as the gestalt principle.

This tendency is native to the perceptive apparatus of many of the higher mammals. The eye is particularly selective in its reception, favoring those photic factors that the rest of the visual apparatus (including the entire optic tract, the thalamic centers and primary cortical radiation) can compose into distinct retainable images. The abstraction of form here achieved is probably not made by comparison of several examples, as the classical British empiricists assumed, nor by repeated impressions reinforcing the "engram," as a more modern psychology proposes, but is derived from some single instance under proper conditions of imaginative readiness; whereupon the visual form, once abstracted, is imposed on other actualities, that is, used interpretively wherever it will serve, and as long as it will serve. Gradually, under the influence of other interpretive possibilities, it may be merged and modified, or suddenly discarded, succeeded by a more convincing or more promising gestalt.

This principle of automatically abstractive seeing and hearing deeply affects the potentialities of art; for it provides another and quite different means of constructing forms, whereby tensions, always created in the process, are subordinated to the unity of a substantive element. Instead of starting with the expression of linear forces which make points of arrest by their intersection, or with points that beget lines by their motions and volumes by expansion, the first productive envisagement may be of pre-eminent bounded shapes, carved out of the total virtual space of the work. What is said here in terms of space holds for all other virtual dimensions.

Herein lies the chief and immediate virtue of representation in art. Far from being a non-artistic competing interest, it is an orienting, unifying, motivating force wherever it occurs at all in the early stages of an art; it is the normal means of "isolating abstraction," or abstraction by suppressing or cancelling all obscuring factors in order to emphasize the intended form. It provides terms in which a visual structure may be seen at once as a whole, and its parts as articulations of the whole. This character usually imparts itself to the entire work, so it comes with a single impact. The semblance of objects serves to objectify the total expressive form.

In European art the imitation of nature became an obsession, beginning with the Renaissance and culminating in the present popular standard of so-called "photographic truth to nature." But the great masters, even while they wrote about "imitation of nature," always knew that the abstractive power of representation lay not so much in giving virtual forms the semblance of being objects, as in seeing and using their resemblances to objects. So Leonardo, in a famous passage of his *Libro di Pittura*, advises painters to gaze at the texture and cracks of old walls, "where you can see all sorts of battles and swift actions of strange figures, facial expressions, and dress, and numberless things, which you can then render in complete and good form; which appear in walls and other such mixtures, just as with the sound of bells, you can hear in their tolling any name or word you fancy" (1882, Part II, p. 66).

The abstraction of gestalt from an actually given object by seeing it as an image of some entirely different thing—a plant, a roof, a boat, a human or animal figure—is a very ancient source of representational art. In a cavern at Commarque, in France, there is a paleolithic sculpture of a horse's head which was obviously suggested by the shape of the protrusion which served as the block. In the realm of plastic art, quite apart from symbolic intent, the intuitive seeing of one thing in another is an invaluable means of abstracting not only shapes, but nameless characteristics. The conception of one thing consciously or even unconsciously held in mind serves as a scaffolding for the envisagement of the other, so the main lines of representation of that other borrow their motivation from both; the resulting gestalt "is and is not" its avowed object. But instead of giving it a profusion of meanings, as the religious symbol-user tends to do, the artist sees the gestalt emerge as something in its own right; and if he imposes another interpretation on it, he does so to see it undergo some further transformation, until it yields elements of pure design. Such elements, then, can be developed through a wide range of motifs, or used without any representational intent.

In Europe, the ascendancy of Greek art and letters gave Greek aesthetics, too, an unchallenged sway, so that its key concept of *mimesis*, translated literally as "imitation," became generally accepted as the obvious aim not only of plastic art but of literature and even music. Representation of objects and actions was measured by its compliance with the laws of optical projection instead of by its service to more fundamental artistic ends. In other parts of the world, however, where the arts also have firm traditions, the use of natural forms especially in painting is differently conceived. Its purpose is understood to be the abstraction of elements of design which may be found in the most diverse contexts in nature, by representing objects in terms of lines, large and small dots variously produced, etc., derived from the envisagement of other objects. In the Japanese canon, for instance, there are eight methods of painting rocks, each based on the use of a highly adaptable unit of design, gathered from some phenomenon where it is clear and striking, such as axe strokes on a tree, the shape of alum crystals, hemp leaves, the wrinkles in a cow's neck. Henry P. Bowie, who had a thorough Japanese academic training in art, listed these standard devices in his book *On the Laws of Japanese Painting* and called them "symbols or substitutes for the truth felt" whereby "the sentiment of a landscape is reproduced by . . . suggesting . . . many of its essential features" (1951, p. 55).

The principle of gestalt or articulation of forms has intimate relations with the principle of dynamic structure or tensive design in all the arts. Either may predominate in evidence, but the life of every design springs from some interaction of these two creative processes. They are not opposed to each other as "motion and rest," for tensions arise from the very existence of closed forms, from within them and from their outward relations, and rest or resolution may result from balance or convergence of tensions. They are aspects, abstracted from the actual sense of life in different and incommensurable ways. Intellectually we can conceive them only by turns, though perhaps very quick turns; but in the visual arts we see them, in the poetic art we understand them, in music we hear them, simultaneously. That is a fundamental fact of artistic structure, and one of its differences from discursive form. Within a work of art this sets up a level of deeper tensions than those which we perceive as such: a permanent tonicity, which pervades the work and is the most elementary source of its apparent life, or "livingness."

Gestalten are multivalent elements, serving many purposes at once. Even the one interest we are pursuing in the present chapter, namely, abstraction, they serve in more than one way; for besides their "isolating" abstractive function, and besides their dialectical interplay with dynamic elements in a work, they have a character which has been called the "physiognomic" aspect of presented forms, and which is one of the most interesting puzzles in the psychology of perception today. It seems to be a primitive sort of "intrinsic expressiveness." Some percepts convey ideas of internal feeling, without being cathected by association with any emotive experiences. Why they should do so, and how their so-called "feeling-content" is received, has been a bone of contention among students of human mentality, especially social philosophers, since the beginning of our century. Like all psychological problems of feeling, this issue has been clouded by two philosophical obstructions—the simple, classical concepts of sensory reception and its intracerebral effects (data being associated, infected with emotion in the process, stored away and occasionally retrieved as memories), and the influence of ethical concerns, which stresses the social uses of feeling-perception before the process itself is understood, and in this way slants its investigation and interpretation toward premature, special problems and axiologically rather than scientifically suggestive wordings.

Several psychologists—Klaus Conrad, O. Kroh, Friedrich Sander and most notably Heinz Werner—have reflected and experimented on the conditions and causes of the non-social phenomenon of "physiognomic" perception, which often precedes or even replaces perceptions of physically describable sensory forms. So Werner reports that according to Sander's findings ("Über Gestaltqualitäten," 1927), "perception is global first, in contradistinction to a later stage at which the parts become increasingly more articulated and integrated with respect to the whole. Furthermore, much of the initial perceptual quality is dynamic, 'physiognomic'; feeling and perceiving are little differentiated, imagining and perceiving not clearly separated" (Werner 1956, p. 347). Conrad, checking Sander's work in his own researches, found that in peripheral vision, too dim light or too brief tachistoscopic exposure, a figure of bright lines on dark ground "loses its structure, . . . but gains a sort of physiognomy (Werner). Certain physiognomical qualities dominate the structural qualities" (Conrad 1954, p. 495).

Under normal circumstances of adult life, the passage from an initial impression of "intrinsic expressiveness" to perception of "primary and secondary qualities" has become automatic and practically instantaneous in most people. But in childhood that process is slow, and in some perceptual experiences may not reach completion at all. According to Oswald Kroh, the spontaneous interpretation of objects as expressive forms belongs to an early level of experience, the time of learning to distinguish and organize the data of the outer world, when autogenic activities still mingle freely with peripherally engendered ones, so that mental functions are not yet felt sharply as subjective or objective. Furthermore, they are transformed into a presentational datum which "mirrors" their dynamism and appears as its expression.

Here, certainly, the concept of symbolic transformation is employed, and all but named. The "transformation" operating spontaneously and involuntarily at a mental level of sheer perception is precisely the projection of feeling—vital, sensory and emotive—as the most obvious quality of a perceived gestalt. To take up this sort of emotive import is a natural propensity of percepts in childhood experience. It tends, also, to persist in some people's mature mentality; and there it becomes the source of artistic vision, the quality to be abstracted by the creation of forms so articulated as to emphasize their import and suppress any practical appeal they would normally make. This is the just ground for the frequent assertion that an artist must see and feel as a child; and it is, I think, the only ground for that widely misused statement. For he must not "feel as a child," and project childish feeling, but only translate feeling into perceivable quality, by intense concentration on the potentialities of forms to symbolize it even for people who no longer see actual things "physiognomically."

Klaus Conrad has made an interesting though incidental observation on the process of artistic projection, prefixed by an account of various phases which occur in the genesis of a closed and objectified form in natural perception, as experiments with gradual illumination, gradually increased tachistoscopic exposures, etc., have shown. A figure thus slowly apprehended seems at first to move and vary; "it shows a certain flickering and wavering life, which is mostly surrounded by a more compact contour. Thus, a compact contour with a flickering core is set up. This tendency to restlessness we call fluctuation. In tachistoscopy . . . on being exposed for the second time, the same figure is seen as totally different from the impression received during the first exposure." This figure, furthermore,

> appears unfinished and incompletely evolved. . . . In the subject, such an experience gives rise to a feeling of tension, and the tendency to give the figure finality. Then, again, one cannot grasp such a figure at will . . . but has to accept it as it inflicts itself upon one. One's mode of experience is changed from the critical to the receptive. I call this, the loss of the degrees of freedom. Only when the conditions of excitation have reached such a degree that the figure appears final, structured and finished, contrasting clearly and distinctly with its background and ceasing to vary in a fluctuating manner, does this tension slacken. The figure detaches itself, so to speak, as an object from the subject, it is released from a much stronger subject relationship, faces us coolly and remotely, and only then are we in a position to perceive the figure freely and at will.

A little further on, but still in connection with the above passage, he comes to speak of the artistic process. "One is bound to assume," he concludes,

> that a creative artist . . . conceives at first a kind of bud of the gestalt. The artistic achievement is thus not fully given and structured in the beginning, but seems to be at first a process pregnant with possibilities, without structure but with a strong physiognomy, fluctuating and without definite shape, not clearly detached. The subject [i.e., the artist] is then charged with an impulse to elaborate the process, but without complete freedom, as [he would be] in confronting the finished creation. Only when the work stands fully finished in front of its creator all this has changed, it is fully structured, clear and remote, is experienced with finality and can be perceived at will, with all degrees of freedom. The . . . *vorgestalt* has evolved into the *endgestalt*. (ibid., pp. 495–96).

The essence of the artist's task, however, is not only to create a form "fully structured, clear and remote," but in so doing to hold in that final objectified *endgestalt* all the phases of the evolving vision: the core of "flickering and wavering life" within the compact contour, the tension, the ambiguity, the sense of potentiality and non-finality, above all the "strong physiognomy" and the cathexis, which appears in an actually emerging gestalt as subjective involvement, incomplete detachment. The artist's "realized" form has to retain all these experiential aspects which an ordinary perceptual datum gives up as it reaches its full objective status; because the ordinary percept becomes a thing for the percipient, but the artist's creation becomes a symbol.

Since art is a symbolic expression, every aspect of life which it can render has to be transformed in terms of its complex abstract presentation; any mode of abstraction that the human brain has evolved, therefore, may be drawn into the processes of our self-comprehension. Even the discursive mode is not necessarily excluded, though its misuse is such a constant danger that its happy employment as an artistic device bespeaks a very sure expressive aim. The sort of conception that guides the primitive art impulse is versatile and unfettered, and finds symbolic possibilities in practically all aspects of actual experience. Just as the simplest given element sets up tensions in its surroundings, so everything that enters into a work has some physiognomy or at least the seed of physiognomic value; not only the gestalt that emerges in acts of perception, but simpler elements, recognizable colors, sounds, tangible surfaces, heat, warmth, coolness, iciness, light and darkness. There is a reflection of inward feeling in the most typically outward, objective data of sensation; their subjectification is practically started with their very impingement on the specialized organ that receives them. Their character is never as fixed and simple as the distillations our conventional store of qualifying adjectives has made from them.

None of these elements keep their character within the art to which they belong, or even in a piece where they recur under different circumstances. The structure of a work of art is nothing as simple as an arrangement of given elements by a half a dozen, or even a dozen, combinatory operations. The techniques of abstraction and projection are largely derived from the opportunities offered by the material, often on the spur of the moment, in a situation that may never be repeated. Those are the highlights of expressive power. But even the most familiar ways and means require other principles of projection than combination of sense data.

One of these is the principle of sensuous metaphor, the symbolic equivalence of sensations that have an emotive character in common. The significance of sensuous metaphor for artistic expression can be illuminated by going to the etymological dictionary. The etymological phenomenon in question is the change of sense which words undergo in the course of linguistic history. The fact that they do change in meaning has, of course, been noted long ago, and some types of change recorded, such as the narrowing of originally wide meanings to special ones, either by some paramount application, or by moral association; also the opposite process, the extension of word meanings, terms being carried over from their original uses to variously related ones. But the interesting exhibit is the shift of meanings in words denoting sensory qualities, which seems to be based on a principle of truly spontaneous sensuous metaphor, and finally to take a turn which reveals a mode of abstraction developed only in works of art.

Apparently the words which lend themselves most readily to metaphorical uses are those which denote light, heat, movement, or faintness, dullness, also pain and threat (which we shall come to presently). All these words either have direct application to mental states and acts, or have close cognates that are obvious extensions to psychical phenomena. It appears that light, smoothness and especially movement are the natural symbols of life, freedom and joy, as darkness and immobility, roughness and hardness are the symbols of death and frustration. Those perceptual impressions which are intuitively received as expressive lend their names quite spontaneously to conceptions of feelings, and at the same time exchange them among themselves.

The sensuous metaphor derives from symbolic elements that intensify the impression. Such elements create secondary illusions that play against the primary illusion of the gestalt. Secondary illusions are semblances curtailed in favor of the dominating primary gestalt and consequently remain only partially realized. They are products of the composition, not given with its material, but created by the development of the material. That is why laboratory experiments, which require definite stimuli and responses, have never yielded any insights into artistic experience; they can test only correlations of simple isolated impressions. But sensuous metaphor is public enough to be a creative force in language, and secondary illusions can be deliberate achievements, because any specific sensation which may be connoted in one's experience of, say, a "musical" effect in poetry, not made by intonation, or a "colorful" symphonic passage, is unessential. Whatever the context evokes will probably clinch the emotive abstraction.

The conceptual processes which the metaphorical extensions of words reveal are manifold. The discovery that basic forms of subjective feeling relate many objectively disparate sensations is not the only formal discovery to which philology leads us. There is another abstractive principle that comes to light if the study of sensuous metaphor is pushed just a little further, and focused on one peculiar phenomenon, which appears superficially like an extreme case of such extension, but actually rests on a different logical intuition and consequently involves a different abstraction.

Many words or "roots" denoting qualities give rise not only to all sorts of derivative terms involving those qualities, but by further departure produce cognates wherein the original connotation is more and more attenuated, ending up in its exact opposite. A stock example of this is the derivation of "black" and words designating "white" from the same root which appears in Webster (1960), if we compare two entries: "*blank* [ME.; OF. *blanc* . . . OHG. *blanch*, white, gleaming . . . IE. base *bhleg-*, to shine, gleam; see Black, Blink . . .]" and "*black* [ME. *blak*, *blakke*; AS. *blaec*; akin to OHG. *blah*; IE. base *bhleg-*, shine, gleam . . .]."

The guiding principle of such changes is an aspect of conceptual thinking which no conventional symbolism can express: the fact that every primitive concept arises and exists in an area of relevance, ranging from its own logical domain to its converse domain, and including all conceptions lying between these extremes. The roots of language usually convey ideas of felt experience, i.e., either of action or of impact, and feeling is good or bad, pleasant or unpleasant, with a continuum between them, which, taken from either end, somewhere (not necessarily halfway) breaks over into its opposite. Sensuously, the change of cathexis usually corresponds to changes of intensity, from too faint to satisfy, to too intense to bear. In every sensory experience there is the threat of evanescence and the threat of intolerability, and the precarious balance between them is implicit in every moment of perfection. A sensible quality, therefore, gives into the artist's hand the whole range of feeling it can express, even the existence of that range itself.

The following chapter will deal with the constructive practices based on these numerous, more or less incongruous, yet often intersecting principles of abstraction in the making of virtual living form. The astonishing complexity which may be found in some apparently simple compositions—small lyric poems, line drawings of one figure or little piano pieces every amateur dares to play—results from the countless elements a good artist can create, interweave and fuse, with so many dimensions of symbolic projection at his disposal. In the course of considering the most significant aspects of the art symbol, by virtue of which it presents us with an image of life and mind, we may encounter even further modes of abstraction, which cannot be discussed apart from their uses; in the study of expressive form, abstraction and creation are not always separable. This chapter has only done some of the spadework toward a survey of the prescientific knowledge of feeling, recorded by those people whose intuitive vision has put them in possession of it.

7 / On Living Form in Art and Nature

So far, our discussion of art has been concerned with its symbolic character, the logical peculiarities of its projection, the objectification of feeling as quality, the complexities of artistic abstraction; now, in the present chapter, we come to the point and purpose of introducing the art symbol into a philosophy of mind, i.e., to the image of mind which it projects. In the artistic projection, human mentality (which is "mind" in a strict sense) appears as a highly organized, intricate fabric of mental acts emanating more or less constantly from the deeper activities, themselves normally unfelt, that constitute the life of an individual. There is no simple dyadic relation which one could call "the body-mind relation"; a "psychophysical" organism is one in which some acts have psychical phases. All acts, including purely cerebral ones, are elements of a life. They arise in it and take shape and have some sort of termination, either in processes propagated outward beyond the organism, or else by spending themselves internally, reaching their own point of rest, or being taken up into other acts as constituents. This means that acts have characteristic dynamic forms; and one of the first revelations gained from works of art is that "living form" in art has those same characteristics.

All elements of a work seem to arise out of that whole in which they may also disappear when they are submerged. All elements may grow into themes, into paramount forms. In painting quite elementary decorative figures may serve to organize gripping representations, as the simple shape of the Cross the fusion of God and man, the crucified Christ. And once an element is created, it influences the entire work.

Elements in art have not the character of things, but of acts. They are "active," act-like, even where they are not "acts" in the dramatic sense nor in the special sense which is sometimes given to the word by people who let it mean only moral acts. In a broad sense, which I find far more useful for philosophical purposes, any unit of activity is an act. Taken in this way, the term has an instrumental value for building up a coherent and adequate concept of mind, and on that pragmatic basis I use it in the broad sense here.

The logical form of acts is projected in the art symbol, though not necessarily or even primarily in images of acts. All artistic elements whatever—all distinguishable aspects of the created work—have formal properties which, in nature, characterize acts. Inviolability, fusability and the revivable retention of past phases in succeeding ones are some of those properties. Another very important one is the relationship of elements to the whole, which is very complex, so that it is ordinarily not possible to designate it as a single relation. Every element seems to emanate from the context in which it exists. This appearance shifts from one created element—tension, gestalt, contrast, accent, rhythm or any that one may select—to another; whichever one attends to carves out a context that is indispensable to its existence. This is, of course, a manifestation of the internality of relations among created forms, which is a principle of art, not of life. But it parallels a biological condition: in life, every act is motivated by a complex of past and/or concomitant acts, and motivates a great number of other acts, among which there are usually some that belong to its own motivating context. It is in this way that an organism is made up of its own acts, and at the same time is the source of all its acts.

The unity of a work of art stems primarily from the interdependence of its elements, and is further secured by this dialectical pattern of their relations. The principle of dialectic is a phase principle; the consummation of one phase is the preparation for another, which in its own consummation prepares its successor, often a replica of the predecessor. Dialectic is the basis of rhythm, which consequently is more than sheer periodicity, or evenly spaced repetition of any occurrence. A rhythmic phenomenon may even involve no exact repetition, but is always a dialectical pattern in which the resolution of tensions sets up new tensions; the recession of one color brings its complementary to the fore, our close attention to the latter exhausts its domination and lets the former advance again; in a good composition of volumes, every boundary of a form is also a conjunction of forms, the surrounding spaces taking their gestalt from the volumes they limit. This mutual conditioning of forms is forcibly apparent in a rhythmic design, where tension and release, upswing and drop, or centripetal and centrifugal impulse do not succeed one another temporally, but are projected spatially (see, for example, Fig. 7–1). One of the far-reaching problems of mind, which we shall encounter in due course, is the organic basis of this visual projection; it seems to be differently developed in different creatures, highly specialized where it exists below the human level (for instance in bees), but in many animals entirely absent. Our clearest exhibit of it is in the arts, which consequently put one on the track of this as of other elementary traits of human perception.

Figure 7–1. Rhythmic Design. (After Alois Riegl, *Stilfragen*.)

The dialectical structure that pervades the virtual object is the main source of its unity, though not the only one. But that object, which is the work as a whole, has more than unity. It has a substantive character, which is, of course, wholly illusory; it is created by the artist, by technical devices, most of which he probably uses so intuitively that he could give no account of them if he were asked how the semblance of substantiality is achieved. There are, moreover, so many ways of establishing, sustaining, momentarily increasing and again etherealizing yet never losing this basic presence to which all the elements of the work seem to owe their existence, that his answer in reference to any particular work would have to be long and circumstantial. But a few practices which normally give body to a composition may be found almost everywhere.

The most essential one is the interaction of the primary illusion with the highly variable secondary illusions that arise and dissolve again, while it remains steady, complete and all but imperceptible because of its ubiquity. The fact that secondary illusions never present completely developed realms of virtual time, space, etc., makes their manifestations appear against the plenum of the entirely developed primary illusion, which consequently seems like a negative background, supplying their complementary forms; and since secondary illusions may be of many kinds, that background has to have a protean character, which gives it an air of indefinite potentiality.

In nature, such indefinite potentiality is the essence of bodily existence, which feeds the continuous burgeoning of life. Life is the progressive realization of potential acts; and as every realized act changes the pattern and range of what is possible, the living body is an ever-new constellation of possibilities. In art the elusiveness of secondary illusions serves to give the work as a whole something of that same character; it seems to have a core from which all its elements emerge—figurations and rhythms and all the qualities to which these give rise. Many elements are but slightly articulated, as their individual developments limit each other; this creates an effect of constant becoming, because partially developed forms seem to be still unfolding. Also, very similar or even identical gestalten may make entirely different sense in their respective contexts, so they seem distinct and yet the same; the gestalt element then appears ambivalent, as though its nature were not wholly determined, but still open to modification by internal or external conditions.

The interplay of identity and diversity of forms is a major factor in the dialectical structure of the art symbol. Especially the use of exactly the same gestalt in expressions of diametrically opposite feelings or impulses is a ready means of projecting the total qualitative dimension which separates yet links its extreme degrees. The explicit image is of two particulars, but the whole gamut is implicitly presented, so that they seem like selective realizations springing out of a matrix or body of potentialities. It is primarily this semblance of qualitative continua that establishes the virtual substance, and the appearance of partial realization that makes elements emerge and submerge like transient aspects of its inward being. The illusion of bodily existence is so strong that writers on art sometimes designate purely visible, imaginable or audible forms as "tangible."

Another condition that gives the art symbol its semblance of bodily existence is its complexity. Its preconceived structure—the "plot," as Aristotle called it, of a story, a painting or a building—may be the simplest of compositions; but in the course of its realization it entails more and more elements, all involved with others as reinforcements and foils and echoes. There are virtual tensions spanning tensions, resolutions that are the poles of new tensions; and on all levels, even that of purely technical construction, there may be mixed projections, mixed for the sake of expressing visual concepts charged with important feeling. All levels of feeling are reflected, explicitly or implicitly, in art. This holds for any successful work, and constitutes its "depth," which therefore varies according to the degree of success with which the work is organized. A very light subject, a bagatelle, may have this sort of artistic depth. It rests on a constructive process that is mainly or even wholly unconscious, and seems to the artist like "the happy hand of chance." But "depth" in this sense is a matter of logical structure, and as such can be understood instead of accepted as a mystery—like many other aspects of artistic expression, which become amenable to serious study only through the ways they are achieved.

It is often surprising to find that the most essential and obvious features in art are created semblances; not only substantiality and depth, but even the unity which is generally considered a *sine qua non* of all good art work, and the individuality or "uniqueness" characteristic of it, are virtual, and usually are achieved together, by the same intuitive moves. The inviolable unity of a total form, especially a highly developed one, is due in large measure to the play of several projections, which cannot be conceptually received at the same time, so that when one is in evidence the others recede, much as one visual gestalt disappears when another emerges, in the well-known ambiguous images of the psychology laboratory; and, for another part, to the "overdetermination" of elements, which makes their cathexes do the same thing. Those possible forms which are eclipsed by the realization of rival ones are still present as the potentialities of an implicit totality created by their dialectic. But they do more than establish that inclusive whole: they constitute the "body" or "organism" out of which its realized elements seem to arise. That is why a good work of art presents itself as a matrix, from which all its sensuously given articulations are derived, while others which do not appear are nonetheless felt to lie somehow in limbo.

Finally, there is a problem of which many people are quite unaware, concerning the individuality of every expressive form. The phenomenon is universally admitted, but what constitutes it, what makes each piece unique, is often a matter of debate. Its uniqueness is popularly explained on the ground that every handmade thing shows some deviations, tiny perhaps, but many, from the conceptual standard. There may be some truth in that consideration, but it does not account for the force of the impression and the importance it has in one's experience of art. Many things (e.g., pipe cleaners, dishmops, cartons), though made on one pattern, are far from precisely identical, yet they do not seem unique. A statue, however, may be reproduced—in some media, such as metal casting, there is no "original," but a perfect democracy of "copies" as long as the mold is intact—yet every "copy" seems entirely individual. There are, furthermore, artifacts of glass, spun metal, etc., which have undeniable aesthetic value depending chiefly on their machined perfection; and they, too, with actually no individual differences at all, seem to be unique in their beauty.

The upshot of these paradoxical findings is that the individuality of a work of art is not a factual condition but a quality, as virtual as all other artistic qualities. It is the semblance of organism that creates the apparent uniqueness of a piece. The work seems unique when it is "alive," i.e., expressive. Consequently this all-important character may grow but slowly under the artist's hand. Instead of being one of the elementary ingredients in the "Idea" with which he starts, it is the reward of his work.

Most, if not all, artistic elements perform more than one function, and as a rule any artistic device can serve more than one purpose. The mutual limitation which possible subordinate forms set on each other's full realization, whereby some are automatically curtailed in favor of a few dominating ones and consequently remain half-realized, has already been mentioned as a source of the apparent fecundity and growth of the work. But it has a further and more elaborate use, in that the competing potential forms may be developed to varying degrees, so as to present a gradient of development. In a Cambodian Buddha statue, for instance, there is usually a perfect elaboration of the head, and a flowing line to the hands, which are given slightly less articulation; the torso and crossed legs are very simply treated as large surfaces and opposed curves. There is a gradient of development toward the head, culminating in the face, and a lesser one toward the hands, that leads up to their delicate form and gesture. Such a figure has the living stillness of a plant; its "inward action" is concentrated in its apex, the head, which consequently predominates without being given any other emphasis by way of extraordinary proportion, posture or features. Its expressiveness suffuses the figure and makes the columnar body seem to subserve the development of the meditative head and the reflection of its poise in the hands; the traditional lotus pedestal repeats the theme of slow and gradual efflorescence.

Gradients of all sorts—of relative clarity, complexity, tempo, intensity of feeling, interest, not to mention geometric gradations (the concept of "gradient" is a generalization from relations of height)—permeate all artistic structure. They also permeate most of animate nature as basic patterns of change and especially of growth; and gradients of growth make the intricate forms of plants and animals. This is the central theme of D'Arcy Thompson's famous morphological study, *On Growth and Form*.

The significant points Thompson makes, with respect to our present subject, are (1) the recognition of organic structure as a record of the processes of growth, a logical projection, in terms of physical form, of their various rates, directions, mutual interference or merging; (2) the consequent involvement of time in the spatial character of living forms which Thompson calls "phase-beauty"; and (3) the appearance of the same logical pattern, which is statically projected as bodily shape, in the dynamic projection of waves running over fields and waters (1942, Vol. 1, pp. 193–94). All three of these conditions throw light on the relation of artistic form to vital form.

Taking these points in their order, we find that the first one, the eventuation of growth processes in articulations of shape, is reflected in the semblance of constant becoming which belongs in some measure to all good art work and in a high degree to its really great products. The sense of becoming, i.e., of process, is symbolically rendered very largely by gradients of apparent completeness, among elements so related to each other that they possess a visual unity and make a forcible impression of evolution from the slightest to the richest articulation of volume, line, surface and implied inner structural tensions. It may be reinforced by many other elements, including motifs, which often determine centers of interest and axes of symmetry. But gradients of all sorts run through every artistic structure and make its rhythmic quality.

The second significant concept borrowed from Thompson is that of "phase-beauty," the simultaneous expression of successive phases in a single form. This is, of course, just a special case of visually projected temporal process; but it is so familiar and almost ubiquitous an example that it explains in some measure the readiness with which we interpret the projection, and "see" the advance of nature in typical forms of life. It illumines the interchangeability of spatial and temporal concepts on an elementary level of human intuition, the level of "natural symbols" or spontaneous interpretation of visual data. What I would stress at present is the naturalness of the symbolic projection of vitality, especially growth and rhythmical activities, in essentially spatial as well as essentially temporal arts.

The third of Thompson's observations—the likeness of phase-beauty in growing things to the form of unbroken waves—throws some light on the oft-remarked fact that in art all motion is growth, although the lines and volumes and tensions that seem to grow never reach any increased dimensions. Wherever those dynamic patterns are projected in any medium, the phenomena which incarnate them assume the appearance of life; for the phases of growth and decay, rise and crisis and cadence, constitute the all-inclusive "greatest rhythm" of life, reflected in every completed subordinate rhythm, and tolerant of numberless variants and deviants among the lesser forms which it spans. The occurrence of such dynamic patterns in non-vital movements like waves, pendulums or spiraling storm winds, just by reason of being non-vital, uncomplicated by the lesser forms (and forms within forms) of life, makes the abstraction of the great overarching rhythm so impressively that it elicits our intuition of "living form" without any conscious judgment. The first such judgment, indeed, is likely to be the false one of taking the symbol for an actuality; but that is a natural stage in the evolution of symbolic thinking, a bridge from mythical to realistic reasoning, which need not be surpassed before the function of symbolic seeing and formal expression may be in full swing. Once the abstraction is made by the eye or ear (the roar of a breaker has a similar cadential form), and spontaneously received as something charged with feeling, it tends to govern the impulse of every stroke or uttered sound or bodily motion. Then the course of art becomes an adventure in the growth and precision of feeling by virtue of its expressibility.

In the previous chapter, surveying the many principles of abstraction which operate naturally and, as a rule, unobserved in the human mind, a little attention to the history of some ordinary words which designate or suggest sensations revealed two such abstractive processes: the distillation of feeling-value by the use of sensuous metaphors, and the unconscious relating of opposite values to each other as the two extremes of one continuum. In the present discussion of gradients in nature and their projection in art, the second of those two functions is relevant; for the tacit recognition of such qualitative continua, which is inherent in human perception itself, is the intuitive basis of our concepts of degree. The deployment of sensory materials by degrees is the chief device of visual and audial articulation. But degree as such, and therewith all increase and decrease, becomes thinkable and appreciable only along an ideal graduated scale.

The immediate relation, sometimes appearing as identity, of sensation and emotion (objective and subjective modes, respectively, of feeling) explains the appearance of sense data as possessing specific degrees in various respects: brightness, loudness, pungency, etc., and implying the entire range of every such quality from one extreme to the other; it is the natural form of internal action that is reflected in the primary, receptive formulation of sensory impacts. The fundamental dynamic pattern of rise and decline, *crescendo* and *diminuendo*, build-up and dissolution, is paralleled by the frame of our perceptual experience, and governs the world presented to us through our senses. Sensations, like emotions, like living bodies, like articulated forms, have gradients of growth and development.

The rhythm of acts which characterizes organic forms pervades even the world of color and light, sheer sound, warmth, odor and taste. The implicit existence of gradients in all sensation reinforces our appreciation of living form by giving it an echo or reiteration, in sense, which is always charged with feeling and consequently tends to subjectify the form, to make its import felt yet hold that import to the projective medium. This is probably the greatest single means artists have of "animating" their work; its importance has made many aestheticians believe direct sensory pleasure to be the prime purpose of art.

Every element in art has many connections with other elements, and every creative technique has many uses. There is no principle of abstraction or organization that is not exemplified in more than one procedure. So the apprehension of gamuts in the realms of sense, which permits an artist to create qualitative gradients that support and substantiate the "phase-beauty" of rhythmic lines or motions, also serves to enhance the fundamental dialectic of elements in the work. When a quality reaches a great height of intensity it seems ready to induce its opposite. Nothing appears more intimately related in art than a value and its contrary. This implicit interplay of extremes is, again, the sensory reinforcement of the many formal elements of dialectical structure which create the substance, unity and livingness of a piece.

The reinforcement of creative functions by what one might term "auxiliary" means is one of the internal bonds of artistic form, and reflects a trait of actual organic form, namely, the fact that in most multicellular organisms there are, besides special organs for the major functions, also some tissues which can take over those functions—perhaps parceling out their several aspects as separate actions—in case the special organ is impaired. Removal of that organ often induces growth of an equivalent one, as in the case of auxiliary buds. In art, the fact that a desired quality may be achieved by more than one means allows a good artist to reinforce his created elements by using one chosen device to establish a particular impression but letting many others incidentally serve the same purpose. This practice, which is intuitive and far-reaching, makes the created work seem like a direct exhibit of life rather than a symbolic presentation, because it obscures the technique in distributing it over many unapparent devices. It also has another, more remarkable, effect: it makes many subordinate features of a work reflect each other, so that each one of them connotes the whole, carrying the traditional and personal style like an "individuality factor" even in separation (within variable limits). That is why a sculptural fragment may still be beautiful, and a mutilated work, especially of sculpture or architecture, tends to close in on itself and restore its organic semblance, sometimes to perfection.

As there are many uses for one and the same device, so there are many possible means to the same end. Where the usual method of meeting a structural necessity or attaining a desired effect cannot be used, either because of physical limitations of the medium or because of internal conflicts, a technical equivalent must be found instead; sometimes it is far removed and indirect, but the created impression is essentially the same. The harpsichord, for instance, is unable to sustain a tone; the composers who wrote for that favorite eighteenth-century instrument contrived, therefore, to make a virtue out of a mannerism that verged on musical vice in their day: ornamentation. In ornamenting a tone with a mordent or a trill, they managed to strike that same tone several times without seeming to reiterate it, for the effect of such a decorative figure is of adventitious tones playing around the harmony note which steadily holds its place among them. The virtual element is a duration, while in fact the tone is repeated; and as each repetition is prepared by a tension which resolves into it, the semblance of rest on a single sustained pitch is created. But the creation is indirect and involves several factors. It is made by the unity of the "grace" as a gestalt, the harmonic identity of the central note, and the directional tendency of non-harmonic tones, which is to come to rest on the harmony note. Unity, identity and repose, deriving from three separate sources, are brought to bear in what seems like a stylistic convention, but is actually a transformation of superficial ornaments into a structural device.

This freedom of artistic creation has a peculiar influence on the created form itself. Even the beholder who is not at all versed in the technique that produced the piece he is contemplating knows at sight that the artist could have done differently; not because that thought occurs to him, but because the work itself expresses intent. With its expression of the artistic idea it conveys a sense of reasonableness, a tacit explanation of its growth. In a good work, every subordinate form appears not only to emerge from the inner substance, but also to be prepared by something else, perhaps by many factors. In a picture, every color or line or even lacuna that sets up a virtual tension does so because other factors are there to meet it. If we start with any feature, its place appears to have been ready to receive it, and its occurrence, in turn, to support the creation of qualities that one would attribute primarily to other constituents of the picture. It is as though a series of preparations were simultaneously taking place. This means, of course, that the sense of preparation is symbolically projected as an aspect of the artistic import.

It is here that Immanuel Kant made his major contribution to the philosophy of art, in concepts of telic form without purpose and perceptible rationality without discursive logic. That such insights could stem from a thinker generally as devoid of artistic leanings as Kant is really astounding, and attests the strength and candor of his mind to meet paradoxical conditions that fitted none of his intellectual habits. The *Critique of Judgment* bespeaks a recognition of the most baffling problems of art—the objective validity of judgments made without reasoning, the "free lawfulness" of beauty, the telic directedness of creation without practical purpose. That these problems are not really solved in the *Critique* is due mainly to the lack, in Kant's day, of the semantic concepts which have grown up in the wake of his own "Copernican Revolution" over a period of a century and a half. Perception, rather than significance, was the central epistemological theme of his time. But his third definition of beauty as the form of purposiveness without any idea of purpose clearly denotes a presentational abstraction; and his fourth definition of the beautiful as that which is "necessarily" recognized, without the aid of a concept, as an object of aesthetic approval certainly expresses the notion of formal intuition. That taste was the arbiter of beauty and pleasure its criterion were obvious assumptions in default of the concepts of artistic import and intuition; yet Kant's definition of taste as the power of judgment of the aesthetic pleasure-value of an object without any other interest, and his imputation of universal validity to the deliverances of such judgment, bring him very close to the idea of the objectification of subjective realities; his "common aesthetic sense" is essentially the appreciation of projected living form.

Actually, the purposiveness of artistic forms is not so purely illusory as Kant thought, but the purpose is one he did not know—expressiveness. And the freedom is not absolute, but is bound to a range of options. In fashioning a work of art, its maker is constantly faced with choices of possible moves, every realized possibility precluding others that might otherwise have materialized, and with them many of their potential consequences; but even as every realization dooms its alternatives, it gives rise to new options. An option is a situation in which two or more incompatible acts are prepared so the performance of any one of them would appear reasonable. The artist's work proceeds from one option to another.

Personal experiences and motivations, decisive as they may be for the success or failure of an artist's work, do not belong to its import. Only one aspect of his creative adventure enters into the artistic projection itself: the sense of movement from option to option, the recurrent progression from potentiality to realization, every decision producing new possibilities and offering new choices. This dynamic pattern belongs to art itself, because it is an inescapable pattern of life. That is why a really "living" work always seems reasonable in every respect, yet not predictable, as though it could, nevertheless, have been different. All its internal articulations are prepared, yet not caused, by their environment; the resulting impression is of motivation instead of causation.

The semblance of motivation is another powerful factor in making artistic elements similar to acts rather than to things. Where motivation appears as a fundamental and pervasive relation, its domain—that is, the work—exhibits the form of the great fabric of acts we call a "life." Motivation entails the concept of acts. But when one speaks of a "motive" in art, the word does not usually refer to what motivated the artist's procedure, but to relations of forms within the piece itself; the variant, "motif," is therefore a justified term as it removes the ambiguity. A motif serves to create a virtual motivation. It prepares a context for a number of developments, some of which are realized, their alternatives thereby ruled out.

The image of life as motivated activity reflects an aspect of animate nature that has baffled philosophers ever since physics rose to its supreme place among the sciences, because inanimate nature—by far the greatest concern of physics—has no such aspect: the telic phenomenon, the functional relation of needs and satisfactions, ends and their attainment, effort and success or failure. There are no failures among the stars. Rocks have no interests. The oceans roar for nothing. But earthworms eat that they may live, and draw themselves into the earth to escape robins, and seek other worms to mate and procreate. They need not know why they eat, contract or mate. Their acts are telic without being purposive.

Teleology is peculiar to vital process, and since it appears in psychical phase as the pattern of aims and voluntary acts, realization, frustration, questioning, solution or bafflement, it is a central theme in the study of mind; but it has had the least successful philosophical treatment of all our major problems. The main reason for this failure is, of course, that teleology is confusedly and yet intimately associated with so-called "free will," with vague notions of purpose carried into cosmology, and indeed with religious and moral issues generally, over which the protagonists of scientific thought and the defenders of the faith fight lusty battles. Let us, at this point, bypass those issues, and look at telic patterns as they appear in the artist's image of life, where no fear of doctrinal words besets their exhibition.

In art, as in life, and nowhere else in the universe as we know it, we find the conditions of necessity and freedom. Freedom is having an option; necessity is the lack of any option. But options belong only to living things, and where the concept is not relevant, as for instance in astronomy, the notion of necessity does not occur either. Only a mythical conception of physical nature leads moral philosophers to bemoan or admire its "unalterable law" and the "necessity" of causal sequences. Physicists do not think of the determinate quantities in their calculations as more "necessary" than indeterminate ones, because indeterminateness does not involve options. Neither has probability or randomness anything to do with choices.

Necessity is as much a vital phenomenon as option; it is the final elimination of all options. Dwindling options and growing necessity, widening options and receding necessities make the "tide in the affairs of men." The semblance of necessity or "inevitability" in art, which has been remarked with wonder since the beginnings of aesthetic philosophizing, is of one piece with that of internal freedom, which is even more widely attested and praised. These two pervasive elements are counterparts, and can enter into all sorts of dialectical relations with each other, even intersect—which they do, indeed, in every optional act: for the agent, if he may choose, also must choose. That is the real "inexorable law" of nature: the perpetual advance of life, from one situation to another, unbroken from birth to death. But the sense of inevitability which all great art conveys is most perfectly made without reference to that actuality. It is created by the fittingness of forms, the build-up of tensions and the logic of their resolutions, the exact degrees to which the elements are articulated, etc.; the idea is completely abstracted from actual life, transformed into quality, projected in sensuous terms. Yet we know it for what it is.

All the traits of "livingness" in art which have been discussed so far are prerequisites for the expression of the most consequential aspect of life, that which ties together its lowest and its highest forms: individuation.

Individuality has been mentioned before, in connection with the apparent uniqueness of every good art object even though it be actually one of many copies. But there is little one can say about "individuality," in the sense of "uniqueness." The conceptual difficulty that besets us here is the same one that we have already met in the handling of "the subject-object relation" broached in Chapter 1; it may be met by a different turn of phrase which simply replaces the concept of an attribute by that of a process. Individuality either may or may not be predicated of an object, but individuation is a process, capable of degree and direction, of being either steady or intermittent or transient, or incipient; it may be reversed, because it has a converse, which will, in fact, play a great part when we come to problems of actual life: involvement.

In artistic organization the mutual influence of forms is patent; they are often involved with each other to the point of complete interdependence. But at any point a subordinate form may take on an active, even ruling function, a motif may develop and detach itself from the fabric of the whole to some degree; it launches on a process of individuation. This is prepared by the semblance of becoming, of something constantly emerging, which is part of all "livingness" in art.

True works of art arise out of the standard artistic practices of a society, when someone who is prone to see the expressiveness of plastic forms in a way of his own modifies the familiar motifs to project that personal mode of feeling. Wherever such a projection of inward vision takes place in the making of a piece, its maker is approaching it not in the spirit of a schooled craftsman, but as an artist, and the piece is a work of art, whatever the success or shortcoming of its realization; its measure is more than vital expression, it is the expression of his idea, his personal conception of the ways of feeling. From the very inception of the work it is not a familiar rhythm, the typical expression of a style, that guides the artist, but his personal idea; and the central feeling on this level is always specifically human feeling.

The same phenomenon occurs in all the arts. Sooner or later, great minds depart from their popular inheritance, and seek to express new and personal conceptions of inward life, especially the rise and course of emotions, and the coloration that each artist's particular "habit of emotion" lends to all the sights and sounds and events of the outward world. In art—any art—the effect of this departure is a new created element: as the artist's work proceeds, the development of forms seems like more than elaboration, it seems like a gradual individuation. The actual procedures—adding, filling, simplifying, clarifying, etc.—are not new, but the semblance of growth is new, for it seems to be an individuating process instead of a typical organic completion.

Where the semblance of growing individuation is paramount, it makes a radical shift in the image of living form. It effects the humanization of artistic import; hence, whenever it gains ascendancy in one of the great orders of art, that art begins its Golden Age. Even then, there are degrees of individuation, which are apparent in the qualities of the average achievements in the work of an age as against the qualities of its greatest masterpieces, where it eventuates in the dynamics of fully developed human emotion and even of thought and understanding.

The process of realization of a work of art is usually the development of various elements that are implicit in the "commanding form"—the artist's pristine "idea"—to unequal extents, giving rise to subordinate internal forms, centers or lines of highest activity. These are distinct within the whole, set off by boundaries generated from within. Their boundaries, however, articulate with other forms, being each other's intaglios, which makes the continuity of the whole. This dialectic of separation and connection is typical of organic structure, and has often been remarked by biologists. Its image in art is the image of individuating force, unequal growth, which underlies all morphology and is the fundamental mechanism of evolution; hence its power to raise artistic expression to a level of complexity that reflects not only universal vital rhythms, but particularly human ones.

Human mentality, however, is not set apart from that of other animals only by a higher emotional or sensory development; its unique characteristic, which makes it something different in kind from animal mentality, lies in the constant stream of cerebral activities which are essentially subjective, having no perceptible overt phases, but terminate as images, ideas, thoughts, recollections, often elaborate figments, entirely within the organism in which they take rise. Those phenomena have a pattern of their own, unlike any other large and well-known order of events; they are elusive, occur without visible source and usually end without visible trace; placeless, yet highly individual, sometimes systematically continuous, sometimes repetitious, at other times madly mixed and rapid in their passage, and usually tinged, if not saturated, with emotional feeling. The most persistent impression we have of such events is that they "are and are not really there." Yet they are generally estimated as the highest values in life, lifting human existence out of the animal world into a different realm altogether. Most people, therefore, ascribe to such purely subjective phenomena a different metaphysical status from that of material objects and physical events, and postulate a separate sort of reality, "consciousness," intrinsically psychical and not a phase of physiological functioning, which embraces them as its own, essentially non-physical, contents. How little any scientist can do with "contents of consciousness" the earnest efforts of great men have long demonstrated; how little can be done while ignoring the intraorganic climaxes of human mental acts psychologists great and small are still demonstrating. The fact is that people operating with familiar physicalist models do not see that the wraith-like character and mysterious coming and going of images and thoughts are a peculiarly interesting aspect of cerebral activity, which has never been studied or even precisely envisaged.

The art symbol, however, reflects the nature of mind as a culmination of life, and what it directly exhibits, first of all, is the mysterious quality of intangible elements which arise from the growth and activity of the organism, yet do not seem entirely of its substance. The most powerful means to this end is a practice which has already been discussed in other respects: the creation of secondary illusions. It figured in the previous chapter as an abstractive device, and earlier in the present one as a way of giving the work just that virtual substance which the image of psychical occurrences must appear to transcend. At the same time, it serves most readily to produce that image, with its appearance of disembodied being.

The semblance of substantiality may arise from many conditions in a work, one of which is the contrast between the permanent, ubiquitous character of the primary illusion and the transient, incomplete character of all secondary ones in its domain. This same contrast stresses and enhances the insubstantial nature of secondary illusions. These result from special uses of the material, which are closely allied in principle with "sensuous metaphor," the symbolic equivalence of sensations. In the emergence of a secondary illusion, such as the sudden impression of color in music, or of eloquence in the lines of a statue, an element is created that seems to belong to a different symbolic projection altogether from the substance of the work. The effect is a sublimation of the expressive form.

In all advanced artistic creations there is some such play of secondary illusions over the unfailing, all-supporting primary illusion, with various effects, ranging from the expression of elementary feeling as a transient phase emerging from the organic matrix (as in rhythmic designs) to the appearance of acts that seem to depart from their somatic source, and form a separate, essentially mental pattern. A secondary illusion may be so elusive that it seems like a purely personal impression, and one is surprised to find that someone else has experienced it, too; or it may be so powerful that no one can fail to receive it. Of the latter sort is "harmonic space" in music, which musicians refer to as familiarly as they do to "tempo," "movement" or "sequence." Similarly, in the plastic arts all movement is a secondary illusion, but its appearance as "spatial rhythm" is so normal that few people realize it is secondary. Yet space in music is not homogeneous and complete, nor is time or motion in visual works; both are secondary, but genuine artistic elements—that is, neither is made by extraneous suggestion, as motion, especially, is sometimes thought to be.

The role of secondary illusions, however, may be a major one, and the techniques that beget them sometimes lift artistic conception to entirely new heights. Then, naturally enough, the astonishing illusion seems even to expert critics to be the very substrate of their art. The phenomenon of "harmonic space" is an interesting example of the creative power which such a principle of construction (as against a principle of art as such) may exercise; for the spatial illusion made by chordal structure has lifted European music to a level unrivaled by any other musical tradition. In Victor Zuckerkandl's *Sound and Symbol* (1956, esp. p. 55) there is a lucid exposition of the way in which simultaneous harmony, based on the complexities of tone itself, the overtones that yield the "cycle of fifths" and the natural relations of keys, conjures up the inescapable secondary illusion of space. In this tonal framework, the intervals between tones become powerfully apparent virtual elements which take on every sort of significance according to their places in the new pattern of musical tensions. "The interval actually heard," he says, "does not extend between two different pitches; it extends between two different dynamic states" (p. 92). Yet the music is not static; the harmony itself is directed "forward," i.e., toward cadence. Most people will agree with his assertion: "When we hear music, what we hear is above all motions" (p. 76). It has been said countless times. But the usual meaning given to "motions" is "melodic motions," which are essentially motions up or down from one tone to another within the gamut of pitches. A progression of chords, however, is not a motion up or down; yet neither is it simply a succession, like a single tone sustained or repeated.

Melodic motion abstracts the feeling of locomotion; it is a sound image of locomotion where nothing is transferred from one place to another. Even if we have a strong impression of musical space, and tones of different pitch appear to occupy different places in it, the movement of a melody from tone to tone is not a displacement of anything. But harmonic progression makes a further abstraction, for it does not even create any semblance of locomotion. It makes a direct and very pure abstraction of a feeling of pure temporal change, which is its outstanding quality.

Here, then, we have the "disembodiment" of an element emerging from organic structures. What occurs in harmonically structured music is a double abstraction, namely, of pure movement and furthermore of change without movement, pure transmutation. It is this double abstraction, made by a single new device—simultaneous harmony—that gives music the power to symbolize the passage and constant transformation of acts which are finally consummated in purely inward events, in the emergence of fantasies, memories or verbally formed thoughts. The "intellectual" quality of such music has often been remarked, yet nothing is more emotional than the harmonic advance of chords. Notice, however, that this advance does not create any semblance of "mental contents," but only of their psychical nature and the dynamism of their fluent shaping.

In most instances, secondary illusions present themselves as intangible elements deriving from some other order of existence than the virtual substance of the work in which they occur. The possibility of their occurrence makes the art symbol capable of reflecting the many-dimensional and incalculable character of experience. This widened scope of its expression may even be attained without going outside of its own primary illusion for a "secondary" effect, because various modes of the same primary illusion arise very readily—sculptural qualities in painting or architecture, pure lyric moments in drama or dramatic ones in prose narrative or lyric poetry.

The interplay of modes in the selfsame primary illusion (while the work as a whole, nevertheless, keeps its particular modal character) rarely has the intense effect of a genuine secondary illusion, which seems to present to one sense what normally reaches us via another; yet both are of the same category. Their fundamental importance is the same, only at different points in the development of the life image. Any secondary illusion, whether it is striking or quite subdued, is perceived as an act of transition from one level of feeling to another. It is transition made perceptible. Such a presentation of pure passage always carries with it an effect of "strangeness," as Owen Barfield observed (1928, p. 189), which more extravagant writers often call "magic." Where it is produced by a secondary illusion of the commoner sort, i.e., incursion of another mode, it tends to enhance the semblance of potentiality to the point where the work seems ready at any minute to take on a different organization. This is what makes an expressive form "exciting" without any daring novelty or representational appeal. It gives it a fullness of life that brings it to the brink of transformation.

A powerful secondary illusion usually carries the virtual life beyond that brink and makes the impression of a real shift from one order of existence to another. Herein lies its intense emotional power: the transition occurs, the higher phase emerges. Many thoughtful aestheticians have puzzled about the fact that so often the quintessence of art seems to lie in a division between two states, in which some mysterious passage or transmutation takes place. Kandinsky has remarked it, though one has to know his language and his peculiar mystique to gather from a brief excerpt what he means (1947, p. 30). Professor Francis Fergusson speaks of a "timeless moment" in drama, in which a destiny is realized (1949, p. 193). A "timeless moment" is one in which action, the mode of drama, gives way to an inward vision, still on the part of the agent in the play (not the spectator), but apparent to the audience as a plastic image would be, though it is not a visible image. It is poetically created, a mental act of the dramatic personage that presents itself as though it were fixed in a sort of mental space.

All secondary illusions, whether they serve primarily to intensify the expressiveness of a piece or whether they create a quintessential moment, have the same character of suddenly coming into existence from nowhere, apart from the virtual substance of the work (which is anchored in the primary illusion according to its proper mode), and fading again into nothing. In their very nature, therefore, they project the outstanding attribute of human mentality, the termination of autonomous acts in psychical phases that resemble those of perceptual acts in many respects; that is to say, the occurrence of images. Like fantasies, secondary illusions seem to have no somatic being; they are disembodied, yet they come out of the created form and heighten its livingness, even to a degree where the form in its entirety seems to be changed.

It has been said that the high moment in any work which achieves such a sublimation is "an unreality between two realities." Some people prefer to describe it as "a reality between two unrealities." That phrasing, of course, expresses a value judgment (and certainly a proper one) on the element of sublimated feeling, the vision or inward illumination or whatever it seems to present; "reality" is a word of better "metaphysical pathos" than "unreality." But, rhetorical preferences apart, the intended phenomenon is the same. It is the element in which the transition from somatic feeling, which is our ordinary reality, to imagination, the autonomous act of envisagement, comes to formal expression. Here is the dynamic pattern of the conceptual act, the strangeness and "otherness" and bodilessness of symbolic imagery, projected in the structure of great art.

That process which symbolic projection brings with it is the objectification of feeling, which continues into the building up of a whole objective world of perceptible things and verifiable facts. But as soon as it begins to build the "world"—and that is probably very soon, almost *ab initio*—it also presents abstractable forms, such as the external world provides us with, and the process of objectification engenders its counterpart, the symbolic use of natural forms to envisage feeling, i.e., the endowment of such forms with emotional import, mystical and mythical and moral. That is the subjectification of nature. The dialectic of these two functions is, I think, the process of human experience. Its image is "the poetic," more generally "the artistic," and it can appear in art from either pole of the dialectical tension—the artist sees it constantly in the quality which he finds in his world, and which emerges in his successful work, and in his best work may even go beyond anything he has ever known.

There is nothing in art that must always be achieved by the same particular means, as there is no definable limit to what a technical device can do. But the creation of secondary illusions is a powerful, not always feasible and controllable process; and the influence it exerts where it occurs involves the whole work. Those artists and art lovers who find the quintessence of art in that sublimation of the primary illusion where the piece seems to be given to more than one sense (taking poetic perception as one "sense," though that is a difficult and deep subject) are prone to attribute that power to art per se. It is, indeed, a key to the mystery of art as an image of mind.

It is hard to prove the achievement of a true secondary illusion, because many appreciative percipients of a work receive its emotive impact without realizing what makes it; also it may fail to occur, as artistic experience of any sort very easily does under unfavorable circumstances. The impression may be brief and seem personal, but nevertheless be made on a good many persons, so one feels that those who do not receive it have "missed" something that is—or was—there.

There is one step beyond that play of secondary illusions in which different perceptual realms seem to intersect, and make a semblance of rising and fading presences that in actuality belongs only to mental images—memory, fantasy and shifting perceptions. This further step I can only call "transcendence," because it seems to transcend the sensory vehicle altogether and make an almost pure presentation of the "Idea." Such a rarified projection cannot stand alone; it arises from a constellation of devices, making a manifold abstraction. Effects of this sort are often designated by awed recipients as "magical."

One more remark may be in order here, before we go on to the study of mind guided by a new image. Generally, when one receives an impression of "sublimation," it carries with it a sense of quite sudden and unaccountable simplification. When life reaches a limit of complexity and intensity it breaks over into a larger pattern that swallows its former elements and exhibits greater ones of its own. The sense of simplification attends that change.

There are many more things to say about art, but they will have to await the time when they become directly relevant. At the present juncture we turn to nature for the reality conveyed in the image, the actual phenomena it brings to light. For an image may—indeed, must—be dropped when it has done its work. To enlist its work at all is a new venture. The use of biological concepts and phenomena to illuminate problems of art is far from new, and has, indeed, a considerable vogue at present. Several writers have also made very serious analytic studies of art based on the analogies to artistic form that are provided by natural phenomena—cell division and replication figuring as formal repetition, organic rhythms as prototypes of artistic rhythms, etc.—much as they appear from the opposite angle which I am taking here. Our difference is not one of findings or opinions, but of purpose. Their purpose is to penetrate the mysteries of art with the help of their biological knowledge; mine is to gain some biological and psychological insights through the suggestiveness of artistic forms. A symbol always presents its import in simplified form, which is exactly what makes that import accessible for us. No matter how complex, profound and fecund a work of art—or even the whole realm of art—may be, it is incomparably simpler than life. So the theory of art is really a prolegomenon to the much greater undertaking of constructing a concept of mind adequate to the living actuality.

# III / *Natura Naturans*

8 / *The Act Concept and Its Principal Derivatives*

Once the image of life is recognized in its artistic projection, where it is seen to include all mental life, we have some measure of adequacy for the terms of a conceptual structure which can support biological thinking of a sort that, in due course, will pose and resolve psychological issues. We are in the realm of nature; actual life, not virtual, is in view from the new angle which the central position of feeling imposes on the artist's vision. That vision remains in the philosophical background, to hold the work of logical construction to its course, from the choice of basic concepts to the most advanced formulation of scientific facts. Such elaborate, advanced factual thinking should arise in due course by the use of concepts which, in the beginning, may be roughly sketched and imperfectly defined; use has to establish their definition, and will occasionally even force their redefinition. At the outset it is better not to worry too much about scientific form, or even about unassailable proof of every assumption, as long as the assumption is known for what it is. But a steady increase of precision, a cumulative growth of decidable issues, a certain ease of technical formulations and a visible tendency toward systematic connections among those formulations may well be demanded of a philosophical theory that claims to provide a conceptual framework for the empirical study of mind. That challenge is to be met.

Turning from the symbolic presentation of life to the phenomena of its actual occurrence on nearly all of the earth's surface, one is most immediately struck by the difference between living and non-living entities, animate and inanimate nature. At first glance these two categories seem entirely distinct: the non-living things exhibiting a relatively simple system of interrelated events, the system of mechanical causes and effects, in which past and future conditions are mathematically calculable and predictable, and the living things defying the laws of mechanics as by some inward power, so that their histories within the framework of inanimate nature are incalculable and essentially unpredictable. But upon closer inspection the boundaries between those two categories appear less and less sharp; there are borderline cases, such as viruses, which are hard to assign to one or the other, and there are physicochemical particles which exhibit no life of their own in isolation, yet have vital functions within organisms, or assume them when introduced into living structures. "Life" is obviously not easy to define.

The difficulty of drawing a sharp line between animate and inanimate things reflects a principle which runs through the whole domain of biology; namely, that all categories tend to have imperfect boundaries. Not only do genera or species merge into each other, but classifications made by one criterion do not cover the cases grouped together by another, so that almost all general attributions have exceptions, some of which are really mystifying. And finally, even series of events, such as the successive stages or phases of plant or animal growth and development, permit no sharp conceptual wedge to be driven between them. No one knows this as surely as the biologist in the laboratory, and the more exactly he experiments and observes, the better he knows it.

But the distinction of phases is not really something entirely artificial. It is, indeed, entirely pragmatic; but in order to be so it has to operate with some form which can be empirically found in the actual event and selected for conceptual manipulation. The continuous process is not composed of discrete episodes, but it has peaks of activity which are centers of recognizable phases, though these have no precise start or finish lines. What we need, then, by way of analytic terms are units with definite centers and labile limits.

Obviously we are not dealing here with material parts of a living thing, but with elements in the continuum of a life. Those elements may be termed "acts." It is with the concept of the act that I am approaching living form in nature, only to find it exemplified there at all levels of simplicity or complexity, in concatenations and in hierarchies, presenting many aspects and relationships that permit analysis and construction and special investigation. The act concept is a fecund and elastic concept. It applies to natural events, of a form characteristic of living things, though not absolutely peculiar to them. Such events arise where there is already some fairly constant movement going on. They normally show a phase of acceleration, or intensification of a distinguishable dynamic pattern, then reach a point at which the pattern changes, whereupon the movement subsides. That point of general change is the consummation of the act. The subsequent phase, the conclusion or cadence, is the most variable aspect of the total process. It may be gradual or abrupt, run a clearly identifiable course or merge almost at once into other acts, or sink smoothly, imperceptibly back into the minutely structured general flow of events from which the act took rise.

An act may subsume another act, or even many other acts. It may also span other acts which go on during its rise and consummation and cadence without becoming part of it. Two acts of separate inception may merge so that they jointly engender a subsequent act. These and many other relations among acts form the intricate dynamism of life which becomes more and more articulated, more and more concentrated and intense, until some of its elements attain the phase of being felt, which I have termed "psychical," and the domain of psychology develops within the wider realm of biology, especially zoology. The work of tracing and understanding that ever-progressive, self-weaving web of life in terms of acts and their interdependent functions will be the substance of what follows in this book. First, however, it is important to have a clearer idea of the act concept and a number of conditions which follow directly from it.

Acts are elements which show as much tendency to become expanded and elaborated into wholes as to yield further and further subordinate elements, to the limits of distinguishability. Their functional subunits, separately considered, close in on themselves to present in miniature the typical act form, and in contrary perspective acts merge and grow into whole lives, still maintaining that same essential structure. The best support for this contention comes from the working vocabulary of our research biologists, geneticists, physiologists, evolutionists and field zoologists. Through all their widely separated areas of work there runs the fundamental recognition of the act as the basic phenomenon.

The word "act," like all words in common use, has different special connotations for different people. One has to divest it of all accrued shadings and apply it rather where its definition (or, failing that, its explicit characterization) permits than where popular associations do so. Restrictions may then be explicitly placed on its meaning for systematic purposes. In the present instance, this liberation from tacit value connotations brings the term "act" into close accord with the sense in which scientists use it, not only for intentional acts but also for unconscious, involuntary or even purely somatic processes, of long or short duration, in plants as well as animals, even down to microscopic protozoa and germs.

Every animal and human movement, whether it be a whole behavioral act (like the twitch of a horse's skin to throw off a fly) or a subordinate element (like the tensing of a muscle in vocalization), exemplifies the basic act form, and so do its further and further constituent elements, down to the smallest units of vital action. This may sound like a sweeping assertion, but it is well supported by the careful, literal language (not the fashionable jargon of industrial metaphors) used by clinicians as well as field and laboratory scientists. Even botanists see the life they are dealing with in terms of concatenated acts.

What gives every act its indivisible wholeness is that its initial phase is the building up of a tension, a store of energy which has to be spent; all subsequent phases are modes of meting out that charge, and the end of the act is the complete resolution of the tension. Sometimes an act is complicated in its build-up, that is, a number of more or less independently originating charges summate to create a synthetic high tension; its inception, then, is widely based in the organism, and despite the apparent singleness of the pool, each contributive charge may require its own release; the act, therefore, has to be correspondingly complex. Also, a tension in process of being spent may be reinforced by a new charge which enters its path and heightens its potential again. The fact that locally developed energies have particular paths of release seems fairly certain, but only a very few such courses are known at all—the reflex arcs, which exhibit complete acts in what appears to be a genetically simplified, schematized form. Even in low animals the acts of feeding and of withdrawal from injury—in many species, the only behavioral acts—are elaborate events with many variable elements. They are usually, perhaps always, responses to specific stimuli, but by no means stereotyped reflexes.

Though the physiologist employs the concept of "act" in his formulations of problems and findings, he is quite clearly bent on the discovery and understanding of mechanisms, and expects to trace acts to purely physical origins; that is, he regards acts as natural phenomena, and the realm of life as continuous with the vastly greater realm of inanimate nature. In the laboratory scientist's thinking, "vital act" and "mechanism" are not incompatible terms. It is true that he does not follow their theoretical implications down to their metaphysical presuppositions, as philosophers of science are called upon to do, and that this might be why the paradox does not trouble him; but it is somewhat strange that two principles which are philosophically conflicting should be so systematically conjoined in all scientific studies of life and mind.

As there is prescientific knowledge of feeling expressed in the work of artists, so there is prephilosophical abstract conception involved in the thinking of empirical scientists; and concepts which serve without stint or hazard in a limited field, where they are freely mingled and manipulated, should be capable of some consistent logical formulation in wider systematic thought, such as is the philosopher's business. If the concepts of mechanism and of vital act seem antithetic in philosophy, one or the other of them is probably misconceived.

The act concept has been so exhaustively discussed by philosophers that one would hardly expect to find unrecognized presuppositions still lurking in the term. But their idea of the mechanism is still the traditional one of a machine made of prefabricated inert parts, powered from a single source and designed to perform a predetermined set of interlocking movements, producing a result intended by the makers and users of the contrivance.

Physicists have, of course, progressively modified their concepts, although they may become explicitly aware of such changes only retrospectively. A thoughtful stock-taking article, with special reference to the demands of biological conception, is John R. Platt's "Properties of Large Molecules That Go Beyond the Properties of Their Chemical Sub-Groups" (1961). The first sub-section is entitled, "Changes of Physics with Changes of Scale," and begins with the observation:

> We generally use a different set of rules or equations for problems of different ranges of size. The basic laws may not alter, but they are combined in different proportions, so to speak; . . . consequently the dominant physical forces and the distinctive properties of matter change, with every alteration in scale.
>
> Small water waves, for example, are governed principally by surface tension, while large ones are governed by gravity, although both forces are always present. Atoms and small molecules must be described by quantum mechanics, but this . . . goes over more and more exactly into classical mechanics in describing the macroscopic properties of large molecules.
>
> In biology . . . the complete change of structure and mechanism with every change of scale is particularly striking. (pp. 342–43)

After discussing the surprising phenomena that arise with molecules of 500 atoms, 5,000 atoms or "in the 50,000 atom range" in formations of linear chains, helices and double helices, etc.—phenomena such as self-replication, electron transfer, muscle action—he concludes: "Evidently many strange phenomena of biology actually follow quite naturally from physics and chemistry, once we have adjusted our concepts to the changed conditions and the changed scale and the changed complexity. What is most important is that this makes it less necessary for us to be dependent on vitalist or epigenetic or other peculiarly biological explanations that have been proposed for these phenomena" (p. 358).

But the philosopher seeking the essence of mind, or even of life, usually has no such elastic and potent concepts of biophysics and biochemistry. Every discovery of physical laws exemplified in animal functions threatens to impose the image of "*l'homme machine*" on his mind, and drives him, in protest, to some form of antimechanism, because on the basis of his entire experience of vital feeling and intrinsic value, his intuitive judgment—perhaps even his sense of humor—tells him that the image is spurious. Yet he has no other image that invites scientific minds to explore its object. So he can only resort to the logically inconceivable, but religiously familiar, animating soul, guiding entelechy, or numberless incarnations of an *élan vital*.

It is here that the artist's symbolic projection provides a principle of analysis applicable to the actual living form his work reflects: the principle of distinguishing, within a dynamic whole (i.e., a whole held together only by activity) articulated elements, which nonetheless are indivisible in themselves, and inalienable from the whole, if they are not to give up their identity. In the preceding chapter I pointed out that artistic elements are "act-like." Their biological analogues in the world of nature are acts.

The analysis of acts leads one, not to inert permanent bits of matter being rearranged by impinging forces, but to further and further acts subsumed under almost any act with which one chooses empirically to begin. At length, some present-day researchers even reach a level of proto-acts—events which belong to chemistry or electrochemistry as much as to biology, because they exemplify the character of acts in many respects, yet not in all, so that viewed in a reverse perspective they would seem to foreshadow rather than present processes of genuine life. In this borderland it becomes relevant and justifiable to ask, where does life begin?—which is equivalent to the question, what are the most primitive full-fledged acts?

Clearly, at that point we are in the realm of science, and seeking the mechanisms of molecular integration in the evolution of organic compounds. By "mechanism" I mean any process we understand in terms of physics and chemistry. The complexity of such processes is beyond the imagination of anyone who does not know some samples of them rather intimately; they grow up into self-sustaining rhythms and dialectical exchanges of energy, forms and qualities evolving and resolving, submicroscopic elements—already highly structured—merging and great dynamisms emerging. The common-sense tenet that such products of nature cannot attain feeling, awareness and thought loses its cogency when one is confronted by the actual intricacies of chemical and electrochemical organization. The bridge to organism arises of itself, and the conviction that "extended substance" cannot think and "thinking substance" cannot have material properties appears as a medieval doctrine handed down to modern philosophy in Descartes' famous dictum, and with no firmer foundation than his word.

It is, in fact, noteworthy that there are rather few elaborate lifeless mechanisms in nature. Geysers and blowholes, volcanoes, tides and whirlpools, the variable yet generally patterned dynamisms that effect cyclonic storms, are spectacular mechanisms, but they are simple; all very intricate natural mechanisms that we know are alive. Now, such vital working systems have no inanimate solid parts assembled and adapted. They show rhythms within rhythms, interlocking timed sequences of chemical changes, electrical fields and currents that induce the chemical actions or, conversely, are generated by them, the most elaborate physical processes under a network of homeostatic controls; the sum total is a matrix of acts within acts, organizing previously unrelated material units at the molecular and atomic levels in an unbroken continuum of activity that builds itself up into the incredible dynamism called a living body, which disintegrates if the creative activity stops.

The study of living functions as acts thus leads backward into the physical sciences without coming to any dividing line that has to be crossed by a *saltus naturae*. Looking forward to the fields of less well-known nature—psychology, sociology, ethics—we find ourselves in possession of a basic concept that can be developed to serve far more difficult ends than workers in those fields have ever dared to set themselves.

Perhaps the first and most arresting feature of the realm of life is that the causal order exemplified in nature as a whole seems to be somehow absent here. A little further reflection, however, makes it apparent that all mechanisms exhibit causal relationships, all movements have causal antecedents; the analysis of acts in terms of such sequences is not impossible, but for some reason it is generally irrelevant. A more important relation among acts is something called "motivation." So far, even professional scholars who have taken account of the difference between causation and motivation have not transcended the common-sense level of so-called "ordinary language." As a result their reasoning generally provides no access to more advanced problems nor leads to further conceptual developments and connections.

An organism's motivation, or, as R. W. White prefers to call it, its "urge that makes for competence," expresses itself in exploratory behavior whereby a creature finds out the nature of its surroundings, and in nosing, mouthing or manipulating objects, whereby it learns its own powers to effect changes, to make things happen in the external world. The aim of such "monkeying" behavior is acting just for the sake of causing and controlling events; the creature finds out what will happen in consequence of an act. The motivation of that act lies in his own previous behavior of exploring the environment, and the changes that occur in his situation are due to his own postural changes and shifts of focus or attention.

It is not only as "causation of the psychical," but as this and more, that I would use the term "motivation": as "causation of acts." Since acts are natural events of a highly variable, yet fundamentally typical form, it is not surprising that their causation by other acts as well as by non-vital, circumstantial events such as "field" determinates, specific isolated external stimuli, or certain conditioned reflexes shows a comparably typical, complex pattern. The entire motivation of an act can never be summed up in a "motive," nor in several motives, although motives are important definable elements among mental acts, to be discussed in due course. For the moment let us consider the peculiar process of motivation, in contrast to causal relationships which do not fall under that heading.

Every act arises from a situation. The situation is a constellation of other acts in progress, often including some which develop with the acute initial phase of peripherally originating acts, such as we feel as impact if they are intense enough to develop a psychical phase. But the substance of a situation is always the stream of advancing acts which have already arisen from previous situations punctuated by previous impacts; centripetally proceeding acts (usually but not always of brief, quickly completed build-up) impinge on that continuous integral process, differentiating and developing its myriad possible forms. All distinguishable acts arise from this matrix, which is their situation.

The process whereby they arise is a basic causal relation obtaining among acts, which may be termed "induction." One act, or a complex of acts, may be said to induce a new act; ultimately the entire situation, whatever its stage at the time in question, induces any and every act. There may, however, be a range of immediate relevance to a given act within the situation. Induction is a very complicated process that is but little understood; this does not mean, however, that we should dismiss it for some less difficult "conceptualization" which will give us law-like formulas with simple predictive uses but no instrumental promise in the face of true scientific problems.

An organism normally exists in a non-living physical environment, which is constantly undergoing changes that affect the active being, the organism, at its center. This environment at any particular time is generally referred to as "the environmental situation," and is the psychologist's chief object of consideration in judging the acts of the organism; the "inward situation," being unsurveyable, is usually dismissed with a phrase of recognition, except where special pharmacological experiments are the issue. But the way in which any event in the "environmental situation" affects the life is deeply influenced by the fact that it is a life, not a non-living physical complex, on which the event impinges. Many years ago, Jakob von Uexküll (1909) called attention to the fact that two different organisms in the same environment were likely to exist in widely differing environmental situations, or, as he called them, different "ambient worlds" ("*Umwelten*"), due to the selective powers with which their respective peripheral organs (their integuments, as well as specialized sense organs) could filter out noxious or even merely useless influences. Besides these differences in the reception of outside influences, there is an immense variation in the value an influence, once received, has for various creatures. This is because the external event can keep its formal self-identity only to the point of making peripheral contact with the system of acts; if it invades that system, that importation falls at once under the sway of the vital processes, and becomes an element in a new phase of the organism; that is, it engenders a new situation. This sort of influence is continually taking place. Energy is fed into living systems all the time, as oxygen, nutriment, warmth or light, from their peculiarly specific *Umwelt*, which is not "the environment" in a usual sense; Uexküll's word, "*Umwelt*," has been translated "ambient," which is the term I shall use.

Such impingement of outside events on an organism is, of course, a causal relation; but it is not a simple causal relation between a non-vital force—the push of an object, or even a current or a ray—and an act produced by it. The only way an external influence can produce an act is to alter the organic situation that induces acts; and to do this it must strike into a matrix of ongoing activity, in which it is immediately lost, replaced by a change of phase in the activity. The new phase induces new distinguishable acts. This indirect causation of acts via the prevailing dynamic situation is "motivation." It may arise from intraorganic sources, too, which is to say from autogenous acts that radically alter the general activity, inducing a new phase (i.e., a new situation); in that case, overt acts of the organism may be motivated by entirely covert events.

An external event that initiates a behavioral act in an organism is a "stimulus." It is quite obviously a cause of the act (the latter being known as the "reaction" or "response"), yet the sequence of cause and effect is just as obviously not a simple transmission of motion, heat, or other physical quantity from one body to another. The disproportion between the impinging force and the action produced in the organism is so spectacular that some thinkers have questioned the applicability of ordinary causal laws to behavioral responses.

Whether there can be sciences of behavior comparable to physics in their abstract structure I am not sure; but there can very probably be an understanding of mental phenomena that would permit us to trace them in a downward direction, at least, to their roots in biological events we have hopes of knowing systematically and precisely.

To this end I have introduced the notion of the act as a formal unit, or modulus, of living processes. A response, such as aggression against a father-surrogate, is an act, arising from a situation that reflects a general, accumulated condition of the organism. The condition stems from acts long past that still affect all emerging situations through their (now completely integrated) traces in the matrix of activities, the organism itself; they have continued themselves in its special form, its disposition. A response such as a sudden increase in saliva flow is also an act, arising from a situation that may be just as complex but less individual, so that analogous acts with analogous motivations may be induced under many circumstances, in countless organisms. A heartbeat is an act, and so are all distinguishable physiological events that compose it.

Returning to the analysis of the act form itself, with its typical phases of incipience, acceleration (with or without growing articulation), consummation and cadence, we are arrested at the very outset by the challenging complexity and importance of the first phase. Most of the motivation psychologists, who conceive motivation as the evocation (or, sometimes, the releasing) of a "drive" by a stimulus, and the behavioral act, therefore, as the overt termination of covert processes in the organism (a concept to which I certainly can take no exception), have observed that "drive" is not simply a general impetus to motion, but is directed to and through particular effectors, and subject to guidance along the course of its swift or gradual expenditure. This specialization in "drives" distinguishes them from inorganic forces; for machine power will drive one machine as well as another to which it may be coupled, but "drives" are discriminate. The direction of a "drive" is toward a particular object or away from it; but the specificity of the drive goes further, according to the particular nature of the object to be approached or avoided. There is, by way of example, the difference between the danger of falling and that of being run over, which are met by quite different movements implementing the "avoidance drive."

Motivation, effected by a stimulus, is thus conceived to be the activation of a "drive." Just what constitutes the "drive," however, is hard to tell. The different drives directed toward goals or away from dangers certainly appear as "intervening variables." They are events in the organism, started by stimulation and terminating in overt acts that have obvious reference to specific things, beings or events (such as electric shocks occurring in particular places).

The conception of behavioral acts as terminations of "drives" has the great virtue of emphasizing the intraorganic dynamism that underlies overt responses, and thus breaking away from the simple "billiard ball" model of causality. But as a principle for the theoretical analysis of life in terms of acts it is not suitable, because it does not characterize acts as such. This is immediately apparent from the fact that not every act is supposed to stem from a drive; some elementary responses, such as withdrawal of the hand from contact with fire or a hot object, are said to be caused directly by the stimulus. Furthermore, the same drive may be thought to terminate in any one of several possible acts, which are formally distinct, though pragmatically equivalent. Above all, one can speak of "drives" only in relation to behavioral acts; but the understanding of such acts requires conceptual terms that can be carried to the microscopic level.

The dynamism of life lies in the nature of acts as such; it is incorporated in their structure and gives them their typical form. Every act, as I said early in the present chapter, has an initial phase, a phase of acceleration and sometimes increasing complexity, a turning point, or consummation, and a closing phase, or cadence. The initial phase is its impulse. This is an integral part of the act itself; it is the incipient act.

An impulse is usually conceived to be a homogeneous discharge of energy, the equivalent in animate nature of a force, or impetus, in the inorganic realm. But an impulse, or nascent act, is an offshoot of a fluid situation which, because of its unstable character from one moment to another, is probably never altogether determinable. Within the active organism, the very matter which is implementing an act may undergo dissolution in the process and be transformed, so that it enters into another mechanism that functions in another situation. The first really identifiable element is the impulse; and this is already an articulated process.

Even in acts which are complete, all-or-none discharges of energy, like the "firing" of a single neuron in the brain, the impulse must be supposed, usually if not always, to be composite. The complexity of the cell makes it unlikely that a simple stimulus normally evokes the act of discharge, although the latter, when it does occur, seems to be always exhaustive of the entire impulse. In such minute acts, therefore, the building up of the impulse may be essentially a summation of converging charges raising the electrical potential of the neuron to the point of release, whereupon the cell, having "fired," is briefly "refractory," unable to act, and perhaps unable to receive a charge; the activity runs through a series of cells as a course of successive discharges, each motivating the next.

In more complex acts, however, various elements of the total event often seem to occur as by a "pre-established harmony," rather than in the manner of a chain where each movement induces the next. Subordinate acts appear to converge with mutually independent timing on the achievement of an integral larger whole. A striking demonstration of this is the swallowing reflex where ten muscles, plus the diaphragm, are involved. Excising or procainizing participating muscles, or concurrent stimulation of hypoglossal or lingual nerves, does not affect the sequence of events in the other muscles. The result is that a dynamic pattern is realized in the occurrence of the total act. Every constituent act has its particular impulse, with its own intensity and easiest path, its possible alternatives if that path is obstructed and its own rate of progress; and every impulse, when it issues in action, resolves the particular organic tension it represents, which is an accumulation (perhaps infinitesimal) of potential energy ready for transformation into some other phase. In living systems such charges tend to form integrated patterns, i.e., unitary but organized impulses, and spend themselves, under the influence of one largest, unifying impulse, in a flow of events that takes the characteristic form of a single act.

The only really decisive way of justifying a new philosophical departure such as we are making in treating the act as the unit of living form is to apply the proposed concepts to some field of empirical research to which they properly relate, and show that they are adequate, or at least more nearly adequate than any older ones, to the logical demands of the material. Fortunately—as it often happens along the broad fronts of intellectual advance—such a test has already been made, with gratifying results, in the biological science of ethology. In a pioneering theoretical article, entitled "A Basis for the Quantitative Structure of Behaviour" (1954), the authors, W. M. S. Russell, A. P. Mead and J. S. Hayes, have taken the act concept as the systematic unit for the understanding of behavior. They limit their theoretical discussion to the treatment of such phenomena as ethologists ordinarily deal with, i.e., the more or less stereotyped, often species-specific responses of animals that have been scientifically observed in field or laboratory.

It is, unfortunately, impossible to present in due order even the main points of the conceptual structure built up in that very systematically written article, but certain similarities between its treatment of acts and mine are: first, the basic unity of the act, though Russell, Mead and Hayes base it on an empirically observed, regular coincidence of elements, and I find it in the singleness of an over-all tension; second, the development of the act from a functional "center," which is not said to be a local mechanism or "brain center," but some sort of intraorganic starting point where the act is formed as a unit charge, ready to be triggered by an external or even internal stimulus—clearly an analogue to my notion of "impulse"; and, finally, the tenet that extraneous influences on the act reach it indirectly, through the act tendency. This leads directly to the concept of the situation, or current phase of the life in which—and from which—the act arises.

The supposition that the act takes its presumptive shape and scope in the initial phase, the impulse, has several advantages, too, for it allows one to define potential acts, actualization (and at a later stage, realization), inhibition, and finally intention, opportunity, choice and the effects of decision. The concept of the potential act is of special importance here, for it has sometimes been said that such a concept, necessary as it is for understanding choice, intent, foresight and any effect of negative conditions (as in "sins of omission"), cannot be construed in terms of natural science, which can admit only actual occurrences to its realm of causes and effects.

A potential act is, then, an impulse. It need not reach a stage of muscular contractions, nor of cerebration that records itself in galvanic skin reflexes. Its overt development may be wholly suppressed by the actualization of another, incompatible impulse; then it remains potential, though it may be so for a long time, continued by repetitive pulses, or held unspent in its nascent state. The impulse, or potential act, is something that really occurs; even without the normal development here called "actualization," an impulse is an event.

That the essential form of a complete act is prefigured in its impulse has been experimentally established by records obtained with microelectrodes inserted directly into individual neurons. The all-important finding in these empirical studies is that the so-called "firing" of a neuron is not a simple discharge, such as we see in an electric spark, but has a typical and often elaborate spatiotemporal pattern. T. H. Bullock, who is one of the pioneers in that field, states as a well-grounded conclusion: "The output of single neurons and of groups of neurons is normally probably always patterned, i.e., temporally and spatially distributed in a non-random way" (1961, p. 48). Several investigators have analyzed the heartbeats of lobsters and crabs, and their findings all converge to corroborate the hypothesis that a prepattern of the act (the heartbeat) is exhibited in the impulse.

Such elementary somatic acts, moreover, are not the only ones that seem to be generally and tentatively, at least, preformed in the impulse, to be modified by situational pressures in the course of their actualization. Dr. Bullock observes such wider connections, saying:

> certain regions of the cortex can be crudely stimulated electrically and complex, vivid audio-visual experiences triggered. . . . Less complex but normally coordinated movements occur in lower forms . . . such as chirping or antenna-cleaning in crickets and compulsive drinking in a goat. . . . Other familiar examples are sneezing, jumping, spitting, stinging, swallowing, seizing, displaying, and the like. . . . It seems at present likely that for many relatively complex behavioral actions the nervous system contains not only genetically determined circuits but also genetically determined physiological properties of their components so that the complete act is represented in coded form and awaits only an adequate trigger, either internal or external. (1961, p. 56)

The use of microelectrodes has revealed unexpected functional specialization even within single cells; it appears that, far from being just storage batteries periodically emptied and recharged, nerve cells have physiologically distinct parts, and their charges and discharges involve those parts in rhythmic sequences for the inception of apparently simple, integral acts. The mechanisms are still in the realm of conjecture, but the fact that the act form is established in the impulse is fairly certain.

The build-up of tension in a single cell can terminate only in a minute impulse, but cell assemblies can form impulses to larger acts. There are billions of cells in a mammalian nervous system; cerebral cells, especially, seem to work in large assemblies, initiating behavioral acts of wide range and duration that go through many phases to their over-all consummation. And for every actualized impulse there are densely crowded others which reach only a momentary state of incipience because the on-going act abrogates their expression, so they terminate as infinitesimal modifications in the matrix of life. Those are the potential acts eschewed by the individual, and they are countless.

Impulses whose realizations would run counter to each other can occur in such rapid alternation that they practically coexist, springing from one and the same situation in the organism. If they originated by separate paths they might even actually coexist. But their respective developments certainly cannot both be carried out; they are incompatible, and the occurrence of both impulses in one situation presents an option. The organism has to select its course. Thousands of options are presumably decided automatically all the time; in lowly animals this may even hold for larger behavioral acts. But whenever an act is induced by a change in the vital situation, such as the life process itself constantly engenders (thereby motivating an endless stream of acts), it is likely that not only the impulse of that act, but also one or more conflicting impulses or alternative potential acts are formed, which are doomed to speedy abrogation. This play of impulses forms the dynamic matrix of life, a plexus even more involuted and compounded than the metabolizing, differentiating, ever-changing structure that is the material organism, because the latter consists only of actualized events, but the life comprises also all the potential acts which exist only for milliseconds or less. Perhaps that is why we feel that life is "in" the body and pervades its actuality. Out of this matrix all mental and behavioral acts arise.

If the basic concept of the act is that of an event, a spatiotemporal occurrence, the act form has to be distinguished by a convenient term; for in any theoretical context it is this abstractable form, which two acts may have in common, that is of interest. This formal aspect of acts I shall call "action." In so doing one really just establishes explicitly what is generally accepted in common parlance, for such typical forms may be found in inorganic nature too, in which case they are usually referred to as the actions of machines, winds and waves, corrosives, etc. We speak of the "action" of pistons or gears rather than of their "acts." It is action that living and non-living mechanisms may have in common. The same action may be performed by an animal's heart and by a pump, or by a rodent's teeth and by a file in a man's hand, or possibly by some electrical circuits in the man's brain and those in a modern computer which therefore is viewed as a "mechanical brain." The term "action" is sometimes extended to specific acts, usually in cases where it is the nature of the action rather than the act that counts, as for instance in impersonal, collective acts, like the conduct of a war. But in the strict sense here given to it, it means the causal pattern, or operative principle, according to which an organic or inorganic mechanism works.

There is one further derivative concept which is of major importance if acts are to be taken as the basic units of all biological thinking: the concept of vital activity. For this we require the notion of action, as just defined, for separate acts may be hard or even impossible to identify in that department, let alone to predict. The situations inducing acts are so unsurveyable that a situation can practically never be calculated with enough certainty to assure the occurrence of any specific act. In the study of life, therefore, any safely acceptable "laws" usually take the statistical form of probability laws. Most of the "laws" which have been established with any degree of certainty in that domain concern acts which are exemplified by thousands of instances, namely, repetitious vital acts, of which the readiest examples at a molar level are ciliary or flagellate movements, heartbeat, and gill or lung breathing. Such acts are very commonly concatenated into series, wherein the same general form is discernible over and over again, often with considerable deviations that cancel out in a larger statistical pattern. I shall refer to act sequences of this sort as "activities," and regard that term as strictly proper to them except where it is explicitly extended beyond its strict meaning. This practice will provide us with a distinctive name for a very important type of construct in the biological universe of discourse, and at the same time not violate common usage; the constant events of life, such as circulation and breathing, are generally called "activities."

The introduction of "activities" brings us very naturally to the all-important topics of rhythm, dialectic, self-continuation and finally to the possibility of defining "agent" in terms of acts. But concepts developed in the course of that undertaking really belong to the next chapter, and will have to wait their turn.

9 / On Individuation and Involvement

To speak of acts without assuming the existence of agents may appear to be an odd philosophical vagary; and those philosophers who begin their conceptual analyses by deciding what is "implied" in the use of selected key words are likely to take exception to the practice, on the ground that an act is necessarily performed by an agent. Their argument rests, of course, on their concept of "act," which is at first vaguely accepted, in order to be precisely established by analysis of its contents or implicit "sense." I have not taken this approach, but have assumed the notion of "natural event," and distinguished acts as events of a particular sort. The defining function of the class of acts established in this way does not entail the assumption of an agent.

To trace the development of mind from the earliest forms of life that we can determine, through primitive acts which may have vague psychical moments, to more certain mental acts and finally the human level of "mind," requires not a categorical concept, but a functional one, whereby entities of various categories may be defined and related. The most promising operational principle for this purpose is the principle of individuation. It is exemplified everywhere in animate nature, in processes that eventuate in the existence of self-identical organisms; it may work in different directions, and to different degrees; that is, an organism, proto-organism, or pseudo-organism may be individuated to a low or high degree, in some respects but not in others, and anomalies of individuality—double-headed monsters, parabiotic twins, as well as properly semi-individual plants and animals—may arise by imperfect or by normally only partial individuation. Under widely various conditions, this ubiquitous process may give rise to equally various kinds of individuality, from the physical self-identity of a metabolizing cell to the intangible but impressive individuality of an exceptional human being, a Beethoven or a Churchill, who consequently seems "more of an individual" than the common run of mankind.

Individuation is a process consisting of acts; every act is motivated by a vital situation, a moment in the frontal advance of antecedent acts composed of more and more closely linked elements, ultimately a texture of activities. The situation, uniquely given for each act (and therefore not amenable to specific description), is a phase of the total life, the matrix, from which motivation constantly arises. The acts that effect the individuation of a being emerge from some larger matrix, such as a biotypic stock; or a generally only semi-individuated organism may undergo a higher individuation in one of its life episodes, as some colonial creatures, for instance corals, have a free-swimming, independent juvenile stage; or again, a species may develop a particular line of individual action, as the hairs of the sundew (*Drosera*), unlike any other parts, and quite unlike the hairs of most other hirsute plants, respond directly and independently to stimulation by contact. Here it is the direction rather than the degree of individuation that is interesting. In some exhibits of the principle, for instance the individuation of tumors within the normally subordinate tissues of plants and animals, both the direction and the degree to which those special acts can go are of prime interest to the pathologist. But it is in the embryologist's laboratory that we find the functional concept of individuation explicitly recognized as more negotiable, and therefore more appropriate to research, than the older substantive concept of "individual."

A very appreciable logical virtue of the concept of individuation is that it has a converse which is also a functional concept, namely, "involvement." The two principles are opposed, yet interdependent, in more intricate ways than simply balancing each other or alternating. In most vital phenomena both of them are in operation, and the processes that exemplify them are numberless. Individuation occurs in cytological differentiation, in parturition, in speciation, in the origination of mind and in the development of personality. Involvement proceeds from the earliest coazervation (if such there was) of proto-organic droplets to the most extraordinary acts of integration—mutual control of cells in a tissue and of tissues in a body, physically connected populations (plants conjoined by rhizoids, stolons or rhizophores, colonial animals by a coenoecium or a coenosarc), bisexual reproduction, and beyond such physical levels, herds, communal nests and hives, processes of human communication, human society. These are but a few of the forms that involvement of acts and of whole lives can take. Most of them—as also the diverse forms of individuation—will require discussion below, because they have played their parts in the long history and vastly longer prehistory of "mind." The development of beings with minds is probably the highest individuation the world has ever known, and its prehistory is the history of life on earth.

If mentality, and more particularly the human version of it which is properly called "mind," is to be conceived as a natural outcome of the irregular, yet cumulatively progressive development of animalian life, we have to look for all explanations of its powers and limits, its mechanisms and vagaries, in the ruling tendencies of the great animal kingdom itself; and these appear, often in their purest modes, on the lowest levels of life that biological investigations have reached, even far below the separation of main orders. Going still further backward, we can only extrapolate the directions and rates of presumable earlier events in the formation of life itself. Yet there, in those events, lies one of the key problems of the life sciences: the origin of agents.

In discussing the nature of acts I have already touched upon the "act-like" character of some non-vital chemical transformations, especially interactions of different substances. Why are these events not bona fide acts? Chiefly because they do not develop into a self-continuing system of actions proliferating and differentiating in more and more centralized and interdependent ways; that is, they do not enter into the constitution of an agent. As soon as they do so, they become acts. An agent is a complex of actions, and all actions that belong to that complex are acts of that agent. All true acts, therefore, are to some extent involved with other acts; very intimately with their own subacts, and with superacts into which they themselves enter, and not much less so with acts to which they stand in some relation—active or passive—of induction. The wider relationships that compose the basic dynamism of life, and are all subsumed under "motivation," probably hold in one direction or the other between any acts belonging to the same organism.

The question of the origin of organisms is, then, how some of the chemical actions on the surface of the earth or in its surrounding gaseous envelope ever became involved with each other so as to form centers of activity which maintained themselves for a while amid the changes of forming and dissolving compounds around them. They need not have been endlessly self-perpetuating from their beginning; in a chemically active cloud, or the "rich oceanic broth" of a lately cooled planet, where such compositions could occur, they would be likely to happen by the million, so the first proto-organisms might have been of short duration—unfixed, unrelated myriads of briefly viable forms—

constantly replaced by means of the same causes that produced the earliest ones, and not yet by means of each other.

The first person to undertake the task of making the system of physical, chemical and electrical events yield a functional explanation of biogenesis and carry it to considerable lengths was the Russian biochemist A. P. Oparin. His book, *Origin of Life* (1936), appeared at a time when its very title aroused skepticism and prejudice; yet it was almost immediately translated into other languages (English in 1938), because even a casual perusal sufficed to show his colleagues that this was an entirely new approach to the old problem. His hypothesis contained three novel features: (1) he thought of the origin of vital processes as a heightening of chemical actions rather than the incursion of an ontologically unique "living spark"; (2) he postulated past, not present, conditions of the earth's surface as the environment of such accelerating changes; and (3) he anticipated an insight which is only now receiving general recognition—namely, that the phenomenon of "life" is a wide, varied and unbelievably complex functional pattern rather than a single attribute or essence which either is or is not possessed by any given physical object. Some aspects of that pattern may be found in a physical region where others are lacking; one could not say, perhaps, that there is life at that point, yet there is action that produces organic structure.

Briefly, Oparin's theory runs somewhat as follows: All action—mechanical, electrical, chemical, organic or inorganic—occurs at some time and in some place of the material universe; that is, it has a physical location and effects changes in the material condition of that place at that time. If any repetitive action (be it the beat of waves on a rock or the passage of an invisible ray through an invisible gas) is concentrated for an appreciable time in a particular location, the matter which occupies that location, provided it continues to do so for a long time, becomes organized in a spatial pattern reflecting the dynamics of the action. Once the imprint of the action is established it facilitates further repetitions, and at the same time standardizes their form by channeling the course of motions, meting out the substances or charges involved (as filters, pores, tubules and electrical conductors do), thus modifying the activity which is itself deepening and distorting its own frame and thereby establishing and modifying itself. The relation between structure and process is mutually adaptive.

Before such organization even of the simplest sort can occur, however, there has to be some stability of substance in a circumscribed locality. In a perfectly liquid or gaseous medium there will obviously be no chance of developing a permanent imprint. Lightning passing through vapors or striking into waters may cause a dramatic molecular reorientation and induce great chemical actions, but all effects are soon lost in the chaotic motions of the fluid media. The first requisite for complex structures, therefore, is an isolated and bounded region in which chemical changes can happen to a self-identical substance. Oparin suggested that colloidal gels, which (following their most notable investigator, Budenberg de Jong) Oparin calls "coazervates," are very likely to have formed in the welter of the earth's early hydrosphere, and possess many properties and especially potentialities to make them probable forerunners of primitive living things. Unlike other colloidal particles, these coazervates—which arise in all sorts of sols—effect a rigid orientation of the water molecules around their envelope of equilibrium liquid, so there is a real shell around the little two-phase particle.

Here, then, we have a fulfillment of the first requirement for an organization of matter by localized activity—a bounded, inwardly active particle. Oparin goes on to describe further properties, such as absorption and adsorption of molecules from the surrounding medium, and how these acts might lead to growth, differentiation, proliferation, growth competition and so-called "natural selection." Some of those further speculations raise difficult problems; but the problems themselves invite experimental tests and, where the findings do not bear out the scheme, alternative hypotheses. The main point is that all the later details are developed from his theory of how the most primitive life was formed, which shows clearly that the theory is conceived in genuinely biological terms.

Oparin was not reasoning in a vacuum. Even the concepts which directed his researches, i.e., the active nature of "living matter," the acceleration and heightening of chemical actions by increasing autocatalysis, and the development of "steady states" in centers of balanced action, were not unshared notions when he professed them. Bertalanffy said as much at just about the same time. So as soon as their relevance to the conception of vital origins was pointed out, the metaphysical chasm between the inanimate world and the world of life began to close, and biological research struck its natural connection with fundamental laws of physical science.

Oparin's theory was only a tentative proposal. H. F. Blum, for instance, found it more plausible to assume that life began not in a chemically rich ocean, but in slowly drying puddles, into which amino acids, formed in the atmosphere, had been precipitated (1957, p. 161). N. H. Horowitz, whose brilliant reasonings, borne out in experiment, will engage us later in another connection, concluded that the first beings were probably not molecular aggregates, but single macromolecules (1959, p. 107).

In the course of such speculations and debates, one fact became apparent to all the participants: namely, that the nature of the earliest living entities is as problematical, as hard for us to reconstruct on the basis of any life that exists today, as their environment. They were almost certainly nothing as complicated as a cell, with a nucleus harboring a chromosomal system of inestimable potentialities; nor is it likely that their metabolism was comparable to that which occurs in even the simplest living cell today.

The beginning of the life process, whether it stemmed from the chance occurrence of a single viable molecule or aggregate, or—as I find far more plausible—lay in a generative phase of the earth's history during which millions of eobionts arose, certainly appears to all scientific inquirers as a formation of patterned activities and their more and more perfect integration until they constitute a matrix in which their own form becomes modified or even entirely blurred, so it can only be found again by analytic abstraction. Such living matrices may have various degrees of coherence and persistence; but they are systems, self-sustaining, and (as we know them) self-propagating, wherein every event is prepared by progressively changing conditions of the integral whole. Every distinguishable change, therefore, arises out of the matrix, and emerges as an act of an agent; for such a vital matrix is an agent.

In the earliest phase of life, however it may have proceeded in detail, the principle of involvement certainly appears as dominant. There must have been strong ruling tendencies toward organization, which led to increasing interdependence of actions and eventuated in the formation of biological mechanisms. The most important factor in that process, the main source of all functional continuity, must have been the establishment of rhythms. Rhythmic concatenation is what really holds an organism together from moment to moment; it is a dynamic pattern, i.e., a pattern of events, into which acts and act-like phenomena very readily fall: a sequence wherein the subsiding phase, or cadence, of one act (or similar element) is the up-take for its successor. It occurs in nonvital as well as in vital processes, but in the latter it is paramount, and reaches degrees of differentiation and intensity unrivaled by anything in the inanimate realm.

Rhythm is not usually defined in terms of the concatenation of the elements which compose the rhythmic series. It is commonly assumed in scientific thinking that the essential character of rhythm is the repetition of any distinct, recognizable event at equal intervals of time; i.e., that rhythm is periodic repetition. But, in fact, not all rhythmic repetitions are strictly periodic. There may even be rhythmic sequences of events which are not really repetitive; for instance, a performer of "modern dance" rarely repeats a movement, yet every least motion of the dance has to be rhythmic. Similarly, if a cat runs across a floor and suddenly leaps up on a table, the leap is as rhythmic as the repeated loping movements, although it is a unique element. It need not even terminate the series; if the animal goes on, leaping down again and bounding away, the unrepeated movements may have broken its course, but not the rhythm of its over-all act.

The essence of rhythm is the alternation of tension building up to a crisis, and ebbing away in a graduated course of relaxation whereby a new build-up of tension is prepared and driven to the next crisis, which necessitates the next cadence. If the series of actions thus engendered consists of alternating contraries, such as rise and fall, push and pull, suction and expulsion, and each element in spending itself prepares and initiates its own converse, the resulting rhythm is a dialectic.

Dialectical rhythms, like rhythms *per se*, are not limited to the actions of vital systems (the swing of a pendulum, in which each fall builds up the potential energy for the opposite rise, or the wave returning down the slope of a beach and hastening the next breaker are familiar examples), but they play such a major role in vital functions that their importance in the activity and even the physical existence of organisms makes them an essential mark of living form in nature, as their virtual image is of "living form" in art. The concatenation of minute acts—close to the molecular level—into continuous series, self-sustaining by virtue of the cyclic structure of their elements, each of which has a definite magnitude measurable from any phase of the cycle to its repetition, is the basic pattern of life. It is carried on by such diminutive and intricate mechanisms that every development of our optical enlarging instruments reveals new functioning structures in what theretofore looked like homogeneous substance. Most, if not all, of the processes we can distinguish as yet are summations of smaller ones; and the summations take the form of rhythmically concatenated acts, which either summate or differentially interact to produce larger rhythms. The parabolic curve which expresses the typical act form emerges again and again, at each level of integration, in the physiological rhythms of every organism; and this form, with its main phases of inception, acceleration, consummation and cadential finish, is what makes the rhythmic pattern, and is accordingly the basis not only of the distinguishable unit acts in a continuous activity, but also of their self-concatenation, and the consequent self-perpetuation of the continuum.

All the transformations found in animate nature take place in the inanimate realm, too, but at incomparably slower rates. Their tremendous acceleration—sometimes several hundredfold—is the work of catalysts; and one of the essential dialectical processes characteristic of organisms (though, even here, not strictly peculiar to them) is the act of autocatalysis, i.e., the synthesis of the catalyzer for a given function as a by-product of the function itself. So the activities of the living matrix become more and more concentrated and rhythmicized; they also become accelerated, by virtue of their autocatalysis, and would presumably reach excessive rates and break up under their own force, were it not for another circumstance, just as remarkable as their self-catalyzing functions, namely, that at some point they also produce checks on their own activities. So a complementary set of enzymes, synthesized by differentiating cells as they approach their adult stages, inhibits the action of their own morphogenic substances at their location and in their vicinity, and very frequently in the whole organism. A new balance of contraries is thus set up, a shift between self-induction and self-inhibition which reverses whenever the structure in question reaches completion or suffers loss. Paul Weiss summarized this controlling action with the statement: "Briefly, each organ or each cell type produces inhibitors of its own growth, and the total concentration of these in the circulation comes into equilibrium with the productive or generative mass to produce a steady state" (Watterson 1959, p. 101).

This dialectic of induction and inhibition may exhibit very elaborate patterns, in which more than two processes become involved to effect the prevailing and continuous balance of life. Sometimes the activity of one functional unit, instead of directly initiating its antagonist and so limiting its own operation, induces the activity of another unit, which then provides the inhibition of the first. Sometimes they become each other's monitors, and sometimes the second unit—the inhibitor of the first—is limited by still another factor in the organic situation. Where many rapid, circumscribed rhythms are going on, some of these may summate and set up new, superimposed rhythms; or powerful periodicities extraneous to the organism may "entrain" its natural rhythms, as the stronger intraorganic cycles always tend to entrain the weaker ones; so the sum total is still further complicated by the fact that activities deriving from widely different sources, from central and peripheral impulses, may intersect and interweave and modify each other in the system.

The resultant steady state of actively maintained balance, which appears superficially as inactive existence, is the tonus of living tissues, the only constant sign of the basic vital process always going on, which makes the difference between the functioning leaf and the withered leaf, the man at rest and the man dead. Without this unceasing, self-inducing and self-limiting dialectic ground base no stimulus can initiate any biological response from plant or animal. Only anatomical structures which are already active can be stimulated. That is, of course, no more than a corollary to the proposition, set up in the previous chapter, that all acts are motivated by other acts, and any extraorganic events which elicit specific acts do so via the matrix of activities, the agent; or, as D. O. Hebb has put it, "an afferent excitation does not arouse inactive tissue but feeds into an activity that is already going on" (1949, p. 121).

The organism is made entirely by processes which are vital acts; not necessarily all its own. Animals, with very few exceptions, are heterotrophic; they cannot synthesize their major nutrients from abiotic elements. They can only take over acts of transformation begun by autotrophs—that is, ultimately, by plants—and continue them in ways and patterns of their own. But from the time an agent initiates or assumes vital acts it performs them in systematic ways, making its more and more deeply involved and integrated matrix, its life.

The materials metabolized by the basic life processes are, of course, minutely distributed and redistributed, held together by chemical linkages, oriented by ever-shifting polarizations and elaborated into a single, vastly intricate physical structure. That structure is the agent's body. The body is the perceptible record of the life which produced it, and still produces it as long as that life continues. Were it not for this cumulative recording of acts in their passage, we could not know most of them at all, because of their infinitesimal scope and often their deep involvement in greater acts, wherefore the constituent cycles are only statistically observable, not singly distinguishable. The body, throughout life, is the "dynamic equilibrium" itself, growing and differentiating into articulate forms. Underlying all its variegation is always the "substrate," the vast molecular structure that includes the cells, the intercellular fluids with their complicated cargo of alimentation products and metabolic by-products, either excreta or precious catalyzers, and the non-cellular deposits of calcium and other inorganic substances. This is the material matrix, the counterpart of the functional matrix of activities, and indeed the product, and therefore the exact reflection, of the latter.

What makes an organism look individual is not the possession of unique features, nor of many slight deviations from a standard, e.g., a known type specimen, but the fact that the ontogenetic processes of its individuation, which may be perfectly normal, are encoded in its bodily form. That is the basis of "living form" in nature; and this projection of dynamic pattern into relatively fixed material pattern holds good to the most elementary level of cellular and even molecular structure. The body consequently is the tangible record of past and passing activities, which have inscribed themselves, late ones over earlier ones, new ones constantly altering the latest summary, so that in a mature metazoan body it takes great acumen and patience to trace back the earlier phases of some lifelong continuities.

The most illuminating exhibits, common though they may be, are the visible gradients of growth and other changes in organic forms, for by following a gradient one can see in spatial projection the beginning and end, the steady or changing rate and the direction, or radiating directions, of a process. Nothing could show the act form more clearly than do the gradients of ontogenesis, differentiation and growth to maturity; every change of proportions in a multicellular organism, normal or pathological, bespeaks a difference in rates of growth between comparable articulated parts; and most developments, whatever their rate, exhibit either an over-all gradient or an interrupted series of processes, each of which has a characteristic rise, acceleration, slowing and termination. Even the deployment of colors in flowers, insect wings or animal skins usually shows gradients of diffusion from a center of highest activity, arrested at boundaries of contact with other processes, so that lines of stopping and stowing mark their interpenetrating extremes.

A good demonstration of such pattern-making is to be found in the literature on insect wings, which comprises many detailed studies of wing growth, veining, mutant aberrations and experimental distortions of wings, at least in the genera *Drosophila* and *Ephestia*, and also some investigations of color distribution in butterflies' wings. The final gradients of pigmentation are seen to arise, in the main, not from the points of origin of the wing, but from several peripheral areas, which induce what R. Goldschmidt termed "determination streams" of activity—mitosis, cell migration and melanin synthesis—that seem to proceed by rhythmic waves of impulse (see Sondhi 1963, p. 294). Such rhythms are not necessarily simple or single, since several areas of the wing are under separate controls, and have been experimentally found to express the actions of different genes. Henke distinguished two types of morphogenetic rhythms in the determination of wing patterns, "diffusion rhythms," which start from an area of earliest activity and gradually extend along distinct lines, motivating successive developments, and "simultaneous rhythms," which start from many centers at once, giving rise to scattered dots, that fall into more or less even spatial patterns by virtue of the competition among the simultaneous impulses (see ibid., pp. 296-ff.).

One of the most significant results of all these highly detailed studies of pattern was Goldschmidt's discovery of the "prepattern," a purely functional condition, primarily a differential rate of mitosis, in apparently similar cells which afterwards exhibit different qualities and degrees of pigmentation. The distribution of colors on the wing is only a final record of processes which have been going on over a protracted period, and which started at different stages of pupal development (if not earlier) and advanced at different rates, so they attain their irreversible, final forms at different times. This means that those scales or other tissues which reach the adult form soonest may block or change the course of others that are still labile in the "determination stream." The pattern is gradually decided, although under normal conditions the outcome is invariant; so the spatial design of typical colored forms really summarizes a complicated temporal process.

Goldschmidt's findings demonstrated for the first time that a primary pattern may be laid down before a visible one occurs. There is, however, another significant aspect to the functional design that precedes the visible phenomenon: it is in the active phase of laying down the prepattern that genes exert their influence. No matter which or how many genes affect a particular process, the final bodily expression of it is still open to other than genetic determinants (for instance, the interference of scientists), so that the phenotype contains an element of accident which the underlying gene complex does not share at all.

Genetic inheritance makes the unity and continuity of a biotypic stock; it is every living being's indissoluble bond to its own ancestry, its commitment to the life of its kind and none other. The gene complement is the one permanent factor in its lifelong, progressive situation. Everything else may change; everything else that motivates the advancing flow of its impulses and its realized acts plays on this anciently established core. Heredity is the primary involvement of every organism with other organisms; not with a "kind" distinguished by characteristic traits, but with its stock defined by its own actual descent and its resultant common ancestry with some—possibly, all—others of its taxonomic "kind." The stock is the largest natural unit of life. The gene complement, with all its possibilities of combination and mutation, is what holds such a mighty unit together, and sets the limits of what may happen within its scope.

But the stream of hereditary life moves with a characteristic pulse of its own, by a constant succession of individuations. The stock may be regarded as a unit of activity, but it is not an agent, an individual, or an organism; such entities arise only by processes of individuation. And here we are at the starting-line of today's most exciting and penetrating scientific researches, which are in genetics, embryology, cytology and related subjects that bear on the origin and development of organisms; for every such development is a course of individuation. The activities that compose a particular life, however, are so many and so variable that even in a single organism individuation may go to different lengths in separate directions, and even its greatest degree may be high or low, so that some living things *in toto* are more individuated than others. But one cannot range organisms in a simple hierarchy of progressive total individuation, because the many directions make a single criterion impossible.

The most primitive act of individuation is the isolation of a protoplasmic unit by a completely surrounding membrane, selectively penetrable under osmotic pressure. The protoplasmic cell is the elementary form of life; it is represented by numberless strains, only some of which tend to individuate as self-sufficient organisms. The majority have special sensitivities to the presence of other cells, particularly others of closely related origin, so that the "daughter cells" created by an act of mitosis remain conjoined, and their "daughters" in turn augment the clump, which may grow to comprise millions. In such an aggregate, however, other potentialities naturally come into play, because each cell has to adapt itself to its position in the mass. A cell at the center has a different ambient from one on the surface. The central one has no access to metabolites from the outside, unless streams of fluids form passages or some system of molecular transport develops whereby vitally necessary chemicals reach it. By the time they do so, they will not, of course, be in the same condition in which they reached the outermost cells. Also, the pressures and electrical tensions at the periphery and the interior, respectively, are apt to be quite unlike; so are the concentrations of waste products and enzymes manufactured by these microscopic agents. Considering, then, the inherent versatility of cells, one can understand—at least in principle—the processes of differentiation that arise spontaneously in a multicellular complex and progress with its increase.

The internal microsituations, together with the original equipotentiality of cells, go far to account for the special articulations that tissues undergo in the development of a metazoan organism. But these changing and interplaying situations are not haphazard in their advance; they unfold in a perfectly logical over-all pattern, one total conformation preparing another in typical succession, and in relative independence of events that do not belong to the differentiating protoplasmic unit. This ever-repeating pattern is peculiar to the stock, and is the basic framework of its characteristic impulses, actualized in the growth and activity of each individual. The course of actualization, however, is always modified to some extent by contingencies of the organism's situation as a whole as well as its internal transient conditions; and the degree to which its deviations from the generic norm can go without destroying the particular life—that is, the amount of leeway in its individuation—is itself part of its heritage.

The vast complexity that results from all the possible relationships of active cells lets processes of individuation take many different directions and continue to different lengths. These processes begin in previously existing protoplasmic structures with which the new organism is all but indistinguishably involved at first, and from which its activities gradually free themselves; but any particular line of its individuation may end before that total superact is completed, so that in some vital stocks the new being retains its involvement with the parent, and through it, with other incomplete individuals. Some coelenterates, for instance, remain physically connected with one another through a common alimentary system, although each of the hydranths which grow from that conjoining organ performs its perceptive and conative acts—trapping and devouring food—in full independence of the others.

The reason for this incommensurability of many aspects of evolution is that the entire process of individuating consists in so many lines of activity, moving at different rates and building up the organism in different respects—stabilizing its outward structure under the influence of an environment in which its ambient defines itself and changes with the creature, developing organs specially suited and also limited to the performance of particular functions—that a considerable degree of unity may be attained, or an impressive complex of interrelated organic structures articulated, even while some mechanisms remain primitive and below the evolutionary level of the organism as a whole. This sort of allometry runs all through the animal kingdom, and makes it well-nigh impossible to plot definite distances, on any taxonomic, physiological or psychological scale, between two members of different orders or even phyla. In the study of human development it becomes of paramount importance, because it directs one's attention to analogues, if not precursors, of human traits in forms of life far removed from our own, or even from the primate stocks we are accustomed to compare with hominids.

First, however, let us turn once more to the elementary steps in the formation of organisms, because physical separation from a progenitor is not the only aspect of primary individuation. There are also degrees in the separateness of organisms from the inorganic world, as parts of the latter may become included in the former to serve physiological purposes. For example, seed-eating birds of many kinds carry gravel in their crops, which serves to grind up the hard-coated grains.

There are other conditions, too, that produce ambiguities in the boundary between individuals and the external world, particularly the exact opposite of such prosthetic "organs," namely, the extrusion of organic products to form part of the animal's ambient. The most familiar instance is the spider's web. It is essentially an extension of the spider's body; the animal's reactions to the slightest touch of anything upon the web are like those of many other animals to a touch on their antennae, or of a person to a contact made with his groping hand, which explores and is ready to grasp. Yet the web can be abandoned; in this sense it is in the spider's ambient, rather than in the confines of the body as an antenna or a hand is. It may be regarded as a physical possession taken of the immediate environment, or as an extension of the organism that is not ended by a subsequent contraction, but by a casting off, like the shedding of hair, skin, milk teeth, and antlers, except that the abandonment of the web is under the immediate voluntary control of the animal, which true bodily castings are not. But the form of the web is due to an organic process, genetically determined, species-specific and subject to characteristic disturbances by various drugs or other physiological influences. Its status with respect to the physical individual is really ambiguous.

Caddis cases, sand dollars, leaf cocoons, honeycombs and paper wasps' nests, though they all incorporate some substances produced by their respective makers, are not primarily extensions of the animal body; they are better described as exploitations of the environment. There are other ways in which living things, plants as well as animals, modify their environment by exuding chemical substances. Molds and fungi often emit enzymes into the substratum from which they draw their nourishment so that part of their digestion is carried out before they absorb their food; their immediate vicinity functions as a sort of external stomach.

Such imprecise division between organisms and their surroundings may lead to curious forms of involvement with other creatures; for just as physiological products released into the circumambient medium—air, water, soil or a particular piece of flesh—may act as digestive enzymes on metabolites occurring there, so they may act very much like hormones on other members of the agent's stock that happen to be in the vicinity. Norbert Wiener characterized musk, or other sexually attractive substances, as "communal exterior hormones" (1948, p. 182).

Involvements may also be progressively established by organisms with others of their own kind, or of entirely different kinds. The first case is most perfectly illustrated by the well-known but still amazing morphogenesis of the slime mold *Dictyostelium discoideum*, a multicellular fungus built up not by division of a parent cell, but out of free, amoeboid cells which come together and find their places in relation to others, whereupon each undergoes some particular modification according to the place it has taken, so that the self-arranging cells form a plasmodium, stem and fruiting crown—a well-formed, multicellular, individual plant. This is probably the most complicated purely organic integration of separate organisms into a true unit that we know; what evolutionary course has led up to it no one (to my knowledge) has ever ventured to guess. But, phylogenetically, multicellular individuals seem to have formed by aggregation of unicellular organisms as well as by the process that is still reflected in metazoan growth, the increase without complete separation of "daughter cells" produced by mitosis.

The making of a metazoan organism by progressive involvement of previously separate cells (or other units) is known as integration, and most biologists prefer the latter term. My reason for using the former as the converse of individuation is that not all processes of involvement are integrations; there are dovetailing functions and forms of life which never become integrated, but always remain distinct and even separable. Consider the numberless phenomena—some of them really bizarre—of parasitism, symbiosis and commensalism, which show all possible patterns of involvement and all possible degrees of histological and physiological integration. The incomplete individuation of social insects, especially honeybees, is the best-known example; but there is one less familiar case—that of the termites—which displays in the life history of each "queen" the passage from a morphologically and functionally complete individual to the colonial condition in which that same individual loses its self-sufficiency, giving rise to a swarm of incomplete organisms that take over most of the functions of the mother, who finally can no longer move about, but is fed and tended by her sterile offspring, while she herself grows to enormous size and becomes, in effect, nothing but an organ embedded in the hill—the womb of the colony. Yet she and her mate, who (unlike the fathering drone among the bees) lives with her in her chamber, and all their small specialized children, though collectively functioning, retain their physical separateness, and interact mainly if not wholly by behavior, and not by physiological integration.

As life began with increasing concentrations and protractions of interactive ferments on the earth's surface, so it continues in an ever-mounting advance of devouring, integrating, self-maintaining activities. The progressive individuation of organisms, especially in the animal kingdom, at present culminating in human individuals, is so striking that it has led many people to regard individuation as the sole principle of evolution. But from a higher standpoint—an Olympian point of view—such an outlook might seem narrow. The gradients of individuation might appear as strong lines in a swirling flow of ecological involvement of species with species, life with life, wherein every impulse to individuation sets up its own course, that may be long and become spectacular on the way, or may come to a stop very soon. Individuation goes on all the time, but it can proceed only in a framework of active involvements with the generating stock and the nourishing substrate of an ambient that is a small detail in the whole biosphere. Often, indeed, the very means of individuation, being chiefly powers of aggression against other individuals, lead to new involvements which become paramount, as with organisms that exploit others to the point of becoming entirely dependent on them. Then the life of the parasite is strengthened and developed in a special direction, as, for instance, the tapeworm's incredible procreative power, at the expense of its general self-sufficiency.

Yet with every acquired involvement, like that of the so-called "social insects," some increase of repertoire is gained even as individuation is blocked or lost. The over-all growth and elaboration of vital activity goes forward, sometimes by processes of individuation, sometimes by the opposite, the amalgamation of individual lives in a joint existence. Nothing in inanimate nature can serve as a model of this aspect of vital process. Life is so opportunistic that every possible avenue of implementation and continuation is exploited, and evolution seems to progress by movements that sometimes are dialectical dynamisms, individuation and involvement pushing each other to growth of activities. In human life, corporate acts are the most spectacular assertions of the species, extending its ambient even beyond the terrestrial surface; but they spring from the most individuating element in each brief life, the mind, and as soon as individuation is seriously frustrated, they also fall apart.

Though we have no physical model of this endless rhythm of individuation and involvement, we do have its image in the world of art, most purely in the dance; for this dialectic of vital continuity is the very essence of the classical ballet. Think only of that perfect example, *Les Sylphides*: individual figures emerge and submerge, *pas de deux* develop and melt back into the web of choric movement, divisions form only to close over what was, for a moment, the path of an advancing stream. And not only in dance but in all choric works of wide range this largest rhythm appears: the "tide in the affairs of men, that, taken at the full, leads on to fortune"; or, in the highest musical form that has yet been developed, the sonata, which is choric in structure whether scored for the keyboard or the full symphonic orchestra: a scarcely discernible new theme may begin a history, but even if it rises to apotheosis it can never transcend the stream, which may finally integrate it with another individual form or even simply engulf it. Individuation and involvement are the extremes of the great rhythm of evolution, which moves between them in a direction of its own, always toward more intense activity and gradually increasing ambients of the generic lines that survive. A degenerating activity is usually making way for the upsetting impetus of another kind of action; under such conditions the organism can persist only by being involved with others of its own kind or of alien kinds that vicariously perform its waning function. Thus the stock itself, which has evolved its own vital activities, may give up one or another of them in the course of its own expanding life.

> Like a child from the womb,
> Like a ghost from the tomb,
> I arise and unbuild it again.

10 / The Evolution of Acts

> Nicht der Reiz, sondern die Veränderung die er im inneren Zustand des Organismus hervorbringt motiviert die Bewegung.
>
> **Ludwig von Bertalanffy**

The complexity of the numberless organic forms which have evolved in the long course of life on the earth never fails to impress the investigator who gives them his attention, though by practical necessity he has to restrict his special studies to a single genus, and perhaps even to a relatively tiny part of that. Our progressive insight into physical, chemical and electronic mechanisms and the scope of their possible functions has led to a general change of intellectual focus from anatomy to physiology, that is, from the description of the myriad forms as such to their description in terms of observed, or imputed, or sometimes purely hypothetical functions. The conception of organisms as self-fueling, self-maintaining and self-replacing mechanisms, and of their internal structures as working or supporting parts, has opened avenues of scientific advance in more than one direction, and made a heroic onslaught against the mystical doctrines of non-physical agencies, special kinds of energy ("nervous" or "spiritual"), final causes, and other ineffable noumena supposed to invade the phenomenal realm to produce physical effects.

The notion of "survival value" in the theory of evolution introduced a practical element into biological thinking that focused the attention of anatomists on physiological mechanisms and the functions whereby plants and animals conduct their lives, feed and defend themselves, keep from freezing, find mates or utilize wind, water and insect carriers to fertilize their seed, and perform all sorts of astounding acts, by virtue of which they survive, on the average, for a length of time characteristic of their species. Once the functional interpretation of all tissue structure became established, the discovery of more and more amazing mechanisms and further "servomechanisms" supporting them became the new line of advance in biology.

It was here that a still further conjunction of scientific theories occurred: this time, the importation of physical models from the advancing fronts of chemical and electrical engineering into biology. Despite the fact that some speculative thinkers are promptly beguiled, by the possibility of finding such models for vital processes, into seeing the human brain as a computer (a pathetically bad one by modern standards), and into speaking of cybernetic machines as "brains" or even "organisms" and of their parts as "organs," the suggestions derived from mechanics and electronics have led to revelations in physiology. The practice of such borrowing is, of course, very old; what gives it a special significance in the present case is that two fast-developing sciences are linked by it to progress together. The perfectly serious use of biological and even social terms for very complex machines shows that their operations are based on schematized biological acts. As for the converse relationship, the influence of electrochemistry and other advanced physical sciences on the development of biological theory (not to mention their tangible contributions, such as high-powered microscopes, electrodes and dissecting instruments), it widens the physiologist's insight into living organs and functions with almost every new departure in purely mechanical principle or practice. Physiology, genetics, embryology, as well as paleontology and related studies, united by the basic concepts of evolutionary natural history, are building squarely on the older and riper sciences, especially by using the feats of modern engineering as guidelines and models.

There is, however, one serious pitfall in the use of technological models in conjunction with the classical concepts of evolution, i.e., survival value, adaptation and "natural selection" of the fittest. Man-made mechanisms are normally devised for some purpose; as a whole and in all their parts, which may be intricate servosystems, they are intended and designed to serve preconceived ends. To meet particular needs is what adaptation, fitness and value mean with respect to human contrivances. Consequently the notions of requirement, adequacy, conscious aim and choice of means are inherent in the thought and language of engineering, whether chemical, small-current or simply mechanical. When this language is carried over into biology, it naturally brings with it the technician's view of mechanisms as inventions and of their functions as dictated by a presumptive user's needs. So all the considerations of economy, time-saving, margins of safety, reserves of material, storage and deployment of power, and the principles of coordination and communication governing our industry are read into the organic forms and functions that have taken shape in the course of evolution. In the structural analysis of living matter, for which the technological models are indispensable aids, this fallacy may be unimportant; but when we come to the philosophical formulation of concepts for broad as well as narrow and detailed biological thinking—concepts that can link all the sciences which the "modern synthesis" has brought into the compass of evolution theory, and can be further extended to cast psychological and moral thinking in commensurable terms—the implicit misconception in the formulative principles becomes seriously misleading. Then it prompts biologists to raise pseudo-problems, and to resort to teleological explanations that pass as "scientific" because they stem from a scientifically grounded technology. The "problems" arise only with the assumption that biological mechanisms are servosystems developed to meet needs.

The obstacle which this economic misinterpretation of living structure and function sets up against a truly biological conception of evolutionary processes is increased by the fact that machines and programs are made not only for a purpose, but by a designer and organizer. Since the assumption of a divine Creator, who might exercise the required foresight and ingenuity, is proscribed in the scientific sphere, the analogy of the industrial plant can be carried out only with a replacement in the managerial and planning departments; and this is commonly made surreptitiously, by a literary trick of using what purports to be a mere figure of speech—the introduction of "Nature" or "Evolution" as the agent who supplies the blueprints and materials and guides the attainment of her (instead of His) purposes. This ready evasion of a difficulty which really shows up the weakness of the machine model has become the stock in trade not only of science writers, but of excellent, authoritative scientists writing on problems of adaptation, organic integration and evolutionary tendencies. The snare may be their conception of the public for which one writes on such subjects, whom they tend to regard as an utterly ignorant laity; but a more peculiar and somewhat suspicious fact is that the mythical agents, ostensibly introduced to indulge the general public's literary taste, find their way into places where they will never meet that public.

Another current device to evade theological implications yet keep the teleological outlook is to attribute purpose, foresight and even social conscience not only to primitive organisms (plants as well as animals), but also to organs, tissues or cells. So one reads of coelenterates "solving the problem" created by their increasing bulk, and slime molds "circumventing" other engineering problems by clever inventions (Bonner 1952, pp. 16, 22–23); of creatures that "succeed in evolving" new anatomical structures (Tumarkin 1955, p. 233); of flowers "learning to mimic" animals, and animals "knowing how to synthesize" chemicals (La Barre 1954, *passim*; see especially p. 336).

This rather recent fashion is fairly sure to be taken as "poetic license." The interesting aspect of the new literary ruse is not the effect, but its source, which is the same as that of the old "Mother Nature" cliché; the ineradicable feeling that something must plan and direct, set goals and figure out ways and means to reach them; if not Nature, then cells, or even "Director DNA." Information is coded by one agent, decoded and acted upon by another, "input" is processed and "output" furnished "as desired" or "as needed," though we are never told who needs and desires it. Instructions go with it from spinal or cerebral centers. Only the factory manager is discreetly left nameless.

The fact that common sense is evidently unable to do without assuming some plan and method in the evolution of animate forms shows that there is, to date, no satisfactory alternative way of conceiving life; no illuminating and systematizing conception of vital events, as natural (i.e., physically determined) progressions, in the course of which such phenomena as needs, values, purposes, means, successes and failures are generated.

Darwin, for all his intellectual daring and reinterpretation of facts, and for all the challenge he proffered to the religious outlook of his contemporaries, did not directly challenge their common-sense image of natural law, which was that of a statute set up by God and obeyed by nature. Darwin's aim was, obviously, to explain the screening out of some characteristics and the progressive development of others as an automatic consequence of competition among organisms for their common means of life; the fact that natural forces limited and channeled the formation of species without anyone to select the breeding stock for desired traits was the core of his theory. The phrase "natural selection" seemed a happy means to connect the genetic principles known in agriculture and animal husbandry with the new theory of evolution.

The most serious influence of the phrase is a formal one; for where a choice is made—no matter how impersonally—there must be fixed forms from which to select. So, in various ways, the language of Darwin's heterodox *Origin of Species* tends to hold his successors to a traditional frame of thought. Every venture into functional thinking comes as a difficult "breakthrough" out of that frame.

One purely practical further circumstance which gave Darwin's brilliant formulation a somewhat rigid character was that all the data on which it was based were taxonomic. This condition, too, we have inherited. Adaptation is the key concept in the theory of evolution; but evolutionary history is long, so most of the materials at our disposal are fossil remains, or else distinct but anatomically comparable living stocks which have been ranged in hypothetical series of progressive development along various lines. What we usually witness, consequently, is adaptedness; adaptation, the actual occurrence of changes to meet special conditions, must be inferred as having taken place in the past. How it operated, and presumably still operates, has been speculatively but nonetheless hotly debated; at present, it is almost unanimously held that heredity, random mutation and "natural selection" suffice to account for the development of all plant and animal forms on the earth from their "eobiont" phases to the degrees of bodily, physiological and behavioral complexity they possess today.

The patterns of heredity are certainly known in the large, at least for fairly high organisms such as flies or, in the plant kingdom, peas, four-o'clocks, corn and countless other spermatophytes; few biologists doubt their determination essentially (if not absolutely) by nuclear genes. That means that any novel trait which arises in a stock and is transmitted from parents to offspring must stem from a change in some gene or genes.

Whether "genes" are infinitesimal organs with individual functions, or (as suggested by Goldschmidt) focal parts each controlling a particular function of the harboring chromosome as a whole, and whether or not the visible bands on chromosomes are really the active "genes," the essential mechanism of heredity has certainly been identified as the "gene complex" that repeats itself in every cell of a multicellular individual. This pervasive and immense repetition is one aspect, often overlooked, of the intrinsic organismic unity which has no parallel at all in the gross functional unity of electronic machines that work faster than any brain.

Upon this minute bearer of heredity rests the initial fitness of the resultant individual to survive in a hard world, and the constitution of the stock depends on the nature of the family lines which in fact do survive. So, on each phenotype that comes to expression, "natural selection" is said to act, letting the new organism live to procreate ("selecting" it), or causing it to be extinguished without replacing itself (awkwardly termed "selecting against" it); indirectly, therefore, "natural selection" acts to shape the gene pool that is the potentiality of the stock, and establishes a statistically best adapted type.

The data for the differential ability of individuals to survive, and for its molding effects on what mutant genes can express themselves without upsetting their possessors' applecart and their own evolutionary continuity with it, are really too full and systematic to leave much question of their significance. Neither can the other factor in Darwinian theory—the heritable character of mutations, for good or evil, once they have occurred—be reasonably denied. Yet the theory of evolution by "natural selection" continues to be attacked as inadequate, oversimplified, "purely negative" and "too mechanical." Part of such criticism may be due to traditional attitudes and affronted feelings, and is to be discounted accordingly; but that fraction would not greatly trouble scientists writing for their colleagues, nor evoke such polemics as one finds in the works of "Selectionists" and their critics. There is something more important that is lacking or askew in our best and most systematic evolution theory, and that fault is philosophical; it lies deep in the conceptual structure which has been built up, by fortuitous, unrecognized steps, on the peculiar Darwinian vocabulary of "traits," "species," "adaptation" and "selection."

The gist of the philosophical failing is that in these terms the environment figures as the principal agent, while the organism is given an essentially passive role. The picture "natural selection" draws of the evolution of high forms of life from lower ones is one in which environmental forces act in concert on the products of randomly varying procreation to select viable phenotypes, and so, indirectly, mold the genotypes by balancing the gene pools of the earth's plant and animal populations. I believe it is this picture—the image of life, not any working model—that is inadequate; and to amend that is a task in philosophy of science, for it requires no new factual data, but a reformulation of the basic conceptual scheme in somewhat different terms, to let the organism count for what it is, i.e., as the agent.

The conception of vital events as acts, or natural processes having a typical dynamic structure, automatically initiates just such a change. Indeed, it does something more than to improve appearances: it leads biological inquiry smoothly from the evolution of organisms to the development, in the zoological realm, of behavior, or spontaneous acts of an animal as a whole, probably with the first glimmering of a psychical phase, or perhaps only some momentary, protopsychical approach to such an intraorganic event. This transition is hard to make in the terms of classical evolution theory, where behavior has to be treated as part and parcel of the phenotype, "selected for" or "selected against" and, in the positive case, adapted by chance to some "ecological niche." As one goes on to the higher forms of feeling, especially in human life, it becomes more and more difficult to extend the scientific frame without breaking it. But the act concept erects a different scaffolding for the same researches. The basic terms it logically provides are act and situation, motivation and actualization; in these terms potentiality, impulse, activity, rhythm, dialectic, entrainment and other essentially biological notions may be defined, as some already have been in the foregoing chapters. And just as the beginnings of life on earth fall within the compass of that conceptual structure, so does the whole evolutionary pattern of generation and differential survival, which underlies the phenomena of mind for which the framework is constructed.

At this point it is unavoidable, I think, to introduce a relational concept that lends itself to more precise uses than "selection" in tracing and describing what happens during the growth, life and procreative success or failure of individuals; that is, a general concept from which many special relations and logical constructions can be derived, and such phenomena as "natural selection" can be analyzed in more literal terms. Although I am reluctant to coin words (a favorite technique of pseudo-science-making), I have resorted to the new word, "pression." The semantic virtues of that term are that in the first place it is not a current word with some previously fixed connotation, yet is an obvious substantive, with a significant "root"; and second, it is capable of all sorts of specifications that do yield familiar words, most of which are definable and usable in the biological realm: impression, expression, compression, repression, oppression, suppression, all capable of grammatical transformation into active and passive verbs or adjectival forms; besides the quantitative term "pressure." "Pression" is a general designation for a class of relations which obtain between situations and acts: those relations that determine the form of an act in the course of its development, i.e., beyond its determination in the generating impulse, and conversely, such as shape a situation for subsequent or sometimes concurrent acts. The advance of life is a fabric of burgeoning acts, in literally billions of pressive relations which automatically adjust the elements of that incredibly complex dynamism to each other, so that it exhibits itself as an inscrutable matrix of "living matter."

Before taking up any more detailed discussion of pression, however, another even more essential relationship between acts and the situations in which they develop should be recognized: that is implementation. Every act requires some support from its environment, be it intraorganic or extraorganic. Breathing is, and must be, implemented by a constant availability of oxygen. The metabolic processes have to be fed continually with their special and essential metabolites. The consummation of acts—indeed, every moment of their proceeding—depends on opportunity given by steadily moving situations that keep pace with the evolving acts. The degree to which an act requires implementation is variable; the very high activity of cell division seems to require little material aid, once the cell has reached a stage of internal imbalance that motivates its division—unless an electrical charge or graded release of some stored energy, unknown to us, is its "supporting cause"; whereas normally acts of hearing, vision, tactual perception or of manipulation require a relatively great and constant implementation. Since an organism is built up by its own acts, its whole structure naturally reflects this need, which is inherent in the act form itself. As for those intraorganic events which seem quite self-contained, acts of differentiation going on in single cells, their implementing situation has been prepared before they began; a cell may well be in a state of awaiting only one outside act, such as the synthesis of a sufficiency of one enzyme, to trigger its mitosis.

Motivation (at the organic level often appearing as "induction"), implementation and the many forms of pression are the influences that produce and shape the evolving system of acts which we see as a life, and in larger extent as the life of a stock. Evolution is primarily a development of acts, and secondarily of taxons; and all the principles of evolution spring from the nature of acts. Each separately distinguishable act evolves from its patterned impulse, through all the modifying exigencies of its course, to whatever consummation it achieves. Each situation evolves, with greater and greater complexity, to give more scope to subsequent acts than previous ones had. Every individuation, or ontogenesis, is an evolution. The evolutionary pattern is inherent in acts, and in all the complexes they form: lives, populations, stocks, and finally the whole history of life on earth that we usually mean by "evolution."

This being the case, the so-called "mechanisms" of evolution have their prototypes in the processes that beget and regulate all acts. The continuity of the vital matrix rests on the rhythmic self-renewal of its activities. In the larger advance of life, however—that is, the stock—this continuity, which is a result of the basic motivation pattern, is complicated by the ebb and flow of successive generations; and here the self-renewal is not a relatively simple repetition of acts, but breaks up, at the starting point of each procreation, into a new pattern of impulses, each one of which stems, nevertheless, from the parent matrix of ongoing or potential activities. This extremely complex and varied phenomenon of rejuvenescence brings us to another characteristic of acts, which is of their essence, though it is seldom remarked except in rare and striking exhibits. Total acts, whether relatively simple or unfathomably involved and synthetic, may expand or contract, without losing the unity of their over-all form that was determined in the primary impulse.

The degrees to which acts may be reduced are astounding. They may even fall below the threshold of impulse, to the level of potentiality, which is a biochemical level. Cytologists today are quite aware that the "properties" of biochemical structures are essentially functional characteristics, potentialities, which (to fall in with today's jargon) are "coded" in their molecular constitutions. Consider, for instance, that a protozoan is capable of reducing its vital activities to such a degree that its periphery shrinks to the minimum of surface outwardly exposed and having to be inwardly maintained, i.e., a sphere, and its inward changes may even come to perfect rest, preserved only as a biochemical complex, a suspended internal situation. In such a waiting state, some microscopic lives such as bacteria found completely insulated by rock salt appear to have remained unbroken for millions of years, and resumed their rhythms of vital impulses when a new ambient, fit to implement their actualization, was given again.

The special relevance of this reducibility or contractility of acts to the conception of life as a progression of activities, rather than a series of anatomical structures made according to a given "blueprint," varied by chance and "selected" mainly by mischance, is that it suggests a process whereby vital activities themselves may be inherited via genetic transmission. Activities as here defined, i.e., dialectically concatenated series of acts (such acts being aptly pictured as "cycles"), even in countless conjunctions and mutual modifications, may be reduced so they are nearly or wholly suspended, if they have only a minimum ambient to implement their progress; they may contract to no more than a complex of electrochemical tensions or sustained patterns. In this state a concentrate of the uniquely structured, enzyme-controlling processes that characterize a particular organism may be physically separated from it to start a new life, alone or with a conjugate in which a corresponding stream of activities is temporarily stowed, chemically encoded, ready to expand into impulse and action. In this way a germ cell carries a "genetic code," not as a "blueprint" to be followed or a set of "instructions" to be obeyed, but as an organically engendered crowd of suspended activities ready to resume their advance whenever possible, in any subsequently possible ways.

The most essential and ubiquitous kind of pression in the whole realm of life is the self-expression of impulses, i.e., acts. Every impulse presses to actualization. Every act, in the course of development, expands as far as its initial impulse and the buffering impulses of acts entrained by it or implementing it can press, and as its situation permits. If the conditions it encounters do not let it come to consummation as a whole, it is repressed; if it never, or scarcely, gets under way from its central impulse at all, it is suppressed, and its abortive dynamism adds itself to the unanalyzable matrix of the agent.

The pressure of billions of impulses, ever pushing to actualization in every single organism, entering or failing to enter the moving stream of acts that constitutes the life of the agent, and beyond the agent, the stock, and enfolding the stock, the whole teeming life process on earth, is a force that fairly defies imagination. Perhaps that is why Evolutionists do not imagine it. But their failure to do so has resulted in the "mechanical," "negative" and peculiarly passive conception of organisms which are, *ab ovo*, determinate future entities being fitted into "ecological niches" by an outside agent, the environment, that performs the acts of "natural selection." The use of the word "niche" for an ecological ambient strengthens the classical image. If, however, one regards the hereditary complex of vital rhythms as the initial datum, which consists essentially of dynamic elements—potential impulses, i.e., competence, in the sense generally used by geneticists and embryologists, coded in chromosome structures in ways which are not yet understood—the fact that the actual evolution of life proceeds by pressions becomes self-evident, for life is itself a central pattern of expression, in which each impulse determines its own obstacles, i.e., its own counter-pressions, intraorganic or external. In this way, each agent defines its own ambient, which is not the environment it shares with other beings, but is a unique tangle of pressive forces that encircles its acts, through which they wind or push their way, and in midst of which they also find implementing and promoting conditions which yield to their advance and take their imprint.

The evidence of such complexities grows constantly with the progress of physiological, and especially genetic, research: on pseudo-alleles, position effects, coincident mutations that may modify each other's influence, multipotential genes, plasmagenes, pleitropy, multigenic controls of development. Every discovery makes the living organism look less like a predesigned object and more like an embodied drama of evolving acts, intricately prepared by the past, yet all improvising their moves to consummation.

In the beginning of a life, as activities emerge again from their extreme reduction in the germ, something more than recurrence takes place in the course of such a rhythmic progression of acts: their passage tends to accelerate, and the cycles to become more precisely alike. Both tendencies stem from the fact that every act makes some impression on the system in which it occurs; that is to say, it sets the stage in some special way for subsequent events. As a rule it clears a path for its own passage, and thereby for that of any other act very much like itself. This pathfinding process is generally called "facilitation." Naturally enough, an act facilitated by a precursor is apt to run its course somewhat more rapidly than one that finds no obvious track to follow. Since cycles of organic activity—metabolism, respiration, circulation, etc.—are facilitated as well as motivated by their immediate predecessors, they are inclined to quicken unless some limiting condition in the system holds them to a maximum speed (as is sure to happen in an organism).

The same influence—the impression of past acts in the maturing system—accounts for the increasingly standardized form of the recurrences, because the readiest way to their consummation is to fit exactly, move by move, into the prepared form. It may also account for the fact that developments once fairly started sometimes continue, and undergo quite excessive elaborations which embarrass the devout Selectionist who can find no survival value for them, and cheer the Orthogeneticist because they so obviously express an inherited unadaptive tendency. Such phenomena as the spectacular evolution and devolution of ammonite sutures, and the well-known progressive exaggeration of saurian armor beyond any possible benefit to its bearers, certainly bespeak a tendency of impulses dominantly established in the gene pool of a stock to express themselves more and more characteristically as long as their actualization is ecologically possible. But it is rarely possible for long—so rarely that ammonites and ankylosaurs are famous. If the champions of orthogenesis build their evolutionary theory on such cases, it rests on slender supports, being founded on exceptional rather than normal facts.

Yet the much-decried principle does exist; only, it is not peculiar to phylogenesis. It is the principle of continuity characterizing all acts, the effect of their original impetus, on which internal and external pressures operate. As a rule it is heavily masked by limiting conditions, especially the processes of adaptation and ecological competition. What the spectacular overdevelopments teach us is that in the fight for survival the tendency to continuous elaboration of started activities is always there; and it is unfortunate that serious study of such implications is often discouraged by fear of an epithet—"orthogeneticist," "teleologist," "Lamarckist," or any so-and-soist that nobody wants to be.

The acceleration engendered by long repetition may also have some important consequences at a deeper evolutionary level, namely, for the building up of the first organisms, because (if one may trust physical models) rhythms with a tendency to accelerate appear to be "pacemakers," i.e., to entrain others of slower frequencies. The earliest established activities in pristine "living matter," whatever was their nature, would then be likely to have assumed a guiding function, and on this simple physical basis provided a mechanism of integration from the very start of life. Similarly, in the course of the earliest individuation and growth, older rhythms would normally entrain younger ones, and keep the harmony of the organism as a whole, in that each new activity would have to reflect, *ab initio*, the inherited dynamism of the oldest complex. That is, indeed, a highly simplified skeleton concept of vital structure; even a bacterium is not only "a population of oscillators." But this skeleton concept does set forth what is perhaps the simplest and most essential principle underlying the original dynamic unity of each vital stock that has continued itself from generation to generation. So much of ancient determination, at least, is encoded in every daughter cell or gamete that passes on to a new life.

The vertebrate heart offers a paradigmatic case of entrainment, in that it has really not only a single rhythm, but several, one of which— the "pacemaker," in most creatures the rhythm of the sinoatrial node— entrains the others, so the "beat" presents as a unit act; but upon removal of the "pacemaker," the several entrained activities on which it had imposed its own tempo resume their original rhythms. This reversion is interesting in that it exhibits a persistence of the original impulse patterns in the older elements, which yield to the faster rhythm, but were not formed under its influence. They are not elaborations, but of independent origin, secondarily entrained by a more vigorous activity. Obviously, in the ontogeny of a highly advanced type of individual, we are not dealing with the simple case of elementary rhythms dominating by virtue of prior development. Yet it is suggestive to find that in so integral an act as a heartbeat subacts are still capable of segregating and running their own courses. The dissociation devised in the physiologist's laboratory shows in reverse the evolution of functional complexity.

Because acts are events of distinct form, held together by the impetus given in an original impulse, they can be partially altered in passage and still achieve a relatively normal consummation. "Pacemaker" action, whereby one process controls the frequency of other processes with which it interacts, is only one of many integrating factors in organic activity. Slow rhythms of great amplitude may entrain, wholly or partially, much faster ones of smaller compass; the variable yet dialectical rhythm of breathing produces some alteration in the much less variable pace of the heart, through a vast intermediary complex of biochemical mechanisms. This whole subject of physiological rhythms is far too great to be pursued here, though the scientific literature on it is almost always relevant to the study of life with a view to the nature of mind.

Some notion of the complexity of rhythms, the constant and countless oscillations that go on all the time in a metazoan organism from the first cleavage of the fertile egg to the death of the individual, may be gathered if we consider that an electromyographic record from one muscle fiber represents thousands, each act in each fiber being slightly different from all others in that same fiber or in others; that a record from one nerve cell is one of many million, all spontaneously active, even if not specially activated, at every moment of an animal's life; and that these do not include any activities of chemical transformation, protoplasmic streaming, cell migration, division and aggregation, or the myriad effects of larger changes such as locomotion, shifts of attention, etc. These present something like a true impression of the complexity of life. Those larger rhythms that rise and fall with our sleeping and waking, moving and eating, are superimposed on the myriad microscopic activities and unconscious repetitive pulses that compose the organic matrix. Little we know how every breath we draw reverberates through the whole vast dynamism of interacting cycles, the internal situation of the next moment of life, that motivates the next breath.

The development of special organs in all metazoa (and of quite specialized organelles even in some protozoa) has long harassed biologists seeking only natural, i.e., causal, explanations of apparently purposeful directedness in nature. The generally accepted view—the only one, as far as I know, set up uncompromisingly against all kinds and shades of teleology—is the neo-Darwinian, according to which chance mutations constantly produce new forms, most of which are deleterious if not lethal, and therefore are bred out again, while a few improve their possessors' chances of survival and procreation, and consequently are established and increased in the gene pool. That such a formative process takes place is almost certainly true, and easy enough to accept as the basic pattern of a universal life stream that consists of individuations—numberless, ubiquitous, competing individuations, which naturally take their forms in any way that the forces around them permit, exercising all the functions they can, and surviving if, and as long as, the essential functions are possible. Note, however, that this constant interplay of forces, which makes shifting obstacles and openings for each individual so that variously equipped organisms are differentially brought to grief, is not a mechanism; the frequent references, in the literature, to the "mechanism of selection" bear witness to the beguiling influence of the term "natural selection," which seems to refer to an act, or at least a function, of some specific power. "Natural selection" is a historical pattern, not a mechanism; it is the pattern of the natural history of life.

As soon as one regards evolution to be a pattern of acts rather than of the anatomical changes that form the record of acts, many such difficulties may be resolved by detailed study of the act form itself and the structured dynamisms it imposes wherever life is in progress. In the first place, random mutation is much easier to imagine (if not to understand) as a deviation from a long-perpetuated activity than as a "loss" of a chemical constituent.

Mutants probably arise long before exhaustion of the substances in question have made their activity evident by leaving them as the sole survivors on the depleted base. But no one knows what other internal processes, controlled by other genes, perhaps whole teams of them, were involved in the new process; or how many other mutants could potentially have made even greater advances, save that the active mechanisms did not accommodate their vagaries. Perhaps this sort of internal discipline is what gives living process an appearance of heading in a constant direction—the evolutionary path, which is not straight, yet as a whole seems to hold a general course. It is a form of pression that would rarely eliminate organisms, i.e., only in the unusual situations in which a mutation might be buffered out that would have saved the whole system; but it is probably a constant controlling influence on the expression of genes, and governs unknowable numbers that consequently never come to light at all. They may, however, be carried along in the gene pool of the stock for ages, and constitute the immeasurable capacity for new developments that seems to be stored in every individual matrix.

New, incipient activities are selectively entrained or incorporated, perhaps rearranged and incorporated, or overridden and suppressed by the established rhythms of the whole hereditary mechanism of the cell, when the time comes for the mutant gene to take effect. Sometimes its influence is too disharmonious to be fitted in and too strong to be suppressed; then the mechanism breaks down, i.e., the mutation is lethal. If, however, the change is accommodated and the organism survives to maturity, its whole activity is somewhat altered, and remains so if it is handed on in the tiny sample packages that are the mutant being's germ cells. In all its future cells the mechanism is modified by the mutation. This sort of "internal selection" of what a new individual is going to present for ecological shaping at all does involve a mechanism, and really is a process of selection. That the physiological activities in cells, tissues and organs constitute very exact mechanisms need not be argued with anybody who has even a popular idea of vital processes.

Yet these earliest conditions, viewed as acts, give one a truer idea of the advance of life than the usual formulation of evolution theory, because in such an intrinsically active and self-harmonizing zygote there is a source of energy to push against extrinsic pressions, and to produce acts characteristic of the agent even when they are deeply impressed with the marks of ecological circumstance (Fig. 10–1). Contracted to a chemical tension pattern in the germ cell, the inherited rhythms continue, and as the new individual is synthesized by its own metabolic procedures, its acts expand in every way possible to find

Figure 10–1. Water Buttercup (*Ranunculus aquatilis* L.) with Submerged, Aerial, and Transitional Leaves. (W. Keble Martin, *The Concise British Flora in Colour* [New York: Holt, Rinehart and Winston, 1965]. Copyright © 1965 by George Rainbird. Reproduced by permission of Holt, Rinehart and Winston.)

consummation. This process may attain fantastic complexity as integration of impulses, reinforcement, elaboration of subacts, preparation of situations that motivate new acts and assimilation of concomitant acts in progress are built up in the embryo of a higher organism.

One principle, frequently stressed in the works of Evolutionists, is that needless structures are bred out of a strain in the course of its adaptation to an environment that makes them unnecessary. Such a statement is probably a dangerous generalization; a deleterious development is usually bred out by ecological screening ("selection against" it), but a great many harmless ones, of little or no apparent use, are carried along for whole biological ages without paying for themselves as they go. One could, indeed, set up a principle of tolerance, as reasonably as the principle of elimination of needless structures. Tolerance is a large and rather neglected factor in evolution. Since useless forms play no noticeable part in the economy of organisms they are easily overlooked; but their existence is really significant for a theory of life, both for what it tells us about origins and for the unexpected role it is apt to play in phylogenetic crises.

The origin of useless or at least unnecessary processes is not harder to understand than that of useful ones: both arise from the matrix of acts which, in its turn, has arisen from chemical complexities in past conditions which we can only reconstruct by surmise. Each germ of life is a packet of potential impulses; each moment of its development is a configuration of occurring impulses seeking actualization among the basic acts already in process of realization. In this swarm of variously proceeding activities of a metazoan embryo each one persists as long as it can, each act that comes to consummation preparing further acts, so that complicated act structures record themselves in the formation of living cells. Some of these structures interact at the cellular level and form tissues, sometimes of great complexity—tubules, sheaths, laminae, cysts, threads and bundles—by chemical syntheses apparently catalyzed at a lower level, in cells, through the never interrupted activities of the chromosomes carried over from the parent strain. Unless these formative processes are stopped by the interference of others, by lack of implementing metabolites, or by destructive extrasystemic forces, they go on to form organs of still greater complexity than their component tissues.

It is here that a larger form of action arises. Over and above the microscopic cyclic acts of chemical transformation, which have already become staggered so that one set of changes supervenes on another (i.e., tissue differentiation on cell formation), acts that involve a whole area, and finally become localized in one of those specialized organs, begin to occur in relative independence of the metabolic rhythms. In the course of ontogenesis those larger acts take shape where and as they can, find their track in the living web of rhythms and expand as far as the developing anatomy permits. Again, the heart presents one of the best examples. It begins to form early in embryonic life, apparently serving no purpose until the incipient vascular system is ready to act with it. In the earliest phases, however, a characteristic function of periodic contraction, the so-called "pulse," appears in many evolving tissues, some of which will cease to exhibit it later, while others will join the cardiac development, so their rhythms will become entrained by larger ones and finally by the circulatory pulse.

The "beat" that precedes heart formation illustrates a basic characteristic of organic function, namely, that its integrated activities are often detectable before their special mechanisms have even begun to appear. Nothing could demonstrate more aptly the primacy of acts in biological existence, and their gradual concentration in those regions of an organism where they can expand, dominate and integrate most fully. This order of development, from differentiating function to specialized location (tissue determination) and finally specialized form (cell determination), has been noted many times by embryologists.

The point of all these embryological observations is that a great amount of differentiation and differential growth is neither needed nor promptly suppressed by essential activities in the actualization of a genetic impulse pattern, but tolerated. Organs develop when and where they can; and the competence of even mature bodies for such development is sometimes surprising. As structures take shape, they offer opportunities to vital impulses to express themselves as they never did before, and total organic acts, such as the digestion of a meal, supervene upon the perpetual microscopic activities of life.

Every act requires some implementation, and any impulse shifts about—or perhaps, is shifted about with the flow of its situation—until it finds a medium for its expression. This medium may be simply a material to act upon, as a push requires some resistant matter in order to be a "push," and drinking entails the presence of a liquid that is imbibed; or it may involve a constellation of other acts, which may be in progress or ready to be induced, to support the actualization of the impulse in question. In the first case it is convenient to speak of the "substrate," in the second of the "means," or (in advanced forms) the "mechanism," of the act.

Now it is a familiar fact (every housewife knows it) that wherever a substrate is given, some living thing is likely to attack it. Bacteria, molds, worms, flies will batten on any suitable organic matter available to them, and where grain is stored, rodents will find it. A coral island rising far out in the ocean becomes colonized by terrestrial plants, as soon as littoral seaweeds and flotsam have formed enough soil on its shores to support a few seeds that have survived passage through the digestive tracts of migrant birds. Bermuda is said to have had at least seventeen species of herbs and trees when it was discovered. All these instances are simple examples of exploiting a substrate. But the opportunism of agents, especially animals, goes much further than that, seizing on every implementation prepared by their own acts or by events in their ambient, and in that way concerting their hereditary activities in relation to original or gradually resultant conditions. That is the active process of adaptation, which goes on constantly in the frame of imposed limitations and the filter of ecological competition.

Something similar happens in the course of a creature's internal development. Wherever a tissue complex is formed, some elaborate hereditary impulse enlists its mechanical or chemical possibilities, i.e., imposes a vital function on it. Just how such a larger activity then induces sundry trophic impulses to develop the organ further in a functional direction would have to be learned in each case; but that it generally does so is evident. The activity and its mechanism evolve together. The tendency of acts to be entrained or assimilated by stronger or more extensively organized ones makes early internal activities of differentiation and growth prone to advance in harmony with the vital round, and be drawn into its repetitive acts so that these make use of the newly emerging tissues and complexes and the substrates they incidentally supply; that is to say, gene-borne impulses to structural elaboration tend to be subjected to the opportunism of the basic life-supporting acts, and modeled into smoothly working mechanisms.

This view of organogenesis receives strong support from the changes of function which many hereditary anlagen undergo in the course of ontogenesis, and the great variety of ultimate developments they exhibit in the phyletic spectra of their adaptive radiations. In embryonic and fetal life some organs serve temporarily for other acts than they will negotiate later; and people who think of them only in relation to their final forms and uses wonder how they can "know" how to assume those forms long before it is time to launch on their predestined activities. Embryologists, however, have long been aware that many tissues and even highly articulated structures are put to one use after another, with successive changes of detail as their ever-changing total situation represses one activity and motivates another. Perhaps the best-known example of such shifts in the functional character of organs during their fetal development is the formation of the mesonephros first as an excretory organ, which acts in that role while the metanephros, the true kidney, is taking shape, and then, in male birds and mammals, gradually transforms its tubules into ductules of the epididymis, participating in the differentiation of the sex organs. But there are many more such functional changes, less evident anatomically. Sometimes even one and the same action has different effects in different stages.

The same principle, the continuity of impulse patterns through geologic ages of unbroken life, through alternate contractions into infinitesimal germs and expansions into new individuations, operates in phylogenetic as in ontogenetic progression. The causes of evolution lie in the dynamic properties of acts and act-engendered entities. From the old, wonderfully versatile gill structures, for instance, all sorts of tissues have arisen in the mammalian and avian orders, in place of the gills that could not develop in their changed situations: the endocrine glands and the thymus and parathyroids from the anlagen of the gill pouches, the meatus of the ear instead of the ancient gill slits, jaws and ossicles from the arches, and supporting tissues of the throat from what used to make up various parts of the aquatic breathing apparatus. As the germ plasm has an unbroken history of millions of years, so has every aspect of its expansions into individuations, though many of these are overlaid beyond recognition by the effects of past contingencies—mutations, inhibitions, distortions and admixtures of new impulses to the primordial ones. There is probably no new impulse that can establish itself without enlisting the support of a primitive one. Yet new impulses must arise with the growing cell assembly constituting higher animal forms in which vaster numbers of interfaces and phasic boundaries produce more energy for contractile functions and nervous discharges.

This capacity to fulfill the vital requirements accurately in many casually varied ways has an interesting parallel in the realm of behavioral acts; there, a similar (perhaps selfsame) directive tendency of a well-formed, deeply motivated act over chance-guided subacts which arise from the momentary situations created as its superior tension builds up to actuality is the physiological prerequisite for the formation and holding of purposes. The reappearance of basic principles that lie in the act form itself, on different levels of life and in many different contexts, goes through the whole realm of biological sciences, and extends to psychology and the historical disciplines. Such pervasive principles connect the phenomena of chromosome structure with the dynamics of ontogenesis, and further with behavior, feeling, nervous development, animal mentality and finally human mentality, or mind.

The action of genes seems to be very largely concerned with determining the tempo of ontogenetic process, and perhaps of lifelong activities, such as metabolism and cerebral rhythms, as well. To say that acts are "encoded" in genes as biochemical patterns means, of course, that the first, i.e., direct, influence of genes must be chemical; and the translation of dynamic phenomena, such as rhythms, into chemical transformation rates is one of the most efficient methods of tracing them back to their genetic determiners. The chemical phases of these basic acts which eventuate in growth, cell movements, embryonic organization, nervous and somatic and behavioral patterns, are of an almost unsurveyable intricacy; one has to isolate the smallest possible complex to track the genetic interactions that finally, by a contrapuntal balance of inductions and inhibitions, guide the synthesis of a single metabolite or effect a single function such as cell respiration.

One further characteristic of acts should be mentioned here, though its full importance will emerge only in a later part of this essay. It is, again, a trait of major importance on at least two far-separated biotic levels, gene activity and behavior, respectively, and perhaps on others. That is the power of subacts, sometimes highly integrated complexes of subacts, to segregate from superacts in which they may have developed as original articulations, and to become involved in different superacts. On the genetic level this separability appears as the famous Mendelian law of segregation; and if so-called "genetic information" is indeed the hereditary continuance of activities, the segregation of subacts is well attested by Mendel's discovery. A detail of action developed in one particular strain of a plant or animal stock may in this way become an element in the future of another strain belonging to the same large stream of life.

In behavior, meanwhile, the same principle underlies the important phenomenon of repertoire. It has been recognized for some time that animal behavior is based on a fundamental repertoire of motions, postures and orientations out of which an individual's instinctive and adaptive acts seem to be compounded. Such repertoires have not been investigated with anything approaching the patience and effort that have been spent on the elements of inherited competence. The best observations of behavioral units, as far as I know, have been made in connection with instinctive actions and with prenatal and neonatal movements, both animal and human.

These are undoubtedly not all the principles of act structure that set the phenomena of life apart from those of inorganic nature; more intimate study is fairly certain to reveal other aspects that are similarly grounded and just as ubiquitously expressed. But the ones so far discussed should serve to support the claim implicit in the heading of the present chapter, and explicitly made in its pages—namely, that "Evolution" is essentially an evolution of acts. It is acts that grow and continue and rejuvenate, and that may come to an end, from which there is no rebirth—extinction.

Besides the basic principles of dynamic structure, there are also functional properties of a less pervasive sort that characterize the ever-growing activity of life on earth: occasional major changes in the implementing mechanisms of some acts, changes which arise from no single sequence of events, but from summations, convergences and (chiefly, perhaps) from overdevelopment of successful functions that leads to excessive complication of structures and steps. Such eventualities beget crises in the existence of the stock that encounters them; but if it survives it usually makes an evolutionary advance, which may even be spectacular.

Finally, over and above the widely spaced yet systematically probable shifts of functions from old means to new and readier ones, there are some extremely rare and intrinsically unpredictable changes, not in patterns, but in the quality of events. They are unpredictable because until they have once occurred they are completely unimaginable: changes of phase in causally unbroken continuities. This is a large and problematical subject, by no means beyond its speculative, hypothetical stage; but its promise of generative ideas for the understanding of mental phenomena is great. And not only that; some light on the philosophical problems of genuine novelty and its emergence seems to come from this direction, too. So a further, searching pursuit of the natural history of acts may be expected to open the approach to a conception of mind and of its origin from the beginnings of life.

11 / The Growth of Acts

Despite the principle of homeostasis, which is apparent especially in the inhibition of enzyme syntheses by an accumulation of their own products, acts do grow. Acts grow in scope, in complexity, and in intensity, according to (1) their chances of implementation; (2) their organizing propensities, which depend largely on the opportunities they create for subacts to develop, and for lesser acts in progress to become entrained; and (3) the energy of their original motivation, which may be greatly enhanced by confluent impulses in the course of actualization. Each of these modes of increase may reach its own kind of limit, where it can develop no further in the same pattern, so a crisis occurs; the creature's activity undergoes a radical change, as the same essential impulse finds a different road to consummation.

The growth of acts obviously leads to tensions and inadequacies which, in turn, produce changes of relative opportunity for different ways of exploiting the environment, of keeping the organism intact, and of procreating, perpetuating the stock. A living stock is not only an "open" system drawing on its environment, but also a hysteretic one, constantly preparing its own next condition and action; its repetitions are never exact, because the very impulse of an act is affected by what lies behind it, and no two acts—not even two cycles in one rhythmic series—have identical histories. The implementation of greater, more elaborated and more integrated acts proceeds on the autocatalytic principle, as steady activities inscribe their form on metabolized substrate materials, building cells and other mechanisms, tissues and higher structures. The increasingly embodied and differentiated matrix motivates more and more concerted and potent impulses that tend to rhythmic, even if greatly variable, repetitions. So the forms of life develop wherever they can, on the basis of ancestral impulses, acts and physical records.

Since the hierarchy of structures in animal organisms—cells built out of elaborately patterned nucleoproteins that present as functional units, tissues composed of differentiated cells, organs of integrated tissues which may be of various origin—thus parallels the increasing intricacy and impetus of vital activities, it seems reasonable, at first sight, to postulate one geminate systematic order of complexity for structures and processes. But the order is not as simple as it looks; very advanced organic complexes may come to serve quite elementary purposes, and vice versa; and this phenomenon, which might, offhand, be viewed as an awkward exception to the general parallelism, is actually an important feature in the evolutionary advance of animal life. So, from the beginning, one cannot expect to match up complexity of structure directly with level of activity.

A major instance in point is the occurrence of behavior, or overt holistic action, in the zoological realm. Since special internal processes, such as circulation of fluids carrying metabolites in solution, arise with differentiated tissues, and larger, cumulative kinetic patterns with the appearance of special organs, one might expect the gathering internal activities to break over into action of the organism as a whole, i.e., into behavior, at some advanced phyletic stage. But that is not the order we find. Behavior is elementary in the animal kingdom. The simplest animals we know—unicellular, free-living amoebae—already perform unmistakably behavioral acts. Yet their internal structure is almost entirely transient, constantly created and dissolved by the changing phases of the protoplasmic stream, so that phase boundaries sometimes take the place of permanent membranes setting functional units apart. Nuclei, mitochondria and Golgi bodies are the amoeba's nearest approach to internal organs, and the provenance of these structures is so different from that of true organs that the comparison is more fanciful than scientific.

Here, however, we meet again with a principle already familiar in the context of ontogenetic acts, namely, the appearance of functions before any visible differentiation of permanent special mechanisms to perform them. As with the heartbeat, oxygen exchange or other vital function in embryonic higher organisms, so with the over-all responses of these lowly little drops of protoplasm: before there is any fixed musculature, the organism as a whole goes into action at the touch of nutritive substances, the impingement of light rays, or when stimulated by gradients of temperature or of chemical conditions in the surrounding waters.

The one permanently structured organ in these briefly individuated little sol-gel systems is the cell membrane that divides them from their environment. It is not only the dividing wall, but also the frontier of exchange between the organism and its external world. It has to let some molecules go in and others out, and bar still others altogether. The importance of the periphery holds for all creatures, no matter what their degree of complexity, size or behavioral freedom; and especially in free-living animals, which may enter new environments, the structural articulation of the surface membranes plays a leading part in the evolution of their organization. So it is not surprising that even in the protozoans any advance in complexity of the creature as a whole involves, above all, a great elaboration of the enclosing membrane, which may be granulated, ciliated, divided into layers, perforated by pores and tubules and fibers that turn one kind of terminus inward into the cytoplasm, and a differently qualified ending outward toward the environment.

In higher animals the outer surface becomes specialized as an extremely complicated *integumentum commune* with many mutually adjusted, if not quite inseparably integrated, functions. From the standpoint of act development it is of inexhaustible interest, for its essential function is a dialectical one—to hold the organism apart from its environment, and at the same time to conjoin the two, and mediate their interchanges. This dual operation is reflected in all aspects of its structure, its variegation, its ontogenetic development and tendency to specialization. The protective function is expressed primarily in the epidermis of flattened cells that become keratinized, successively die, and are sloughed off, to be replaced from below, from the dermis, the "true skin." But its conjoining, mediating actions are involved with its many detailed subordinate forms, which amount to millions of distinct and self-contained organs—sweat glands, sebaceous glands, hair follicles—as well as minute piloerector muscles, and above all the countless nerve endings, largely unmyelinated, with a variety of sensory functions. In its exposed position, the skin has grown to be the most adaptable of all organs, able to meet the multifarious and often times sudden changes of conditions in the surrounding world. Often the skin as a whole seems to be a highly multipotential sense organ.

The peripheral surface of an organism develops from the very beginning in a systemically uncontrolled situation. Contacts with extraneous substances are radical changes of situation for active tissue, in which its activity is usually increased, sometimes in directions that were not apparent at all theretofore, and sometimes in its normal course. That is what it means to say that foreign substances tend to be inducing, which may be seen *in vitro* as well as *in vivo*. Changes of situation motivate acts. The outermost parts of any organism consequently are kept in constant and very variegated action, and such action records itself in a great complex of highly developed structures, mutually fitting and fusing as best they can all the time, and differentiating by virtue of their native impetus to continue in their respective actions and the diversity of pressions and opportunities each one encounters. The outer surface is geared to meet emergencies, and motivated all the time to specialize, diversify and intensify its growth and other functions. It is always in a state of development, not unlike a young, individuating organism; consequently, even in the highest animal forms and at full maturity, the skin is a neotenic structure.

The great evolutionary importance of this constant and inveterate activity of the peripheral surface in animals is that it probably engenders the first acts of such intensity that they enter a psychical phase, a moment of intraorganic appearance as sensation. There are several reasons to believe that sensory acts are the earliest ones to be felt, perhaps in a wholly indefinite psychical instant, at the highest concentration of impulse coming to expression under extreme contrary pressions, either sudden, or built up gradually to a maximum. Such fleeting moments of something felt would be unlikely to have any determinate qualitative character. Neither could they carry "information." They would presumably occur as the organism goes into action motivated by an acute situation; but it may have made comparable responses to "stimuli," received by proto-sensory organs, at a slightly lower pitch of activity countless times before the process culminated in some faint little gleam of feeling. That momentary event, in itself, may have no perceptible effect on the organism's behavioral acts (wherefore we cannot know when and where it may occur); but it would be prone to prepare its own repetitions, so that psychical phases might become more frequent and finally common in some kinds of situation.

At such points, true novelties emerge from conditions that did not presage them, though retrospectively they may be seen to have set the stage for them. A truly novel phenomenon is one that could not have been imagined or conceptually constructed before the first instance of its kind had occurred. It has, therefore, the semblance of a *saltus naturae*; but it is possible, with some philosophical patience and thought, to treat such genuine novelties as emergent presentations instead of resorting to new metaphysical noumena, and thereby hold to the unity of nature that underlies the possibility of any natural science.

If sensibility is indeed the earliest kind of feeling, it does not, of course, have distinctive character as such in its most primitive setting; nothing could feel "external" to a sensing creature before something also felt "internal." For long ages, scattered tiny psychical episodes might mark the most intense acts of some animals in those sudden developments of situation that are called "stimulations," without changing the normal round of actions in which the agents periodically meet such situations. But with the increase of acts which at some point in their passage enter a psychical phase, a creature's behavioral actions fall under the influence of its felt encounters and become organized to anticipate repetitions of such episodes; more and more, then, behavior—the acts of an organism as a whole in relation to extraorganic conditions—comes to be guided and developed by feeling, which at this level had best be termed "awareness." It is presumably momentary, and at the end of a stimulated response may be simply extinguished. Between stimulations there may be no feeling at all; even the response may not be a felt act, but a disappearance of feeling, as the concerted excitation subsides and falls below the threshold of psychical presentation. Such considerations give some likelihood to the supposition that the first felt acts were sensory.

With the concertment of responsive behavior, however, the counteractivity gradually attains its psychical levels, too. At this juncture a basic division of felt action takes place, the division into what is felt as impact and what is felt as autonomous act: objective feeling, or sensibility, and subjective feeling, or emotivity. This dichotomy is probably unimportant in the lowest forms of life in which it exists at all, and it certainly attains its greatest significance only on the human level; but it has some very interesting aspects in the middle ground of animal development, too, especially in the problematical realm of instinct, which will engage us in later chapters. At present let it only be said in passing that our persistent failure to understand the actual, progressive motivation of elaborate instinctive acts, such as the building of an oriole's nest, is largely due to a preconceived notion of instinct as something automatic, not involving any mental acts; and this preconception rests, in turn, on the identification of mentality with intelligence. As soon as one classes as "mental" all acts which have a psychical phase, i.e., a felt passage, however faint or brief, the whole basis of animal mentality broadens; and instead of seeking out tiny bits of resemblance to human knowledge or reason in it, one is led to search the human mind for little-known elements of feeling, directly available, though rarely noticed, to furnish clues and hints for a hypothetical construction of subhuman motivations. But this large topic must bide its time.

Our concern just now is with the growth of acts beyond the development of the matrix itself and its internal functions, that is, with the growth of behavior. The chief characteristic of behavior is the massive release of energy, not at regular intervals, as when chemical or electrical forces, constantly engendered, periodically reach a threshold and motivate cyclic functions, but as much larger impulses to movements of the whole animal, or of its appendages, in its surroundings. Such acts also arise, just as the organic activities do, out of the matrix; no external event can cause them except through its influence on the situation of the agent, in which external and internal elements intersect and interact. The change of situation effected by a single, acute external event may be so sudden (even though it be transient and trivial) that the motivated behavior seems to be directly caused by the "stimulus" (which psychologists today like to call the "input"); yet the most careful experiments indicate a much more complicated causal relationship. Their results really fit better into the conceptual frame of acts and motivating situations than into the simpler frame of stimulus-response concepts.

The experiments here referred to were actually made on neural rather than overt (muscular) responses; but since the former, especially when elicited by external stimuli, are normal commencements of behavioral responses, the observations recorded and discussed in connection with them by the experimenters are surely not irrelevant here. In the course of the Princeton Conference on Nerve Impulse, Dr. H. K. Hartline declared that the response of the visual receptor, rhodopsin, to a short flash of light has a significantly long delay during which it becomes "fully determined," even while "there is as yet no sign of it" and while "the initial part of the response process is out of reach of the stimulus" (Nachmanson 1954, pp. 44–45). The response is certainly the functional counterpart to the structural phenomenon of "prepattern" (cf. R. Goldschmidt's findings in Chapter 9). But what is happening while the initial part of the act—the part that should receive and transmit the causal influence—is "out of reach of the stimulus"? It is taking shape at the impulse level, under the influence of the motivating situation altered by the stimulus, and it takes tenths, rather than thousandths, of a second to work itself out before it comes to expression as the effect of the external cause.

That behavioral acts have the characteristic form of "pre-set," gathering impetus, consummation, and cadence or "finish," does not need to be argued at this point. The act form is most obvious in overt performances, and only found to be exemplified by intraorganic events upon attentive observation, comparison and generalization. But when it is found throughout all organisms, something momentous happens to the whole panorama of biological facts, from the chemistry of protoplasm to the psychology of man: they are seen to be of one piece, no matter how far apart in its vast structure. "Organic form" then appears in nature as it appears in art, and no matter how much scientific analysis may fragment it, every part still reflects and represents the whole; the image of life is restored, and all the models that mimic vital mechanisms in simpler terms do not destroy it, because the structures which their lifeless parts represent are clearly conceived as something else than ultimate changeless parts; they are conceived as tension patterns expressed in substance, which hold their form by a staggering complex of rhythmicized acts. Such dynamic patterns are not parts, but elements. Down to the structure of protein molecules, they determine the nature and potentialities of living matter.

The parallels between vital processes on different levels of organization lead us at this point to an interesting question about a fundamental principle of life: nothing less, indeed, than the question of adaptation to a normal environment. We are wont to look for adaptedness in animal structures and functions, and certainly we find it in the countless vital mechanisms which have taken shape and survived in ecological competition to the present day. But adaptedness is a result and tangible record of adaptation; and a great deal of adaptation goes on without leaving any such material evidence. Adaptation is a process, a characteristic of acts, which constitutes the leeway of life; it goes on all the time; and where it is not difficult for a being to adapt its activities to given circumstances, any closer adaptation of its structure to its normal environment would give it no particular advantage over its rivals. It might, indeed, be slightly detrimental, because every refinement of one function in an organism is bought at the price of some other development, so that perfection *praeter necessitatem* is quite generally no asset. That is probably why a great many "pre-fittings" in nature are not very close. They are adequate, and if they are adequate there is no evolutionary pressure toward their further specialization. The adaptedness of organisms to their ambients is important in inverse proportion (very roughly speaking) to their powers of current and constant adaptation to circumstances.

The term "adaptability" has two meanings which have rarely, if ever, been formally distinguished: one may be called "genetic adaptability," consisting in mutability of a stock with considerable strength to produce viable mutations, i.e., a wide potential adaptive radiation; the other, which I would call "functional adaptability," is the leeway of individual action in a situation.

The interesting bearing of functional adaptability on evolution theory is that it sets an automatic limit to some progressions of genetic change toward bodily specialization, by abrogating the need, and therefore quickly reducing the survival value, of the latter's further increase where active adjustment can take over. This consideration throws some light on the twenty-five-hour intrinsic cycle of human activities, which a person slips into under experimental conditions of isolation. It is a discrepancy from the standard common multiple of all of man's periodic activities, the twenty-four-hour day, that has never been bred out, because it does not matter to man's viability.

Perhaps no environmental influence at all originally set the round of human organic paces to coincide in approximately twenty-five-hour total cycles. Instead, it may have been the rhythms that were paramount in the beginning, and changed only with internal developments of catalytic enzymes: the periods of chemical turnover, integrated in the metabolic acts. All the periodicities in a stock must have grown from these smallest and oldest time units in the course of phylogenesis. In the twenty-five-hour cycle of man we have another instance of that persistent constitutional standard, the whole act, unchangeably itself no matter how masked, that we have encountered before in the intrinsic rhythms of the heart, which yield to a pacemaker but reappear when that modifier is removed.

On the fundamental metabolic and trophic activities, the functional patterns of the special life-sustaining organs are superimposed in the course of embryonic development, and form a system of larger internal acts of the organism. Some of these processes have only intraorganic conditions to meet, but some have to negotiate more uncontrolled situations, because the organs in which they occur have some contact with the extraorganic environment through openings in the body wall.

The great organs of behavioral action in the metazoa are the skeletal muscles with their peripheral adjunct organ, the skin. Their one inherent special activity is contraction, which goes on persistently without particular occasion and may fall to a very low level—so low that its constant presence was a discovery once upon a time, the discovery of "muscle tonus." It has its rise and fall, which is slow, like organic changes. But superimposed on this basic activity is another system of contractile acts, characterized by massive impulses, very rapid rise and strong tendencies to entrain other acts or to become entrained, to wait for implementing acts that are forming and to suppress and supersede incipient obstructive acts. These acute motions of the organism in its *milieu externe* constitute its behavior.

The potentialities that lie in the kinetic properties of protoplasm, first expressed in the flagellate movements that are common to a great many unicellular organisms (plant-like as well as animal-like ones) below the level of separation into two "kingdoms" of life, are subsequently realized in the animal kingdom to such a degree that their development has become a major principle of metazoan evolution. The progressive increase and organization of contractile tissues has, in fact, given behavior the leading role among survival mechanisms in all the higher animals, and expanded the range of their actions so enormously that entirely new ecological pressures have become paramount in shaping their adaptive modifications. The vast numbers of interfaces and phase boundaries in metazoan organisms, producing myriads of electrical potentials, probably provide the massive discharges that allow large units such as visceral or skeletal muscles to contract. The general absence of behavioral acts in the botanical realm and the anomaly of their limited, exceptional occurrence might then be accounted for by the simpler chemistry of plants, and their fewer internal tensions.

Any great increase in the scope and strength of movement without concomitant developments of protective or restraining mechanisms would soon bring the phylogenetic adventure to an end. An example of that dangerous discrepancy is furnished by our own infants between one and two years of age, when they are able to walk and run, seize things and topple them, but have not yet developed a proportionate awareness of imminent situations. So, since many very mobile animals have evolved and survived to their present state without a baby-sitter, their increasing mobility must have been always counterbalanced by sufficient other changes to meet the emergencies it created.

The first such change was probably the high elaboration and activation of the skin which in many animals is the source of all their external sensory organs. But a protective and reactive—even perceptive—outer surface is not enough to safeguard the unity and coherence of a being of large impulses that eventuate in overt acts. Many of its muscles are too remote from the periphery to be under its control. In very small organisms there may be some direct transference of impulses from one somatic cell to another, but with increasing distances this could not be effective. Something more made integrated behavior possible—something derived from the same embryonic source as the skin, that is, from the ectoderm: the nervous structures. These penetrate the interior of the living system and extend the acts of specialized epidermal loci along sinuous courses to stations of similar specialization, forming either nerve nets, or long fibers and synaptic plexuses of a central nervous system, established in the gastrula stage of the higher animals and culminating in a brain.

The skin is closely related to the nervous system even at the highest level of neural development. In ontogenesis, the neural plate as well as the epidermis is formed from the ectoplasm. Phylogenetically, the organs of hearing, wherever they occur, are formed from the skin, especially from its complex surface layer, and in low forms of life eyes are of epidermal (or analogously outermost) origin. Only with the higher development of the brain is the photosensitive part of the eye derived from the diencephalon (sclera and cornea are still developed from the skin). In a larger scheme of life, however, the organ of vision may still be viewed as a highly specialized center in the single structural unit, the ectodermal component of the animal body, which comprises skin, nerves and receptors.

The matrix of impulses in so complex an individual, and even at some lower levels of organization, is so dense that every impulse meets some competition; consequently wherever an actualization occurs there has been an option which the actualization has decided. This fundamental structure of animate process is what makes life irreversible. Most options are decided almost instantaneously and by millions, but the fact that potential conflicts lie everywhere indicates that options belong to the very nature of acts. The optional character of life is so pervasive that it presents not as a structural feature but as a quality; one of those elements of which we have as yet made no tangible or even mathematical model, but which is projected in works of art, and is perceived qualitatively as "vitality."

Out of the flood of unfelt options arise the larger ones that resolve themselves in behavioral acts. The emergence of motility in the course of ontogenesis is closely linked with the differentiation and maturation of the nervous system. One of the notable features of central nervous systems is their division into two sets of fibers and associated "centers," sensory and motor. This differentiation is the anatomical expression of an early division of animal acts into two principal classes: acts precipitated by a "stimulus," i.e., by an acute change of situation, which usually arise from peripheral impulses, and, if they have a psychical phase, are generally felt as impacts; and those which arise from interior impulses, motivated by more gradual situational changes, and, if felt, are normally felt as autonomous acts. The interplay of these two impulse patterns in the single dynamic system, the agent, is the foundation of behavior.

It is fairly certain that behavior arises in ontogenesis from many sources, just as organic functions do. The patterns of their respective developments are, indeed, very similar. Just as organs gradually assume their characteristic activities and adjust them to the conditions imposed by the rest of the system at each moment of their continuous history, so the organism as a whole performs all the acts its situation permits, fitting them into the conditions of its ambient. It develops motions of distinct and integrated form. A stronger and more concerted act may entrain previously articulated ones of small scope, or override them, or force their shift to an altogether different consummation, just as maturing organic processes do among themselves. Some of the latter, e.g., the activity of the lungs, verge on behavioral action from the beginning. The skeletal muscles gradually, in postnatal life, attain a limited amount of control over respiratory cycles. This is a major step in establishing the power of vocalization in many animals. Other prenatally prepared patterns of motility are clearly recognizable in the subsequent instinctive acts that arise, in most cases, with as true a systemic timing as the staggered fetal organic functions.

The basis of instinctive behavior is not primarily the desire to cause changes in the environment, together with some unlearned knowledge of how to do it, but the consummation of impulsive acts; and the whole gamut of articulated, essentially repeatable, overt actions of which an animal is capable is its repertoire. Highly elaborate acts are synthetic products of the instinctive repertoire, formed under the pressures or implementations, encouragements or discouragements of the outside world. Since behavior always does change the agent's ambient in some way, it automatically achieves good or bad situations for further acts;

and such results quickly motivate acts incorporating favorable results in their normal consummations. The result need not therefore be preconceived by the animal; it is anticipated in that the tension set up in the impulse is not resolved until the practical change occurs, or some other change that takes its place. Beasts and even men may not know that the aim of an act in progress has shifted.

A complex that has reached a high articulation by virtue of its micro-ambient becomes involved in one organic activity after another, so that its earlier functions are often—I would venture to say, usually—not primitive stages of its ultimate specialty at all. A new situation causes it to realize some quite unforeshadowed potentiality. It is often surprising to learn what ends a receptor has served in its phyletic past. Sometimes it continues to do so even after a newer function has become paramount, so its previous ones may go unrecognized in future. The non-visual activities of the eye are a striking instance. Its primitive function seems to have been light reception and propagation in connection with metabolic and trophic processes. Parietal eyes, some ocelli and very probably the eyespots on the backs of certain slugs are held by many physiologists to serve in such capacities rather than for vision. The mammalian eye still carries on this sort of function, through fibers that leave the optic nerve tract to enter the hypothalamus and in some cases terminate in the hypophysis, with somatic effects on skin and hair pigmentation.

Evolving processes are forever differentiating, so that distinct functional elements and associated structural articulations constantly arise. These follow their specialized courses with gathering impetus until they reach the limits set by the rest of the system, or until their own activities become overtaxed or overelaborated; then there is often a radical change of activities as another mechanism, which has formed just a little more slowly but with similar potentialities, takes over the function.

Such changes constitute crises in the course of life, phyletic or individual. Biological crises are not necessarily precipitated by external events or abnormal inward conditions, though of course they may arise that way; but ordinarily they occur as normal crests in the wave-like acts of vital development. For almost every physiological mechanism that achieves a high degree of differentiation, there are other commencements of potential structures, large impulses that could use the same opportunities for expression, but remain in abeyance or are diffusely enacted through other channels as long as the previously started rhythm is progressing freely; but if that rhythm flags for any serious reason, an easier and freer act complex, fitting into the same total organic pattern, is apt to be ready to displace it. This sort of functional shift has already come to our attention as a systematic phenomenon in ontogenesis. It also occurs in the wider sphere of behavior with the maturation of each individual. Few people realize what radical changes in the enlistment of muscles and other organs occur in the course of learning such acts as walking and jumping. The shift from one mechanism to another is still more pronounced in the development of higher abilities, such as reading; while basic acts that are generally not even recognized as performances, acts of perception, seem to undergo similar changes in the course of special training, which lets one conjecture that such shifts occur quite normally in the course of maturation, too. In tachistoscopic experiments, imagery and the truly visual phases of the perceptual process tend to disappear as the perceiver approaches virtuosity in perceptual tasks. Emphasis shifts to the motor aspects of the whole perceptual act (Renshaw 1945, p. 218). Here, as elsewhere, the characteristics of growth and progressive articulation, functional integration, and adaptation that belong to physiological processes reappear, sometimes in larger and more striking form, as typical properties of behavioral acts.

Throughout the evolution of an animal stock its activities grow in extent, diversity and intensity. With such increase, of course, the ambient of its individuated lives widens and becomes richer in opportunities for action. All life is opportunistic; every extension of the ambient—which is not only *Lebensraum*, but also the spectrum of sensory impressions, the range of awareness of external conditions as substrates or means of action—is also a further extension of behavior. Growth is the perpetual trend of life; the material self-enlargement of organisms is only one manifestation of it. Acts and ambients grow and diversify, reintegrate and shift to higher levels, together. That is the course of evolution. The power to negotiate a larger and more "difficult" ambient is often taken as the measure of evolutionary advance.

But growth—in nature as in art—is not always expansive. Acts may grow in intensity, where more and more diversification in a limited compass implements their progress, while they gather impetus by entrainment of other incipient acts, pooling of impulses. Such acts finally break over into the purely intraorganic phase of being felt.

This is not a shift of functions, but the emergence of an entirely new phenomenon, "feeling" in the broadest sense, or consciousness. It is a crisis in natural history as great as the emergence of life from physicochemical processes; the emergence of a novel quality in the evolutionary course of life. This momentous crisis may not have been a "crisis" in the ordinary sense of a single, more or less cataclysmic, event, but a vastly distributed, protracted process taking eons to develop. As it did so, however, "life" in another than physical sense originated with it—"life" as the realm of value. For value exists only where there is consciousness. Where nothing ever is felt, nothing matters. Biologists speak of "survival value" with relation to organisms to which they do not impute any felt acts, but the term is really inexact, and reflects the natural and world-old belief that all individuals not only automatically strive, but desire, to live.

But this is all anticipation of later chapters. At present our concern is with the growth of behavioral acts and its harmony with all other evolutionary patterns, as far as we can survey them, from the simplest forms to the most elaborately organized. The significance of mental acts in this connection is that they prepare very rapid advances in behavior and concomitant growth of animal ambients, and themselves have such power of growth and such flexibility in mutual adaptation that they shift from one course or one mechanism to another, and build up a whole functional response system, which we refer to as the agent's mentality. The study of these processes belongs to psychology; but the basis of that study is the conception of living form and function, which takes one from biology into psychology, and further into the strictly human part of that discipline, the investigation of mind and all its reaches and expressions.

For in one primate stock—the hominid stock—all the developments of special talents seem to have tended in one general direction, which was toward cerebral activity; and at some fateful juncture in the history of that genus, there occurred a shift—doubtless long-prepared—of a systematically and practically unimportant cerebral function that took all related ones along, somewhat as the turn of an odometer that has reached 99,999.9, starting with the decimal figure, replaces one 9 after another by 0, until at the left end of the line a new space is filled by a "1": 100,000.0. Such was the great shift, the shift from animal to human estate, that initiated the development of mind. To reconstruct in theory what probably or even conceivably happened in actuality is still a large undertaking, to which the next part of this essay will be devoted.

IV / *The Great Shift*

12 / *On Repertoire and Instinct*

The most important concepts to bear in mind in dealing with the problematical issues of animal behavior are (1) the wholeness and typical form of acts, (2) the advance of situations, and (3) the fact that an organism always does everything it can do. These fundamental ideas have been employed, so far, mainly in relation to physical development, growth and organic function. But, as already stated in the previous chapter, primitive behavior is an extension of the internal functions, and is governed by analogous (though not identical) controls. In its simplest form it resembles the homeostatic interactions of organs, which is a dynamic system of stimulation and inhibition; stimulation by a perpetual stream of changes in the internal situation, constantly motivating new impulses, and inhibition of vast numbers of their presumptive enactments by stronger, rival acts or act products, so the somatic impulses which finally come to overt expression represent only a very small selection. The main difference between such intraorganic activity and the lowest forms of behavior is that the decisive conditions controlling behavior are external, the somatic elements being largely permissive.

A modulus of reactive behavior may be seen in the rising and sinking of plankton in adjustment to light conditions and to the day and night surface temperatures of the water. Plankton locomotion is dependent on drift horizontally but "voluntary" (I would prefer to say "facultative") vertically. This capacity to escape from an environment that is becoming too hot or cold, bright or dark, acid or alkaline, etc., is sometimes treated as a power of choice, and perhaps it could be so designated; but before having proffered any definition or discussion of "choice," I would rather say that the animal had a behavioral option, because this option may be resolved very much like the millions of physiological options that make up the advance of organic existence. Certainly in these minute animals tropisms are dominating impulses, and behavior consists of immediate reactions. The creature moves to escape discomfort, not to reach a goal, and comes to rest where the conditions are tolerable, without knowing in advance where that will be. In this way its ambient is very widely extended, but never defined or organized. This is very much like the homeostatic influence of organs on each other by means of their respective products or activities, except that the two nocent extremes between which the congenial balance (not necessarily 50–50) obtains are external to the organism and motivate its counteraction as a whole, i.e., by locomotion or change of posture.

Aimless motility is the lowest form of behavior, but develops, of course, in concert with the vague ambient which it expands enormously by every specific act. Its forerunner is the all-important power of bodily extension and contraction which might be considered still on the biochemical level, save that it already shows the complexity of causal pattern here called "motivation." The external cause operates as a stimulus, that is, through the matrix of activities which is the organism, to add its influence to the prevailing condition of that system. In a swarm of unicellular beings like the zooplankton, the effects of a stimulus are statistically predictable but not individually certain. The stimulus creates an option which, at this low level, the internal state of the agent decides. But even here the decision is between alternative acts of the typical form: impulse, rise, consummation, cadence, amid pressions that limit and shape the response and may distort or frustrate it.

In higher animals a repertoire of behavioral acts is prepared, if not actually exercised, *in ovo* or *in utero*; and it is this fetal forerunner of adaptive behavior that furnishes the elements from which instinctive acts are formed, by much the same sort of process that engenders elaborate organic functions. There is, indeed, a continuity between somatically functional prenatal or neonatal behavior and the subsequent uses of the same inherited elements of overt action in the maturation of instinctive or otherwise adaptive behavior. In many situations organic activities are normally supplemented by facultative acts ranging from probably unconscious responses, steered by simple though often variable stimuli, to clearly voluntary movements directed toward ends rather than away from external pressures.

A case of purely physiological activity which is, nevertheless, behavioral in character is the gemmation of sponges. The cells that make up the gemmule aggregate to central collection points where the sponges form. Their behavior is probably unfelt and certainly unaimed, motivated by chemical or electromagnetic forces which are not entirely understood at present. Their separate potentiality is relative to their degree of individuation during a given passage of their total history. When a migratory cell enters into a gemmule it gives up its individuation, and its behavioral competence is lost without being actualized. The significant aspect of such loose organization in pseudo-metazoan structures is that it shows how elementary overt action is in animal life; wherever there is even transient individuation there are potential concerted acts of the individual as a whole. The amoeboid actions of slime mold cells, which finally compose an orthodox plant producing windborne spores, present another example; the influence exerted by *Fucus* eggs on each other, and even by a single one on itself, by means of "exterior hormones" illustrates the motivation of group activity by the products of individual members, singly and collectively.

At the low activity level of plants, which is normally a purely somatic level, contacts with environmental stimuli motivate unequal rates of metabolism and mitosis, so roots grow vigorously toward a source of food, buds open fastest where light and warmth reach them most freely, etc. It is typical of animals, however, to unfold their behavioral acts particularly under the influence of external events, so that more or less acute outward changes are reflected in the motivation of overt acts, making those acts appear like direct mechanical effects of the stimulus. The fact that an isolated organ, dissected out of a living animal, often can be activated without any total bodily matrix to motivate its response supports this view. But this is really an interesting example of act contraction and expansion, appearing at the level of individual existence as the principle that mutilated organisms—each kind within its own limits—tend to reorganize their activities almost immediately on a new basis and adapt them to their new condition. While such macabre behavior lasts, it may look like a lifeless "output" of motion effected by the electrical or mechanical "input"; but it really represents an artificial heightening of endogenous processes, and fails when there are no more such processes to heighten.

A further step in the external supplementation of internal balancing mechanisms is taken by animals that seek out places with comfortable microclimates in the midst of generally adverse conditions. The advance, however, is not simply associated with evolutionary advance. From his studies of an excellent example of active, responsive adaptation, C. M. Bogert (1949, p. 209) holds that endothermy was developed from a particular coincidence and integration of mechanisms which had been separately elaborated for behavioral control of temperature in various reptile species. This hypothesis fits well with the conception of shifts of function through over-elaboration of mechanisms which, becoming somewhat trammeled by their own complexity, allow a different, simpler action to emerge and perform their function on a higher level of organization. But I am inclined to doubt that the basic processes of homoiothermy have been evolved from behavioral thermoregulation. The mechanisms to which functions shift when their old mechanisms become unadaptive are usually far removed from the old. Genes that have long been suppressed can come to expression in effective impulses when more anciently established operations, which have long inhibited them, give way for any reason. Then the repertoire of the stock seems to show new elements, out of which apparently new acts can be formed; but the potentiality may have been there from primitive ages, only held in abeyance by the prior development of competing activities.

The change to endothermy must have begun in a steadily increasing and statistically more evenly distributed rate of energy production, and led to the remarkably constant consumption of the excess energy as body heat. But there is no indication that the new mode of living arose as a higher development of former ways. It is much likelier that an independent physiological advance overtook some reptile species and motivated the entire new complexes of behavior appropriate to avian and mammalian life.

The neural potentialities of response to changing external conditions seem to develop on the same principles as the neural controls of somatic functions; that is, they develop to varying degrees *in utero*, and sometimes express themselves first in forms which may or may not look like the behavioral acts into which they are destined to enter postnatally. Not every stereotyped response of extrauterine life necessarily has a recognizable intrauterine precursor; the characteristic pattern may be engendered only in the radical ontogenetic shift of situation at birth (or hatching, metamorphosis, etc.), or in later stages, for in most of the higher animals the process of maturation continues through a period known as "youth." An act may also be so composite that the innate factors are masked by mutual modification, or eclipsed by the much more evident external factors to which they are adapted in practical use. But I think there is convincing evidence to be found—though only on close study and reflection—that all animal behavior below the level of concept formation is instinctive; and the conceptual level is very high on the evolutionary ladder, not far short of human mentation, if short of it at all.

The building up of instinctive behavior from the matrix of trophic and somatic activities is not a simple ascent; behavioral acts may supplement autonomic processes, as the quokka's licking instead of sweating heavily and the poikilotherms' selection of suitably air-conditioned stations; or the advance may proceed on the opposite principle, such troublesome methods being gradually obviated by the development of physiological mechanisms, like internal temperature controls, which automatically and constantly perform the necessary functions. In evolutionary progressions, just as in taxonomic classes, there are no simple patterns and definite constant directions. The course of progress from lower forms of organization to higher ones is zigzag, and, like categorical divisions, is sometimes blurred; there are no sharp lines between organic specialization and competence for behavior, between reflex action and behavioral action, repertoire and instinctive acts. Most biological processes are, in fact, dialectical; that is to say, they go forward as an interplay of opposed but mutually determined phases. The essential forms of vitality repeat themselves on all levels of life, from metabolism to ratiocination. Sometimes they are most apparent in elementary functions, sometimes in very high, superimposed attainments. The principle of dialectic was originally discovered by Plato as the pattern of philosophical thought. It is also the basic biophysical pattern, the principle of cyclic concatenation of acts, whereby the cadence of each consummated act is the preparatory phase of the repetition of the act. This is the dynamic form known as "rhythm."

Homeostasis, long recognized as the source of "steady states" under conditions of constant biochemical activity, has its analogue on the behavioral level in the interactions of impulses with their coordinated "inhibitors" and "releasers" (inhibitors of the inhibitors). In organic behavior (breathing, peristalsis), inductor and inhibitor substances, which can evoke or block the muscular acts involved in each cycle, are fairly well known, even with respect to their origination in the body. In reflex action, specific stimuli and selectively responsive sensory organs, as well as many of the neural paths and plexus over which the stimulated impulses are conducted, have been found; and in organisms of relatively simple structure, such as most arthropods, the inhibiting "centers" (e.g., abdominal ganglia) which hold the reflex activities in check can be located by excision experiments which release unlimited mechanical movements.

In higher forms of animal behavior, too, there are stereotypic actions, sometimes of considerable complexity, that show very little variation from one individual to another within a species, but great interspecific differences. They are the actions that are generally referred to as "instincts." Their endogenous nature is evident because the first time an animal attempts them it executes them in typical fashion, just as it carries out its first breath, yawn or whimper without "trial and error." The course of the act, which may be an elaborate series of movements, is prepared by the creature's developing anatomy. The chief difference between the operation of an "instinct" and of organic behavior is that the former is fitted to external conditions and requires extraorganic substrates or means. Its distinction from reflex action is that it is prepared by related acts, or "appetitive behavior" which culminates in the consummation of the total act, i.e., in a subact, quite properly called the "consummatory act." Consummatory acts are the most stereotypic movements, but also least peculiar to any taxonomic division below the largest, e.g., class or even phylum. It is mainly "appetitive behavior," and the less noticed cadence which follows consumption, that are species-specific, and provide the defining characteristics of the various "instincts."

The pattern of a total instinctive act does not seem to be controlled by fixed neural mechanisms. The locus of an electrode which yields one stereotypic act in response to a first stimulation produces a different one upon a later stimulation of exactly the same frequency and intensity; and, still more disconcertingly, if electrodes are left in place in a chicken's brain stem and the experiment extends for several hours, the selfsame area yields (apparently in random succession) now this, now that unit of instinctive behavior—preening, cackling, fleeing or what not—with occasional intervals of no overt response (von Holst and Saint Paul 1960, p. 410).

Such experimental results do not lend much support to a theory of act-specific centers as the mechanisms of instincts; rather, they point to a variable use of most, if not all, stations in the brain, a great versatility of its nuclei, as though they were junctures in circuits rather than fixed organs with specialized functions. The nearest to a fixed neural mechanism in control of overt acts is the spinal reflex arc, which, however, appears on close examination to be much less simple, far more involved with the brain, than its early investigators ever suspected. The long and short of it is that we have as yet no physiological knowledge of the brain adequate to explain the phenomena of animal (let alone human) behavior.

The chief reason why the study of instinct has made so little headway, despite the wealth of empirical data which we owe largely to the patient field work of the ethologists, is its lack of usable basic concepts in terms of which problems could be framed and hypotheses mooted. Its weakness is philosophical; that is why research in its domain falls apart into antagonistic schools. A. N. Whitehead once remarked that the only ideas opposed schools of thought have in common are their tacitly accepted presuppositions, which are fallacious. Something like that holds for the instinct theorists and the learning theorists: what they hold in common is the concept of "behavior" as a reaction of a fixed mechanism, which may be a whole animal or a special part within the animal, to a distinct stimulus or series of stimuli originating in the environment. As a phenomenon, this is what we find. But what one finds as an objective datum depends on one's units of thought; and units of thought have historical origins, but only pragmatic credentials. The main shortcoming of the stimulus-response unit is that it builds no large frame of biological thinking in which organism and organs, vegetative functions and strictly animalian functions, special mechanisms, reflexes, "conditioned" responses (which may be reflexes or not), sense impressions and guidance of behavior, instinct, adaptation, options, voluntary movement and learning all have some common denominator. The lack of such a common denominator, or basic conceptual unit, has made it seem necessary to study some major psychological phenomenon by a special approach, in its own special terms, and to treat all the rest of psychology as an extension and generalization of the concepts and principles used in that particular study.

To find divergent lines of evolution springing from different anatomical possibilities, with consequently different principles of action, is disconcerting; none of the hypothetical cause-and-effect patterns can be expected to serve as a modulus in the systematic study of all forms of life. To understand the evolution of instinctive acts from early forms to the amazing complexities presented by advanced nesting and food-getting acts, one has to have a more abstract and more inclusive conceptual scaffold. The conception of animal life as an advancing stream of activity instead of a pattern of overt acts induced by external stimuli or a fixed number of internal "drives" suggests such a versatile treatment of instinctive behavior. It does not contradict most of the generalizations which have been made, often with great logical circumspection, from experimental findings recorded in the traditional terms; rather, it tends to show their full implications by shifting the emphasis to different aspects of the established facts. In such a conceptual framework the notion of a stimulus, for instance, as a "trigger" needed to release a pre-set physiological mechanism appears as a highly simplified mechanical model; for an actual "stimulus" is a crucial item that completes a situation which motivates the responsive act. The concept of physiological "triggers" or "releasers" is a valuable one in neurology, where its use is naturally limited to the study of particular nuclei and circuits, and in exactly such contexts it is legitimate and useful in psychology, too; but it harbors a danger for the unwary imagination, namely, the suggestion of the mousetrap ready to close, but doing absolutely nothing until the trigger is released. No living mechanism is ever doing absolutely nothing. If its normal and special action is inhibited, something is covertly going on, there are changes with the maturing, proliferating or perhaps aging processes of the surrounding tissues; the inhibited complex is waiting, and waiting is a physiological activity.

There are, in fact, several kinds of species-specific (which means, of course, hereditary) acts: (1) pure reflexes, elicited by particular acute stimuli, and requiring no conscious intent; (2) autogenous acts motivated by changes of internal situation, prenatal or postnatal; (3) direct responses to opportunities for action offered by the ambient, which are made in characteristic ways by different species—the typical movements generally recognized as examples of instinct; (4) special proclivities, such as the raccoon's to dip its food into water, the cat's to bury its feces; and (5) apparently purposeful, elaborate acts, like the sunfish's fanning his brood, the nesting and feeding habits of many birds, the astounding performances of sea otters, dolphins and apes.

These acts are all instinctive in animals. That does not mean that they are never done intelligently, nor that their performance is "unconscious" in the sense of being unfelt by the agent. Animal intelligence is the perception of opportunities to perform instinctive acts without suffering any harm—that is, with a weather eye for dangers; and animals differ widely in intelligence. But that subject belongs to the next chapter. Our present concern is with the organic substructure of behavior, which is the native repertoire developed by every individual according to its kind, not necessarily in very early youth, but by the gradual articulation of its organs, sufficient accumulation of their products, and perfection of muscular and other bodily mechanisms by growth and use before another instinctual element can come into play. Instinctive acts have their proper time of life, though some of their subacts may occur before or after that time, in other behavioral patterns or alone. Even in maturity, an animal may perform a new act in typical form at the first attempt, without guidance or example; sexual and parental behavior occur when the organism is ready, and are perfected by repetition, but are not changed to different ways.

No matter how cleverly the environment may be exploited to implement the actualization of animals' impulses, I submit that their acts are all made out of elements in the agent's native repertoire and steered by the current advance of the motivating situation, organic and ambient, from move to move. The sort of behavior classed above under the headings (4) and (5) can be traced to the native talents listed as (1), (2) and (3). (There may, of course, be other and better classifications; such schemes should never be taken too seriously.) The natural forces which cause the evolution of behavior are the same ones that cause the evolution of organs and their interacting functions, and spring from the formal structure of acts, which determines the peculiar organization of causal relationships here called "motivation." The same principles operate from the beginnings of life, at the borderline between chemical interactions and primitive organic activities, to its highest forms. The basic processes that build up elaborate behavior patterns have physiological versions in the activities of the simplest animals and of the organs of higher ones. For instance, the tendency of acts to perseverate unless repressed or disrupted by dominant acts appears in the continuous action of the frog's olfactory bulb and also pieces of the brain, even *in vitro*. Even trophic processes—which are all composed of genuine acts and proto-acts—have the repetitious character which is behaviorally known as perseveration; its material record is the replication of structures. The occasional supplementation or even replacement of organic processes by behavioral ones shows one form of transition from somatic to voluntary action, and even closer relations may obtain between the ambient-sensitive autonomic system and the volitional, perceptive and conative acts of higher animals through the participation of that system in the balancing and grading of the energies spent in behavior. The push to action comes from central sources, from the matrix, the organism as a whole, which is always doing all it can as energy is brought in or drawn in, bound in constantly self-restoring protoplasmic structures if its immediate expenditure is prevented (which is largely, and constantly, by action of the parasympathetic system), and meted out again in thousands of enacted impulses, whenever and wherever the ways are clear.

The complexity of animal life, certainly at the vertebrate level and perhaps in the highest invertebrate forms, is such that every behavioral act arises from a texture of activity which is full of gradients, summations, urgencies, inadequacies and abnormal substitutions. The intra-organic situation motivating an act is only statistically estimable, and our experimental control of it correspondingly crude. The environment is more readily controlled; it is there that we establish thresholds of stimulus intensity and vary the "input" to elicit quantitative and qualitative variations of an animal's "output." Sometimes we change the internal situation in gross and abnormal fashion by injecting chemicals or excising parts of the organism, and by such methods a great deal has been learned; the extent to which mutilated animals can reorganize their functions, the participation of many mechanisms—including dispensable ones—in most facultative acts, the balanced round of hormone actions, the chemical unity and individuality of higher animals and relative divisibility and tolerance of lower ones and, indeed, nearly all the general physiological facts that serve to explain animal behavior have been established by cumulative series of experiments and the statistical tabulations of their various results. But the necessity of watching one controlled factor at a time, or at most two or three in conjunction, tends to obscure the fact that what is a factor in the scientist's picture is an element in the activity of his animal preparation. The superimposed records, especially when smoothed to a general curve, yield what looks like a direct causal correlation of "input" and "output," and for the purpose in hand that may be desirable. It must be remembered, however, that for the larger purpose of understanding animal life, the deviations from the norm, which the statistician properly ignores, are significant; for while in an inanimate mechanism they would be trivial, caused by jarring or by uncontrolled changes of light or temperature which could be eliminated if greater accuracy were demanded, in an animate system they signify the underlying and largely inscrutable processes which motivate overt action or progressive changes in metabolic and organic activities such as hypertrophy or degeneration of tissues. The facilitation or inhibition of microscopic acts which summate or culminate in behavior is always a variable element in any individual preparation, affecting its every reaction; so the spectrum of deviations which are smoothed out of the statistical curve representing an experimental sequence is an index to the relative depth and complexity of the matrix on which the stimuli impinge.

There are gradations of intensity in acts as well as in the stimuli (bodily contacts, temperatures, lights, etc.) in a creature's ambient. The lowest level of activity is that of obscure impulses summating into a dense and constant potentiality but not coming to expression; this massive background of impulses is the field of options in which every consummated act—microscopic or macroscopic, overt or covert—determines by its own realization the abrogation of countless other incipient acts. It is lower in activity than the fabric of minute but realized somatic acts which constitute the tonus of a living body; even beneath the muscle tone and the metabolism that upholds it there is the continuous possibility of activation, whether for growth, internal change, cyclic functions or behavior. But that deepest stratum, the vitality that exists in dormant eggs, seeds and suspended lives generally, goes almost entirely unrecognized.

It is from this depth of potentiality that the history of an act should ideally be traced. But in seeking to construe and understand the data we actually have on any particular instinctive act form, we have little hope of carrying back our study of its evolution to the earliest motivating conditions, and demonstrating step by step what elements have entered into its formation, so that now the behavioral pattern in question characterizes the stock which shares in that long life history. We have to begin with some hypothetical "primitive" stage of the stock, at an evolutionary level where it is recognizable as a probable forerunner of the animal in question. Yet it makes a great difference in the relative powers of psychological theories whether they are couched in terms that suggest and invite a biographical view of the structure as well as the action of living bodies, so the image of physiological mechanisms appears as a detailed picture in the context of a huge relevant whole, any part of which could be drawn in and handled in the same terms, or whether the terms suggest unphysiological mechanisms, such as industrial and communication machines, built out of independent parts and operated by a devised system of signals, triggers, couplings and prearranged emergency switches, while nothing in natural history corresponds to the designing, manufacture and setting up of the machines.

The best starting point in the study of instinctive behavior is probably *in medias res*: that is to say, with the organism's postnatal repertoire of acts which show some degree of stereotypic form the first time they occur. These overt acts consist of many subacts which in themselves would hardly be appreciated as units, though they are recognizable in several different complexes, as distinct patterns of breathing may be seen in crying and in sleeping; and they in turn subsume overt and covert acts, some completely integrated in the larger whole, others partially entrained, borrowed elements of concomitant processes, down to organic acts like breathing, which in most animals is an autonomic activity rather than an instinctive performance. Spinal reflexes, sometimes modified by intrauterine conditions, provide ready-made movements to be incorporated in more precisely adaptable responses.

Every instinctive act is motivated by a situation that is deeply prepared in the organism, by gene-controlled stages, to produce massive impulses to muscular action, intrinsically patterned in hereditary forms. Those dynamic forms are products of evolution just as certainly as the taxonomic forms that characterize the agent, which means that they have a phylogenetic past and an ontogenetic course of individual progress, just like bodily structures. As long as vital acts are entirely internal, like heartbeat and peristalsis, involving mainly or wholly involuntary muscles and autonomic nerves, their status as evolutionary products is rarely questioned. But when they are directed outward, something more than self-perpetuating organic rhythms may enter in to determine their courses, namely, substrates to act upon and sometimes means to find or reach such implementing conditions. If the necessary environmental complement is directly given, the organic pattern of a hereditary act is scarcely modified; sucking, for instance, seems to be a complicated movement which occurs even without implementation.

But not all neonate activities are so preformed that they need only to be spontaneously exercised to have a favorable effect on the agent's situation. The thrashing, kicking and other typical movements of newborn babies, though they may have physiological value in building muscle or aiding circulation, make no practical changes in the infant's surroundings. Yet it is interesting that from the start these muscular expressions are total acts; the avenues of impulsive discharge have been prepared *in utero*.

Such short, unadapted, but fairly well-defined and repeatable motions are not strictly speaking instinctive acts, since they do not in themselves serve to negotiate the agent's life in his ambient, but they are the instinctual elements out of which true instinctive acts are made by gradual integration, maturation and the molding forces of pressions from within and without. Instinctual elements, rather than a collection of "instincts," compose a creature's basic behavioral repertoire.

To trace the highest developments of animal behavior back to their instinctual sources one has to abandon the common-sense standpoint from which they appear to have arisen in response to special needs, and ask from what beginnings such elaborate actions could have grown to their present complexity. Here we have, on the level of instinctive behavior, a problem already met on the lower level of metabolic action—how a sequence of acts could have evolved in which the earlier members serve only to prepare later ones which are going to be appropriate to a subsequently given situation. This question arose earlier with respect to molds and other autotrophic organisms which regularly synthesize chemical compounds from which they can ultimately produce the metabolites they need for their living. N. H. Horowitz (1955, pp. 299–300) speculated that such preparatory acts were not evolved in ascending order, but in reverse, the final consummation being originally possible without special preparation, but becoming more and more difficult until only those mutant strains which synthesized the necessary metabolites could survive. These strains, which soon became the whole continuing stock, again and again met the same sort of situation through which they alone had been able to pass; and there was another crisis and another, at each of which the stock was nearly annihilated by exhaustion of an essential metabolite, save that each time some mutant organism—in molds, possibly just one, though in view of the astronomical numbers of individuals probably more—synthesized the rare chemical and continued while millions of normal colonies perished. Gradually the vital activity of such autotrophic organisms has become a stepwise process in which only the last step is really metabolic.

In this kind of evolutionary change, one might say that a change occurs in response to a need; but the statement has a weasel character, since actually the change had already occurred in part of the stock, no one knows how many generations or eons ago, and a new need only made the existence of the genotype apparent as the phenotype proved to be preadapted. Most evolutionary novelties arise without total destruction of the older forms; hence the prevalence of species and varieties, related genera and even orders presumed to have common ancestors. But the great mutant forms that leave no representatives of their ancestral stock on earth may have taken evolutionary spurts under severe circumstantial pressions; many evolutionists, led to the problem of fast and slow phases of physical and behavioral change, have remarked that the most spectacular alterations and departures occur at low points in the phyletic history of a stock, when it is "defeated," and its individuals are small, few or precariously supported by their environment.

We do not know what goes on in the forming of each individual genome; but if one thinks of this essentially biochemical process as a dynamic system of organic acts, then each behavioral act appears to rise from the physiological matrix exactly as every heartbeat, breath or peristaltic contraction does, to take shape as an articulate directed impulse under the restraint of competing impulses, to find its implementation by ambient conditions, through preparatory preceding behavior and constant, concerted perceptual acts, and to be sustained by the dynamics of the act form itself—rhythmic perseveration, which in behavioral acts becomes facilitated repetition—elaboration, entrainment and integration, and especially an over-all tension that is resolved in consummation. These main aspects have been discussed in Chapter 8, and have only to be borne in mind; they dictate the working principles stated at the beginning of the present chapter, which seem to me to throw a different light on the tangled problems and exhibits of "instinct," "learning" and other cognate phenomena.

The most important principle for a biological interpretation of such behavior, and indeed of all animalian acts, overt or covert, is that an organism always does everything it can do at the time. Everything it does not do is precluded by what it does do or has done, or by lack of opportunity in its ambient. Its growth has created countless possibilities and limitations, its whole past underlies every situation that emerges for it from moment to moment. This raises an interesting question with regard to so-called "inhibitor" functions. Every voluntary muscle that goes into action inhibits its antagonist, but the inhibition is automatic, incidental to what the active muscle is doing; a muscle cannot simply inhibit another's act, without performing a rival function of its own. Similarly, every "center" in the nervous system that is found to be holding some specific act in check is probably doing something in the vital round, incompatible with the inhibited function. The "releasing mechanisms" postulated by Lorenz, Tinbergen and other students of instinct must then be thought of as yet further acts, motivated by outside stimuli or inner processes, which interfere with the normally present inhibiting activities. It is not necessary to postulate specific mechanisms; in the play of rival impulses, any physiological mechanism can act as an inhibitor, and its own inhibition would disinhibit any impulse or impulses now no longer prevented. This is, of course, just Sherrington's "principle of reciprocal innervation," explored and extended since his day by many physiologists and some psychologists.

The same essential condition of life that limits and inhibits growth and behavior by competition—namely, that an organism is always performing every act it can at any given time—also makes up the pervading opportunities of living things. Under the spell of orthodox, single-minded selection theory, some Evolutionists do not appreciate the fantastic lengths to which this opportunism may go. But it is really the obverse aspect of the "unoccupied niche"; the force that makes "niches" in the first place, the automatic trend of impulses toward implementation of their active expressions. This trend may be a constant shifting of central activities (perhaps a groping expansion in various directions) until implementing conditions for the act, or part of the act (subact), are met and the overt phase develops. Something like this must occur in the transition from impulse to behavior, or the many unusual adaptations could not have arisen; simply to note that they have survival value and were "selected" is not enough to account for their emergence in the first place; no physical trait and no action can prove valuable, and consequently be "selected" (i.e., be able to continue), until it has actually occurred.

The constant development of opportunities for the carrying out of incipient acts thwarted in their most direct paths to consummation, and the fact that every consummated act provides some facilitation, however slight, for its repetition, probably work together to give hereditary changes of physique and behavior the tendency to develop more and more according to the openings they find in the surrounding world, which George Gaylord Simpson (1949, Chapter 3) refers to as "oriented evolution." The constant transformation of every environment by geological and meteorological causes, the rise and decline of floras, the coming and going of animals (think only of the Grand Banks built of minute exoskeletons of formerly innumerable creatures) make heredity and mutation only a moiety—though perhaps the greater one—of evolutionary advance. No being, and no living stock, can ever arise in maladaptation to a fixed environment and subsequently become adapted; but changes, slow or relatively fast, in an environment have to be matched by changes in the genotypes it supports. That is a generally accepted concept today: the evolution of ecosystems. What is less well known, perhaps (no study, so far as I know, has ever been made of it except incidentally), is the scope of individuation and aberration, the freedom of action permitted by a creature's place in the ecosystem which frames its existence. Undoubtedly some ecosystems are more exploitable than others, so they encourage the enlargement of at least some of the *Umwelten* they comprise. This highly variable factor, this leeway of life, is of prime importance in the origination of novelties, and in some respects certainly underlies the growth of instinctive behavioral acts and the ambients that expand with their growth.

13 / *Animal Acts and Ambients*

As already stated in the foregoing chapter, I hold that all animal behavior is instinctive, arising from organic sources as impulse seeking expression in motor action, and guided to direct or indirect consummation by acts of perception. To understand a creature's aims and methods one has to consider in what sort of *Umwelt* it lives, that is, what it is able and likely to perceive. The most natural thing is, certainly, to assume that animals—not only dogs, horses and other familiar kinds, but also birds, fish, insects, and all forms possessing eyes—see forms and colors much as these appear to us. Laboratory studies, however, have led most investigators to the belief that mammals with the exception of the primates have little if any color vision, whereas birds and fishes see colors as we do; insects, too, are credited with this "higher" ability, originally conceived, of course, in strict accordance with our own.

It has long been known that most mammals have a much keener sense of smell than men—probably as long as people have used dogs to follow scent trails, and have had to hide their own trails and their food stores from animals. The distance vision of hawks, the night vision of owls and nocturnal beasts are familiar examples of sensibility surpassing our own. But that there may be sensory qualities entirely unknown and unknowable to us is a sobering thought for a scientific thinker, who is of necessity an empiricist. Ultraviolet vision is only one such manifestation; its discovery was quickly followed by that of the bats' echoic hearing of their own squeaks in ranges which are supersonic for man, whereby they seem to steer their courses in the dark among obstructions and track their flying prey. This aural function is pragmatically so different from ordinary sound perception that one may wonder whether sound and ultrasound form one sensory continuum for the animals or two sensory modes. I suspect the latter, because the over-all result of a bat's high-frequency vocalization and echo reception is a spatial frame in which the animal acts, while its low-frequency hearing seems to be alertive, episodal and geared to the range of its own emotional utterance, like the hearing of most other mammals.

Still more recently (1959, 1961), Yngve Zotterman brought experimental evidence that some animals, but not all, possess a taste organ which responds to pure distilled water; overt behavior as well as electrical recordings from the gustatory nerve indicate a taste reaction to water dropped on the tongue. The most baffling aspect of these findings is that the ability to taste water neither rises nor declines with advance on the evolutionary scale. Frogs appear to have it, also pigeons and chickens; cats and dogs, but not rats; and most surprisingly, rhesus monkeys, but not men. Again, we can form no idea of what pure water tastes like. The same researches make it very probable that some animals cannot taste sweet, some cannot taste bitter, and so forth. Also, a substance we find bitter, sour or sweet may excite, in another animal, the nerve fibers which characteristically respond to NaCl.

The discovery that many animals have percepts entirely unknown to us has naturally led to a wide search for still further senses which might explain the ability of many creatures, notably birds, to perform feats of migration and homing which are quite unaccountable in terms of human means of pathfinding. Hypothetical percepts include use of polarized light, radio waves and radar signals, Coriolis force, magnetic currents from the earth, inertial pressures, and perhaps other possibilities that never reached even the stage of a "preliminary report" in a professional journal. Experiments in such a field are hard to devise and carry out. So far, certainly, artificial conditions set up to establish special modes of perception by undiscovered sense organs or more diffuse bodily feeling have indicated no such sensory endowments. There may, of course, be influences of local conditions that rise above the threshold of perception, as some human beings feel electric charges in the air before or in a thunderstorm, and a good many people feel low atmospheric pressure; but that does not mean that they can use such feelings to guide them from place to place.

All the other possible means of pathfinding that have been seriously contemplated are geographical—guidance by river valleys, shores, mountain ranges, etc.—or else celestial, the use of constellations and especially the sun as skymarks for the cardinal directions. Many theories have been based on possible (or supposedly possible) ways of steering by the sun's position in the sky, even involving extrapolation of its path from a short observation of its movement. Excellent naturalists have credited birds with "true navigation" by heavenly cues, and even with maintaining a course under cloud cover by memory of compass points taken from such cues on a previous day.

The great stumbling block to all the "sun compass" theories of animal pathfinding is the fact that the sun's position relative to any given spot of the earth changes with the day and the pattern of change itself changes with the seasons, so a bird using the "sun compass" would have to make allowance for very complicated spatiotemporal factors. We are so accustomed, today, to the engineering metaphors of "automation" and information theory that the notion of birds taking bearings and computing the distances and directions on long flights does not strain our credulity.

And as there are inexplicable animal abilities to challenge our powers of theoretical interpretation, so there are equally astounding and inexplicable blunders and apparent stupidities. The obliviousness of many animals—insects, birds and mammals—to what we would consider the goal of behavior, when that "goal" is displaced or removed, is quite puzzling. With our natural, common-sense assumptions of what animals should be responding to, some of their behavior is flatly inexplicable. We are really forced to the conclusion that animals do not live in the same sort of spatial milieu as man. There are several well-attested conditions which make that proposition plausible. The most important is that animal perception is more intimately bound to overt action than ours; in fact, it is established in the performance of instinctive acts, which are guided by feeling, both central and peripheral—that is, by felt impulses and felt sensory impingements, or sensations. Percepts are often very indirect deliverances of interacting sense impressions of mingled sorts. The principle of their formation is selection, among all the elements in the external aspect of a situation, of those that will implement whatever acts are in progress. That includes evasion of obstacles, especially death-dealing ones. In other words, the primary characteristics which animals see are values, and all the qualities of form, color, shape, sound, warmth, and even smell, by which we would naturally expect them to recognize things, enter into their perceptual acts only as they enter into their overt behavior as values for action. A young animal creeps under any living or non-living body that is warm and soft. A cat generally chases anything that runs or flutters. That does not mean that the young one would recognized a fur-lined boot in which it had slept as the same object if the boot were on someone's foot, or that the cat which had chased a roller skate that was pushed across the floor would pay any attention to it if the skate stood in a rack.

It is hard to believe that cats and dogs may not see chairs and tables, cage doors and corridors just as we see them. Yet experiments really support that conclusion. E. L. Thorndike, an early experimenter (1911), even entertained the idea that animals do not perceive permanent, well-defined objects as human beings do. Like Jakob von Uexküll, he was aware that an animal's ambient is not what we imagine as its "environment." It may not see what we see, when it does not act as we would act.

A few years after the appearance of Thorndike's book, *Animal Intelligence*, Hans Volkelt published a monograph on representations in animals' minds. He had access to the facts collected by Thorndike, John B. Watson and K. S. Lashley, Albrecht Bethe and von Uexküll, as well as to the interpretations those authors had offered, and like them he concluded that animals had no store of images and memories of past occasions, and that even their current perceptions were not of physically defined, permanent things, to be met with again and again under various conditions. But he pushed his very careful and well-grounded speculations beyond those of von Uexküll and Thorndike to the problem of what non-human creatures do perceive. His first realization, based on a long, though chance-inspired, observation of his own, was that the crucial property of animal percepts, which apparently determined all their other properties for the perceiver, was their value in the current situation, and that this value depended on what activities were in progress or in readiness at the moment.

Fully half a century after these early demonstrations that animals do not perceive events and things in their surroundings apart from their own impulses and acts, some quite similar experiments by R. Held and A. Hein have shown this principle to operate in even more radical ways: their surrounding space itself is perceptible to them only by means of their own activity in it. The inherence of their sensory acts in larger behavioral acts is clearly apparent from a series of learning experiments in which young animals (kittens) were prevented from using and seeing their own limbs, while they were passively transported through a territory which they could view in passage, as one watches the landscape from a vehicle one is not guiding. The apparatus was a circular track in which one kitten walked in a halter suspended from a rotary arm above, so it could walk only forward, while the opposite end of the arm moved a gondola with another kitten that could move but not see its limbs, and could not walk, as it was carried passively around the same track. It could look forward and somewhat laterally; the walking kitten wore a shield restricting its vision in the same way. The result, briefly stated, was that the passively transported kittens learned nothing about the terrain, though they could see it, while the walking ones easily learned to place their paws and move or stop as they wished. This, in itself, was not surprising; that paw placement would profit from visual and tactual feedback is reasonable enough. But the next experiment on the same pairs of kittens showed the full effect of autogenic action on the development of visual judgment.

The second test was on the so-called visual cliff, a path with an illusory drop on one side, a shallow shoulder on the other. Denoting the actively moving kittens by A and passive by P, the experimenters report:

> All A's behaved like normally reared Ss.... each A descended to the shallow side of the cliff on every trial.... The P members... were tested on the cliff on the same days as their actively exposed litter mates. They showed no evidence of discriminating the shallow from the deep side.... Following the 48 hr. period of freedom in an illuminated room [all the experimental animals had been reared in the dark], the P members... displayed normal visually guided paw placement and performed all descents to the shallow side of the visual cliff. (Held and Hein 1963, p. 875)

So it appears that space itself, as an animal knows it, is action space, and that even its visual presentation is not simply given, but made by the agent's own exploitation of its possibilities. The immediate recognition of the "visual cliff" appearance by cats which had never made a descent, but had explored a track with paws and eyes, indicates that for cats at the age of walking and seeing any natural incentive to space perception suffices to start all the mental acts required for its further development from one moment to the next, that is, from one situation to another. The feelings of direction, distance, contact and progression seem to be extended almost at once from actual to potential movement.

Such learning does not exemplify any of the patterns recognized in learning theory or assumed in setting up the usual learning tests; yet here it is, demonstrated in the animal laboratory, and one cannot but wonder how it could have been recorded there without arousing any surprise that "incidental learning" should so far exceed the predicted effects of reafferent stimulation. The canons of scientific method require that animals be presented with specific, controllable stimuli which seem simple to the experimenter, such as black squares and circles and triangles on a white ground, or vice versa, white on black.

But it may be that animals trained to distinguish squares, triangles, etc., as black-and-white figures never see them as such at all; that they distinguish black holes from white obstructions, or even just see black holes, and see nothing noticeable at all (the white shapes on black) if the background does not look like a dark alley. In viewing the standard black triangle they may never notice the apex, but see only the equivalent of a trapezoid, which would be the part required to admit a rat's body, and would do so as adequately as a square or oblong aperture. The angle formed overhead by the sides is irrelevant, whereas the horizontal base is not. But neither a possible hole nor a white "thing" plays any part in the food-reaching act that involves a choice of doors. It takes long training in the unnatural, simplified setting of cage or apparatus to establish a visible "sign stimulus" for an animal that does not use such things in its normal ambient.

The findings here collected and many others like them corroborate the judgment which Volkelt based on the few examples he knew— Thorndike's cats, Bethe's bees, Watson and Lashley's terns: that animals have no representations, and so can call up no images of things met in one situation to recognize the same objects in another. What animals perceive, according to his conclusion, is above all a qualitative character, a "complex-quality" of a total situation. Any change of some contained element in a total situation may change the "complex-quality" of that situation, so the animal may change its behavior without being aware of any specific new stimulus. As Volkelt put it, "In animals, the relationship of perception and action is not that the presentation of a thing-like complex evokes a correlative act; nor yet that the act is correlated with an atomistic sense impression. The behavioral acts of a primitive organism are adapted to the presence of certain holistic complex-qualities which may comprise even the entire motor, visceral and emotive condition of the animal itself" (1912, p. 90).

Every past event, therefore is assimilated to the agent's reactive scheme; instead of recalling former experiences and "associating" sights and tastes, smells and movements, with consequent pleasures and pains, and then imposing such remembered patterns on similar sense stimuli encountered thereafter, an animal relives its act with its whole previous qualitative complex; "all at once, the entire past experience is present again; for the earlier total experience affects the present one assimilatively; the old one virtually repeats itself" (ibid., p. 117).

The literature is full of observations indicating that what we see as permanent, essentially unchanging objects may have no such qualitative stability for animals. Paul Leyhausen, in his excellent study of the hierarchy of moods observable in beasts of prey, especially various species of cats (viverrines, ocelots, African genets, civets, African tiger cats, servals and others), noted how the appearance of a rat or a mouse, which the experimenter saw unequivocally as "prey" for his felines, seemed to change even from one subact of the killing process to another; and as a subact might be elaborated, even in the course of the usual totality, to draw in subacts of its own and become temporarily the dominant act in progress, there is a play of moods, a relative hierarchy of motivations at every moment, in which the prey animal is successively (or alternately) a target, a toy, a victim, a morsel or what not.

From these and many other examples it appears that if we would venture any guesses at what an animal perceives we should first study the nature of its acts, behavioral and, as far as possible, organic; for all non-reflex behavioral acts are continuous with internal preparatory acts, and any intimate study of overt responses must reveal something of their total form before we can reasonably infer anything about their covert, psychical phases. A few general aspects of animal acts, which become apparent only through a wide survey of patterns in very many, very diverse species, may account in some measure for the basic differences between human and non-human perception and capacities.

Instinctive acts are behavioral wholes from their beginnings, i.e., their respective main impulses; and where an avenue of expression is free, they go through characteristic phases of development. In the most established act forms which have not become highly elaborated, such as a frog's or a toad's hunting pattern, the sequence of stages from the motivation of the impulse to the consummation can be fairly well seen and analyzed; more complex acts, by comparison, then corroborate the findings. One of these most general observations is that adaptation to external conditions is made chiefly at the commencement of the act. Dr. Mathilde Meng (1958) recorded this fact. The consummatory phase is the most reflex-like and, indeed, in the acts which she studied, involved reflex movements, for which all the voluntary behavior furnished the proper conditions. Once the preparation is made, the act may even be completed *in vacuo* if the implementing conditions suddenly fail—for instance, if the target flies away before the hunter leaps or lurches for it. This increasing automatization has long been noted, and inspired the theory which Lorenz and Tinbergen hold of a hierarchy of neural "centers," each controlling a lower one, down to a reflex "center" which triggers the consummatory act. Their neurological picture may be somewhat too simple even for the anuran brain, since so far, at least to my knowledge, the series of "centers" has not been found (which does not imply that it doesn't exist); but certainly the characters of the earliest and the last subacts are patent, though the graduated order of automatization claimed for the intervening acts is more assumptive than demonstrable. There is convincing evidence that in the lower animals, at least, the situation that obtains at the beginning of an instinctive act engenders the total performance, even a day-long succession of cycles, so that any modification of the course of the act has to be introduced very early, while the impulse is forming under the influence of exteroafferences. The preparatory phase is the phase of adaptation.

The fact that the first stage of a protracted or complex total act in a relatively simple nervous system is the decisive stage for adaptation to ambient conditions, as well as the "pacemaker" for all its own repetitions, shows the unitary nature of instinctive acts. The main impulse, once it has been perceptually directed, really initiates a rhythmic continuum, or activity, for the day. We human agents hold our acts together by a conception of purpose and means, involving causes and effects, which holds us to our original intention; and we survey the results of our total performance to judge whether it is complete, and whether it was appropriate. An imaginative presentation of the conditions we hope to effect is contained in the purposive concept. But that is a human method. In animal acts, the over-all tension is preformed in the impulse, and the act is apparently not controlled by an image of external conditions to be achieved, but by a constant internal pressure toward its consummation.

As the earliest overt phases of instinctive acts, which are continuous with covert ones in the realm of impulses, seem to be the most intense, and in low animals the only ones sensitive to impingements from the external world, so the last phase, the consummation, whether successful or abortive, also has its special character: it is the most fixed element of the total act. This fact was already evident to one of the earliest analysts of instinctive behavior, W. Craig, who pointed it out in an article which is still valued and referred to by the ethological psychologists: "Appetites and Aversions as Constituents of Instinct" (1918).

This is essentially the pattern of instinctive acts which Heinroth, Lorenz, Tinbergen, Kortland, Thorpe and many other observers have found. The beginning and the end of the act are its essential elements—impulse and consummation—spanned by a single arc of nervous tension. The consummatory act has its own subacts; in a protozoan the whole process may be comparable to that which, in most metazoa, takes place after the consummatory phase of "eating," i.e., after the swallowing reflex has made sure of the catch. Even internal, chemical and kinetic actions undergo great evolutionary changes; but in their phylogenetic courses they fall under the control of the autonomic nervous system, whereas the orienting acts fall to the motor action system, the voluntary muscles and their nerves. Behavioral impulses generally arise from the latter system. In some lower forms of life, such as anurans and urodeles, hunting consists of perceptual orientation and then an unguided leap or lurch with open mouth ready to close, on the prey or on emptiness. With the evolutionary advance to higher forms it comes to include many very elaborate subacts—tracking, digging, the various forms of fishing practiced by birds, bats, raccoons and even by water-shy cats.

Now, the respective characters of the first and last phases of a relatively simple instinctive act, such as a frog's fly-catching—the first essentially an act of perceptual orientation, the last so stereotyped that it simulates a reflex—together may long have constituted the whole act. Early aquatic ancestors of our amphibians probably moved without aim, as many fishes do, snapping at such food morsels as they might meet on bottom or by nosing along under the surface, or, perchance, in the body of the water. Then there was no introductory alerting and orientation; the feeling of contact, at best presaged by a small aura of scent, was so close to the consummatory snap and swallowing that there was hardly a moment of expectancy between them. But with the development of a live-insect diet and terrestrial habits, the beginning and the end of the feeding act moved apart; only those individuals that could withhold the snap long enough to fixate the prey, which is apt to make the fixated object or spot a terminal of motion (as every learner on a bicycle knows), escaped starvation. The act expanded into a sequence of perception, conative posturing, and finally the strike.

This hypothetical but very probable expansion of a basic instinctive act is reminiscent of the growth of somatic acts which N. H. Horowitz observed in *Neurospora*: a successive increase of preparatory chemical activities synthesizing metabolites essential to the plant, when the autochthonic supply of them was exhausted. The final metabolic act was old and generally unchanging; but its rise from the trophic impulse evolved as the cultures which could not perform it any more on their depleted substrate died, and left the field to the few mutant strains that synthesized the needed compound.

One fact supporting the parallel between the evolution of instinctive behavior and the biochemical evolution in the molds is that several investigators of instinct have found the rising stage of such complex, species-characteristic acts the most plastic, and in higher animals most steadily and minutely guided by peripheral sense. The fact that here the ontogenetic development of a complex behavior pattern presents a model for a possible phylogenetic process demonstrates the pervasiveness of the act form in all vital phenomena and the recurrence of evolutionary principles on the most widely separated levels.

The capacity of some large acts to span long periods of time in waiting for the appropriate situations to develop which will implement their progress and consummation has also been observed in behavioral contexts. One of the most variable and often intricate performances in the mating of animals is courtship; this behavior, preceding copulation, has both internal and external difficulties to meet: inwardly, an abnormally high emotional tension with violent impulses pressing for enactment, and outwardly a need for concomitant, complementary acts of another individual. It is the frequent failure to find a partner momentarily ready to join the rising passion and implement the sexual act that motivates the evolution of courtship activities.

As acts can be expanded, so they can also be contracted. On the somatic level, down to the cellular and even the molecular, this occurs in the higher forms of life between generations in the continuity of a stock; but it may also take place in behavioral acts, where it appears mainly as a sort of "telescoping" of stages, together with some reduction in the spatial scope of movements. E. A. Armstrong (1955, p. 124) remarks that a male wren's nest-invitation display may be curtailed if the female already knows that nest; H. Hediger, whose main studies have been of mammals rather than birds, found that the successive phases of the procreative act—oestrous, coition, pregnancy, birth, lactation and again oestrous—could be "telescoped" to various degrees by curtailment of one phase through premature onset of the next (see Klein 1956, p. 340). Another example of act contraction, more strictly behavioral, is given by Noble and Bradley (1933) in their study of mating procedures in lizards. These observations, by the way, revealed the astonishing facts that in the species investigated the females have no sexual "drive" (so that the frequent statement that the male's display "attracts females" is without foundation), and the male will subject weaker males to his sexual passion as often as females; so it is only because of the constant activity of the males that probably all females become impregnated sooner or later. The authors describe the four steps to consummation, the first of which seems to be a purely organic excitement on the part of the male. The second step is seeking a mate. The next phase is the most complicated, since the partner (male or female) is fighting the rapist, but their further acts need not delay us here. As the whole process nears its consummation, the intervening subacts are still adaptive, contingent on the behavior of the partner, who is gradually immobilized by a process of rubbing, which may be persuasive—that is, pleasant—or hypnotic, or paralyzing, then suddenly all groping and guiding responses cease, and the stereotyped movements of copulation supervene.

The point illustrated by all these instances is that the large instinctive acts of animals arise from apparently quite massive impulses, so their tensions may hold over long periods of time from inception to consummation, tolerate a good deal of interference without breaking, accommodate if not entrain a great many lesser impulses (such as responses to concomitant sensory impacts), and expand or contract in adaptation to the progress of the ambient situation. Such a view of animal life is very different from any that one can formulate in terms of stimuli and responses. An organism activated from moment to moment purely by successive external stimuli could never carry through large acts like some hunting techniques, procreative patterns or animal peregrinations. There is no reason why stimuli should arrange themselves so providentially that millions of organisms should find them well ordered to produce appropriate responses from moment to moment. Many creatures do often react to entirely fortuitous details in their ambient, which may be properly called "stimuli." The result, however, is not a wonderful display of adaptive behavior, but an exhibition of senseless, rapidly shifting responses, usually in an anomalous situation.

Under normal circumstances countless impulses touched off by casual peripheral impingements are overridden by current acts stemming from larger impulses. It is the nature of these large impulses, motor and locomotor, that really shapes the ambient of an instinctively enacted life. They have not been studied with anything like the attention that has been given to perceptions, yet they probably are as important to what various animals perceive as the sensory capacities themselves; for in the frame of instinctive impulses and their expressions percepts function otherwise than in the human sphere. If we would speculate on what an animal sees or fails to see in its environment, we must start from what it is doing; for it sees whatever will implement or frustrate its acts. Their implementations may be materials, special places, and above all vistas and avenues permitting an act in progress to continue, unfold from one move to another; that is, the creature has an eye for enticements, openings and options, perhaps not far ahead, but arising as they become relevant. In this serpentine, ever-developing ambient, impending frustrations of acts, ranging from small obstacles to threats of instant death, appear with the same continual emergence as the successive opportunities.

The reason why animals, operating without concepts or symbols, can function as effectively as men might do in similar situations, and sometimes more effectively than men could, is that their major instinctive acts are highly articulated, phylogenetically developed units, unconfused by any awareness of merely possible exigencies, possible errors, or thoughts of other possible acts. Their instinctual evolution has been as gradual as that of the agents themselves. Their successive stages are often physiologically expressed in a homologous pattern of hormone production in which one biochemical phase engenders, and merges into, another; it is through this pattern (today called a "code") that the species-specific forms of instinctive action are heritable. Such complete patterns are not found in human lives; all their elements may occur, but they have been fragmented by the pressions of conceptual processes so that there is no automatic sequence nor order of detailed, unpremeditated action any more. That subject belongs essentially to Part V, but the reason for mentioning it here is that it explains our difficulty in imagining instinctive behavior as more than a simple "drive" to copulation, self-defense or participation in mass hysteria. The large instinctive acts of animals are not only "triggered" by impinging conditions—meteorological, seasonal, communal or what not—but sustained by the bodily changes these impressions motivate when a creature is otherwise ready for them: those changes are hormone actions. Most hormone actions are gradual, sometimes cumulative, so they may present a different hormonal pattern at each station of their development, and consequently can sustain a complex total impulse throughout its progressive phases.

As the ambients of higher animals are made by their acts, their places are created largely by instinctive activities, and reflect those behavioral patterns. The fact that a sea bird may be momentarily confused by radical changes in the surroundings of its nest site, such as removal of trees or spectacular pieces of flotsam—stranded barrels, wreckage, etc.—or the addition of new objects, does not mean that these things make its memory image of the site whereby it finds its way back to its nest. The bird gives little evidence of having anything like the memory images whereby we would find a colony we had visited and a particular nest in it; but the fact that it can fit a fairly close repetition of a former act into the re-encountered scene makes this "the same place," one met with what may be the most important feeling for space-construction in animal life—familiarity. Human beings are so used to identifying "landmarks" that we tend to overlook the fact that in driving along a known road, for instance, we see all the unremarked stretches between such special markers with a nearly, if not wholly, subliminal sense of familiarity. In the birds which have amazed ornithologists by their apparent oblivion to visual cues, that general sense of *déjà vu* may be all the identification of objects that they need or make.

"Places" are not geographical regions, but pragmatic entities, locations of felt events; as such, they may expand or contract with the expansion or contraction of the life to which they belong, which may have several places—feeding, nesting, hiding, courting places—each with its unique, inherent feeling tone, and its own special sense of familiarity when it is revisited.

If, now, we consider this intimacy of an animal's local adaptation, springing from the mutual influence of acts on spatial configurations and of the evolving space on acts, and put it together with the evident need of locomotor acts for the establishment of "place" demonstrated by Held and Hein, we may gain a new possible interpretation of the puzzling process of "imprinting" in the young of many precocial birds and possibly some mammals. Like most ethological terms, "imprinting" has been conceptually blurred almost from its very inception by the two chief malpractices that bedevil psychological theorizing: (1) applying the term beyond its original domain, to habituation, attachment and sundry other effects, and (2) defining it in words that carry a heavy load of dubitable assumptions which consequently are taken for granted—not only "inhibitors" and "releasors" and "sign-stimuli," but also more universally accepted ones like "filial responses" and "social conditioning." I shall use "imprinting" in its strict sense, to denote the frequently observed phenomenon, distinctive enough to deserve a name of its own, that a relatively large object moving at pursuable speed over the floor entices newly hatched chicks (the exact optimum age, in hours, varying with species) of many gallinaceous and anserine birds to follow it about.

We are so beset, today, by social problems, so aware of social relations, that we are inclined to look for their analogues in animal life wherever a behavior pattern suggests such a parallel. So the juvenile following of a moving object, observed in many walking or swimming birds, was no sooner generally known than it was hailed as a "mechanism" to "socialize" the chicks, attaching them first to their mothers and then to their kind.

Controlled experiments in field and laboratory have brought a good deal of evidence that calls the primarily "socializing" function of imprinting, *sensu stricto*, in question. If its motivation is really an impulse to be near a particular other animal, it is odd that chicks and ducklings will follow cardboard boxes, balloons and cylinders as readily as they will follow an adult bird, and that they may even be imprinted more readily by such socially absurd objects than by a life-like decoy. I have so far learned of no case in which a chick imprinted by a cardboard box extended its attachment to other boxes of "the same species" (presumably, the same brand and manufacturer's number), preferred them later in life to birds of its own feather and tried to mate only with a box.

It has taken good ornithologists and other animal observers a surprisingly long time to suspect that the impulse of young chicks to follow a moving object could be anything else than a "filial response." It is, of course, normally exhibited in a complex of filial relations prepared by the parent's brood-raising act, but that does not make the isolable following response itself filial. The fact that it can occur quite apart from any possible "social" concomitants certainly suggests that its immediate motivation, at least, is something else than an affective attachment.

The chicks that follow inanimate objects are not becoming imprinted either by their own kind or by a lifelong home. The imprint is temporary, serving only to keep the chick in contact with a particular leader while it develops its space feeling and spatial perception by locomotion. The tendency to follow is compounded of visual fixation, which may be momentarily learned, like foot placement, and of the drawing influence of a fixated point if it moves, that is, of a lure, which makes the pristine action-space a path. The further the chick moves behind its leader, the more its action-space becomes structured; wherever that space collapses into nothingness, the animal becomes lost and frightened; hence the ardent pursuit of the direction-giving lure. Muscular feeling seems to enter crucially into the space experience.

Such examples may suffice to justify some doubt as to the "filial" nature of the following response. Under natural conditions it is, of course, normally made to a parent bird (in some cases the father, not the mother), so that species bonds should become established at the same time in which the young animal is articulating its action space and engaging its powers of perception. That perception develops gradually with maturation of organs and interested exercise is a generally accepted tenet. From the very beginning of the chick's pursuit of the moving object, it is doing two things—establishing not only its lacework of paths, but also its visual object constancy. For the latter activity the plainest forms are best; for the spatial integration of vision and motion, one lure may be as good as another.

The great intimacy of relationships between animals' perception and action, the way their space awareness seems to reflect not only the general act form of rising, culminating and being spent, but the special forms of particular acts, may also contribute to our solution of those other major mysteries of animal movements, migration and homing. These two phenomena may not be manifestations of the same principle, though I think they are related, so let us consider, first, only the large and spectacular act of migration. The tendency to move periodically over relatively long distances, keeping a steady direction, is a trait that appears in animals of astoundingly diverse stocks—e.g., butterflies, bats, turtles, sea otters, lemmings, grasshoppers, eels, hummingbirds, geese. It is so widespread in the animal kingdom that it may be expected to appear in almost any phylum, class and family, in one genus and not another, and even in one, or a few, or in all but one, species within a genus. The great and at the same time odd distribution of the migratory impulse, which is certainly a hereditary trait, makes it appear like the effect of a very ancient gene (or gene complex), perhaps lying unexpressed in vast numbers of creatures, and easily blocked by circumstances even in stocks in which it normally comes to expression. The inheritance of such a tendency is not hard to accept theoretically, since it is known to be linked with hormonal rhythms, and hormone patterns seem to be essentially gene-controlled. But the impulse is all that we can attribute to heredity; the question of how animals find their way when the spirit moves them to travel remains unanswered.

All the speculations which have been made on avian means of knowing and keeping a desired course assume, quite unwittingly, a human concept of the space to be traversed, and consequently of the directional clues which might be found in it. In our thinking, the structure of space is so obviously a geometrical one, with north, south, east and west defined by effects of the earth's rotation, that any line of movement is to us a division of space into areas composing its total expanse. Also, we find it axiomatic that a directed movement is directed from one place to another, i.e., from a starting point to a goal, and when the goal is reached the locomotory act is finished. This human way of seeing space raises the questions, for us, how an animal stirred by the migratory impulse knows the direction of its goal, and how, having determined that, it keeps its course exactly in that direction; for a small deviation at the beginning of a very long journey would make a large displacement at the end.

If, however, animal space is built up by non-conceptual acts—which does not mean unconscious, automatic action—and is essentially a complex of paths and actively evolved places, the possibility of instinctive migratory behavior may be given with the formal character of locomotory acts themselves. The conditions that motivate great or small seasonal movements, over seas and continents or merely from one altitude belt to another on a mountain, in a mass migration, or a partial one, some of the population staying behind or settling along the way (as our robins do in winter), are so diverse that every species has to be considered on its own terms as to routes or flyways, mode of departure, resting places or uninterrupted through-travel, and so on; but one feature appears to be common to all the larger locomotory acts of animals, and that, I think, underlies their mystifying navigational powers.

As animals live in psychologically established "places" rather than locations, their movements beyond a familiar place are ventures which originate and terminate in that place; that is, their wider movements are excursions. This circular character is prone to appear whenever a departure is not complicated and masked by serving other acts such as search for food, pursuit, escape, standing at bay, hiding, or other practical behavior not in the creature's own territory. Young animals chasing each other may run a long course, but it is circular; it tends to repeat itself again and again, unless the pursued one is suddenly pressed into a deviation. Play is the least practically modified behavior, which might be expected to show a primitive basic pattern in its purest form. But wherever a relatively large locomotory act without a direct goal (e.g., a quarry) is performed, it tends to begin and end in an established place (not necessarily a permanent "territory" of the individual or group).

The significance of this basic form of animal travel is that migration should, perhaps, be viewed as a round trip with "stopovers," rather than as a passage from one locality to another, with a known goal and a method of navigating by particular landmarks or skymarks. The apparently purposive travel to better nesting grounds, climatic conditions, food supply or safer existence during an incapacitating molt of flight feathers may have started with quite different motivation, from taxonomically much more disseminated, elementary impulses; nothing more, perhaps, than the very common hormonal disturbances that are reflected in the seasonal restlessness of many animals, known in man as "spring fever" or "itching foot." Since such restlessness in non-human creatures usually occurs at the commencement of the breeding season, it has been attributed without much question to the influence of the increscent sex hormones; Maurice Fontaine, however, found that in fish the effect may be concomitant with any state of the gonads (1956, p. 156). His researches make it appear that any disturbance of the iodine balance inclines a fish to become restless, to venture into rapid or open water and to react to stimulating conditions—flood, moonlight or what not—and so start its journey, for which it may otherwise be, physiologically, in greater or lesser readiness. The thyroid activity starts a dominant behavioral act that overrides other tendencies, and suppresses whatever lesser acts it cannot entrain. If, now, the fundamental form of animal peregrination is cyclic, that hormonal-inspired venture, whenever it occurs, is an excursion which normally will end where it began, no matter how protracted the "stopovers" (one or several) on its course may be.

One cannot generalize from fish to birds, but avian behavior provides its own versions of the "round trip." The most telling aspect is the circling form of the group action; as the birds rise together they also land together on the lawn or field from which they started. If one does not consider the natural circularity of animals' locomotion these flights seem purposely "organized," and as the purpose is not apparent, they are interpreted either as "practice flights" intended to train the young, or—more fashionably just at present—as "ritualized" acts with some symbolic social function.

In phylogenetic history the rhythms of glandular activities have, of course, developed in mutual adjustment; no seriously disharmonious species could survive and, indeed, no extreme disharmony can develop, unless some impulse, otherwise held in check, can profit by the abnormality and give the whole system a new functional pattern. The great wealth of unrealized possibilities in every being makes even the major activities adjustable to one another at every level of organic functioning. So, in those species which have a periodic urge to travel, this impulse and the procreative impulses have fallen into some mutually advantageous pattern, though not the same in all species—not even, necessarily, in closely related ones.

The elasticity of the "appetitive" stages of behavioral acts is what makes such large cycles as migration amenable to all sorts of elaboration. It also permits their progressive growth; and herein we may have a key to the mysteries of orientation and guidance. That migrations have evolved from small beginnings is certainly not a strange idea. It has been proposed many a time. Changes of season, coinciding with a mild restless period, would start a movement in the direction suggested by the warm appearance of the southern skies, or (where the discomfort is heat or drought) by the cool azure of the north. There may also be changes of climate. Such climatic changes are slow; if the animals had a strong "place habit," and their migration were gradually timed with the season of severest cold or heat stress, its circle might expand vastly. Environmental conditions, such as the lure of the new climate, would tend to encourage the expansion in a special direction and draw the cylcic excursion into a long ellipse such as we see in most avian migration routes.

It is on such extended flights, however, that the problem of navigation becomes acute; how do the migrants hold their course? There seems to be fairly general agreement among investigators that the sun somehow keeps them on it, though the difficulties presented by its own movements tend to call every sun-compass theory in question. Yet I think the sun may guide the long line of flight wherever guidance is necessary; the simplicity of birds' brains and the strength of their impulses make it possible, on a principle we have met with in lower animals of various kinds—wasps, crabs, toads—that the ambient conditions prevailing at the beginning of the act govern its entire performance. Perhaps the rising of the sun, which is always from the east, is enough to orient the flight, which then proceeds independently of subsequent changes of light or any other circumstances, until the energy of the travelers flags, and that subact of the total flight is finished. It may even continue under overcast, until the next clear sunrise starts and directs it again (for night migrants, sunset would play the same role). What is the length of an act (in *Bembex*, the day; in *Bufo*, the separate foray; in *Ocypode*, the "building episode") is not always easy to tell in the case of subacts of a long, overarching tension from a massive and complex impulse to its consummation, which, in the case of migration, is return to the starting place. The main point, however, is that directional guidance along the migratory course of animals probably plays a minor role.

The direction, originally established on a small scale, is regularly reestablished with the start of the instinctive act. What long-past condition motivated it cannot be generally known, but would have to be determined for each species or even population. But once initiated, the excursion simply continues to occur, its form becoming more fixed and sure not only by repetition, but probably also by a concomitant increase in the hormonal activities—as processes encouraged by unrepressed enactment tend to increase—and thus, perhaps by favored micromutations, could gain some representation in the gene pattern. Differential elimination of the weaker migrants would play its usual major evolutionary role.

Opportunities always shape the growth of acts, for species as for individuals. The features of earth, sea and sky, although (to judge by the behavior of animals toward visible objects irrelevant to their acts of the moment) probably not specifically remarked, do have a subliminal familiarity value for the creature moving among them; and as quickly as they offer support to a progressing act they are exploited. Such facilitating conditions have been observed and remarked in the study of some migration routes.

Several animal psychologists who have made observations under natural conditions have likened the sensory guidance of animals to the progression of a melody; as each movement furthers the motivating situation for the next, so the implementing situation advances from chance to chance, the creature progressing as its need is met. This is Santayana's "animal faith"—going on, using the moment, without knowledge of death at the end. Volkelt, after concluding that animals possess no representations, declared:

> According to our view, the landscape which a carrier pigeon sees beneath it does not resemble a "map," but appears to the pigeon relatively unarticulated and diffuse. . . . The successive impressions do not compose an internally ordered series of mutually limited, distinct images, but present something like an optical melody. And likewise, what the carrier pigeon's memory contains is not . . . a vast sum of isolated impressions; but melody-like qualitative complexes, that will unroll at the touch of sensory impressions, constitute its available stores. By these optical melodies it finds its way from landscape to landscape, as a person reproducing a song finds his way from one tone to the next. (1912, p. 126).

In a similar vein, more recently, J. J. Gibson pointed out that even in man's goal-directed, object-bound visual experience the underlying physiological activity of seeing proceeds in this same instinctive way (1950, pp. 158–59).

To construe animal acts in non-conceptual terms requires great care in wording not only statements, but questions, and consistency in interpretation to make systematic observation possible. The following chapter presents an attempt at such a coherent treatment of instinctive action, by offering possible alternative interpretations for the alleged "social," "rational" and "ceremonial" practices of animals in more animalian ways, as acts formed in impulses and guided by the melody-like passage and growth of sensible and emotive feeling, to consummation or failure.

14 / On Animal Values

The non-geographical, act-engendered nature of animals' space is so different from our visually given and implicitly relational space that it makes one suspect that their perception of events and their motivations may be equally different. To form any hypothesis of the evolution of human mind from its presumable animal origins, we need first of all a much clearer idea of animal mentality than we are employing in zoology and psychology today. What we ourselves are prone to feel or able to feel, objectively (i.e., as impact) or subjectively (as impulse and autogenic action), must have grown to its present developed stage from much less systematic, less coherent animal feeling. Without the benefit of protocol statements the occurrence of any psychical phases in animals can, of course, be only speculatively asserted, and any further conception of their nature must rest on what we know directly in human life; yet such conception need not be naively anthropomorphic if the significance of the differences between human and animal action be constantly kept in mind, and those differences themselves pursued and reflected on. The possibility of sensations may be largely inferred from physiological data; their actual occurrence or non-occurrence where one would expect them—for instance, the incidence of pain with gross bodily injury—may sometimes be experimentally tested on a basis of behavioral reactions. But for the most part any psychological notions we can form of animal capacities, levels and modes of feeling must be theoretical constructions, working concepts.

So far, however, the conceptual frame of our animal psychology is loose and flimsy. The "working concepts" do not work very well. Each set governs some area of the total field, but beyond that area may conflict with more systematically established facts, as the Lorenz-Tinbergen hypothesis of "act centers," "inhibitors" and "releasers" (inhibitors of inhibitors) does not fit into the fast-advancing neurological theories of total brain functions; or the use of a basic hypothesis may be limited to artificially controlled phenomena, as the unquestionably true principles of reflex action and "conditioning" can only be applied in the insulated environment of the laboratory, so they give little explanation and certainly no constant guidance to the observers of creatures in the wild. We have so far found no biological concepts on which to base any indirect methods for the study of psychical phases in animal life. This leaves us with the direct, natural method of imputing an essentially human mentality to non-human agents, and two attitudes toward that practice: simple acceptance of its naive anthropomorphism, or a really equally simple, summary declaration that there is no way of finding out anything about animal feeling, so the best policy is to deny or at least ignore its existence. The first is a misguided approach, the second an acceptance of failure at the mere sight of the task. But the task itself is to find a means of using the natural approach and systematically correcting its errors; that is, assuming that animals' acts rise to psychical phases as ours do—a fairly safe assumption, on the ground that we are animals, and the general nature of acts is the same throughout the zoological realm—to discover how and why whatever other organisms feel might differ from what is felt by human beings. If the psychical moments of animal acts are different from ours, it means that the acts are different, perhaps from their very impulses to their consummations.

The best way to gain some understanding of the mentality of various high and low animals is, therefore, to discover step by step how their acts call our anthropomorphic image of their lives in question. They will do so from almost each observation to the next, if we do not overlook the small deviations from humanly specialized reactions, or refuse to dwell on their significance in order to feel ourselves constantly in rapport with the animal. All concern for maintaining an attitude, whether a sentimental or a scientific one, for avoiding a conclusion that would be theoretically disappointing or might lay us open to the charge of espousing an obsolete "ism," is ruinous to research. Negative findings, especially where the expected positive results seemed so certain that the experimenter practically deemed his experiment a formality to satisfy the demands of his methodology, are exciting mysteries, the first indications that familiar facts may need new interpretation. That is the route of systematic correction which leads almost imperceptibly, stepwise, to philosophically advanced standpoints, far from the naive beginnings of theoretical conception.

The previous chapter was devoted to this sort of study of animal space perception and its role in shaping the ambients in which animals live. When we discover how different their psychological space is from ours we are led on to further questions: why is man's space experience geometric? And, if beasts have few or no permanently self-identical things, how do we come to have so many, and to find and accept them so readily that our world is given its structure primarily by physical objects? Nothing is more natural to us than to think in terms of permanent, simple substances with variable attributes. If animals do not perceive objects in this way, yet obviously deal with them, how do they know what to do with them, when to seek and when to avoid them? There must be differences between their object perception and ours, as great as between their ways and ours of possessing space.

A widely disseminated, well-nigh universal assumption made by observers of animals in the wild and in captivity (zoos, farms, homes and even laboratories) is that animals communicate with each other by sounds and other "signals." To entertain even the possibility that animals have no social intercourse comparable to human language, no code to signal their demands, warnings or new discoveries to each other, is difficult for most people. Communication is, in fact, such a problematical phenomenon that its exact meaning with respect to animals needs very careful statement. A correct formulation of the terms in which it is to be conceived is likely to hold implicitly the concepts that will automatically rearrange our empirical and theoretical views of mental evolution. The numerous inconclusive attempts to link human and non-human mentality in a continuum, which fill many serious books today, are perhaps all obstructed by the same weakness, the lack of adequate ideas of the animalian forms of perception and action from which our own development has taken off in its great expansion. A coherent view of animal mentality, without immediate reference to our own, might provide a foundation for surer insights into the fateful evolutionary shift that has taken place in the hominid stock.

To construct such a conceptual framework requires, however, the abandonment or at least shelving of practically all the basic notions in general use today; not only hypothetical entities such as the hierarchy of "act centers" in the brain stem, "inhibitor mechanisms," "innate releasing mechanisms," even the innocent-looking "sign stimuli" and "social signals," the older "memory traces" ("engrams") and "contents of consciousness," but also many slipshod generalizations embodied in words and phrases, that is to say, in the uncritically accepted ways we refer to the objects of our descriptions and interpretative discussions: using "stimulus" for every motivating condition, specific or general, even for things the organism is expecting or seeking; or talking about "mechanisms" where we really mean only functions and act patterns and have no idea whether these arise from special mechanisms or result from interactions of processes otherwise accounted for; and so on. In this way the key words of discourse lose their precision, and problems are sidestepped.

But the most detrimental practice is the carrying over of words from anthropology and ethnology to ethology, with a radical change of meaning, which reflects back on their proper meanings in their proper places, and wipes out all conceptual accuracy in both contexts. Those words are, specifically, "symbol," "ritual" (or "rite") and "ceremony" (or "ceremonial"). To apply such terms to stereotyped animal movements requires their redefinition on the basis of superficial resemblances of such movements to human acts which have quite different motivation and really symbolic, ritual and ceremonial values. All findings based on these terms rest on the interpretation of animal acts, which are behaviorally convergent with human acts, in terms of human motivation. The convergences are not even always very pronounced; a superficial similarity, such as that of the posturing of animals which dare not attack each other to the prescribed moves of men in a fencing match, is enough to elicit the judgment that the non-human opponents do not wish to kill each other, but only to measure their relative powers in a conventionally limited contest.

The motive to such anthropomorphic psychologizing is the desire to find the evolutionary continuum of animal life, and especially mental life, from fish (if not from protozoan) to man. A child's experience shows up, very clearly, how the non-human and the human phenomenon differ. Fear of darkness in children, as I can remember all too well, results from the occurrence of uncontrollable imagery, unchecked by the reassuring sight of familiar surroundings. A child's imagination, and memories elaborated by fantasies, run wild in the dark. The motivation of that fear is precisely what the child does not share with other animals; but the species-specific unrealism of mankind is often played down in favor of practical intelligence, which seems to be approached by some animals, or it is vaguely linked with stereotyped animal acts by calling the latter "superstitious behavior." That terminology suggests, of course, that the "superstitious" monkey, rat or pigeon, like a superstitious person, believes its formalized act to have a practical effect. Such verbal vagaries and foibles, as well as the reading of symbolic intent into canine or simian gestures, are designed to eliminate the dividing line between animal and human existence.

Oddly enough, however, the various attempts to establish the continuity of animal life from the foot of the evolutionary scale to the present estate of man by removing that line militate against our finding the genuine continuity, because in nature every division is also a meeting line where the most intricate relations occur, so the smudging or masking of any crucial boundary obliterates the relations between taxonomic groups and the unity underlying evolutionary shifts. Therefore I shall follow a different method here by dwelling on the principles of animal motivation and interpreting the ethological data as strictly and consistently as possible in non-human terms, up to the point where the "great shift" becomes imminent. Many first-hand observations in the field have been recorded which offer factual material for such an alternative treatment.

Most of the principles of animalian impulse and perception which seem to underlie the evolution of feeling have already been discussed: the character of acts, especially their wholeness, their potential expansion and contraction, their comprisal, entrainment and induction or repression of other acts, and their constant competition, from the impulse level onward, for complete actualization. These basic properties of all acts produce the patterns of tensions which constitute the continuous lives of organisms. The courses which particular acts take, however, are of unsurveyable variety, starting in the thousands (indeed, millions) of specialized impulses—each specialized according to its moment in the progressing matrix—and running as they can through the fabric of circumstance to consummation in recognizable or hidden ways, or to repression, adding a new potentiality to the agent's cumulative past. It is in the covert stages of actualization that differences of motivation between human and non-human acts become effective, so that psychological experiments on animals with "stimuli" based on humanly conceived values sometimes have astonishing outcomes.

Yet to make really fundamental differences accessible to our theoretical imagination requires some hint of the alternative possibilities that lie open to an advancing act, either in very striking anomalies of practical behavior (such as a tern's detour "around" a branch which has been removed long ago) or else in some generally unrealized, chance-detected psychological experience of our own. A suggestive finding of this sort comes from the human psychology laboratory, where several experimenters have found that the recognition of words in tachistoscopic presentations seems often to be preceded by a subliminal reaction to their good, evil or mildly disturbing meaning. There is some premonition of value in the process of recognition which, in the case of negative value, retards the reading of the word.

This finding raises the problem of how a word, an image or any presentation can be evaluated before it has been recognized. That no response can be made to the character of an object before that object has been identified is an axiom of common sense. The situation could be described in terms of the perceptual act, consummated in human agents by the intellectual event of object perception, but starting as a deep, complex, gradually gathering enactment of a total sensory impulse; an impulse elicited from the peripheral receptor organ by the impact of some ambient event, but propagated through the brain via many paths, and entraining all sorts of impulses—defensive, conative, or more vaguely emotive—as elements of itself along the way. Its psychical phase develops gradually, however fast its completion may seem; perception is not an instantaneous act followed by discrimination and evaluation, but is built up by processes of discrimination, each of which imposes some value on the ultimate form.

The significance of these findings in human psychology for our necessarily speculative judgments of animal feeling, perception and motivation lies in the objective demonstration that value may be adumbrated before perception of forms is complete; indeed, the expectant, covert anticipation of the full percept appears to be an emotively tinged process, missed in our ordinary introspective analysis because of its minuteness and transitory character. The complexity of the human perceptual act, which culminates in the recognition of a word, an image or some other closed form, allows earlier phases to be felt in other than cognitive ways, either as an uneasiness about the coming presentation or an eager expectation of it, growing as the percept emerges. This premonitory phase R. S. Lazarus and R. A. McCleary have named "subception." They define their new term to mean "a process by which some kind of discrimination is made when the subject is unable to make a correct conscious discrimination," and refer to it elsewhere as a distinct level of perceptual activity (1951, pp. 103, 120).

If our recognition of sensory data builds itself up to a degree of intensity at which the receptor organ achieves focus and epicritical distinctions on a basis of lower but increasing motivation, it may well be that for other creatures the stage before such full cognitive action is the most important, perhaps undergoing elaborations for which it is given no time in man because the peripheral mechanisms overtake and entrain it (this subject will presently be discussed). In that case, animal perception might be normally a matter of locating situations for action, in which a center of highest value draws the agent's interest; that center—for us, the "object"—presumably has sensory properties which the animal recognizes without conceiving them descriptively, i.e., without distinguishing them as shapes, colors, surface feelings or even characteristic smells; recognition is not necessarily judgment. Generalization is inherent in all acts, since perfectly identical situations do not occur, so "repeated" acts would be impossible if they could not allow for ambient changes within a fair range of conditions having similar implementing values. Perhaps what is "the same" for an animal is the sense of satisfaction with substrates and aids to progress and with whatever situations emerge as successful acts are consummated; or, inversely, the sense of effort which may rise to desperation when an act is blocked. Impulse and the feeling of passage are remembered in reenacting a performance, and how much of that remembrance is a psychical event and how much is effective without conscious recall may differ widely from one kind of animal to another, in conjunction with the relative degrees of intensity to which acts normally rise in each species and the height they may attain at their utmost concentration. An infusorian may not feel as much of its activity as an animal with a central nervous system, yet its acts show the same characteristics of facilitation by repeated successful performance, progressive sensitization to motivating conditions, abbreviation of the preparatory stages and, consequently, more rapid consummation, which makes the impression of purposeful aim at the usual result. Whether such acts express entirely unfelt chemical "affinities" or have their moments of intensification in which they go into psychical phases we have no way of judging.

It is hard to conceive of perception and behavior without human ways of identifying and relating objects, first of all, by their attributes of color, shape, size, etc.; in spite of all theoretical realization that human standards do not apply to the mental acts of birds, beasts and fishes, we use them in judging their behavior as clever or stupid, random or purposive and even egoistic or altruistic. When Tinbergen remarks on the gull's lack of intelligence in rolling a displaced egg back into its nest laboriously with the underside of its beak, when one sweep of its wing would accomplish the whole desired change in a second, he supposes—as a human observer naturally would—that the gull's purpose is to push the egg back into the nest, and that it knows no better than to reach for it in a difficult, inefficient way. If, however, one views the total complex of relations of gulls to their nests, eggs and young, it appears very likely that the bird retrieving an egg has no such purpose at all, no idea that the egg ought to be brought back by one means or another, the easier and quicker the better; it seeks contact with the egg, and makes it at a part of its body that seems to be especially sensitized for contact with the young, the underside of the bill. This is the location of the famous red spot at which the chick afterwards pecks, a sense organ and effector organ in one, an organ of interaction with the new generation (Tinbergen, 1953, pp. 6, 242).

The need of contact between a bird's bare, feverish brood patch and the smooth and cooler eggs, perhaps heightened by the sight of the eggs, is sufficiently comparable to the varied feelings in the breast of a nursing woman, with the sudden increase of lactation when her infant cries, to be quite comprehensible in terms of human experience. The notion of such local sensitivity can be carried over to explain the gull's use of the underside of the bill, as well as several other phenomena. But occasionally one meets a response, or absence of response, that is hard to understand by any analogy with our own ways of feeling; and when one reflects on the differences it suggests between animal and human motivation, these may prove to be far-reaching. Tinbergen's "stupid" gull is a case in point: as soon as one applies animal measures to its inefficient acts, it becomes apparent that labor-saving is not one of its values, that the practical results of acts are not motivating ideas, but that bodily feeling and immediate desire, fear and a medley of other fleeting emotions control instinctive performances, rather than any humanly acceptable "goals" or purposes. That is a basic insight gained by the observation of a relatively small deviation from rational behavior.

Another apparently trivial phenomenon which ultimately draws one of our natural assumptions in question is the behavior of female pigeons which, by all signs, are physiologically ready to lay, but will not do so in solitude, though they will start laying as soon as they can see another pigeon—male or female, or even their own reflection in a mirror. In a gregarious bird like a pigeon the need of companions for the development of normal instinctive behavior is not surprising. But what is indeed surprising to a human psychologist is that the very audible cooing of pigeons in adjacent cages hidden from the experimental bird has no influence on her readiness to lay. To us, the sound of other persons talking in an adjacent room would be just as suggestive of their presence as the sight of them.

Because sound is so obviously a social medium in human life, we are prone to assume that utterance is always communicative, that animals, like men, listen to each other and that their sounds are intended to be heard and automatically interpreted by other beings, i.e., received as warning, lure, advertisement, identification or other sort of "signal." The first important relation between utterance and hearing may be that the animal hears itself. The two functions, expressive and auditory, stem from different phylogenetic sources; audition certainly served originally for information of general ambient conditions, and was preceded by vibratory sensations with which it still merges, for human sensibility, at the lower end of the audible frequency range. Vocalization and its various functional substitutes, wing-rubbing, leg-rubbing, bill-clapping, etc., are originally expressive acts of inward excitation, and it is quite conceivable that their basic motivation is self-expansion, enlargement of the act in its noisy consummation. Both erotic and angry excitement evoke the desire to feel large, and lead naturally to any way of expanding the body—by piloerection, wing-spreading, gular inflation or whatever the animal's native repertoire provides—acts known as "display," and universally supposed to be performed to impress a partner or adversary (as the case may be). Vocalization may well be a part of fighting and mating behavior, but to what extent it impresses either rivals or females may vary according to species, from a powerful influence to none at all. It may, of course, have either or both of those effects; it may even have communal functions, such as the mutual encouragement of frogs in a chorus. There is no message carried in their sound, but a suggestion which spreads like a chain reaction throughout the frog assembly in the pond. Suggestion and suggestibility are the bases of most exhibits of so-called communication among animals. The trouble with calling sounds and motions "communication" or "signaling" is that these words connote not only an effect on the hearer, but an intention on the part of the performer to produce that effect—to warn, direct or solicit another creature. Even "attracting females" may well be a by-product instead of a motive of courtship utterances and antics. Those overt acts, which normally evoke the responses of a partner, were probably not purposive in their origin, but purely autistic, spontaneous acts of self-enlargement, enhanced by the hearing of the agent's own resounding accompaniment.

If, then, an animal's own autogenic vocal activity became an effective part of its self-inflation in high excitement, this aural feedback would have a new path to the ear—internal conduction—and a separate feeling tone, more allied to kinesthesis than to peripheral perception. In the pristine stages of its development it might have influenced the locations of the organs of hearing and of sound production in relation to one another. In all animals so far known which utter emotional sounds, these organs are close together; the development of their conjoint functioning may have induced the origin of the sonal apparatus near the auditory, or—if they were of equally ancient origin—encouraged their mutual approach in the course of their evolution.

The important aspect of such a widely based history of hearing would be the peculiar emotive character it was destined to give, at a later stage, to the reception by one animal of sounds produced by another of the same species. Objective and subjective feelings—i.e., the senses of impact and action—are easily mixed in creatures having no conceptual functions to define the subject-object boundary (which can be ruptured even in human experience); in hearing utterances of fellow beings, that boundary, indistinct and unstable as it is in animal feeling, would be quite normally effaced, and the result would be an empathic yet outwardly oriented response intrinsically different from the purely practical impulse pattern guided by ordinary ambient conditions.

At what stage this empathic hearing would become an important bond between animals might vary extremely from species to species. As instinctive behavior, it is always individually motivated, both as a cyclic whole and from move to move in its enactment. It is neither egoistic nor altruistic; those are moral terms which have meaning only in human society. But it is always egocentric. This is one of the cardinal facts to keep in mind in tracing the motivation and trying to understand the feeling of animal acts.

In protracted instinctive acts such as the complete cycle of procreation, a sequential order of impulses is guided from one consummated subact to another by a closely similar sequence of waxing and waning sensibilities. The great hereditary behavior patterns have two essential internal mechanisms of control, the nervous system and the endocrine system. Impulses seem to arise in the former by both central and peripheral stimulation, while the highly specific, often temporary feelings that guide their active expression depend mainly on chemical balances and chemical changes in the organism. The process of endocrine influence appears largely as a differential sensitization of perceptual systems—not only receptor organs, but their whole inward extensions—to ambient conditions, i.e., to lures and possibilities for action. Hormonal and some other chemical phases of the vital round impose special values on perceptual objects in harmony with the growth of impulses; not only procreative impulses, but also those to seasonally fluctuating activities, such as food consumption in frogs, which reaches a peak in August and early September, then dwindles steadily until hibernation sets in, and does not fully resume until after spawning in the spring.

Changes in responses to sensory stimuli are less often dictated by any physical alterations in the stimulant objects than by an organically motivated shift of cathexis from one sort of thing to another. Such shifts may be gradual, as in the seasonal use of materials which at other times have no value for the agent, or they may be quick and transient, as though the perceived object suddenly seemed different for a moment. In the latter case, of course, one cannot assume a direct hormonal influence, which is always slow and only preparatory in nature. The currently prevailing chemical balance is a general condition underlying the play of perceptions, and as these are essentially emotive perceptions of momentary values the animal's total awareness is governed by the inward pattern of sensitization. Ardent search, for instance, stimulated by the finding of one or two special morsels amid grass or forest leaves, sensitizes the exteroceptors involved in it to respond to the wanted smell or sight and raises the threshold for other perceptions.

We can discover a similar though perhaps somewhat less pronounced phenomenon in ourselves; if we go into woods or pastures to find, say, flat stones to pave a garden walk, we are likely to see such stones by roadsides and in crumbling walls, in quarry rubbish and old cellar holes for days afterwards when we are not looking for them. Our eye is sensitized to those flat gray objects, but generally only within fairly definite limits of size and some standards of shape. The source of that visual selectiveness, in us, is a guiding envisagement of a planned act, which exists concomitantly with many other quite unrelated plans of action, that may be thought about in bewildering succession and alternation and put into effect bit by bit and by turns. As we may think back to the laying of a slab walk long after that plan has been realized, our visual reaction to possible materials persists for a while beyond our need of them. I doubt that non-human creatures find act values in things through remembered needs. They are differently motivated in their gathering and storing food and in their building operations, though these processes may overtly resemble human behavior. But in trying to envisage their mental actions lacking conceptual guidelines, such small contact points as the act-determined sensitization of a receptor organ to special percepts, which we do seem to share with most animals, point to one of the physio-psychological substructures of all mentality, and also indicate—if only implicitly—the differences of development from that common organic groundwork to the respective mental phenomena of man and beast.

There are other kinds of elementary feeling which we can still find in ourselves and consequently understand subjectively, though they are not of major importance to us, but which enter into animal lives as prime determinants of behavior. Two of these, I think, are controlling functions in the so-called social behavior of animals, which for just that reason is not really social, but communal, however organized and sanctioned it may look. These two functions are empathy and suggestion.

Empathy is sometimes equated with sympathy, but is really something else; it is a much more direct physical reaction inherent in the perception of other beings, especially of the perceiver's own kind. We experience it when, for instance, the sight of a very sore eye causes our own eyes to water before we have had time to imagine how it must feel, or when the mere sight or sound of vomiting revolts our own stomach, or watching a steeplejack climb to a perilous height makes us dizzy. Empathy is an involuntary breach of individual separateness. Sometimes it does not even involve that breach but, contrariwise, is a stage in the loosening of a closer bond, actual identity, as in parturition, where a new separateness, long prepared, begins. In animals it is probably a fluctuating, gradually fading intimacy of feeling that unites a parent animal and its brood for an indefinite yet transitory period of time. In human life, where conception and imagination pervade the whole fabric of sensory reception and its immediate uses, empathy is largely replaced by sympathy or some other semi-intellectual response; but in animal life it exists unrecognized, unchallenged and operative at all possible levels and to all degrees.

The same is true of suggestion. We know its influence on our own thought and action, but this is probably very weak compared to its motivating power for animals. Although there are many phenomena of "mob psychology" in human behavior, the part played in them by suggestion is hard to isolate from the effective context of publicly held ideas, social attitudes and individual motives which go into each participant's act in the crowd. In animals, however, such mental conditions are not operative, and suggestion has free play. The speed with which it operates where it is unobstructed has made human observers assume that in such suggestible creatures as flocking birds or schooling fish there must be a special signal given by a leader, which reaches all the members of the group at the same moment, like a conductor's signal to an orchestra.

Upon close examination, both in laboratory tests and in less formal observation, it is quite generally found that what is loosely called "imitation" in animals is really suggestion. The distinction between these two phenomena is neither trivial nor verbal. Imitation is a progressive act of watching another creature's movements and repeating them, one by one, in the same succession; imitation can stop in the middle of a series of moves, without breaking any unifying tension, consummation or cadence. Suggestion, on the other hand, motivates an impulse similar to that of the individual setting the example, but may eventuate in a very different expression.

Imitation, *sensu stricto*, is rare in animals, if it occurs at all, which is not certain. Even in apes, which are said to imitate each other's and their keeper's acts, direct imitation of postures, movements or step-by-step procedures has not been recorded; to "ape" another individual is to follow his suggestion in the use of a situation, but not to watch his behavior closely and copy it as faithfully as possible. Animals are not inclined to watch each other objectively; they see the act a companion is engaged in, and at once have an impulse to do the same thing themselves, but they may do it by a different method. Suggestibility is their forte, and makes some species so sensitive to one another's impulses that the first "intention movement" runs through a whole drove of individuals. This is one of the alleged "mechanisms" holding the members of herds, flocks or swarms—constant or temporary—together. It is not a special mechanism, but a heightened degree of a general feature in animal psychology. In close individual relations, sexual, parental or possibly sibling (e.g., in play), it is likely to be so entwined with empathy and other reactions that it becomes impossible to isolate.

Animal perception, then, is not simply an impoverished version of human perception. It contains possible sensitivities to impingements that we cannot feel, and where it parallels our sensory modes it is limited or extended by the values that enter into the animal's instinctive life. Not everything that is physically perceptible is necessarily noted and utilized by dolphins, songbirds or monkeys, any more than by men. But I am inclined to believe that signals, and especially communicative—intended and interpreted—signals, play a very minor part among even the highest non-human beings, if such devices occur at all; and that directly felt inward and outward acts, springing from impulse and ambient pressures and opportunities, are sufficient for all animal needs. There is a tendency to sweep aside the undeveloped and moot notions of "instinct" and look for signs of rational action and approaches to human ways of thinking wherever an animal performs an act which simulates such processes. In studying the so-called higher animals—primates, cetaceans, Corvidae, elephants, dogs—our whole interest is slanted toward the demonstration of conception and reasoning in them.

If, however, one views all animal life, including man's, as a great texture of impulses and enactments, in which special patterns emerge somewhat as the forms prepared in low relief on a background, and perhaps scarcely visible, emerge when pigment passes over them in a rubbing, the wholeness of instinctive life appears much more vital than when it is conceived as a product of interlocking mechanisms or concatenated involuntary reflexes. It is pushing from the matrix of impulsive organic activities all the time. There is no need of looking to animals for the specialized human functions of concept formation and symbolic expression, not even to apes. What does distinguish the "higher" animals is a great increase in emotionality, which entails a corresponding increase of perceptive functions, not necessarily by virtue of better receptor organs, but of increasing values imposed on what anciently developed senses convey. Without a true appreciation of the richness and completeness of life built on instinctive action, and of the heights to which discriminate sensibility and emotional reaction can rise on that foundation, one cannot recognize the critical point where an overcharged system of mental operations breaks over into imagery and symbolic conception, and the great shift from animal mentality to mind begins.

15 / Interpretations

The conception of instinctive behavior as a product of countless, competitively enacted impulses raises the question of motivation in an acute, ineluctable way; a problem which the hypotheses of hierarchically arranged "act centers" and that of integrated reflexes both sidestep and replace by the alternative assumption of innate mechanisms predisposed to perform typical acts. The basic assumption here proposed is the constant guidance of overt animal action by feeling, both peripheral and central, i.e., perceptual and emotive; the complex and often puzzling observed phenomena of non-human behavior—the part of the ethologists' contribution with which I rarely could or would quarrel—must, therefore, be constantly and consistently interpreted in terms of direct individual impression and equally immediate expression. This bars any explanation in terms of "social" usefulness or prevision of future conditions. All the conditions are "now," and the guidance, from the total impulse to consummation of the fully elaborated act, is by the agent's own feeling. The motivation of a behavioral act has to be conceived as a felt element in the situation from which it arises, that is, as something with a luring or driving value for the performing organism, not only as an inherited reaction established by "natural selection" for the good of the species.

There are behavioral patterns hard to explain, involving subtle reflections on animal situations and feeling. One phenomenon that immediately comes to mind is the alleged "magnanimity" of a wolf which has overcome another one in a fight; according to report, the loser, when he gives up, crouches and offers his most vulnerable spot, generally his throat, to the victor, who thereupon stops his attack, apparently satisfied to be acknowledged the stronger (Koenig 1962, p. 172; Lorenz 1957, pp. 206–7). There are two versions of the subsequent act; according to one, "after waiting to make certain that the loser is not going to move, the victor urinates on any nearby object. This is an act of dismissal and the loser then departs hurriedly" (Evans 1968, p. 104). But in the version given by Lorenz—romantic enough, without carrying the "magnanimity" of the victor beyond his refraining from biting the exposed throat, neck or whatever the loser seems to present in his "gesture of humility"—the moment the cowering wolf changes his attitude, the aggressor resumes his attack. The submissive gesture and noble acceptance of it produce only a momentary suspension of the fight. Finally, however, the winner feels the urge to urinate, and as he backs away to seek a stump, tree, or perhaps hydrant or lamp post to do so, the underdog makes his escape. Lorenz says nothing about an "act of dismissal," i.e., a signal to the loser that he may go.

Robert Ardrey, in *The Territorial Imperative*, declares that "when wolves indulge in final debate, the loser rolls over on his back, exposing his belly to the victor; the winner, incapable of attacking him further, walks away. It is a behavioral gesture in no wise different from the human gesture of raising one's hands in surrender" (1966, p. 340). Neither Lorenz nor Koenig claims to have seen the victor simply walk away. Yet even Ardrey's nonchalant top dog is supposed to understand and honor a formal gesture. It is this statement, explicitly made or subscribed to by all the authors here quoted, that I would challenge.

In animals, movement which may terminate in a posture characteristic of a mood, an intention (the covert part of an act, usually felt both emotionally and somatically before the overt phase is reached, if it ever is) or an expectation is a direct enactment of an impulse motivated by the situational complex of the passing moment. A wolf's yielding to superior strength is not a gesture, but an actual collapse, in which the loser can still use mouth and feet in purely defensive action but gives up all aggressive tactics, so the casual fight is really over, and the victor gives up the encounter, too. Its original fury is generally not sufficient to carry it to great lengths. An older defeated animal no longer finds the puppy habit of lying on its back and struggling with all fours the most natural defense; it cowers and looks up at the foe to counter his moves, groveling abjectly and, of course, watching. I can see no indication that it means to expose its throat. No matter what posture a shrinking animal takes when fear overcomes it and holds it motionless, it is sure to expose some vulnerable part—throat or nape, belly or skull. To see any intention of registering humility in its attitude is an arbitrary "in-reading" of symbolic human values.

The interesting problem is the action of the superior wolf, which is supposed to be inhibited by the "appeal for mercy." If the ethological principle of interpretation, the treatment of animal movements and postures as formal acts, with communicative intent, is to be dispensed with in judging the cowering pose, the winner's alleged recognition of the "appeal" also has to be treated in a more strictly animalian sense. The empirical fact, attested by many observers, is not to be doubted, namely, that the top wolf's aggression seems to be suddenly inhibited. The only problem is to explain the motivation of that apparently "social" limitation of his fighting spirit. The statement that it has survival value, though probably true, is no explanation; neither is the allegation that "a mechanism" must have evolved which "shuts off" his aggressive behavior at a critical point. The question is what mechanism, if there be a special one, or else what interplay of general psychological operations effects the sudden abstention from further attack.

The answer, I believe, can be found in the principles of animal motivation offered in the previous chapter as alternatives to those of the ethological school: the complete egocentricity of acts, even those usually classed as "social," their guidance from move to move by progressively developing psychical phases just ahead of the next major impulse, and the lability of individual separateness, which facilitates episodes of empathy and raises the normal levels of their intensity and frequency above those of man. It is possible—though I certainly would not assert it categorically as a psychological fact—that the groveling posture of the worsted animal suddenly evokes an empathic sharing of the animal's emotional tensions in the victor, as though he himself were wholly overcome and suffering what is happening to his victim. The fight no longer has two participants; it is no longer going on. There is only this cringing underdog. Quite possibly, such shared and indistinct feeling governs the whole conflict: as long as both antagonists attack each other, empathy might heighten the bellicosity of both, but give no behavioral indication of its existence. Certainly a fight would be a more intimate joint act if the movements of each angry attacker struck into the other's sense with something like the emotive quality of the impulses behind them.

Naturalists and photographers in the wild have given us a wonderful store of factual knowledge, and with it some very jumbled and wavering, largely anthropomorphic commentary, mixed with constant warnings that we must not think of even the higher mammals in anthropomorphic terms. This shows that there is no systematic frame of animal psychology, in terms of which they could easily and freely interpret the behavior they have so closely and conscientiously observed. Such a framework is, indeed, not easy to construct, and to remember that all animal acts fit into it and not into our own conceptual system of mental action takes practice before it becomes easy, just as switching from our traditional measurements in feet and inches to the metric system does at first. But once we have a few major operational concepts I think it can be done, and the sign of its feasibility is that more and more facts are drawn together under the same principles of interpretation, while the latter all lead back to the same basic generalizations. The assumption that animal behavior is guided by feeling, not envisaged purpose, and that this makes it consistently egocentric although it may encompass acts and even needs of other beings seems to me a promising start, although—like all theory that goes beyond *ad hoc* explanation of gross empirical fact—it involves some speculation and indirect evidence where direct verification is impossible. Perhaps the most convincing test of its validity would be to reinterpret, one by one, in these non-human terms the main accepted facts of animal behavior which are currently supposed to rest on symbolic communication, ritual, codes, property claims and other conceptual functions. Such an inductive procedure is, of course, impossible in the confines of a chapter; so I shall select typical phenomena and their usual interpretations and try to reveal the anthropomorphisms implicit in them (which are sometimes plain, but also sometimes subtle), and propose, in each case, a more zoological conception in terms of animal values, impulses and immediate feeling, sensory and emotive.

Let us return to the fighting wolves. One of the distinctly non-human aspects of the formal surrender is that it does not end the hostility, but lasts only as long as the "appeal for mercy" itself is being made. This does suggest strongly that the inhibition springs from momentary feeling and ends with it. The possibility that it is a product of empathy has several supports, in that this hypothetical assumption would explain some attendant facts. For one thing, the winner's "magnanimous" or "merciful" act is bound so closely to the despairing partner's active expression that it seems to spring from the sight and feeling of the latter's yielding body and probably the smell of his terror, as though these all melted into one overweening dread that communicated itself, for the moment (a psychological moment may be long), to the top wolf, and inhibited his attack. That would explain why his "mercy" lasts no longer than the loser's "submissive gesture": if a sudden wave of empathy interfered with the winner's aggression, any change in the beguiling *tableau vivant* would naturally break the induced restraint. Another fact such an empathic basis would elucidate is that the inhibiting mechanism works only among members of the same species.

In the canine encounters described by several ethologists, the fight ends when the victor withdraws to urinate on some upright object. The most widely accepted interpretation is that the victorious beast marks the place of his recent triumph as his own. But in animal memory a finished act probably has no retrievable form which could impress its value on the place of its occurrence. Animals do not celebrate past achievements. Perhaps the successful fight has done a great deal to make its location a "place" for both animals, not necessarily to be sought or avoided, but known as a station on future courses, and urinating close by helps to give it its place character. But one does not need to attribute to animals any intention to leave the mark which the maker of it and many others afterwards sniff, and are seen to "renew," or to "cover" with a different scent, according to whether the observer judges the visitor in question to be the originator of the scent post or a different individual. The first act of micturition was a most natural one after a fight; any excitement causes most animals to urinate. No one seems to have noted when and where the defeated animal next relieves itself, perhaps because no one has invented a symbolic value for the act, which obviously can only be performed at a safe distance, after the underdog has made his escape.

As for the subsequent uses of the post, this involves a further basic principle of motivation which plays a more important and constant role in the life of lower vertebrates than at the specialized human level: the principle of suggestion. The smell of genus-specific urine is enough to evoke micturition especially in male dogs, and, according to the few available accounts, other canines. Even human beings know the suggestive character of the sight or sound of this act, and even of running water. Many animals seem to be similarly affected; dogs going the round of scent posts in their familiar range urinate briefly at each one. The difference between male and female postures for that purpose lets the males develop the use of such stations in much the more visible pattern, and points to a subtle difference in motivation, which illustrates how motivational patterns in general grow up and become articulated by integration of quite separate, opportunely coincident elements. The male dog's ability to lift a hind leg laterally lets the musculature of the groin pull the penis in a similar sidewise direction as the animal stands on three legs, so the urine is sprayed toward a definite point beside instead of beneath the agent. This evidently gives vent to another impulse, namely, to orient toward a goal, which we see especially in aggressive gestures, such as the spontaneous aiming of missiles at another being by apes, usually without practical effect (another revealing fact in animal behavior, to be considered), but enacting the inward focusing of feeling on an external object overtly in a self-expressive gesture. The goal need not be a creature, nor need the emotion which momentarily cathects it be aggressive; a scent post is of intense interest, so it evokes a directed response, an extension of the organism in the form of a shot of urine, which is facilitated by the convenient shape and suggestive smell of the post. The female cannot combine the suggested urination with the emotional expression toward the communal post, so the formalized response of the male does not develop in her, and even the impulse to relieve herself at the site is not as automatically carried out.

A similar combination of the same two motivating conditions in the production of directed urination, and—in this case—defecation, too, probably underlies the action of howler monkeys observed by C. R. Carpenter; according to his account, "an animal may break off dead limbs and drop them, or fecal matter may be released with reference to the observer" (1934, p. 27). Here the two impulses, aggressive advance toward the intruder and the visceral response to general excitation, are only loosely integrated in that the latter, too, often seems to be directed; and as it is released from above, it requires no such technique as the adult male dog's, but can be practiced by young and old of both sexes.

In his monograph, Dr. Carpenter is very precise and as literal as possible in his statements and especially his interpretations. It is fairly clear that he regards the monkeys' actions here recounted as intentional. His judgment is probably correct. But real forms of attack on the disturbing person or his blind they are not, or they would be performed by the gathered group, like the "mobbing behavior" of some birds, which seems to give super-avian courage to otherwise shy and fugitive little individuals. Each monkey pauses in its course over the human watcher to throw a branch or excrement at him; sometimes, apparently, a single animal ventures to approach him for the purpose and quickly withdraws again. The author, furthermore, remarked previously that this performance was only one of five possible reactions of howlers to man. The motivation of the "attack" is evidently not simply hostile, nor is it entirely unintentional momentary excitement.

An act which does not fit exactly into any of our preconceived categories of animal motivation is a challenge to our theoretical inventiveness and powers to construct further hypotheses. In the quest for alternative interpretations one has to be guided by hints and pointers from other animal acts, mainly in the same species but sometimes in very distant ones, and by such basic principles as underlie one's analysis of animal behavior as a whole. In this case, a suggestion comes from far afield, from an observation made by J. L. Kavanau on deer mice that were given access to a running wheel which could be started and stopped by the experimenter or by the mice, according to various arrangements. "Once male deer mice, *Peromyscus crinitus*," he says,

> have learned to turn on a motor which drives a running wheel (for a set time), they repeatedly perform the act and run the motor driven wheel. Given control over both the onset and the cessation of rotation, they turn the motor both on and off themselves, running the wheel (for varying periods) on a purely volitional schedule. But they will only run a motor driven wheel

when the rotation is self-initiated. As often as the motor is turned on by the experimenter, they doggedly press a lever (within seconds) that turns it off, even though this entails giving up wheel-running entirely.

. . . similar behavior results when deer mice control ambient illumination. Animals repeatedly press certain levers . . . that turn light off in steps, after it is turned on by the experimenter; conversely they press other levers that turn light on in steps, after it is turned off by the experimenter; while if given complete control over illumination, they repeatedly run back and forth between levers, stepping light on and then off. (1963, pp. 251–52)

These experiments certainly reveal a long-ignored animal value, namely, opportunity to initiate a perceptible change in the external situation, not necessarily for the better, but simply a change which completes the consummation of a novel kind of act. If the effect can be reversed, the first change of situation offers a new lure to action; the alternately encouraged impulses may even become rhythmicized into a continuous activity. Rushing to and fro between widely separated light switches is, of course, a behavioral artifact of captivity; but nothing could illustrate better the principle that an organism always performs all the acts its situation allows. If it does not engage in what looks to human beings like a momentarily possible act, the normal reason is that it is doing something else; not necessarily something overt, let alone as spectacular as pressing levers—it may be completely busy digesting, sleeping, sunning, purring, etc., at a low level of bodily tonus; or at fairly high tonus, perhaps rising toward the limen of active behavior, for a while it may be inwardly playing off incipient phases of more acute acts against each other so none of them develops to the stage of gross muscular movement, and the organism still maintains a motionless posture.

Monkeys are active creatures, and although howlers are less so than many other species, this is only a comparative impression, strengthened by the fact that they become indifferent and withdrawn in captivity. In the wild they appear to be stimulated as much as any sociable beasts by unusual situations. The presence of a human being who does not really frighten them is an enticement to make that being move, without treating it as an antagonist. The howlers may be primarily motivated in the same way as the deer mice controlling the running wheel and the lights in their cages: what they try to turn on and off is Dr. Carpenter.

The behavior of the howlers is especially interesting in that the directedness and concentration of their impulse is expressed in their throwing twigs and branches toward the intruder. Animals with hand-like paws naturally grasp things and drop them, and chimpanzees have been quite clearly observed to throw in an oriented fashion. The howlers do not do as well; but both species show a complete indifference to the suitability of their missiles to harm or even reach the supposed antagonist. This may bespeak a purely self-expressive function of the directed gesture, prolonged as it is by the departure of the projectile; in that case, the character of the hurled object is really of no account, so our judgment that they do not perceive its physical attributes is misplaced, even if true. But an equally plausible interpretation is that in throwing wood, leaves or bark they do try to hit the human observer; if that is the nature of the act, their lack of feeling for the basic mechanical properties of inanimate objects is indeed astonishing.

The use of excrement for the same purpose provides an example of entrainment of a basically unrelated act for the implementation of an intentional, direct one. The animal knows from experience the process of approaching a challenging quarry, or perhaps an antagonist, as an exciting act which involves the feeling of visceral evacuation as part of its consummation. The occurrence of that phase at the moment when the monkey has ventured to a place directly over the disturber is probably a purely autonomic release of tension that has reached its height.

The intense empathic reactions of animals toward each other contrast sharply with their lack of intuitive judgment of firmness, balance and tensile strength in objects. All their feeling seems to be for action. But acts may involve two or even more agents and still be felt as each one's own, and passive materials transiently—though perhaps repeatedly—enter into acts as enticements and means. While such things are functioning they are embraced by animal consciousness, but what to us is their "objective" character apparently does not exist below the human level of mentality. This is, of course, a hypothetical assumption; but if we hold to it seriously it demands several reinterpretations of reported animal behavior, such as "staking out" territory, warning, display, and the larger acts of cooperation, imitation, leadership, communication and the alleged beginnings (or even complete mastery) of language.

To begin with territorial claims, these are generally said to be established by "marking" with urine, and sometimes feces, the boundaries of the pre-empted ground. The nature of animal space and the making of "places" have been sufficiently discussed in the previous chapter to require no further argument here against the anthropomorphic conception that the marked locations are points on an imaginary boundary line enclosing the territory the resident animal will defend. But since, at least in some cases, they do indicate the more or less permanent whereabouts of their producer, the true function of their frequent renewal has to be explained. One incentive to that renewal has already been considered in connection with the scent posts of dogs, which generally do not indicate the private domains that most domestic dogs possess and know very well as their own. A single animal, especially in the wild, will be stimulated to repeat its micturition at the scene where its own smell suggests it. On animal paths such deposits surely act as a pheromone, but not necessarily with respect to other animals; thus I. Eibl-Eibesfeldt, in a study of the common house mouse (*mus musculus*), decided that mice, which constantly defecate and urinate as they run about, are "marking" their paths and stations to make them familiar to themselves rather than as a deterrent to other mice (1950, pp. 561–62). That seems to me a likelier effect of most "marking," intentional or (as surely in this case) unintentional. Some ethologists, however, have thought to see signatory functions in various "marks" deliberately made to convey information to other animals.

The chief danger to animal psychology in such established interpretations is that they tend to impose themselves directly on the data of observation; the observer simply sees the behavioral act as an example of the intentions he has previously imputed to the agent. As all excretions are self-evident ceremonial marks, all utterances are just as obviously "signals," and every alternation of sound-making between two animals, "communication." If he scares up a ground-nesting bird that runs away from its eggs or chicks dragging one wing, he can see that it is trying to decoy him from the nest.

The extension of one wing, throwing the body somewhat off-center, is a natural posture to birds in several situations: sunning, preening, stretching and brooding a single chick. Such one-sided action seems, in fact, to be a primitive repertoire element. The other major instinctual element in the "injury-feigning act" is the cowering attitude which makes the bird appear to be physically unable to run or fly away. This same posture appears in all the "gestures of submission," but also in many courtship movements of birds and other animals, where it is unlikely to have any such significance in reference to the sex partner. From the standpoint of feeling, however, it may have the same value and be the same subaction in the different behavior patterns that contain it.

The emotional feeling expressed in the cowering posture may be viewed, hypothetically, as desperation, being overwhelmed by circumstances. In human experience this is an ultimate degree of terror, and as it is apt to be a direct reaction to immediate conditions in us as in birds and beasts, the assumption that they feel it much as we do is a fairly safe one. Such an emotion is natural when a creature can do nothing at all to counter the danger that is upon it. The bird chased up from its nest by a huge predator, moreover, is torn between two impulses, to cover its brood and to flee; the dragging wing points nestward and bespeaks its reluctance to abandon the young, the flight impulse strains irresistibly away from the deadly foe. It may even subsequently pass by, come full circle back to the nest as if nothing had happened; but if the enemy suddenly looms up again, the "distraction display" may be repeated.

The same sense of helplessness at a moment of total defeat may motivate a turkey to fall prone in midst of a fight, or a dog to cringe beneath a conquering antagonist. The intensity of emotion which pervades such a spontaneous gesture of giving up the struggle runs through every quiver, every erecting feather or hair of the loser's skin, and in a mammal through every sweat gland exuding the smell of terror. In this extremity the presumptive destroyer suddenly suffers an empathic pseudo-identification with his victim and, for the instant, cannot strike. If then the victim tries to escape, the emotional contagion is broken, so the conqueror resumes his attack; but if it is the latter that leaves the spot, the fight is ended.

Now, what about the courting bird that periodically ducks and creeps around a coy or unresponsive female? His situation does not look desperate, overwhelming, hopelessly frustrating. Yet so it may be. The human observer looks beyond the female's current act, and expects her to yield in good time, when she becomes sexually ready; but the male bird, with the female in sight, under pressure of his mating impulse frantically seeking enactment to consummation, may be suffering recurrent moments of desperation. He does not know the asynchrony of male and female rhythms, nor that they will ultimately coincide, as the ethologist foresees, to whom the bird's acts are stimulus-"triggered" or "released" antics phylogenetically predesigned to attract the female. The bird is motivated by feeling which engages the entire organism for its expression. In watching the sexual excitement of a small bird, e.g., a wren, it is interesting to see practically all of his repertoire elements emerging in kaleidoscopic sequence during such ardent courtship.

The purpose of these reinterpretations is to offer a psychological approach to zoological phenomena which so far have been treated without any consideration of animal mentality as we know it from other angles. The assumptions implicit in the notion of "distraction display" and ruses to decoy an enemy from an animal's nest, den or horde are assumptions of characteristically human mental acts: imagining one's own appearance to other creatures and speculating on the way such creatures would react to their own impressions of the deceiver. Short of such conceptual powers, intentional deception is impossible; consequently, I hold that no animal can deliberately feign, deceive, distort evidence, or invent any ruse to trick an antagonist.

The roles that interindividual grooming among mammals, birds and insects play in animal lives are but little understood, and perhaps too simply and superficially conceived. Closer observations on the practices sometimes called "allo-grooming" (that is, grooming another creature's skin or feathers, without further relational concepts such as are implicit in the terms "mutual" or "social" grooming) raise questions of animal feeling, both cutaneous and emotional, that merit more than a reference to beneficial effects like "group cohesion," or "social" practices such as rank-holding, submissive gestures and leader-recognition.

These terms may all fit the acts of grooming, licking or scratching other individuals, but it is highly dubitable that the animal agents themselves know anything about rank, dominance orders, leadership, their own submission (which they are supposed to declare symbolically), or even the fact that they belong to a group which their interaction with its other members holds together. Their acts are not motivated by social aims, but by their own felt emotional tensions and constantly emerging perceptions.

If, then, we can muster the patience to suspend the advanced ethological approach to animal behavior and analyze some elementary aspects of interindividual bodily contact, we may come to the problems of "allo-grooming" and related actions with a somewhat deeper insight into the potentialities of such contact *per se*, and their expressions in cutaneous sensibility, from mere touch, tickle, prick, scratch, etc., to emotionally significant impingements, caresses and abuses, and the reinforcement of intense interactions as between mothers and young.

Allo-grooming has been so commonly observed in many kinds of creatures that the oldest interpretation of it as a service rendered by one animal to another for cleaning the latter's skin, especially in inaccessible places, is generally accepted as the obvious, sufficient explanation. Mothers groom their young; similarly, adults help each other out in awkward passages of self-grooming.

But the cleanliness of a comrade's skin is ordinarily not a value to an animal whose own skin feels comfortable. The great eagerness of some animals, especially lemurs, monkeys and chimpanzees, but above all the baboons, to groom their companions, which often appears—upon behavioral evidence—to exceed the beneficiaries' desire for the treatment, indicates that what induces and guides the act of examining and handling another animal's skin is primarily an impulse on the part of the groomer, not the recipient of the service. Sometimes it is initiated by the latter, which presents its itching surface in a suggestive fashion, but where grooming is one of the most prevalent interactions among members of a company the usual motivation is something else, and can only be guessed at by observation of the normally attendant circumstances and the typical relations between the two creatures involved in each case.

Unexpected conditions may come to light when observation goes beyond the superficial stage of finding the most evident facts of animal life and giving them sociological labels—"staking out territory," "submission" and "recognition of status," "problem solving," "training the young," "cooperation" and "communication." Every one of these categories imposes the image of human society on the activities of animals, and not even only on gregarious ones. But a single odd fact such as the passion of many primates for grooming others of their kind immediately raises questions about the motivating situation, and paradoxical findings like the baboons' tendency to approach a threatening individual rather than flee from it may require far-reaching systematic interpretation. Such interpretation can rest on various principles. Thus, behaviorally judged, a dominant male shows intention to attack; ethologically, he asserts his dominance and command; psychologically, he seems to feel his competence as self-enlargement, so the signs of fear in another monkey promptly make him expand and display his own strength. Because my interest is to trace human intellect and society back to its beginnings in animal feeling, I am following the psychological method, i.e., seeking the most probable mental acts to explain overt behavior in each animal species on which sufficient observations have been made by reliable persons, professional or self-trained.

Two further imputations of human psychical capacities to animals require an alternative treatment in non-human terms of instinctive action directly felt from move to move: the relatively simple case of cooperation, and the moot and difficult question of communication. The reason why an explanation of cooperative behavior is easier to give no matter on what theory is that we know what empirical events we mean by the word, which is not true of "communication." Let us consider one or two typical instances of animals' cooperative acts and try to account for them in terms of impulse and immediate feeling.

Division of roles according to a generally accepted plan is often attributed to packs and droves of animals in pursuit of a quarry, but no one, to my knowledge, has ever described how the plan is made and the roles are assigned in advance. The fact is that every pursuer tries to reach the quarry, but since most running animals tend to take a circling course, the predators on the inside of the curve (however slight) have a more open track to dash around the rest of the pack and intercept the victim's course. The act requires no plan, but springs from momentary opportunity and individual perception of a special chance.

There are, however, acts of genuine cooperation among animals, and these are the ones that put the principle of interpretation in terms of immediate feeling to the test. C. R. Carpenter observed some unmistakable cases as he watched troupes of howling monkeys move along arboreal paths, which required some crossings from tree to tree where the closest branches were several feet apart. In at least two such cases he saw a female, followed by a young one, suspend herself by a tailhold on the last branch of one tree and a handhold on a branch of the next tree, gained by jumping, so her body made a bridge over which the young one—after long hesitation—finally crossed (1934, pp. 73–74).

The principal elements in this rather elaborate joint act are ordinary enough: carrying the young, waiting when it does not follow. The little one had outgrown the riding stage, so it went forward as soon as it could jump to the second tree, but its mother's back was still the needed and natural vehicle. Each move of each animal emerged from the motivating situation; the two agents needed no plan or directive communication. Animals that carry their babies as constantly as monkeys do must feel them as part of themselves so intimately that, even when they no longer ride, the awareness of the young one's reach, strength and jumping span is empathically felt by the mother; she stops and waits between trees, especially where her following offspring falls back, afraid of the leap.

There are few situations in which cooperation between animals has been observed without involvement of the mother-child relationship. The famous St. Bernard dogs, which were kept especially as trackers of lost persons in the Alps, and in other environments have been known to save many a human being from drowning, work best alone; in a quandary, another dog would be no help. The only genuine cases of collaboration I know, carried out as if by one organism, are among colonial insects, which are semi-individuated beings. Vertebrates may cooperate by chance, the action of one animal giving opportunity for successful acts by another, but each one is trying to realize an impulse of its own all by itself. Dogs have been trained to help human beings—the work of our "seeing-eye" dogs is a spectacular example—but that is not entering into an act with a joint aim; the human partner conceives the purposes and the dog has been taught to play its role on command. Other working dogs, even closely associated in a team (as in the arctic) or in a hunting pack, never watch each other's moves to cooperate in the attainment of a common aim.

In the laboratory, experiments have been arranged to test the capacity of chimpanzees to join forces in the accomplishment of an act which promised the same "reward" for them both. The results were "positive" to some extent, in the sense of meeting the experimenter's wishes, but anomalous in that they did not demonstrate any spontaneous cooperation. In the first place, the conditions, task and learning processes were so highly artificial that the records of the experiment tell more about chimpanzees' trainability than about their interest in the "problem," let alone any spontaneous insight into the way to solve it by cooperating. Each move was learned separately by each animal; at last the pair was caged together and trained for teamwork (Crawford 1937). After that, of course, the trick was often practiced by the animals even without reward; captive apes use every possible act of their fully developed repertoire in play, and incite each other to join in the game. Paul Schiller argues that play, not "problem solving," is the basis of learning skills (1957, pp. 268–69).

All the genuine instances of cooperation which I have been able to study seemed to rest on direct or extended parental impulses, sometimes modified or enhanced by other characteristics of animal action and feeling, such as empathy, physical communion (as by trophallaxis and mutual licking), self-enlargement, etc. Today, the most spectacular instances and the most enthusiastically discussed in the current literature refer not to primates, but to a distant order, Cetacea, especially dolphins of the species *Tursiops truncatus*.

It is in the dolphins that mutual aid among adults, which is rarely recorded in other animals and then uncertain, can be clearly observed, sometimes by several watchers together. That such aid is really given to sick or injured *Tursiops* is, I think, beyond dispute; the attentions of strong and healthy individuals to incapacitated ones is claimed to be so reliable that trainers and keepers of dolphins in captivity have learned to leave the tendance of the sick—which requires help to rise for breath every one-half to five minutes, around the clock—to one or two other dolphins in the same tank. Even a single animal can perform this service, which would be impossible for a human being, because of our basic rhythm of sleeping and waking. In such an indefinitely protracted activity we would have to pause for variable but finally ineluctable periods of rest and inattention. That the dolphin apparently needs no respite from its task is certainly as remarkable as the fact that it voluntarily assumes it; but because the latter phenomenon can be regarded as a "social act," and ethologists at present are avid for social relations, social life and social organization of animals, the strange physiological aspect has been generally ignored. Yet when it is earnestly investigated the findings bear heavily, though in a roundabout way, on the intellectualist school's theoretical foundation.

There seem, in fact, to be some peculiarities of the dolphin's brain which make it functionally less similar to man's than many a lower animal's in which the general mammalian brain structures (cortical layers, thalamic nuclei, pyramidal tract, etc.) are less developed than in cetaceans. There is as yet no way of knowing how much cerebral activity in any being is redundant; and one peculiarity in the dolphin's behavior suggests that redundancy in his brain may be very high—namely, his ability to stay awake indefinitely and carry out a voluntary activity for twenty-four hours a day. Dr. Karl E. Schaefer noted this possible reason for the size and apparent complexity of the central nervous organ. In a symposium paper on physiological adaptation of marine animals, he remarked: "The dolphins have a unique sleeping and waking rhythm. They are awake at every breath and always sleep with one eye open. It seems that they are constantly surveying their surroundings with at least one eye, which means maintaining afference to half the brain. That may explain the great weight of their brains, which is required if one part is to be in a waking state while the other is recovering in sleep" (1968, p. 188).

Whatever the capacities and motivations of dolphins may really be, there certainly is great scope for hypothetical explanations. No matter what premises one adopts as a framework, there always could be some alternative hypothesis; only, some interpretations fit better than others into the general system of zoological concepts. This seems to me to hold for the notion of animal values as permanent or transitory cathexes, imposed on objects by their immediate entrance into what William James called "live options" in the active progress of life. So, instead of judging dolphin behavior in terms of "intelligence," "problem solving" and "learning," it may be wiser to approach it first in terms of animal feeling, as an expression of impulse, steered by the perception of opportunities and the felt fluctuations of ambient conditions, and developing from within by a constant generation of reinforcing or competing impulses.

Having, then, at least an idea of how a dolphin could be capable of tending a sick comrade unintermittently day and night, we may return to that rare exhibit of cooperation among adults to question what instinctive proclivities could initiate it and what feeling could support it. An extraordinary response in a species bespeaks a coming together of several behavioral potentialities through the development of an integrated emotive pattern; in this case, apparently, an extension of the parental relation to any individual, young or old, male or female, that relapses into the helplessness of the newborn in immediate need of air. One reason for the dolphin's readiness to respond in this motherly way may lie in the fact that its mode of life reduces early physical contact with the young to a minimum, compared to the constant hugging, grooming, carrying and cuddling of little monkeys and apes by their mothers. The maternal responses which cannot develop maximally in marine mammals upon giving birth, but are restricted to nursing and vital first-aid care, still lie partly in abeyance—perhaps from the beginning of life to the end, with or without any actual motherhood. Because there is so little physical contact to support and sustain parental feeling, it must be intrinsically strong; and perhaps the dolphin's great neural and muscular versatility is reflected in the wide scope of its centrally engendered feelings and its ambient emotive lures. The proclivity of an occasional dolphin to play with human beings on beaches, which has been demonstrated repeatedly and beyond doubt, points to the same readiness to transfer companionship from one sort of individual to another, even creatures of remote species.

Another cardinal reason, though I can adduce it only hypothetically, may be a very strong tie of empathy between dolphins. Since the surfacing for breath in these animals is irregular, which suggests that their moments of oxygen requirement are variable, a dolphin playing nurse to a sick comrade evidently feels, somehow, when its charge is in need of breath. There may be a two-way adjustment, the invalid falling in, after a fashion, with the respiratory periods of its nurse; but there surely must be some fusing of felt somatic tensions to implement the cooperative activity. That points to a close empathic relationship. Now, empathy is a typically animalian form of communion; so it is a supreme development of non-human capacities, rather than an approach to human intellect, that is strongly indicated in the dolphin's care for its sick.

There are, moreover, some fantastic-sounding yet well-authenticated stories of *Tursiops'* pushing wounded creatures—not only their own kind, but large fish and even human beings—into shallows and up on beaches. This practice has always been regarded as a further elaboration of the "care-giving" behavior toward the sick. On this natural assumption, however, it presents some very puzzling aspects, both as a whole and in special cases. As a whole, it has been extolled as a rescue operation because its most spectacular and publicized instances have been those in which a human being has been steered ashore by one or sometimes two dolphins, and thus saved from drowning. But to be beached, especially on shores where the tide periodically goes out, would be no blessing to a disabled dolphin, as the breathing aid in water is; also, the "succorant" acts of carrying and pushing are often administered to dead creatures, sometimes for days, both in the wild and in captivity.

In such acts, it seems, the consummation may be achieved before the impulse is spent; then the act has to have a long cadence, which a human being, to whom the physical change effected by its consummation always seems the "aim" and rational end of action, can only regard as useless motion. Yet the extension of an overt act to give expression to every subact implicit in its total impulse may be a necessity to an animal, and sometimes even to man. We try to counteract, displace or sublimate an internal pressure which has overshot its goal; for instance, if we are working passionately to achieve a particular political change, woman suffrage, abolition of slavery, or the like, and the change suddenly, fortuitously, takes place through events quite apart from our efforts, we have to reorganize our emotions and conations, and switch our actions to another "cause." Animals do not attempt such rational control of their impulses, but seek the most complete actualization of them even if their central drive was quickly consummated. Their performances are not always finished when we think they are; some subsequent acts may still be parts of the supposedly completed ones. A familiar example is the behavior of a cat which has caught a mouse and proceeds—as is popularly supposed—to "play" with it. The belief that the cat follows the act of catching the mouse (which may include subacts of watching, stalking, muscular preparations, building up tensions for the crucial leap) with a playful act in which the mouse becomes a toy is universally accepted. Yet in terms of impulse and feeling it is really a questionable interpretation; more likely, the cat is protracting the hunt which is too quickly successful, by repeating the final phase in a telescoped fashion, letting the mouse just start to run away and retrieving without killing it until the impulse with all its contributaries is spent.

The aim of animal psychology is to understand whole acts as the elements of behavior and the indicators of feeling, whereby the evolution of perception, emotion and ultimately more and more specialized cerebral functions, the characteristically human ones, may be traced to their evolutionary sources. Prevision of changes in the outer world, i.e., envisagement of the results of acts (including very complicated acts), is probably a late achievement; perhaps—as I strongly suspect—a mark of humanity.

Motivation is the ever-recurrent key problem; and where our interpretation of a behavioral episode meets with some disturbing anomaly the chances are that our assumptions of the motivating situation in which the animal is acting are wrong—over-simplified, anthropomorphic or hastily carried over from some other case which they fitted. What closer study shows is that very different impulses may underlie similar overt acts, or to put it conversely, a given mode of behavior may arise from any of several emotional tension patterns. Such patterns may even lapse for intervals which are filled by other impulses upholding the performance, especially if it is repetitious and has become rhythmic. To identify the basic motivation of the whole strange phenomenon is not easy, for often the appearance of an instinctual unit in a new context casts doubts on its most accepted meanings.

So it is with many of the cetacean interactions which are generally interpreted as social services. The propensity of dolphins to help disabled ones breathe is, perhaps, the clearest case, known only in captivity, and possibly elicited solely in that condition. An equally well-attested phenomenon, observed mainly in the wild, is the support given to stricken whales by their companions, two of which immediately rush to the shot or harpooned beast's sides, closing in to hold it upright and sometimes swimming away with it. Naturally, the accepted interpretation of that astounding response is that the uninjured whales come to save the disabled member of their group, but where they take the victim, which is usually dying if not instantly dead, is unknown; the ocean keeps the secret.

There are two principles of animal psychology involved in this interpretation of dolphin behavior as instinctive: the first is the constant development of new motivating situations from minute to minute in the course of a life, which has been sufficiently discussed. The second is the rise and decline of values, the slow or sudden change of cathexis which an object may undergo as it enters or leaves an agent's transient "world." Animals, having no relational concepts, can only feel relationships in moments of their acute changes, i.e., abrupt emergence of a new relation or sudden break of an old one. This principle, too, can be traced through biological act forms to much deeper levels than mental processes in such high animals as cetaceans. It operates in the perceptual mechanisms themselves, which respond with vigorous action to the beginning or sudden cessation of a stimulus, but drop to low levels between, even if the stimulus continues unabated. The same effect of a break in a stream of generally redundant stimulation has been found to underlie the perception of lines and contours in vision and acute tonal changes or accents in hearing. It applies even to non-visual functions of the retina, as R. N. Danielson discovered in studying the effect of light, received through the eye, on the color of the skin in fish (1941, p. 101).

The literature of ethology, though not yet old, is already large, and has established a language of its own embodying highly anthropomorphic concepts which go unchallenged because they are brought in as part of the jargon rather than as explicit assumptions with recognized and accepted implications. The reinterpretations of a few phenomena proposed above are only random samples, meant to show that animal ways may be viewed as acts based on self-centered impulses and courses of immediate feeling. So far, so good: but here, finally, we come to the Asses' Bridge of animal psychology, the problem of communication.

This entire subject, as already remarked, is confused and obfuscated by the stretching of its definition to cover everything from speech, writing and "the media" to the chemical transmission of a fear reaction among fish in an aquarium, and even the eating of one animal by another. William Evans and Jarvis Bastian, for instance, define animal "communication" as any sort of interaction among animals, and then spend paragraphs demonstrating by "deduction" that in animals interaction and communication are identical (1969, p. 427). A definition that permits no distinction between phenomena which analytic thinkers are trying to bring into systematic relation is pragmatically a bad definition.

I am inclined to say, "communication is the intentional transmission of ideas from one individual to one or more others." If the intention miscarries, i.e., no idea "goes across," the individuals fail to communicate, though they may interact closely, elaborately, even violently. I would not first declare that dolphins "communicate" in some sense, and then establish the sense by definition and let that authenticate their possession of language, but in consequence of accepting the strict sense of "communication" I would make bold to say that dolphins do not communicate, any more than other animals—crows, elephants, chimpanzees. It is better to start systematic thinking with precise though narrow concepts and proceed to widen them by stepwise generalization than to start with highly general notions which, being carried from one context to another, change their meanings.

If, then, animals make no communication, what is the nature of their mutual bond apart from sexual union and fighting? I would call it communion. It is practiced and felt without highly cerebral responses, and differs from communication in having no propositional contents— nothing that could be paraphrased in words, such as "that looks dangerous," "this is mine," "column right," or "I mean no harm." Communion is a mutual awareness, a sense of safety in nearness and, amongst gregarious animals, sometimes in numbers. It is not established and upheld by signals, gestures of submission or dominance, but primarily by physical contacts, extended by smell and, in some species, sounds and movements which pass on bodily feelings, large or small alarms, expectations, impulses. A school of fish or a swarm of locusts move as one body. Many animals are so suggestible that the first "intention movement" toward an act, made by another individual, evokes their own impulse to perform the whole act themselves. If we analyze an animal's behavior, noting its incidental postures and vocalization, grimaces and tail switches, we may decide that this or that item in the characteristic pattern is a "social signal" noted and understood by others as a demand or proposal, i.e., as a vocal or gestic communication. Then we see a leader making his followers form their ranks according to a preconceived marching order, or a dominant animal expressing his dominance while another signals submission, mothers giving instruction to the young, experienced elders teaching cubs to hunt. These are all naive anthropomorphisms. G. B. Schaller speaks more correctly when he says, "A dominant male who stands motionless, facing in a certain direction, indicates that he is ready to leave and the other members of the group crowd around him" (1965, p. 344). Note "that *he* is ready to leave"—not that they must do so. There is no reason to believe that he gives an order or intends to indicate anything.

In animal communion signs do not refer to acts or situations, but are always genuine parts of acts; and where they function as cues, they are genuine parts of situations in which the recipients of the cues initiate or change their acts. Consequently an act that arises in a situation prepared by other creatures (conspecific or not) embodies the subact or subacts which entered into its motivation, and is to that extent already a conjoint act. Furthermore, what animals perceive seems to be not so much expressions, positions and movements of others as whole acts, sometimes to be countered (so we think the antagonist has anticipated the next move as "most probable") or completed, like the egg deposition of a female fish followed by the male's fertilization of the eggs. What looks to human eyes like cooperation to get something done is perception of an act in progress which functions as a lure to pursue its development, literally to "get into the act" and carry it to completion. The practical result need not be preconceived or foreseen at all; but if it entails relief from empathic stress (as in the case of freeing or aiding a fellow or a young one), it is "reinforced," i.e., its repetition in other situations is encouraged.

The most striking instances of communal instinctive action are found among insects, where it looks most deceptively like planned human labor with different tasks assigned to different classes of workers or even to individuals. Yet it is in insects that the purely animalian nature of conjoint acts is easiest to see, upon analysis unencumbered by metaphors such as "state," "queen," "dancing" and "instructions" of honeybees, and, with reference to ants, expressions like "slave making" or "tool using" (the latter for joint acts of adults and larvae). Insects have simple responses, but not simplified human ones; their own principles of behavior are masked by figures of speech borrowed from man's political, educational and social institutions. A hive is not a state, because it is not governed; its individual members have no rights and obligations, and there is no reason except the influence of an anthropomorphic model to think of it as an ideal republic. Also, there is no other reason to believe that a "dancing" bee sends out other foragers with factual information and instructions where to go and what to look for. The nature of her abreactive oscillations and the smell and taste of the nectar she carries motivate the next cycle in the foraging act, which is performed by bees that have been in physical contact with her, joined her movements and tasted what she brought in. The similarity of their excursions to that which she just completed rests on the cyclic nature of the total act that is handed over from one highly sensitive semi-individual to others. The "queen" bee, likewise, is not a queen. She gives no orders, no verdicts, neither does she lead a swarm that gathers around her as it leaves the hive to start a new colony. The only thing that has caused her to be popularly called the "queen" is that she does no work and receives constant feeding, licking and tending from the pseudo-females, the ordinary bees—a truly popular concept of royalty: "The queen was in the parlor, eating bread and honey." The derivation of a name for the one large fertile bee from such a source would be just one of many philological accidents, theoretically of no significance, save for the fact that it has long and insidiously shifted the emphasis of functional analysis from organic to organizational patterns, and masked what is probably the motivation of the "royal" treatment this all-important female receives. She is the womb of the colony; as such, she embodies all feminine sexuality and in so intersensitive a group as the denizens of a hive she represents every sterile worker's sex organ. Their tendance rests on their desire for contact with her, and emotively is more like masturbation than like rendering a social service. This is one possible spontaneous source of behavior which so far has required the assumption of a special "instinct" in the workers to take their turn at a necessary task. Bees are emotional, their moods are affected by temperature and light, but above all by acts going on around them, which may elicit feeding in the presence of larvae and—perhaps for a dozen situational reasons—also of adults (a returned forager, circling and waggling, gives the bees that make contact with her little tastes of the nectar she has), and the queen bee is an excellent big mouth to feed. All kinds of cathexis may attach to her, and a constant mild tension somewhat like a sexual excitation seems to surround her wherever she is. When a swarm moves, she is usually deep inside it.

As for the ants, they show even more clearly the principles of holistic act perception, suggestibility, rhythmic perseveration even in overt behavior, empathy, and communion by constant touching, licking, sharing food by trophallaxis. One expert myrmicologist, Derek W. Morley, says of the ant colony, "it is a system of fluxion. The emotive forces flow outwards from each individual to his neighbors and in the opposite direction at varying *tempi*.... This flow of the nervous energy of ants throughout the community is a definite and little understood phenomenon. Nervous tension can be produced by the physical conditions of a thunderstorm, or rather of the tension prior to the actual storm" (1953, p. 170). One is reminded of the "electric" feeling of which some human beings complain, and which others who are immune to it cannot imagine; evidently to ants it is a major emotive pression, perhaps a sensation.

In the first chapter of his book, Dr. Morley described the work of some exceptionally responsive and energetic ants in each colony, among the average, relatively passive members; these moving spirits, always first to find what needs to be done, stir up the other ants to conjoint action. He called them the "excitement centres" of the community. Of this he concludes: "The mystery of the ants is in their empathy, the bond of nervous tension which builds so quick a response one to another that it seems more akin to a response to a nerve-carried impulse within a single individual than one involving two quite separate and recognizable characters separated by space" (ibid., pp. 173–75). Disregard of the suggestibility and empathic relations which let two or more animals participate in one obviously holistic act has led many excellent naturalists to apply anthropomorphic concepts to their behavior.

Animals never order each other around, because without language they cannot communicate a demand or any idea of something they wish to have done or not done. This holds as much for mammals as for insects. The frequent statements found in popular writings (and all too often in learned ones) that birds and beasts send others on missions, assign tasks to them, or forbid their taking or doing something without physically preventing them are all fabled.

A team of psychologists staged an interesting experiment with rhesus monkeys to find out whether a dominant animal, put into a position in which it could not obtain food except by coercing its subordinate cage-mate to operate the apparatus that yielded the usual pellets, would learn to use its dominance to that end. At first, pellets were released only when the subordinate monkey turned the handle, so the other one could obtain food only by snatching it before its cage-mate had a chance; when it had learned to do so, its partner was fed, and returned to the cage without any hunger incentive to operate the machine. The experimenters say, as the essential part of their findings: "The dominant monkeys failed to demonstrate, during three successive presentations, that their prior training taught them anything concerning the function of their partners. This suggests a similar interpretation of the processes involved in primate observation learning and communication.... Thus we think the monkeys learned a chain, not a concept, when coercive actions were obtained, and that the effectiveness of shaping [teaching the dominant monkey, one step at a time, to simulate the hypothesized response], when required, is in keeping with this view" (Horel, Treichler and Meyer 1963, p. 210).

One obvious explanation of the failure of animals to give any commands is, of course, that they have no words to convey instructions or proposals. But this may be too simple a solution. There are, today, several chimpanzees which have acquired a considerable vocabulary in the standard American Sign Language (ASL) used by the deaf. The two psychologists, R. A. and B. T. Gardner, who trained the first of these animals, Washoe, to use words in that language knew from earlier records that vocal expression in apes is limited and ejaculatory, and auditory stimuli not readily noticed, let alone distinguished, while arm and hand movements are quickly made and elaborated. They had the excellent judgment to exploit the native talents of their subject, by teaching her speech in a mode that was natural to her. Despite her extreme youth (she was still an infant, wild caught, not more than fourteen months old and perhaps a good deal younger when brought to the laboratory) she learned easily to imitate gestures. To associate them with objects was a harder task, but was gradually mastered, so that today she has command of about a hundred and fifty linguistic items.

Her training was one of the greatest experiments ever made on the psychology of language. It has revealed unexpected aspects of language which will come under discussion in a later chapter of this book. For our present purpose, however, it has shown above all where the true line between animal interaction—both emotional and pragmatic—and genuine communication lies. In their report, the Gardners wrote: "We wanted Washoe not only to ask for objects but to answer questions about them and also to ask us questions. We wanted to develop behavior that could be described as conversation" (1969, p. 665). This, however, seems to lie beyond the frontiers of animal mentality, and from this outermost edge one can look back and see that all her acts, even those that look most like human acts of conception, may be understood in non-human terms. The most intriguing of these is her spontaneous naming of objects she saw but apparently did not want, such as a mug full of toothbrushes.

One is immediately reminded, of course, of the famous passage in the autobiography of Helen Keller, in which one rare human being who could recall her first recognition of a word as a symbol, not a means to get something or a move in a game, described that sudden, world-opening experience. But here is just where we stumble brusquely on the difference between Washoe and the speechless human child. The world of speech and conceptual thought did not open for the chimpanzee. She subsequently used other words in the same spontaneous way, but I cannot see any convincing evidence that there was, as the Gardners claimed, "no obvious motive other than communication"; no indication that she would not have made a gesture at the sight of the toothbrushes if she had been alone. Object and gesture were closely associated for her in a non-symbolic learned response, chiefly to the sight of the object and the stimulus ASL words: "What is this?" Later the sight alone could elicit the spontaneous completion of her part in a game she usually played with human companions. It would be wonderful to know whether Washoe, if housed with a naive simian companion of appropriate age, would try it on that playfellow, and whether any part of her repertoire would be passed on.

In all her contact with people who speak to her in sign language, this ape (so far as I know) has never asked a question or made a comment, i.e., a remark about anything. Besides immediate demands and protest, all her verbal behavior is naming directly perceived things, or sometimes—rarely—missing counterparts of them. Conversation has no sources in her word-stocked brain; as Goethe said, "Wörter machen nicht Worte."

To take up every kind of ethological misconception and propose a more instinctual and zoological interpretation of the behavioral acts to which it is believed to apply would make this chapter a book. The purpose of the samples I have offered here is to show how very high the development of instinctive life can be, how far and how variously it can expand before the pressure of felt impulse and the impact of perception becomes too great to let the most advanced organisms advance any further without breaking the framework of their mental functions. So far, all treatments of instinct have aimed chiefly at depreciating its functions and proving that "clever" animals have concepts, see causal relations, and make plans of purposive action. Without a more solid theory of instinct than that, one cannot appreciate what must have happened at that critical line which the human stock has crossed, and the highest other animals have not. Also, without a real appreciation of animal mentality we cannot discover and understand the functioning of instinct in human life, confused and masked as it is by conception and the communicative power and peril of language.

16 / *The Specialization of Man*

The phenomenon of mind, arising in just one primate stock, is such a tremendous novelty in animal evolution that it could not have occurred without a peculiar prehistory of coincidences, leading up to special developments in the organism that produced it. The shift from animal to human mentality is so radical that any serious philosopher, analyzing those two types of cerebral activity in their respective highest forms, i.e., animal intelligence and human understanding, is apt to balk intuitively at theories deriving the latter by simple steps from the mental activities of other primates which show analogous behavior in some respects. The growth and elaboration of feeling in man which culminated in the making of mind must have been a story with many beginnings and long, obscure preparations; a story one cannot hope to tell in a brief fashion, because it involves too many facets of evolution. No single principle, however great (for instance, differential survival, adaptation), is likely to explain the rise of language and thought in one primate line, the Hominidae, which involves the whole nature of that line itself, before and above the pressions and opportunities it encountered to form its destiny.

There is an interesting theory regarding the unique character of the human genus, according to which man owes his versatility and adaptability to the fact that he has undergone no specialization. This thesis, which seems to have been original with Louis Bolk, was independently proposed at almost the same time by Otto H. Schindewolf, and subsequently developed by Arnold Gehlen in *Der Mensch: Seine Natur und seine Stellung in der Welt*, which has enjoyed a wide popularity with the general intellectual public in Europe. Gehlen's book builds up a picture of man as a helpless, unadapted creature without any natural defenses, who had to develop his brain power in order to survive. This he was able to do precisely because he was unspecialized; all his potentialities were still at his disposal (1950, p. 109). The very lack of specialization had an obverse side, namely, that this creature, so lacking in physical adaptation, still had all the potentialities which other animals lost when they realized one set of them to the exclusion of others. His inadequate physique expresses his supreme advantage as well as his disadvantages, for in his adulthood he still has the receptive, malleable character of a child, open to environmental and social influences; his form is pedomorphic, possessing permanent fetal traits.

There are several important ideas in that book to which I can give unqualified acceptance, and we shall come back to them in due time. But many other statements and basic notions in it are downright impossible, especially the conception of man as unadapted to the natural world, physically inadequate, defenseless, i.e., originally a creature of wants and deficits. No organism can be unadapted *ab initio* to its surroundings, or it could not have evolved there; and had one been wafted from some other sphere into this unfriendly world, no pressure of need could have caused it to develop a saving brain in time to meet the crisis. Like millions of animals it would have been summarily extinguished.

Yet extended pedomorphy may sometimes have been an evolutionary factor, if the immature form had some advantage for the individual which was destined to lose that asset at maturity. But that is not the same as keeping the infantile state of great potentiality, which Gehlen considers man's highest advantage; for permanently unrealized potentialities are not assets to an individual. Pedomorphy can only be maintained if the creature in its youthful phase can already cope with all the vicissitudes of its environment and, moreover, can support the great physiological disharmony known as "neoteny," the growth of its sex organs to maturity while the rest of the body remains juvenile. If such conditions occurred, the species could settle for life in its most favorable state and ambient, and in the course of millennia prove ancestral to a higher species, genus or even family, i.e., to organisms which can negotiate a greater ambient by virtue of more complex bodily mechanisms and behavioral acts.

The theory of neoteny as a possible condition for evolutionary advance was originally propounded by Walter Garstang. The crux of Garstang's thought is that adaptation is not solely an adult process, but that every stage from the egg onward has to be adapted to its ambient to perform its essential functions. In many low marine animals, which are sessile like plants, there is a need to disperse their progeny, as there is in plants. Many such permanently anchored adult animals and also benthonic, bottom-creeping ones, in their youthful, larval phases were free-swimming, drifting as plankton, sometimes also self-propelled by cilia or flagella. Their larval business was to disperse their species as widely as possible, while their structure gave them freedom and mobility, until its advancing change of phase would pull them down to the safer, restrictive life of the sea bottom. But it may happen in organic development, which depends upon hormones controlled by vast, shifting complexes of genes, that general somatic development and sexual development do not keep step with one another in the normal fashion, so procreation may occur before the organism has realized its standard adult shape. By neotenic sexual functioning in the free-swimming state the bottom-living phase would come after the procreative, and ultimately be eliminated altogether. In this way some stocks might evolve into free and active creatures which only inquisitive scientists would ever think of tracing to their humble benthonic forms.

In A. C. Hardy's summary of Garstang's work, he says, "There is one group of the Tunicata, the Larvacea, which has every appearance of having done just what Garstang supposed the ancestors of the vertebrates to have done; they are pelagic adult forms and there can be . . . little doubt that they are in fact permanently neotenous one time larval forms now specialized for their particular mode of life" (Introduction to Garstang 1962, pp. 9–10). The significance of the hypothetical prolonged pedomorphy of the parent type lies not in its continued potentiality without specialization, but in the chance that neotenic development may give rise to a new and different specialization.

The striking pedomorphic features of man which Gehlen interprets as signs of a neotenic organism may have had other origins than arrest at an infantile stage of primate ontogeny, and be a deceptive appearance produced by very different means. But, although his concept of the helpless creature which had to develop a supreme brain in order to survive may be biologically impossible, the supreme brain is certainly real, and is both anatomically and functionally as genuine a specialized organ as the elephant's trunk or the bee's honeysack. Its extraordinary development, moreover, has been implemented by other specializations.

Every animal makes use of its bodily assets, such as the structure or placement of its eyes that may make them particularly fit for distance vision, as in hawks, night vision, as in nocturnal hunters, water-surface vision, panoramic vision or whatever other kind. Its life habits are determined by its developed talents, chosen by phylogenetic chance and coincidence from its potentialities; and in the struggle for development many possible advantages also go by the board.

The potentialities, however, include behavioral acts as well as trophic and physiological ones; and in the advance of evolution, facultative behavior becomes more and more important in the lives of animals. Where physical endowment is really rather poor, it is often made to suffice, or even put to new uses beyond the obvious old ones, by specialized yet unpremeditated and even unconscious instinctive responses. One of the behavioral devices to which some animals of widely separate classes resort to attain greater accuracy of vision than their laterally placed eyes can negotiate by looking directly at an object is to scan the presented scene by moving their heads as much as the structure of the neck permits, in that way gathering a complex impression in which the forms that interest them are passed across the retina or even from one eye to the other; something like an image of a static object may be made in that process. The physiological condition which invites this substitute for binocular focusing is that immediately successive visual impressions fuse subjectively, as we all know from the moving picture illusion. Perhaps that is why lizards of various sorts, some short-necked sea birds, as, for instance, the Atlantic murre, and at least one large mammal with small, widely spaced eyes, the rhinoceros, all share the habit of standing still and nodding their heads when confronted with another being, as if they sought to improve their sight of it. In most birds, the ability to rotate the head is highly developed, and several species have been observed to turn their heads from side to side so they fixate a target alternately with one eye and then the other before they react to the object by approach or flight. Specialization, far from always limiting a creature to one possible way of life, may invite further developments by realizing more complex impulses as a basis for such advance.

An evolutionary course, being a long-term tendency growing with successive generations, requires some constant ambient conditions to let it proceed; and conversely, just about every possible age-long repetitious situation has been exploited by animals which could specialize in its opportunities, so it is reflected in biological shape, physiology or behavior somewhere. That is the explanation not only of the oddities which occur in nature, the variety of forms and activities, but also of the amazing convergences in organisms of entirely different sorts, such as in the shark, a primitive fish, ichthyosaur, a reptile, and dolphin, a mammal. It brings home forcibly the vastness of the pool of unexpressed genes in every stock, ready to take advantage of any new opportunity given by changes in external conditions and in physiological patterns which reach a new integration or, just as often, a new separate elaboration. Learning in animals, states of being "conditioned" or trained, as well as discovering foods or techniques of living in the natural course of maturation, are all expressions of inherited poten-

Figure 16–1. (*Left*) coral; (*right*) sponge. (Photo by Philip A. Biscuti.)

tiality finding usual or unusual opportunities for enactment. The unrealized potentialities of an organism are existent biochemical structures which, however, are currently or permanently quiescent. Most of these structures, though perhaps not all, lie in the chromosomes, i.e., they are genes; and as any action of a gene requires a distinctive chemical situation to elicit it, organisms always contain vast numbers of inactive genes, many of which may never encounter the conditions that would activate them. The odd results one may get from putting animals, and even excised parts of animals, into abnormal conditions shows the enormous range of potential responses which normally do not occur.

Very different organisms may make similar adaptation to an ambient requiring specialized modes of living; that is spectacularly evident in the convergent forms of fast-swimming fish, reptiles and marine mammals, mentioned above. Sessile animals of unrelated sorts, too, show similar environmental influences by similarities of their gross shapes; an example is two colonial organisms which are even of different phyla, one a coral and the other a sponge, where the same water action is reflected in their respective forms (Fig. 16–1). More complex approximations to a general pattern often result, too, from influences having nothing to do with each other, because the vital impulses of organisms tend to come to the same expression. Radial symmetry, axial symmetry, spiral and annular structure, fibrous and tubular and fan-shaped growth, division, lamination, etc., are basic principles of organic form which operate under so many kinds of stimulation and restriction that they may appear in the most distantly related organisms developing in the most diverse situations. Wherever an opening for trophic activity is given there seems to be a living stock to capitalize on it. Prehensile tails have developed in many kinds of monkey, but not in all kinds; in the common opossum, *Didelphis marsupialis*, and several related species, but not all; in the true chameleons, *Chamaeleo* spp. and three or four lesser genera; in a fish, *Hippocampus*, the sea horse. Any animal having such an appendage naturally puts it to use, but species which can grasp and hold with that added member have not displaced related ones that are caudally underprivileged. There are so many alternative ways of living that no asset seems to be indispensable until it has become so by being exploited. Only then, mainly within the species, differential survival sets in and promotes phylogenetic development of the trait. The distribution of unsuspected genic capacities brought to light in this way is often surprising.

The intimate connections between animal forms and the conditions under which they develop are further shown by the way many traits arise again and again within a phylogeny, apparently independently, after the divergence of species, genera, families or even classes, though with a common path of preparation which may be devious and obscure. Some potentialities find repeated opportunities to come to expression in the life of a stock, with long terms of reduction or total repression between. An instance of such reappearance may be seen in the history of those birds which today are swift runners with wings unfit for flight, like ostriches and emus; while they seem to "recapitulate" the primitive condition of birds just departing from the ancestral reptilian form, ornithologists are fairly well convinced that they have evolved to and through the flying stage and secondarily lost that form of locomotion when ambient conditions encouraged a re-development of powerful running legs. The ancient genes that developed the bipedal stance and running power of pre-avian reptiles may be actively engaged again, but in a total organism so transformed that they function in another context and with another history than they did millions of years ago. Produced under such different circumstances, the old and the new phenotypes are really convergent rather than identical.

A specialization that may be put to a particular use requires several conditions for its development: an initial tendency from which it can arise, an inductive influence, or a succession of such influences, during its ontogeny, and an ambient into which it automatically fits as an asset to its possessor. The first of these requirements has its chance of fulfillment in the enormous potential hidden in every hereditary gene pool. The second, the presence of an inductive embryonic milieu, constantly though perhaps variously operative, is the most fortuitous condition, and the fact that it is ever met at all rests on two general aspects of acts *per se*, which have already been mentioned: that every articulated structure in an organism tends to take on any function which it can perform, however transiently, and that this activity gives it what looks like a protected path of development in the competitive struggle of cell aggregates for continued existence. The first of these two characteristics is a corollary to the principle that an organism, or even a living part of one, always does everything it can; the second, to a less certain, but more and more generally apparent physiological fact, that the regular performance of an organic function has a trophic influence on the performing structure. This encouragement may also spring from heightened action of associated tissues, so that any unit that is drawn into a larger functional assembly tends to hold its own in the ontological competition and also to develop the complex of activities around it. It protects itself, and needs no preferential treatment because of future teleological value.

Specialization is one of the cardinal principles of evolution; its expressions are immensely various, for it really governs the whole process of adaptation. Organisms which tend to evolve with the changes of environmental conditions and widen their ambients as they do so are adaptable, specializing rapidly in many small ways to meet and exploit new opportunities, sometimes putting their old specialties to new uses by behavioral tricks for thousands of generations until encouraged mutation and differential survival motivate long-dormant potentialities to develop.

There are different types of specialization; some of them do, indeed, fit the animal particularly for one sort of life and preclude all others. Moles can live only in fairly soft, rich earth, where earthworms and cutworms occur, and a mole's feet can dig tunnels. Their underground life, already close to extinguishing their powers of vision, offers little scope for behavioral advance or a widening ambient; exaggeration of digging and nosing, and perhaps some specialization of food-seizing organs, seem to be the main evolutionary records of the species. Yet by the measure of survival and continuance, moles are a successful kind, because the conditions they can meet are simple, and common the world over. The same is true of a much more interesting and versatile animal, the beaver, almost as specialized as the mole for one particular way of life; in the beaver it is not only paws, tail and other fairly plastic parts that are modified to fit his ambient, but that most honored badge of zoological order, the dentition. Specializations, in short, may be extreme, yet not lead to any foreseeable extinction or, as in the oyster, stagnation, a dead end of evolution.

The notion that all specialization must lead to fixation in a narrow ambient or to over-growth of special features—horns, tusks, scales—finally making the species unviable seems to me to rest on an overly simple concept of biological adaptation. There are several kinds of specialization, notably adaptation to special conditions, which may lead to the evolutionary stagnation of many marine organisms, the same today as in the Cretaceous; and, by contrast, specialization by progressive refinement of an organ, appendage or talent. This latter kind is seen in the cat's mouth, where the conjoint aim of the canines is coupled with nervous developments that lead to great sensitivity in "mouthing"— using teeth and tongue, without mutual interference, for carrying, grooming, selecting and manipulating quite apart from grabbing or fighting. This sort of specialization, far from limiting the agent's individual powers of adjustment, increases them, and may even lead to a point where new functions are induced and new physical developments encouraged, as in man. The elephant's trunk is surely a specialty derived from the trophic possibilities of the elongated and somewhat movable nose that is found today in the tapir, the hyrax and the anteaters; but far from condemning the animal to a small ecological "niche," it has allowed his great increase in numbers, in size and in animal intelligence, i.e., capacity to realize his instinctive impulses. The happy condition that supported these advances was that the specialization took place in a highly important sense organ, the nose, which implements two primary senses in most animals, smell and touch; by making this organ a prehensile effector as well as a double receptor, the development of the elephant's nose into a trunk has given him an asset surpassed only by the human hand.

Behavioral acts are, of course, more variable than acts of growth and form, and can change more radically in a short time. So, because of their freedom to take advantage of any constellation in ambient events, there are more convergences in hereditary behavior, sometimes so odd that they seem utterly accidental, as when Paul Leyhausen observes that a wildcat's technique of manipulating its prey is perfected in the maned wolf, *Chrysocyon brachyurus* (1965, p. 419); or when E. A. Armstrong, in his monograph *The Wren*, compares in detail the courtship antics of that bird to those of the three-spined stickleback. K. S. Norris and J. H. Prescott report (1961, p. 322) that the Pacific dolphin, *Tursiops gilli*, slaps his flukes on the surface of the water as a beaver slaps its tail (which, of course, has been interpreted in both cases as a warning of danger, but does not bear the interpretation very well), and D. K. Caldwell tells the same story of *Stenella plagiodon*, the spotted dolphin (1955, p. 469). The flat appendage and the ability to leap out of the water seem to be all it takes to provide a noise-making talent which is duly exploited wherever it exists.

Some special traits, behavioral or anatomic, found in very distantly related animals are, however, probably not convergent developments, but similar potentialities at different stages of realization. Any highly specialized form or function characterizing a species or a larger taxon is likely to have rudimentary analogues in other creatures, which may represent quite remote hereditary lines. It is surprising, to say the least, that physiologists have found a striking similarity between the digestive systems of many ungulates specialized for rumination and those of langur monkeys, which, oddly enough, show no behavioral adaptation, such as regurgitating and rechewing, to that peculiar organ. The same sort of analogy between highly developed forms in one or a few species and rudimentary forms of the same traits in others holds for behavior as it does for bodily shapes and mechanisms. The incubators built by the mallee fowl of Australia are the result of a fantastically elaborated behavior pattern; but a similar impulse seems to be in the repertoire of the Egyptian plover, which makes some moves to utilize the heat of the sun in similar fashion, though it has developed nothing like the techniques of *Megapodius*.

Examples could be almost endlessly multiplied, demonstrating the wide range of potentialities which come to fruition only under peculiar circumstances in a few animal stocks. The point of the whole discussion is that vast possibilities are handed down from unimaginable antiquity, to be brought to light by coincidences of organic and ambient conditions. Almost anything can happen in the course of time, on no other basis than the inherent growth of acts in competition with each other, and the opportunities created by the flow of ever-changing situations—even the emergence of mind in animal evolution. Man seems to carry no more genes than countless other beings on earth, even plants, but the particular turn his development has taken has shifted his mental functions into a new dimension, which makes it hard to believe that in his advance he carries some rudimentary abilities which have more admirable parallels in lower animals. There is probably no reason for regarding them as "vestiges"; they may have had a greater day, but are more likely to be unrealized potentialities.

Man is probably as full of unrealized potentialities as the lower creatures. And just as we carry rudimentary organs and functions which other stocks have exploited, our own assets have analogues—sometimes well-developed ones—in other forms of life, not always obviously related, i.e., not necessarily primates. The grasping reflex in the toes of human infants is found in the feet of fledgling cuckoos, as well as in those of monkeys; but it is only in the latter that the analogy has been noted, because there it supports an established view of our evolution, the quite unshakable assumption that man was once as arboreal as most monkeys and apes are today, and owes his chest expansion to a period of gibbon-like brachiation. But some recent paleological finds call the doctrine of a long, wholly arboreal phase of his prehistory in question.

The discovery of *Australopithecus*, which S. L. Washburn aptly described as "an animal with a human ilium and an ape's head" (1950, p. 68), led to a renewed study, both speculative and empirically demonstrative and in both respects exciting, of the gradual evolution of the human skull. Between the snouted heads of apes and the domed crania and rounded, reduced jaws of modern man, the skulls of extinct hominids show almost every transitional stage. But we have no fossil evidence for the supposed back-mutation of the pongid hind foot to the human, plantar extremity; we have no prehensile proto-human foot. The nearest simian foot is the gorilla's; but that is chiefly a basic, phyletic likeness, not a physiological one, for despite the large hallux and sole of the gorilla, the weight of its body is not borne near the inner edge of the foot from heel to big toe, but along a more central line terminating in the gap between the opposable hallux and the other toes. The ball of the foot consequently gives no leverage to throw the weight forward, but the animal's balance shifts mainly sideways from foot to foot and allows only a flat-footed, waddling advance.

Naturally the question has often enough been raised how the hominids came by their upright stance and especially their stride, with straight legs, on the soles of their hind feet. Various theories have been offered, but they all seem too casual and trivial as explanations of such a momentous characteristic. The latest of these proposals, known as the "food-carrying" hypothesis, is inspired by the acts of Japanese monkeys which have learned (supposedly without suggestion from men) how to walk on two feet while carrying trays, even entering the water to wash the sand out of the scattered grain they have scooped up. But there is no evidence that this new use of legs and hands (for their paws are really four prehensile hands) has affected their mode of walking apart from the grain-washing act. It seems highly plausible that the main reason why upright walking does not become the common habit of locomotion in these animals which are capable of it is that their feet are not preadapted for it; they are walking on hands, which is not an easy mode of progression even when the hands are in the right anatomical place for footing it.

The fact that, so far, we have found no evolutionary halfway station between the simian and the human foot nor, for that matter, between their respective associated leg and hip structures indicates that this anatomical specialization of the Hominidae goes farther back in prehistory than our fossil record; and as the upright posture may have played a large part in the spectacular brain development which followed its achievement, and certainly in the human use of the hand, it has very probably been the decisive change that precipitated the divergence of our ancestral stock from the rest of the incipient Hominidae, as several Evolutionists hold today. A mammal walking habitually on straight hind legs is certainly an anomaly; so much so that to reason from its obvious relatedness with the pongids to its own derivation from typical early pongids, already specialized for locomotion through the treetops, may be reasoning from shaky premises.

If the human foot has really undergone a reversion from the prehensile simian foot back to the older, common cursorial form, that change must have taken place with extraordinary speed, between the development of the manus-like hind paw of the apes and the time of the bipedal man-apes with their human extremities. We are so convinced of an arboreal phase in prehuman life that it is regarded as axiomatic. Yet to take such a former way of life in our phylogenetic past simply for granted on the basis of our anatomically obvious relation to the apes may not be a perfectly safe backward extrapolation. Despite all skeletal similarities, mankind may have had its own behavioral specialties from an early stage of the primate radiation; for instance, the hominids might never have been entirely arboreal, yet excellent climbers, that lived in dense coverts under the trees but fed largely above, in the branches (they might even have been driven or held to that way of life by the ancestors of today's pongids, if those animals had taken to the treetops even as branching trees developed, and had made a faster and fuller adaptation to the uplifted feeding grounds in which they finally lived). Much climbing, but still sleeping and freely moving on the forest floor would have induced the slightly deviant development of man's foot, the flexible toes and flattened nails, not by back-mutation from prehensile monkey feet, but by ordinary progressive evolution from an older still cursorial type in which the metatarsal of the hallux lay parallel, as yet, to the other four. Our primate foot might simply never have gone as far in its modification as the ape's.

The human hand and arm, however, show the typical anthropoid form, specialized for climbing and reaching, clinging and swinging, catching, holding, perhaps even brachiating, so there apparently has been some arboreal adaptation in our pre-history. Why, then, should our single primate line have remained terrestrial, and become bipedal instead of four-handed?

One important condition favoring this odd development may have been the wide range of the early hominids' diet. Monkeys and apes are mainly herbivorous and fructivorous, living on leaves, fruits and young shoots (though many will occasionally kill and eat other warm-blooded animals, and possibly all eat some insects). With the spread of forest trees they would seek their food more and more aloft, if their stock derived from an archaic progenitor capable of climbing. The Hominidae, on the other hand, may always have been partly carnivorous, and have hunted as well as harvested from day to day. Those animals which had effectually abandoned the terrestrial milieu and lived aloft went on evolving prehensile feet, for there was no fixed ground to negotiate. So it may be that the greater evolutionary change took place in the apes and monkeys, paradoxically leaving the hominids, which actually underwent less of a mutation, as the more specialized in posture and locomotion.

The next question that arises is, then, whether the upright posture has played a crucial part in the evolution of the "large-brained, small-faced bipeds" of today from some ape-headed bipeds like those of the African early Pleistocene (if not those very ones), and if it did, what was its role. The answers are not simple and, being speculative, not really scientifically confirmable. But some which have been offered are convincingly reasonable. The thinning of the cranial bones and their tendency to expand upward into a domed calvarium occurs for obvious mechanical reasons in the gibbon, which is usually hanging by its front paws. The gibbon has a very small face and rounded skull, but the muscular development in its arms and shoulders, which is required and enhanced by its brachiating form of locomotion, exerts great pressure on the cranium at the areas of muscle insertion and militates against the enlargement or changes of form of the brain cavity. This ape is usually vertical but not standing up. When he walks he generally holds his arms in their normal position above his head so that even when he is erect the head is still sunk between his shoulders. His usual walk is along a branch, where his prehensile toes come into play. When he is suspended his hind legs hang loose, the knees are somewhat flexed and the feet used mainly as hands, i.e., for reaching, holding and gathering things. In sharp contrast, the upright posture of man is a stretch against gravity, from his feet—especially the halluces and their metatarsals, bound to those of the other toes —through the straight knees and hips and continuing in the same direction up the spine to the atlas, on which the head is balanced.

This balance of man's head on the supporting (not only anchoring) vertical spine is probably the main source of its human modification; for it made the powerful neck and jaw muscles of animals with front-heavy, snouted skulls unnecessary, as it also obviated the thickness of the simian calvarium, the adult gorilla's bony crest, the heavy brow ridges of all apes and early men.

E. L. Du Brul and D. M. Laskin, in a theoretical and experimental study, demonstrated quite convincingly how a skull borne on a vertical spine would be influenced by evolutionary forces, and even mechanical ones operating during each normal life, to be "rolled in" upon its axis, and to expand at the top and converge round its support so the *foramen magnum* would tend to shift toward the fulcral point between the chin and the occiput. All the ancient structures, the limbic lobes and sensory relays, in the human head are crowded into the bottom of the skull around the rearing brain stem, instead of being deployed freely on its horizontal dorsal surface. Du Brul and Laskin also showed, by experimental interference with the cartilaginous base from which the embryonic skull starts, what effects were achieved in animals by ablation of one of the two synchondroses, i.e., the spheno-occipital and spheno-presphenoid, which form the crux of that base. The more anterior synchondrosis, i.e., the spheno-presphenoid, was the target of their operations, and the results varied, presumably, with the relative completeness of its removal in their many rats.

One of the notable features in the distortion made by the removal of the spheno-presphenoid synchondrosis (which, in the rat, involves a series of cartilage plates) is its effect on the base of the skull, which becomes extremely short and concave, and forms a deep hollow ending in a raised rim at the spheno-occipital fusion. "The back of this hollow," the authors observe, "houses the hypophysis (reminiscent of the hypophyseal hollow in primates). The plane of the basiocciput then bends sharply down to simulate a clivus as in man." The loss of basal cartilage, then, hampers the normal expansion of the skull. "However, as the brain still grows a bit, it must bulge out at the cranial roof" (1961, p. 121).

The "fetalization" of the skull of a long-headed animal may thus be produced by artificial means; and what a relatively simple ablation of a controlling factor such as a basal synchondrosis may effect could also be the work of a gene. Indeed, two other experimenters, J. A. Dye and F. S. Kinder, working more than a quarter of a century earlier on endocrine influences on development, (1934) had produced almost exactly the same modification of skull shape in young puppies by ablation of the thyroid gland. Thyroid formation and action are under gene control. Thyroidectomy in dogs three weeks old effected a shortening and incurvature of the base of the skull, essentially like the distortion more recently achieved by Du Brul and Laskin through excision of the anterior synchondrosis in infant rats.

Du Brul and Laskin (ibid., p. 124) remarked that a similar shortening and bulging of the cranium occurs in calves deformed by the expression of the "short-spine" gene carried by some cattle, which is lethal to the phenotypical offspring after a brief postnatal existence.

To a calf, that grotesque genic deviation is fatal, but in another animal a very similar influence may be perfectly tolerable; some comparable gene, though perhaps quite different in its other actions, evidently proved viable in the phylogeny of the ocean sunfish, *Mola mola*, for it is normal in its heredity today. The entire growth in that species is in harmony with the short spine and huge, shortened head, and the fish occurs in no other form. Perhaps a gradual increase of this trophic expression was possible because the deep body form was already present, as it is in the boxfishes and trunkfishes to which *Mola* is related, so the exaggeration could be accommodated by the rest of the genome. As a rare occurrence in a generally elongated animal such a disharmonious gene produces a monster.

The bipedal bearing of man must have met with many fortunate conditions to permit and uphold the ever-increasing difference between his progeny and that of any other hominoid, instead of initiating a hereditary line of apes with an anomalous bodily form which shortly would make them unviable. Every further development that was induced by the extraordinary posture apparently was at least tolerable by the organism, and, in fact, tended to promote the most important result of the adaptive change in the skull, which was only just launched in the australopithecene man-apes: the specialization of the brain. That specialization is often regarded as primarily an increase in the weight of the brain; such increase it surely entailed, but actually, I think, the crucial next adaptation was a more subtle, yet more radical one—the gradual reorganization of its many substructures, and some consequent changes in the relative rates of advance and elaboration of their respective functions. With the crowding of the limbic parts into the lower spaces around the brain stem their trophic potentialities became rather severely restricted; and as every organic structure is in competition with its neighbors, the repression of their growth gave proportionately great opportunity to the unobstructed neopallium to expand and differentiate. Elaborations of the neuropile in the opercular lobes appear to have spread outward during phylogeny and occupied the cortex as they developed; for, in reptiles and perhaps some higher classes, the cortex is still essentially a protective, mainly lipoid covering, but just such a tissue as reaching and expanding axons could easily invade. That is undoubtedly the way the cortex in typical placental mammals has become an integral part of the highest cerebral areas.

In man, where the operculum is particularly favored by anatomical conditions, its cortex seems to have taken the lead in the evolution of his entire central nervous system. The latest-developed mechanisms in a living being are, as E. B. Titchener observed, the most active, and in the nervous tissues where electrical and chemical processes are normally of highest intensity they are most ready to attain psychical levels. This leads to a great refinement and quickening of every sort of feeling, peripheral and central, i.e., receptive, somatic, emotive, or of nameless other kinds; and it is in this advance that further changes, facilitated or even motivated by the erect carriage, have fallen in with the paramount change, to support it on its evolutionary course. The most obvious of those auxiliary assets was the freeing of the hands from any involvement with locomotion or bodily support, such as walking on knuckles like the great apes, or clinging to branches while moving or at rest in the trees. The manipulative ability of the human hand has usually been attributed to its long and fully opposable thumb; in fact, that superior, flexible thumb has often been praised as a direct cause of man's ascendancy over all other animals, but Thomas Barbour stated that there is a frog, *Pseudis*, which has a fully opposable pollex and is thought to make use of it, too, grasping stems, without becoming an intellectual superfrog. The gene complex which produces the hand-like front foot of *Pseudis* does not coincide with an otherwise ready genome to incorporate the manual talent for further ends. Even in much higher animals, the monkeys and apes that have true thumbs, it has not met with all the conditions that would make it a major asset for humanization, although the manipulative skill of some simians is close to that of an untrained human being, and would probably improve if the animal found more uses for it. If an ape could envisage a shelter, a garment or a receptacle it could probably make one; but even under pressure of discomfort, chimpanzees—generally deemed the most "educable" of the pongids—never think of thickening the protective foliage over their heads to make a roof.

What will be an auxiliary advantage to a particular development depends on many coincidences as well as on the fundamental anlagen of an animal stock. The foremost condition for making an animal's paw become a hand was, of course, the fact that it was a primate paw, with a tendency to lengthening phalanges and supple joints (the same suppleness is found in cats' paws, where it does not meet with extraordinary phalangeal growth or any incipient independence of the pollex to make them prehensile).

The greatest role of the hand in our evolution is probably due not so much to its manipulative power as to its gradual specialization as a sense organ. The sensibility of the hand is not only high, but epicritical beyond any animal's tactual sense, except possibly that of the elephant's trunk, which has never, to my knowledge, been really tested, but only estimated and praised. The responsiveness of many creatures' vibrissae is quick, but apparently not epicritical; it seems to indicate contact without further perceptual details. But the human hand is a complex organ in which the distribution of sensory nerves and the extremely refined musculature coincide, as they do in our eyes and ears, to implement perception of form, location, size, weight, penetrability, mobility and many consequent values. Its measured movements and the coordinate orientation of its parts, which permit fingering of objects, make it capable of judging the qualities of surfaces—rough, smooth, varied, patterned—and their characteristic ways of absorbing or reflecting heat, which give us information of temperature contrasts and gradients. The two hands working together can negotiate a single complex impression, as J. J. Gibson has remarked (1962, p. 481). Also, all the sensory reactions of the skin and underlying structures are engaged together in the tactual perception of substances: feelings of pressure and release of pressure, of warm and cold impingements, pin-pointed encounters with resistance, oiliness, wetness, and mixtures like sliminess, hairiness, stickiness. The result is that we have not only a report of surface and edges, but of volume imbued with multimodal, often nameless qualities.

There have been few studies of the tactual sense (or better, senses), and Gibson, in the article mentioned above, suggests as the likeliest reason that it was difficult to range this mode of sensibility with the other distinct modes which have their circumscribed special organs. The two earlier psychologists who did give it due attention, David Katz (1925) and Géza Révész (1944), were led to it largely through their studies of perception by blind persons, in whom the tactual mode is, of course, most highly developed. Katz, in consequence, centered his interest largely on the detection of form for purposes of practical judgment, identification and comparison of objects, and such general information as seeing persons usually gather by vision. Révész, writing some fifteen years later and having Katz's work to draw upon, came to the interesting realization that the world built up by tactual means, which Katz conceived as a world of tactual forms, was not filled with completely given or imagined forms, analogous to visual shapes, at all. Distances and directions, terrain and the location of things are its framework, but "things" are not simple sensuous presentations in any mode. They are functionally known and identified, often by a cursory touch, as by a glance; and although they are bearers of aesthetic qualities, they do not immediately present artistic values. Perhaps this lack of artistic significance made both Katz and Révész overlook the cultural importance of the aesthetic perceptiveness of the hand, and pass over it rather lightly, though it certainly has had its own unnoticed evolution: the reception of aesthetic qualities, purely tactual pleasure as of cool or warm waters, living grass, leaves and petals, fur or human hair, and, contrariwise, repellent impingements of crude, grimy or decayed matter, unhealthy skin, contacts which may invoke disgust and even downright horror. That seems to be a human response; apes will pick up the filthiest items. Aesthetic tactual values have importance for man because his experiences of them readily take on metaphorical significance; expressions for "hard," "soft," "liquid," "rough," etc., seem to have entered into his most peculiar achievement, speech, from their earliest uses to designate more than tactual qualities. Like all his aesthetic perceptions they meet and merge with emotional elements which are not current sexual, maternal or hostile feelings toward other beings, but modes of consciousness, felt attitudes, which motivate the earliest artistic expressions, dance and vocalization. But that is anticipating a theme of a later chapter.

Animals, meanwhile, derive direct emotional stimulation from touch, almost entirely from the touch of other creatures, which is a part of their actual involvement with each other. Such physical contact is found in the social insects. Maternal licking of the young is seen in most terrestrial mammals, and in gregarious ones such as wild dogs is carried over to mutual approach of adults in meeting. Where contact involves the use of front paws, as in the grooming activities of monkeys, apes and to some extent lemurs, it does not appear to further cutaneous aesthesis so much as manipulative control, largely implemented by vision. Physical intimacy is sought with many parts of the body; and though apes may reach out a hand to touch each other, it is the palm or the back of the hand, not the fingertips, that makes the contact.

The increase of perceptiveness in the hand of *Homo* is only a part and an instance of his high development in sensibility, especially in articulated, usable sensibility. What makes his peripheral receptions so usable is that most of his heightened nervous functions involve some centers in his forebrain, instead of going more simply through the lower centers of the spinal cord to issue in muscular responses. The cord, in man, is small compared to the brain, and many of its functions seem to have been crowded upward into the brain, just as some work of the human limbic lobes has been gradually taken over by the operculum and its hyperactive cortex, bringing the reflex actions under the control of consciousness and will. This crowding in the vertebral canal, too, looks like an effect of the upright posture, via the exaggeration of the double curvature which is incipient in most primates, but very conspicuous in man. Furthermore, the fact that in all the higher primates—monkeys, apes and men—the eyes are forward-directed is another chance asset for the enhancement of sensibility, for such eyes can be focused together on an object, and for near vision binocular focus certainly yields greater precision than any other method of fixating objects. Apes make full use of this talent; if they can't read, the trouble is not with their eyes. We share most of our blessings with many animals, but with none of them the whole complex that has led to humanization.

This most remarkable product of evolutionary coincidence, the human brain, is, however, not without its dangers. The cerebral activity threatens to overgrow the basic functional patterns of animal life and cause the species to break up on the insuperable heights of its own specialization. This brings us back to Gehlen, for the most notable theme of his book is the difference between man's mentality and that of any beast, however highly developed along animalian lines: the production and use of symbols and their paramount value in all our further mental functions, their distinction from the alleged "signals" of animal communication and from symptoms or other indicators, and the subjective-objective dialectic pattern that builds up "experience" of the human sort. Gehlen proposed that this unique character (which he would not admit to be a specialization) arose from the extreme receptiveness of the human brain, which consequently is overwhelmed with stimuli and overloaded with perceptions, so its possessor has had to lighten his burden by finishing many impulses not physically as direct responses, but in the brain, in mental acts. This is a defense against unbearable overstimulation. The eschewed behavioral consummation of a started impulse is replaced by the formation of an image in the visual system, especially in the cortical part, or by some comparable, purely sensory event; or perhaps by a momentary tensing of muscles and a fleeting fantasy of aggressive response, which stands in for the unperformed act.

But the overstimulation, having introduced a new activity, goes further in its effects than to take up the surplus of impressions; the new activity in its turn encourages the agent to observe things that play no direct part in his current business, just to make images of them, probably without knowing that he is doing so. This practice widens his ambient inestimably far beyond any other creature's.

Several psychologists and neurologists have arrived at the same hypothesis, apparently by independent approaches. The investigation of physiological processes underlying the covert acts of dreaming—producing entirely subjective, intraorganic perceptions, hallucinating situations and events—has led to the problem of what might motivate such deceptive experiences occurring in sleep, and suggested the theory that dreaming is a cerebral completion of acts which could not be overtly consummated. Ian Oswald has remarked that image formation is apt to occur spontaneously in moments of hesitation or frustration while facing a new task, and also that it bears some resemblance to the "displacement activities" frequently seen in hard-pressed animals (1962, p. 84); a "displacement activity" is a makeshift completion of a frustrated act which has got under way—however slightly—and vainly presses for normal consumption. It certainly is but a step from this concept of image production to the interpretation of our vivid, multitudinous dream images and fantasies as cerebral endings of started but blocked responses to excessive outer and inner stimuli. Another investigator took that step, and has written (in the currently fashionable computer jargon):

> the data-processing capacity of the central nervous system is insufficient to allow complete on line processing of input data with respect to its more remote implications, while at the same time carrying out the activity and decision making required by waking activity. In the absence of sleep, recorded unprocessed data would thus accumulate in sufficient amounts to interfere with the normal activity and decision making of the waking state, and this interference would be experienced as a need to sleep. (Shapiro 1967, p. 74)

In weighing this theory of vicarious completion of impulses which are constantly elicited by excessive sensory and central stimulation, one may wonder how so great a novelty as a fictitious image could emerge, even in the most specialized brain, without more broadly based functional preparation. The fact is, however, that the imaginative act is not unprepared, but that most if not all its elements are presented at lower levels of nervous activity. Other than human brains seem to be affected by stimuli of which only some terminate in efferent organs, while many serve to sensitize or, on the contrary, to lower the receptiveness of the brain, and change the "set" or "mood" of the responding organism rather than to elicit overt reactions. We cannot know what experimental animals perceive or otherwise feel, but in ourselves we can test many indirect effects of stimulations, sensuous yet centrally produced, as, for instance, a red after-image where no red stimulus object is given, but a green one was presented some seconds ago; a fully shaped negative image and its positive counterpart usually alternate on a white or grayish surface actually confronted, until both fade away. This alternation is a perceptible phase of a retinal activity. So far, the phenomenon still bespeaks a peripheral influence within a relatively short and easily measurable time span. But some persons tend to produce purely fictive original percepts, either involuntarily (as in dream) or by volition, which are followed by after-images, just as externally induced object visions are. This fact points to a cerebrally started neural activity involving the visual system and actually producing a retinal image, a real percept, though not of an external thing or scene. Such evidence certainly indicates a neural mechanism of visual imagination, and suggests its derivation from the common optic structures of primate brains.

The underlying unity of the central nervous organ, the brain, could be expected to carry the function of imagination into other sensory systems, too, and finally establish it apart from any special sense as a cortical faculty in its own right. Here it becomes the groundwork of symbolization, conception, and all other peculiarly human forms of cerebration; the evolution of mind is on its way.

17 / Symbols and the Evolution of Mind

> Der Gang des Geistes geht nicht gerade aus.
>
> W. Harburger

The Hominidae, whatever their beginnings may have been, have certainly undergone a tremendous specialization of the central nervous system which culminates in the forebrain, and above all the cortices of the cerebral hemispheres. To effect such a high, steady, ever-accelerating development requires constant activation, which may come from one major source or from a play of many influences that mount up to a round of stimulations. Both types of energizing support may be expected in such a reception center as the brain, which has its outposts in the special sense organs, open to chance excitations, and its own rhythmic processes furnishing periodic, if microscopic, stimuli.

The impingement of any act on another—most obviously, the impingement of peripheral acts, sensory receptions, on intraorganic acts, but also that of centrally motivated somatic or cerebral acts on each other and on peripheral ones—effects a change in the situation of the act impinged upon; and a change of situation is what motivates a new impulse. This may reinforce the original impulse to the affected act, facilitating and enhancing its expression, or it may alter, complicate or even block its development. Conversely, every change, such as an increase or acceleration of an activity, requires a change in some circumstantial condition. Several investigators have, in fact, discovered that processes which were deemed continuous are actually upheld by long series of separate stimulations. In order that separate, successive impulses may be similar enough to be repetitive and cumulative, there have to be other acts interspersed throughout the succession, or else a cadential phase of each response must occur to make space for each subsequent impulse in a series of renewals. A good example of the former alternative is the pattern of attentiveness which, according to D. O. Hebb, underlies the apparently steady perception of a simple shape, such as a solid-colored triangle on a contrasting homogeneous

background. In such a perceptual act, vision centers successively on the three differently oriented angles, a, b, and c. The gaze may go to and fro among them in varying order, so the dynamic pattern is something like a-b-a-c-b-c-a-c. "This 'ideational' series with its motor elements," says Dr. Hebb, "I propose to call a 'phase sequence.'" After a more detailed analysis of supposedly steady gazing, he concludes that "perception of a simple pattern is not a single lasting state, terminated by an external event, but a sequence of states or processes," and subsequently: "The stability of perception is not in a single persistent pattern but in the tendency of the phases of an irregular cycle to recur at short intervals. . . . the train of thought is also a 'phase sequence' of the same kind, but more extended, consisting of a series of phase cycles" (1949, pp. 97–100).

All sorts of quick, ignored impressions—including the well-known momentary alternations of foreground and background—intervene in constantly rebuilding the fixated shape, which emerges from their association. Hebb has designated that integral total shape by "t," the complex that is reiterated in recurrent acts of form perception spaced out by arbitrarily varied, intervening sensory events, so that his final representation of the phase sequence is something like "a-b-t-a-c-t-c-t-b." Such internal reactivation of long, complex processes by the influence of their own minute elements on each other is a basic bodily procedure which probably occurs in all vertebrates, and in our own experience is unfelt, either as a continuous act or a complex sequential one.

This is one of the above-mentioned alternative ways of sustaining a so-called steady state, which is really not a changeless state but a slowly advancing act: by frequent, though irregular, recurrence of an effective stimulus in a phase sequence of related acts. The other possible pattern of renewing the impulse to a protracted activity is given by the tendency of directly repeated acts to set up a rhythm by their own characteristic rise and fall; there is some evidence that brain processes which are not reactivated by sensory impingements may be supported by virtue of this inherent, essentially formal property of elementary acts. Hebb, in a passage quoted above, states that trains of thought have the same structure as sustained perception; but an incidental finding made during a differently oriented study, by a different neurologist, suggests a simpler organic mechanism for such covert acts of (perhaps peculiarly human) cerebration. Several decades ago, A. G. Bills found what he considered primarily as a principle of mental fatigue and error, a fairly (though not wholly) regular pattern of lapses in neural response, which makes the phenomenon of sustained thought appear more like a series of acts than like one continuous process (1931, p. 230). He himself remarked that other investigators had seen in this finding an explanation of the greater endurance in mental work than in muscular work. His principle of fatigue seems, indeed, to be an internal source of mental sustainment. Having failed in attempts to correlate it with larger bodily rhythms, he considered it related to refractoriness, an inherent characteristic of neural processes (p. 244). One would naturally expect to relate it directly to the familiar attention rhythms, as Hebb did, but its wave form is different; this may reflect the fact that while the attention rhythms depend on peripheral stimuli and vary with the sensory modalities involved, the rhythms of thought seem to be determined by central action.

Evidently the brain has its own central patterns of activity as well as those stemming from its peripheral contacts with the extraorganic world. As for the latter, the experimental use of "sensory deprivation" has shown with considerable detail and certainty that a constant welter of changing, adventitious perceptual acts supports the unity and flow of waking consciousness. But what of the sleeping brain's activity? The sensory barrage of stimuli does not reach it; its current stimulation must come from intraorganic sources.

The most notable phenomenon discovered early in the systematic study of sleep was the occurrence of rapid eye movements (so commonly referred to as "REMs" that this abbreviation is really necessary to remember) for more or less protracted periods during sleep, which generally but not exactly coincide with periods of dreaming. The first interpretation of this activity was, of course, that the dreamer was scanning the scene of his illusions; but the nature of the saccadic movements is not that of waking eyes watching any kind of event and, moreover, the movements are normally preceded by a slow, rhythmic rolling of the eyeballs. Several interesting coordinations of REM periods ("REMPs") with subjective experiences of dream have, however, been experimentally established, making the existence of some direct or indirect relation unquestionable.

Yet the proposed direct relation of the spectacular eye movements as following the hallucinatory events in the dream meets with many theoretical difficulties. In the first place, highly visual dreaming does occur to some extent without REMs, and non-visual dreams of situation—fears of things not present, expectancies, messages, etc.—may occur with REM accompaniment; and second, only a few actual visual experiences, such as watching a tennis game, could evoke such oscillations of the eyeballs. Finally, also there is the slow rolling of the eyes which usually precedes the more rapid phase and sometimes underlies it, and corresponds to no acts of watching movements or scanning a scene in waking life.

A more fateful stumbling block to acceptance of the picture-scanning interpretation of the eye movements peculiar to sleep is that they are found in newborn infants, both human and animal, including kittens before their eyes have opened, and even fetuses still *in utero*. Such young beings could hardly be looking at visual images. The fact that the abrogation or prevention of REMs seems to cause no disturbance of vision or eye mobility but great changes in behavior and especially emotional response suggests that their influence is primarily on brain activities other than visual use of the eyes.

H. P. Roffwarg, J. N. Muzio and W. C. Dement, in their valuable article, "Ontogenetic Development of the Human Sleep-Dream Cycle" (1966), quite definitely treated rapid eye movements not as an index to perceptual acts, but as an independent process with its own dynamic pattern, probably an elementary cerebral function. The influence of REMs on dreaming may be general rather than specific; they may be periodically—not always, nor always concomitantly—necessary for the occurrence of dreaming and perhaps other brain activities. They may constitute a homeostatic mechanism that has allowed animal development to take a course which would not have been possible without such activation: the steady increase and concentration of acts in the nervous organ leading to a high articulation of feeling.

The occurrence of a psychical phase seems to require an advanced development of the act which culminates in that phase, but what is an "advanced" act may be relative to the rate of evolutionary progress of the species. Many years ago, when psychologists were still speculating on the nature of consciousness, E. B. Titchener proposed the theory that any phylogenetically "young" action, behavioral or even somatic, is felt by the performing organism (1911, pp. 451–52). The notion of "consciousness" as something added to mechanical acts which makes them conscious was a metaphysical assumption implicit in the language of psychology at the time Titchener wrote; but allowing for that outdated vocabulary, his proposal fits the conception of life as a vast system of events whose fundamental units are not atomic, ultimate constituents, but are themselves highly structured forms of organic action, so what is primitive in terms of acts is not so at all in terms of the physical sciences; the boundary between organic chemistry and life is fluctuant and imprecise. Yet once we are certainly in the biological realm, the idea that in the course of phylogeny the line of behavioral advance is the line where activities are differentiated and intensified to the point of having psychical aspects (perhaps faint and momentary in simple lives) sets up a possible structure for the evolution of feeling.

We do not know where feeling begins; let us assume, then, as a hypothesis that it begins with behavior. But where behavior begins is another moot question. That somatic acts we normally do not feel were felt in early epochs of our ancestry is certainly possible; at some time they probably were the highest activities of the archaic creatures. Even today, watching lower animals such as frogs, turtles or crayfish, which sit still for hours after a feeding, one may wonder whether they are not sensuously engaged in digestion.

When the species progresses to more elaborate functions, particularly by the evolution of special sense organs, those new functions arise in the context of the older ones which have settled into such perfectly habitual patterns that they are no longer felt, and largely no longer amenable to feeling by any concentration of attention. The total activity of the matrix has been raised to a higher level, so that the variable acts of seeking and meeting food, seizing, eating, maybe rejecting things, as well as many responses to other changes in external conditions, are now the typical felt events of the animal. Inwardly, the fluctuating rhythms of hunger, sexuality, sleep and waking (where these occur), etc., may rise to psychical phases and sink back into the unfelt round of vital being. Even the most intensely felt moment of existence has its unfelt elements, and certainly its preparation in the non-psychical substructure of all higher processes.

The point of this retrospect on an old-fashioned speculation is that the rapid eye movements of mammalian sleep may be an observable passage in a variable yet constantly present cerebral activity, which may change in intensity to exhibit or not exhibit that spectacular phase, dream, but which reaches some or all the higher systems in the brain and keeps them at a normal level of activation. There are several phenomena connected with REM that point toward the presence of such a physiological mechanism. In the first place, the very early appearance of REMs in neonate and even premature babies (human and animal), and their frequent and long periods in early life, may be aiding the brain in meeting the sudden demands of the extrauterine surroundings, and be stimulated by those needs to work at high tension (the same sort of explanation might fit their decline with advancing age, when most of the cerebral functions have become routine and require only minimal reinforcement). In the second place, the fact that they do not seem to originate in the oculomotor apparatus suggests that they are part and parcel of a larger, general stimulative process; the eye movements proper may be present only during intense activity of the mechanism, for they seem to be easily abolished as soon as the eyelids are opened and the oculomotor muscles are pre-empted for visual purposes. If the REM phenomenon is part of a general restimulating activity, its function would be performed during waking hours by the watchful eye's constant saccadic movements, which make irregular but continual changes to restimulate the visual apparatus and probably the whole participating brain. The winking of human eyelids, usually unnoticed though easily accessible to attention, supplements the oculomotor changes with tiny lapses. But in sleep these influences are lacking, and it is likely that REMs take over their non-visual task.

Now, what have the eye movements to do with dream? Probably, nothing and everything. Nothing direct, such as recording dreamed events or starting the hallucinatory process; but everything, in that the periodic reinforcement of forebrain activity is essential for hallucinations to occur. These are superimposed on the high-tension passages of that activity, wherefore they may occur whenever the tension is high enough, but are apt to be most vivid, continuous and memorable while—or just after—stimulation is received.

Dream may be a further development of the mammalian sleep pattern through stages of progressive intensification and elaboration to the hallucinatory phase, marked especially by the occurrence of cerebrally produced images and illusory experiences. We do not know where this phase begins, i.e., whether any animals have imagery in sleep, but it is not impossible. Curt Richter made the interesting observation that sloths, mammals living in predator-safe treetops and generally unresponsive to external stimuli, may have imagery (see Pieron 1956, pp. 699–700).

There is a real problem of what such a stationary, motionless animal is doing. Its fairly advanced brain suggests that it may be dreaming, letting casual, uncontrolled images take shape and melt away again—records of visual impressions of its leafy surroundings all seen against the sky. Impulses do have to be finished—even mere peripheral stimulations like sensory impressions—and these animals give no signs of overt response. If, indeed, they are able to undergo a half-waking dream, this indulgence might become obsessive, and encourage their physically passive life.

This is, of course, a piece of pure speculation, not even a hypothesis, since there is no way of testing its truth value. If it were true, it would be an instance of extreme specialization, a spurt of evolutionary advance for which the animal finding its peculiar conditions—safety, ease, freedom from wants—all together, was not ready. But in a more normal state of affairs, amid the usual needs and dangers of life, we know that sensory impressions can terminate in this fashion, that is, be consummated in the brain rather than the musculature: that is in man. The expansion of his cerebrum has apparently not been without influence on his sense organs, especially the distance receptors, which his elevated posture calls constantly into play, so his acts of perception chase and crowd each other and start a veritable flood of incipient responses which cannot possibly be all overtly carried out. But (in all likelihood, I venture to say) they are held in abeyance, in waiting, until further external stimuli are abrogated by sleep and the accumulated sensory impressions can be finished in the partially relieved brain. Their consummation is, first of all, the dreamed image.

We make a still further use of the images that emerge, without volition and apparently without effort, in our brains. For we are overburdened not only with excessive sensibility, but also too many emotive impulses, certainly more than can be freely, overtly spent, especially in the social context of human life. So, while animal hallucinations (if there be any) probably pass in kaleidoscopic fashion without any interest except change (emergence, fading, succession), ours tend to pick up emotional values; and their doing so is not a simple process. It is, in fact, the greater part of what Sigmund Freud, in his early book, *The Interpretation of Dreams*, called the "dream work." Emotional reactions are always to our own impulses in situations which do not immediately let them pass into action, that is, obstructions, long or briefly unmet needs, and especially conflicting motivations, which may be large or almost imperceptibly small. The small ones are the neglected ones, of which we may take no notice at all. They just belong to the fabric of the ever-moving situation in which one lives. Yet they may summate to impart a general feeling tone to the passage of life in its situational context.

No one knows just where and by what mechanisms dreams are generated, but their elements have been traced with some certainty and detail to remembered, unremembered and often jumbled past situations in the life history of the dreamer. The images which punctuate the dreamed acts and situations may have sources quite apart from the biographical fragments underlying the intracerebrally produced events. These visual images, which are commoner and probably more primitive than auditory ones, show one of the most important functions of the human brain—composition. A dream vision is one presentation, no matter how it may subsequently change; it may embody many old sensory impressions, but they enter into one momentary apparition. What they all contribute to achieve is a quality made visible—sometimes an innocent enough object, a bag, a fishing pole, a restaurant counter—but with a feeling of unknown significance; or a creature, human or animal, with physiognomic character above all other traits. This expressiveness is what dominates the "dream work" of composition.

Some images seem to separate themselves from their context, when the context has dissolved to a great or small extent; images tend to remain, like illustrations of a story that has become illegible. We know they were more than images; they somehow concentrate the significance of the vanished story in themselves. What they really have taken on, however, is the whole cargo of emotional acts which have been finished in the course of the dream. The awakened dreamer cannot recollect the events of the dream, but they color the remembered image and make it exciting on every recall, for they belong to its nature as intimately as its form and literal meaning.

Dream images, are, in fact, symbolic forms; they have no practical value, for they were only figments, of purely organic origin, and their emotional charge is not appropriate to the dreamer's known experience and behavior. But it is highly appropriate to primitive impulses, wishes and fantasies which cannot be allowed to enter into waking life and consequently are relegated to the covert activity of dreaming. One of Freud's most revolutionary ideas was that forgetting, rather than remembering, is a purposive cerebral act, a process of repression, which allows nothing to remain in memory except symbolic images that disguise their meanings as they convey them. Dreams have no regard for morals or decencies; a mechanism which wipes them out as we return to waking life saves us from conflict and shame. Brain action at the level of dream production, thought ("the dream thought") and moral conflict, no matter how primitive, appears so involved that no simple schema of traces and actually known neural links holds out much hope of a model for those cerebral performances. We do not know how images are formed, but only that they are; how they become imbued with emotion, but only that they do carry charges of such feeling, sometimes great, sometimes low-keyed, yet always present; that the distortions, contractions and substitutions which Freud recorded in his early works have proved to be characteristic of dreams; and also, that dream materials are apt to be derived from unnoticed or unimportant details in previously perceived situations, events, pictures and communications.

But though we are not able even to speculate in any reasonable way on the physiological mechanisms which produce and uphold the phenomenon of mind in man, we may nevertheless note such empirical facts as these. Especially the last mentioned, the usual triviality of dream sources, was remarked by many of Freud's predecessors (whose contributions he discussed at some length), and has been carefully investigated and corroborated since then, first of all by Otto Pötzl (1917), in experimental and clinical studies. Pötzl found that no matter what is the reason why a perceptual datum is not properly taken in—too little time, too little light, too great a distance, distraction or some unavowed motive for not wanting to see, hear, or recognize the presentation—the result is the same: the datum is what he calls "indirectly perceived," never at the focus of the percipient's attention, so it is not remarked, and in reflection not recalled. He found that such items were favored dream material, perhaps just because they were full of incompletely seen forms. Such forms lend themselves most readily to fantastic distortion and interpretation; the images constructed at their suggestion are the readiest to take on symbolic value, which seems, indeed, to influence the process of their formulation.

Later psychologists have recorded the same pre-eminence of trivial or even entirely unconsciously received visual impressions in the perceptual sources of dream imagery. The crucial fact in the present connection is that many aspects of a perceptual act may motivate the failure to note a detail, and sometimes even a whole, sizable portion of a picture. The latter circumstance seems to stem from our normal way of looking at things, "from head to foot" rather than vice versa, so that a very brief exposure may give us only the upper part, or not all of the lower part, of a picture. Many existing forms are lost because the areas which compose them figure as "spaces" in the picture, under the domination of the obvious represented objects; they are the elements used in puzzle pictures, "*Vexierbilder.*" In our ordinary picture perception they go unnoticed, but in the formation of dreams they sometimes give rise to the most important images. Yet all these "peripheral" impressions, no matter what caused them to be peripheral, once they do appear in conscious perception as visions tend to undergo the same fragmentation and recombination, inversions, substitutions and often bizarre distortions as those which Freud found to be originally suppressed by fear or disapproval; and just like the emotionally rejected material, the most casually obscured, unrecognized forms—obliterated by retinal defects or bad presentation—lend themselves to such elaboration and interpretation and are ready vehicles for symbolic values. So it may be doubted that the cause of their indirect perception is what primarily motivates their function in dream, hallucination and fantasy. What, then, inspires the use we make of these trivial, subconscious or unconscious, indirectly seen forms?

I think the answer embraces the findings of Freud, without belittling the far-reaching principle of "psychopathology of everyday life," and also extends to the deliverances of "indirect perception" due to lesions in the visual apparatus and to partially subthreshold exposure; above all, it relates the phenomenon to the general nature of acts. All neglected, unrecognized though physically received impressions are unfinished business. The impulses they touched off were nipped in the bud and not used up in conjunction with other responses, as thousands of starting and pooled impulses are automatically completed (often by entrainment) from moment to moment of actual life. Pictures, speeches, well-formed sound patterns like bird calls or bell tones are somewhat special elements, impinging on our sensibilities as holistic forms amid the flow of the "specious present." That is why their impressions, however poorly retained in conscious memory, are filled with fragmentary as well as completed forms. The normal course of a sensory impulse engendered by such a presentation is an act of clear perception, though it probably always has some uncompleted aspects. Pictures, distinctive sounds and rhythmic motions are natural sources of spontaneous images, which occur especially when current stimuli are reduced—in sleep, in drowsiness, or hypnotic gazing at hearth-fire, moving water or the like.

Imagination, I think, begins in this fashion; its lowest form is this organic process of finishing frustrated perceptions as dream figments. In primitive stages of hominid specialization dream may not have occurred exclusively or even mainly in sleep. For eons of human (or proto-human) existence imagination probably was entirely involuntary, as dreaming generally is today, only somewhat controllable by active or passive behavior, in the one case staving it off, in the other inviting it. But what finally emerged was the power of image-making. This, too, must have had its evolutionary course, starting with that of dream. At first dreaming may have been limited to the optic apparatus, which took up the first great excess of stimuli. We cannot know, but in visually oriented animals, birds and primates, the "optic thalamus" has largely replaced the rhinencephalic stations which the thalamic nuclei constitute in macrosmatic brains; the shift seems to be demonstrable in all degrees. Likewise, the cortical activating work known only through rapid eye motion and its experimental manipulation, though it probably originated in the vestibular system, in man has struck intimate relations with visual functions, especially in the completion of unfinished perceptions by the production of subjective imagery.

At present, however—and there is no knowing since when—dream experiences are not only visual, but involving hearing, touch, and indeed all modes of sense which we know in real life, and above all many non-sensuous forms of awareness whereby we appreciate situations. A dream is a series of events in which causes seem to operate, facts are known though a source of knowledge is seldom presented, future events are fearfully or confidently expected. Yet dreamed reasons and causes are apt to be specious, situations may be quite impossible just as often as they may be possible, and their developments are often completely *non sequitur* shifts of scene or action.

It is the passage of dream events that is so elusive and ephemeral that often we cannot hold even the barest plot of the hallucinated story in memory. As a rule we have to hurry to verbalize what happened in the dream before the action shrinks to a vague surmise of what it may have been—if even that. What permits that modicum of recall is a peculiar paradox in the constitution of dreams: for, while the memory of events dissolves like smoke in air, many images are not only retained without effort, but may be actually haunting for days and weeks, sometimes for years or for life. We pin down the happenings by the images of things, places, people; once in a while—though less often—we have a vision of a being or object in motion, but the motion, in that case, belongs to the object as one of its peculiar qualities. The vision is still an image, self-contained and essentially pictorial. Herein lies, I think, the source of the paradox in our dream recall. A visual percept is given as a single, closed form, because all its parts are simultaneously presented, so it needs nothing to make them cohere; but events can only occur successively, and to have any structure they require causal connections from moment to moment, in a complete, fixed framework of space and continuous time. Otherwise their very nature falls apart, and one cannot even say, in the usual past tense of history, what happened, because there are at best fragments of sequences, but no coherent passage from one situation to another. There is no real "when" and "where," let alone "because." Such experience has no conceivable form, except for the bits the dreamer sometimes does remember, in which acts of his own usually constitute the recollected episode (or episodes).

One aspect, however, the two major elements of dream, imagery and virtual history, have in common: the intensity of emotive feeling which imbues them both. The visual phantasms, whether they be clear or vague, have always a predominantly "physiognomic" character; the most commonplace object, a slipper or a teacup, may have a mysterious quality, or an inviting or forbidding look, or some other air of non-pragmatic value. Its appearance is expressive, though nothing in the dream accounts for that attribute or even for the occurrence of some of the odd things hallucinated in sleep. Only since Freud proposed, and went far to prove, that such irrelevant items are standing in for entirely different ones belonging to another story, namely, the complex of memories, wishes, fears and expectancies not consciously entertained but emotionally effective in the nervous system, has the study of dreams made any headway toward psychological insight. One thing that has become fairly well established is that the driving force of dreams is emotional, and another, that their material is drawn from two sources: very recent perceptions (vestiges of the day) and old memories, often very old, from early childhood. The revival of forms seen during the day is not necessarily an emotional experience; it often occurs before sleep has begun, with closed eyes or, in darkness, open, especially if one has looked long at repetitious forms such as fence pickets, coins, or less monotonous but basically uniform objects, daisies in a field, berries, cockle shells, reeds. The resulting visions may be individually eidetic, yet formalized in their deployment; they tend to cover the visual field more regularly than they did in actual perception, somewhat like a wallpaper pattern, not overlapping; sometimes they may be more formalized, all assimilated to one simplified, repeated shape. Some people find that they come and go, others see them in fixed relations, and can even turn attention from one item to another and back again. Such hypnagogic envisagements are not after-images, yet like those familiar photisms they seem to be essentially retinal. They appear quite autonomous, involuntary and what is commonly called "physical." They are not completions of fugitive "indirect seeing," but revivals of fully formed percepts, as after-images sometimes are; though an after-image may show formal properties which its recipient had not noticed in the original impression, but which the retinal pattern reflects. The images here in question differ from after-images in that they do not alternate positive with negative phases; and from dream-like hypnagogic visions in having no metaphorical function and consequently, in themselves, no emotional value.

What makes them interesting is that, without being true products of the imagination, they nevertheless show formalizing influences which certainly are not exerted by the eye, but by deeper nervous structures, though these may quite possibly all belong to the visual system. The repetition of forms derived from recent sights (like the grasses and daisies mentioned above) or geometric forms of windows, spots of sunlight, etc., is not haphazard, but evenly spaced out in a design covering part or all of the field of vision. This is the phenomenon of revived but spatially modified visual impression; the modification, consisting of the repetition and the orderly deployment of the repeated forms, is obviously a centrally furnished ingredient in the subjective event. I have had it many times without being sleepy, though probably beset by eye strain, once after identifying delicate feather mosses around a rock. The interesting aspect of this retinal reactivation is that it shows the source of some basic principles of design and primitive pictorial representation, namely, the separation and completion of forms and their spacing out on a ground, to lie in the operation of our visual system itself.

The reason for dwelling on the purely ophthalmic reactivations of perceived forms is that they offer a rare chance to see a relatively bare, physiological process of formalization operating below the generally recognized level of imaginal composition, and remind the speculative theorist that so great a cerebral function as imagination is not likely to be the work of any single neural structure or even subsystem in the brain, but probably draws on many parts, many specializations with different evolutionary paths and origins, so that like most complex living forms it is polygenetic.

The great formative process, however, is a higher development, the relegation of blocked, curtailed, started but uncompleted impulses to perceptual and conceptual mechanisms in which transformations, typified in a lowly way by the patterning distortions of purely optic revived impressions, are more elaborately made, and produce the normal, nocturnal phantasmagoria of dream. In man this process has certainly reached astounding heights, reflecting almost all aspects of his life; and if it does have the source and significance here imputed to it, it shows the range and depth of human awareness and especially the plethora of impressions besetting us. It is in dream that the imaginative powers are born and exercised without effort or intention, unfold, and finally possess all departments of sense, and activate another great class of largely uncomprehended phenomena, the products of memory. Remembered sights and sounds, often unrecorded in conscious experience, sometimes whole situations especially of early life, tactile and olfactory and muscular impressions come together to form the profuse, unsolicited imagery our brains create in sleep.

But the most extravagant imagination, if it occurs only as dream, involuntary and unamenable to conscious control, is no direct asset in waking life, however great its physiological use in the cerebral system as a whole may be. What we ordinarily think of as "imagination" is a directed process, an entertainment of images and often verbalized concepts whereby we organize our practical knowledge and, especially, orient our emotional reactions to the ever-emergent situations which form the scaffold of life. The transition from the automatic completion of started acts which were curtailed in the melee of impulses seeking expression to the deliberate envisagement of things not present and situations not actually given is another major move in the shift from animal mentality to mind; and it springs from the further function of dream figments, after the finishing of sensory acts, the completion of autogenic, emotive impulses, which involves the genesis of the decisive humanizing process, symbolization.

A genuine symbol is, above all, an instrument of conception, and cannot be said to exist short of meeting that requirement; that means that an ape thinking symbolically could think of an act he had no intention or occasion to perform, and envisage things entirely remote from his real situation—a termite hill while he was in a laboratory cage far from natural surroundings, etc. Picking up a stem and carrying it even quite far to such a hill in the wild bespeaks an extended act with a preparatory phase in a large, really given situation, but not by any necessity a concept symbolically entertained. Symbolism is the mark of humanity, and its evolution was probably slow and cumulative, until the characteristic mental function, semantic intuition—the perception of meaning—emerged from the unconscious process Freud called the dream work into conscious experience. In the deep, unfelt operations of the brain the generation of symbolic forms may have had a long history, making images that departed from their sensory originals to draw in older, forgotten experiences and gather up their emotional values, until the cathexes they carried were out of all proportion to whatever manifest object-character they had. Only this strange, exciting quality betrays the fact—and then, not to the dreamer—that the ordinary things hallucinated in sleep stand for something not presented. The mechanism of symbol-making is there, but the symbolic relation of the image to the concepts it could serve to express is not evident yet.

Now, all these automatic processes of condensation, distortion, and substitution of pictorial elements for unportrayable ones and, finally, sensuous presentation of the cerebral products in dream are still apart from waking life and its public, external world. At this juncture, however, another characteristic of dream may have played a crucial role in the making of mind—as so often, a factor of no practical value: the paradox already mentioned, that dream events are fugitive, but images tend to be remembered and even to haunt us long after the action, the dreamed story, is largely or wholly forgotten. In this way the image is culled from its context and may occur in recollection without any context at all or in an incongruous one of waking perception. In animal mentality, objects seem to figure essentially in situations, and derive their characters from them and the acts they implement or hinder. Otherwise they may not be noticed, certainly not touched. Even such visually inclined beasts as monkeys pay attention to new but clearly inedible things only where stimulation by interesting ones is pathetically low, as in captivity. But the pure apparition of a memory image without its setting in actions and events is arresting; and since in human memory it usually has some aura of its dream cathexis, this sudden fantasy looms up as an abstracted form, usually with a "physiognomic" appearance. Apart from action, albeit only the virtual action of dream, its notable features are visual traits of shape, color, attitude and expression. Even things and surroundings may be remembered with the peculiar intensity of dream images, while the story that involved them has left no trace of its passage.

Once the pure form is abstracted and remembered, it may be suggested by actual perceptions of waking life; the identity of form is seen in all possible concrete instances, even such as depart somewhat from the model. That recognition of sameness or similarity is an intuition, as form perception itself is; but while the latter is first practiced in sleep, the logical intuition of similarity, which involves sameness and difference, seems to occur only in non-dreaming states. Yet it is intuitive, not learned from experience as the useful or hurtful properties of things are, and the whole development of logical thought and semantical insight to which it ultimately leads belongs to our waking hours. Originally, however, the material of such rational cognition stems from that more primitive deliverance of dream, the memorable image, to which real percepts are spontaneously assimilated if they fit it and from which they derive a more definite form than they are apt to have in animal-like empractic seeing. But in shaping them, the imaginary model also gives the new actual percept some of its emotional quality, the expression of central feeling it had to hold and finish in the dream or half-dream state; and some vestige of that feeling pervades all things seen to partake of that visual form. In this way the appearance abstracted by the paradoxical nature of dream memory carries the symbolic character of a dreamer's involuntary fantasies over into waking envisagement.

That is the momentous step, from form perception to the sense of significance—at this point probably not of the symbol but in the symbol, presenting, at first, more as a feeling of awe than as any real comprehension of meaning, yet marking the first, fleeting acts of ideation. Once the awareness of form had taken place, it would not take a dream episode to negotiate every further such abstraction; intuition, however it may have come into being, is a natural human function and, like Freud's dream work itself, once it is initiated it will seize on every possible material. But seeing expressions and symbolic values in physically presented things may have been involuntary and non-practical for millennia, impressive, sudden, without being available for autosuggestive use, i.e., symbolic thinking and systematic envisagement; more disturbing than advantageous. There are some indications that apes tend, at least in captivity, to see some objects in this way.

In the brain of the ape, some intuitions evidently occur, while others never do, so one can gain some idea of the several intuitive functions, which ones seem to occur most easily, perhaps even in lower animals (though that would have to be determined for each species); and finally, in human mentation, which ones are elementary in that they are required in order to carry the crucial, humanizing intuition of meaning. The recognition of forms is obviously spontaneous in infant chimpanzees, though it is a product of abstraction in them as in us, and some time in the long past of their race as of ours it must have had its beginning—perhaps in excess of vision, making pure shapes in the dark, as it does for us.

One other intuitive perception which underlies the great human departure and shows at least a beginning in captive animals is physiognomic seeing, the immediate reception of expressive value in visual forms. In man it is stronger during childhood than in later years. Finding the semblance of gesture or power in the sheer configuration of objects, with or without true or suggested faces, is an intuition of expressive form that goes beyond the function of form perception as such. In human life it has played a major part, I think, in the evolution of symbolic seeing and thinking, and has been, in fact, a preparatory step toward the emergence of speech.

The intuitive apprehension of symbolic import in sounds, movements, shapes and rhythmic changes like swinging, revolving, and flowing may have had a long development, millennia at least, in prehuman natural history before such import became vaguely felt to belong intrinsically to some objects or phenomena: clouds, flames, fantastic rocks or huge trees and the places they defined, but also small articles with intriguing or suggestive shapes—smooth, hollow, serpentine, eye-like or what not. Their import was sensed without any further exegetics, as it is today by superstitious people who cherish amulets, *churingas* and other magical charms; their significance is felt as a power rather than a symbolic value, their intellectual potency as physical potency. That is a phase of symbol appreciation which probably preceded any real, conceptual use of symbols in thinking, and consequently any coherent thought. But in it we can see a step in the rise of true symbolism; for it may well have sprung from physiognomic seeing, which is rare and episodic in the highest animals but has developed in human mentality to a distinct kind of intuition, which begets at first the abovementioned feelings of vague import, and finally leads to the development of a high symbolic form, the metaphorical symbol, discussed at some length in Part II of this essay.

The first startling effect of a proto-symbolic impression of emotional import received from an object would probably be a sense of awe in its presence. The more one looks at an expressive figure the more its expressiveness grows. Purposely constructed forms especially, set up in an open place for view, take on this aura of vague significance which embraces the whole place that belongs to them and evokes a primitive sense of "holiness." That is the first obvious gathering place of hominid hordes in a state of excitement, where any individual's emotional expression would be enhanced, seen and felt by others, but assimilated for them to the nature of the place rather than to the presence of the single being giving vent to his actual impulses. The figure commanding the place epitomizes the nameless value as an objective quality of its own, making it appear to the members of the horde as a fearsome power residing in that post, tree or devised bogey (this last may belong only to a later hominid stage than the pre-linguistic, pre-cultural beings here assumed).

At this point, again, a biological function we have already found operative in image-making affects the evolutionary process: the tendency to formalization, which seems to govern operant actions as well as vision and hearing. This tendency imposes order and repetition on bodily movements that are not guided by practical intent, but spring from emotional impulses. Such formalization is familiar from animal behavior, where our ethologists have given it entirely human designations—"ritual," "ceremony," "symbolic acts" and even "superstition." Here, at last, we reach the great divide where these terms become legitimate; and at this point we can see how the biological principles of repetition and formalization, which sometimes have spectacular effects in animal behavior, really enter into the etiology of the acts of human beings performing holy rites. As usual, the new mental phenomenon seems to have arisen on a complex substructure, a meeting of several coincident developments. The tendency to formalize non-practical movements, especially expressive, emotionally engendered ones, is certainly the first crucial physiological factor in the advance toward ritual action; another is the fact that probably all hominids, like most of the higher primates, are gregarious, suggestible and interested in each other's doings, so any outwardly expressive, spectacular movement, such as wide-flung arms or top-like whirling on one foot, lifted hands, and vocal accompaniments would evoke imitative responses, perhaps long trains of them. The tendency to repetition which is often seen in play, both solitary and collective but especially the latter, naturally produces some formalization of the repetitious act (most individual perseverative behavior springs from sexual excitement rather than play, and builds up elaborate forms under growing emotional pressure, but it is communal formalized action that leads to genuine ritualization, though in itself it is not enough).

How genuine ritual actually began we shall never know; in the evolution of mind, it is the behavioral aspect of the past lives constituting our heredity that could really tell the story, but that aspect is irretrievably gone. Fragments of fossilized bones are all that remains. But apart from anthropological speculations on which there is no scientific agreement such exhibits do not tell us whether the beings who could fashion those crude spearheads, arrowheads, choppers and blades could also speak.

To ask when man began to speak is a bootless question, because speech itself has probably gone through so many phases that it is wiser, perhaps, to ask from what natural anlagen the process of speech as we know it in all men today can possibly have arisen and attained its unrivaled importance in the great evolutionary shift from animal existence to human estate.

Speech is a process which has created an instrument, language. These two phenomena present somewhat different theoretical problems; the existence of speech in all normal human beings after infancy is a biological trait, but the divergencies and interrelationships of languages, and the laws of language change and grammatical development (which have many characteristics of natural laws), defy all familiar biological canons and methods. Psychological factors abound in the acquisition of speech, and likewise in the history of language, but different factors operate in those two distinct fields of research. At present, it is the evolution of speech that concerns us.

A major fallacy concerning that evolution, I think, is a principle which is sometimes avowed, often tacitly accepted, and sometimes—but very rarely, and then only casually—rejected: the assumption that because a cardinal function of speaking today is directive communication—i.e., warning, commanding and conveying information—the desire for such communication must have been the original motivation of the utterances which gave rise to speech. It follows as a corollary to this assumption that the precursor of speech was some cruder communicative system, perhaps pantomime accompanied by grunts, clicks of tongue and lips, or cries and variable, senseless babble. The latter would merely have developed the articulating and phonetic capacities of the race, and furnished "phonemes" from which "roots," or primitive words, could be chosen. Some authors think of speech as something purposely invented, and adopted by agreement; most scholars today, however, realize that such high intellectual acts would be beyond the reach of man-apes not already equipped with powers of language, and give special credit to theories which derive that amazing human attainment, the fulcrum of the "great shift" in prehuman zoological evolution, from animal beginnings and the special proclivities of one primate family in which coincident developments have repeatedly sparked fateful novelties.

Yet very few anthropologists seem to have studied general evolutionary principles enough to discover that most really new actions did not arise from older processes serving the same ends. They usually take shape in the course of quite unrelated activities which, perhaps, overgrow the agent's needs, and presently find a new use in the organism's economy. The new function is unpremeditated, unintended, yet not accidental; it has been slowly building up with the development of all its elements in other quarters.

So, I think, it must have been with language, which involves so many elements of human specialization that no simple, pragmatic motivation could have initiated it, and permitted the operation of "natural selection" to develop it. There could hardly have been any desire or felt need to communicate among prehuman beings before there were definitely symbolic utterances to evoke ideas, associated with them by their producer, in the similarly disposed brain of a hearer; that means that the utterance was already more than just a sound to both of them, but part of a remembered act in which they had both participated so that their memories converged sufficiently to have a common outside reference—that is, an objective, even if vaguely conceived, denotation, the same for both.

What may have led to the formation of linguistic utterance and understanding was a prior sort of symbolic action, the vociferous accompaniment of the earliest communal expression of formalized feeling, ritual dance. Its motivation was not communication, but communion, though not the sheer desire for bodily contact or at least intimate nearness of ape and monkey bands; what found expression in the dance was the sense of a power residing in the horde as a single agent, pervading the holy place, and perhaps made visible in a fetish—a mysterious central tree or a nearby, terrible "bush-devil," made by nature as a chance form, or by primitive but fantasy-guided hands. The reason for formalizing the expression of group feeling was that in this way it was enhanced, sustained and upheld when subjectively it might have breaks and lapses. The sense of power it bestowed on each individual was a previous value, and to produce it an exhilarating act; to make men (or proto-men) enter into a dance undoubtedly required no persuasion. So it is not altogether surprising that, as Curt Sachs said in his *World History of the Dance*, "the history of the creative dance takes place in prehistory" (1937, p. 62).

The change from simian gregariousness to such organized assemblage as even the most savage true dance requires, though both, perhaps, were still equally based on wordless communion, was already part of the radical shift from animal mentality to mind; for it was the symbolic element—however vaguely sensed—that made dancing entirely different from prancing, and celebration from play, even if group play looks to the human observer like a rite. All animal acts which are repeated, whether for vital purposes, emotional release or in play, tend to become formalized; but to call this tendency "ritualization" is a grave mistake, ignoring the whole psychological aspect of such performance on the one hand and of ritual on the other.

With the overgrowth of mental functions in hominid phylogeny, which seems to have led to fantasy and symbolic or proto-symbolic functions of the brain, the need of contact between individuals, found in all degrees in various animals, undergoes a change from bodily contact to mental contact. Communion becomes an elaborate emotional need, in which the simple impulses to grooming, clinging or going to sleep in each other's arms are gradually replaced by symbolic collective acts: the expression of union with the horde in dance, and of the fear of outside powers—storm, earthquake, attack by real or fantastic dreaded creatures—in seeking refuge round a fetish or in a "holy" place. All primitive divinities, or what goes before divinities in the way of mystic animals or dream figments, are terrible as well as protecting demons; and the mental contact among the proto-human beings which displaces the constantly needed physical contact of gregarious simians is most readily made by celebration, dance, choric shouts and gestures, centering around some symbol of potency. By such acts all the participants are joined in one performance and feel themselves one.

By the time the pre-Adamites—whatever species may have existed at the time or times when language arose—had progressed to the point of symbolic expression, the physiological mechanisms for articulate utterance must have been fairly well complete. The same may be said for the discriminative ear which takes in patterns of sound, the nervous structures that control utterance by coincident inner and outer hearing and the suggestibility of sociable primates that makes choric action the most natural behavior in a group concentrating on one intensely cathected symbol, whether an object or a progressive movement. In such a situation, both movement and shouted ululation would tend to become formalized and be precisely repeated, with more and more articulation at the recurrent high moments of the rhythmic round, which—in its emotional, proto-symbolic setting—was already genuine dancing. At these points, also, the excited brains of the actors are most likely to have generated images, probably visual-kinesthetic envisagements, reactivated by every repetition of the passage that had first inspired them—each dancer his own images, of course, but in a public framework, and perhaps the same crucial context wherein other participants had their private visions too.

These assemblies, if they existed at the dawn of human history (and they are certainly very old, as cave paintings and traces of apparent "sacred places" show), were the first communal rituals, or rather, awesome aesthetic precursors of genuine ritual. This idea, especially of the humanizing importance of primitive dance and the vocalizations developed in connection with it, was propounded long ago (1891) by J. Donovan. It was Donovan's idea that words were not primitive elements in human utterance when it became symbolic, but that meaning first accrued to longer passages, which were gradually broken or condensed into separate sections, each with its own more and more special sense. But what he did not say was how conceptual meaning accrued to any vocal products at all. The symbolic function—in effect, conceptual meaning—begins with the occurrence of imagery; and by the time a particular image can be called up by some known means, imagination is coming under a degree, however slight, of voluntary control. In the fantastic development of tribal dance all individuals of the primitive horde became familiar with the vocal sounds that belonged to various sequences of steps and gestures, some perhaps mimetic, others purely expressive, working up to climaxes of excitement. The "song," or vocal part of the dance, became more and more differentiated with the evolution of the gestic patterns. Donovan suggested that renderings of the drum beat might have been an early motif. In the overstimulated brains of the celebrants, images must have been easily evoked at these points of action and special vocalization—images that tended to recur in that context, until for each individual his own symbolic images were built into the familiar patterns of tribal rituals. A dance passage takes time and energy, if not actually several persons, to perform, but the vocal ingredient can be reproduced with little effort and in a minimal time by any individual. To remember the festive occasion would probably bring the vocal element to his throat; as the memory or thought of a conventional wedding might make one hum the ineluctable Lohengrin march. Our lives are too individualized and various to relate the tune to the same memory for everyone, but in that most primitive, still speechless, barely human life, where the dance was a high and exciting occasion, the fit would be close and quite the same for all concerned. If the action at that point was, say, swinging a club, or even felt like that expansive act, the image may be of swinging, or of whirling clubs, lifted arms or what not; but whatever it is, it symbolizes the activity, the people and objects involved in it, and especially the emotional values of the event. The image with its whole cargo of feeling is the marginal effect of the sound pattern when it is intoned apart from the dance.

The image is a genuine conception; it does not signalize or demand its object, but denotes it. Of course, this conception itself is not communicable, for it is covert, purely private; but the things remembered are public and the sounds activating the private images are public; they evoke images in other persons, too, by arousing memories of roughly the same moments of dance action. Within a fairly wide range it does not matter how different the private images are. They are equivalent symbols for the act and the objects that mark those stations in the ritual where the vocal bits belong which may be uttered out of context by some individual; and suddenly the symbolic function shifts from the several private images to the vocal fragment that evoked them all concomitantly, so meaning accrues to the phrase, other beings understand, repeat the sounds or supplement them with a gesture that demonstrates their memory of the same act or thing awakened by the well-known utterance. If, then, the high ritual act involved a physical object such as a spear, this one element which is not transient like the action outlives the dance, and every so often, in mundane life, suddenly brings to mind the bit of chant, the syllables intoned, the melodious wail, or whatever vocal passage is associated with it. A proto-human being would possibly utter some bit of the chant that came into his head, without any further reason or any purpose, as he handled or suddenly noticed the spear.

The question has been raised more than once why a particular oral sign should be generally accepted as the name of that object. Donovan's notion offers an explanation: the process of naming anything went through a long preparation before the hominid celebrants were aware that their sounds had come to recall special acts or objects involved in them. No one chose a name at all; no one had any idea of what a name was. Very possibly, for centuries after genuine reference to ritual acts and objects apart from the actual ceremonies had come into practice, only such acts and objects had any symbols to represent them. But as savage dance is apt to draw all things from tribal life into its domain, those which were mentionable may have been a large moiety soon after the habit of using the voice in reference to special elements became established.

I suspect that the first meanings of such secularized vocalizations were so vague that the symbols could not really be called "words," let alone "names." Swing a club, hit a man, kill beast or man, whirl and hit, swing a club at the moon—such ideas, perhaps suggested or even mimed in the dance, may all have belonged by turns to one long utterance, in which the separate articulate parts need not have had any separable meanings. But as some fragments were used more and more to call up ideas, perhaps combined with others from other dances to emphasize one possible meaning, the utterances themselves probably became merely suggested, hummed, rather than sung or roared as in the dance; and so they would be gradually reduced to the speaking voice, even if they retained "tones" of inexact but distinguishable pitch as formal elements. That would encourage buccal articulation, i.e., the use of consonants and vowels, above musical and gestic elements. The power of conversing could only have accrued to the symbolic utterances in a more manageable phase, when the vocables in combinations could be so freely and quickly produced that they attained the "transparency" they have today, conveying ideas without being themselves remembered in their precise order.

My only reason for giving so much weight to Donovan's old and purely hypothetical proposal concerning the rise and earliest development of human speech is that so far I have come upon no other notion that fits as well into the evolutionary theory of human origins conceived in the general frame of primate phylogeny: the adaptive radiation of lemuroid, simian and hominoid forms, and the long, mainly single-track history of the terrestrial Hominidae, perhaps terrestrial and bipedal longer than is generally believed. We have no real clue to give factual support to the "festal" thesis, which can only be classed with the familiar pictures of prehistoric scenes depicting dinosaurs in lakes and tree-fern jungles, sometimes conscientiously labeled "artist's conception." But it must be possible to set up other, equally plausible hypotheses concerning the earliest phases of that unique hominid trait, language. Perhaps the greatest stumbling block to original thought in that domain is our present preoccupation with communicating devices and the analysis of factors "coded" in communicated information. This present fashion has led to a completely unpsychological and unbiological treatment of language in other connections than "computer" technology, translation schemes and techniques or (on a somewhat more intellectual level) comparative linguistics, all of which have good use for such systematizing procedures. But formal analyses of fully developed language, like Noam Chomsky's currently influential work, throw no light on the beginnings of speech, which must have come with the gathering force of symbolic expression at a very early period of cultural life. There are so many elements interacting to make up language that some of them may be ancient and common to many animals, some peculiar to the Hominidae, some to mankind alone. So, for instance, the two quite separate elements of reference and of direct address to one or more persons may stem from different sources and have entered into language at different times. But surely the catalyst which precipitated the new and unique power of speech was symbolic conception, the intuition of meaning.

This intuition, too, must have gathered slowly and gone through bizarre, emotional, irrational stages. Unrealistic fantasy is probably more primitive than any intellectual grasp of causes and effects. If, then, we cast about for an alternative to the "festal" theory of the beginning of speech, we are not likely to find it in such practices as assigning names to objects, making statements of fact and directing the acts of other people. Géza Révész, in his *Ursprung und Vorgeschichte der Sprache* (1946), holds that all the essential functions of language reduce to three: command, declaration, and interrogation. Although I cannot but reject many of Révész' assumptions and assertions, especially his cardinal principle that every element of language must have sprung from a desire for communication, and that this supreme human distinction presupposes the prior existence of minds capable of thinking, questioning and commanding, I do find in his book a key idea, the need of contact between fellow creatures. That is what has largely shifted from actual to symbolic levels. In animals, there is usually a need of close, physical contact between mother and young until the latter can feed, groom and protect or hide themselves. In some animals, such as sheep, there remains a frequent demand for physical contact, body to body; in others the permanent need is satisfied by a sense of nearness. Between these two kinds of contact one may find all degrees, such as the tendency in some species to crowd close and seek real contiguity in case of alarm, or the apparent desire to reach the utmost union by penetrating another animal's fur to the skin, although ordinarily each individual goes its own way as far as it can without losing sensory connection with the group as a whole.

Contact between individuals is a reality for all the higher animals, whether it is limited to sexual and parental relations as in the arboreal sloths, slightly exceeds that minimum as in the cats, which have agonistic encounters, too, and in youth play with their littermates, or governs most of each member's normal activities, as it does in truly gregarious kinds. In animals this relationship is almost a physiological condition, a felt communion of action and emotion and desire; in man that communion is progressively weakened by the growing tendency to individuation which comes with the increase of mental activity that eventuates in dream, fantasy, memory images and the mechanisms of symbolic transformation, the fateful specialty of the human brain.

But even as we lost the old empathic bonds, the symbolic function has moved into the place of our broken instinctive unity. Its development had to be high and intense before it could enter into ordinary life, and this high pitch was almost certainly reached in more concerted mental acts than enlisting help or directing another subject's practical behavior. All a man's (or man-ape's?) imaginative powers must have concentrated on a symbolic act to develop and hold the nascent conception at the heart of it, and to let other equally vague figments become entrained by its formulation in the course of its awesome, prerational, gestic and vocal expression. The possibility of festal excitement as such a source has been discussed, but it is not the only conceivable starting point. Even the symbolic celebration of communion, still on the instinctive level, might have developed without quite reaching the crisis of freeing a fragment of the vocal pattern for other uses and for a conscious extraneous application. But the next step in such conceptual and expressive indulgence comprises more elements of thought and envisagement: that is magic-making.

The earliest notions of magic probably were centered on objects that had some suggestive form, like the root of the mandrake, many naturally sculptured forms of stone or wood, physiognomic aspects of old trees, and things with mysterious properties, such as flints from which sparks can be struck and conch shells wherein the roar of the ocean sounds when they are held to one's ear. In any event the weird syllables were intoned, probably with equally weird gestures, over and at the objects which symbolized the power the magician sought to possess, and which consequently were imagined to contain the power. It is characteristic of pristine symbolic expression that symbols are regarded not as meaning something apart from themselves, but as themselves the objects or facts presented. In this way the element of address to another being would be inherent in the conjuring rite, and receive the cathexis of that imaginative performance. Not only that, but the power of the utterance, conceived as physical power to direct the course of events, is the essence of magic, only helped by the overt acts of witchcraft that carry the spell. The directive element, too, is contained in the great unrealistic performance, the enactment of a fantasy, in which feeling rises to a higher level than in any actual business of life.

One could undoubtedly make more guesses at the first sources of language, and still have no measure to apply to their relative probabilities. The only extreme improbability seems to me to be that language arose from some kind of previous communication by improvements that had survival value. Animal contact is not communication; animals may perform joint acts, even pick up an act one from another at some juncture, as bees seem to pick up the food-getting act in a round, without asking or telling anything. Suggestibility and a general community of feeling are enough. It is human mentality that does not remain in the animal pattern. The great individuation made by subjective activity, the symbolic finishing of excessive nervous impulses within the nervous system itself, breaks the system of instinctive responses and begets the first processes of ideation, which eventuate in wild expressions, dance, magic, then the wishing of curses and blessings on other creatures and investing implements such as arrows, fishhooks or weapons with potency and luck by solemn rites, and hallowing the places for dancing or feasting with sacrificial bloodshed. Speech was born, I believe, in such high reaches of proto-human activity, and gathered form when one individual knew by the symbolic utterance of another what that other was thinking about. For with such concentrated expression came real envisagement, the beginning of reflection, thought.

With that achievement, everything really was given. The intuition of meaning was no longer an elusive sense of import, giving emotional value to non-practical vocalizations and gestures, but became comprehension of the idea in the head of the utterer. Such insight probably elicited an echoic answer; the accompanying act was understood, since the articulated phrase itself could be repeated faster than the overt gestures and manipulations; they were called up in imagination by the formula, instead of performed; and that is mentioning, naming. The name, or pseudo-name, may long have covered the magic action, the imagined effect, the sacred object addressed and adjured, perhaps even the magician. But once an idea of anything—act, agent, personage, magic power or symbol of it (e.g., the sun, the moon)—was communicated to someone by a syllabic complex, speech had begun.

After the inception of speech, the very first conveyance of personal ideas, the process may have grown and spread like wildfire; and what was communicated was not necessarily sober and useful information. That is not what a dawning mind, a rapidly evolving individuating brain, would be likely to live on and live for. But with communication a change would also come over the human imagination, recording and amassing its intangible products, instead of leaving each dreamer to find the bogeys and wraiths to embody his own terrors and desires, so that the vertiginous dances, drums and vocalizations of pre-Adamite sacraments really celebrated a different dream for every individual. Strange ideas which nothing but speech would realize and hold could now be shared, and those which appealed to many members of the horde would be accepted, perhaps modified by fusion with others, and taken as realities. None of these hominid creatures in the heyday of fantasy is likely to have suspected any difference between imagination and fact.

One change, however, occurred so quietly that it has seldom been remarked; the change from animal memory to human recollection of past events, which made the time dimension of the mind. But this change is so great that it requires many-sided consideration of its effects on the human ambient as well as on the organism itself, so it belongs more properly to the next chapter and will be treated there.

With the development of language came, of course, its quotidian uses, which most theorists speculating on its origins and elementary forms take for granted as its earliest phase (most of them are convinced that primitive man was entirely realistic and knew nothing but material nature). Certainly those uses became its essential ones: it was in everyday, realistic situations that various degrees of precision became necessary; times, numbers, relations had to be specified and, above all, the use of language tended to become more economical and speedy. The elaborate syllabic formulae with omnibus meaning were more and more broken into smaller semantic units, until speech consisted very nearly or wholly of words with separable, limited (though not always strict) meanings. Relations were implicitly given by suffixes, prefixes and other modifiers, some of which became inflexions, where they were not expressed by actual differences of words used in different typical situations (as "go" and "went," or, for nouns, "cow," "bull," "ox," "calf," "heifer"). The burgeoning of vocabulary and proliferation of grammatical and syntactical forms which must have been very rapid in early periods are mainly products of ordinary practical intercourse, argument, gossip, transactions. Such alteration still goes on in any living language and reflects the cultural changes that are the real movement of history. It belongs pre-eminently to the common idiom; only religious, legal, and in some societies theatrical languages are conservative, sometimes archaic to the point of being incomprehensible except to people steeped in the linguistic tradition.

The rise of language in the Hominidae marked the completion of the "Great Shift" from animal to man. The power of speech transformed the genus *Homo* and every aspect of its ambient; for with speech came thought and remembrance, intuition, conception and reason. With words—in dim, distant and very long ages—some strange, unimaginable ancestors of ours built up the human world.

18 / *Symbols and the Human World*

Language makes every speaker, and even every deaf-mute who has some equivalent for speech and its reception, a thinker; ideas of things, of moves to make, and of possible events fill his mind, and things, acts and happenings which realize or contradict his ideas fill his senses. Words designating things carve out and fixate our objects, quite apart from the acts in which they figure, giving them a defined status they probably do not have for animals, for which they seem to be built into acts so they are parts of acts and may not keep their identity from one situation to another. How animals see objects we cannot know, but we know that among human beings not all thinking and perceiving is as firmly centered on physical things as ours, which is governed by Indo-European, Semitic, Indo-Chinese and other mainly Asiatic forms of speech. Students of Australian indigenous languages have repeatedly pointed out that verbs—words of action—are more frequent and more important in those tongues than nouns or adjectives, and their various forms usually express what substantives or properties of things and events are involved in the acts they mention. Human thinking, in the frameworks of such languages, is different from that which rests chiefly on concepts of objects as fixed items of experience, designated by nouns, which are further elaborated by adjectives and related to each other by verbs. In this way, the influence of language on human life goes much deeper than communication; it is intrinsic to thinking, imagining, even our ways of perceiving. Conception, far from being abstracted from sensory experience, has grown up in constant interaction with the latter, and often—by spurts—in advance of it. A concept is born of words, its exemplification found in the perceptible world. But those Baconian methodologists who think one should simply check a hypothetical concept against direct observation don't know what a help in that business a lively imagination can be! The part played by imagery in the formation of concepts shows the intimate relation of perceptual and intellectual processes at all levels of human mental action.

Animals do not have a continuous world in which one or more coherent orders are to be found. In our so-called objective or outside world, there is a predominant order, the basic classification of things according to kinds, big general classes subsuming more specifically defined ones which, however, first meet the general definitions; that is, an order of genera and species, in which every object which is designatable by a common noun is a member of the class defined by that noun.

Classification is much older than Aristotle; not the particular mode he systematized, but the notion that every individual object, act, being, condition (e.g., sickness, luck, heat) or event such as rain, lightning, earthquake is at the same time a kind of thing, act, event, etc. There are many possible ways of classifying, but the people using any particular way do not know that; to them it seems that categories are part of nature, given in direct experience. That is because no one, originally, consciously imposed them; they are ways of thinking and seeing that express themselves in language, in the process of naming acts or agents, objects or places. Alf Sommerfelt pointed out that Aristotle could formulate his logic of substance and attribute, relation, assertion and negation, because these categories were implicitly given in the Greek language; to all speakers of Indo-European languages the classical syllogism seems to be a logic of "natural inference," because they speak and think in subject-predicate forms (1938, p. 9).

So much for ways of thinking; but the influence of language goes even further, for it extends into people's ways of perceiving what meets their senses. Those of us who have grown up with subject-predicate languages see self-identical objects with all sorts of properties; the properties may change, but if their bearers disappear we stand confounded: "They have made themselves air!" We can see a cat with or without a grin, but not a grin with or without a cat, for "a grin" really denotes an act, and in all European languages an act points to an agent or several agents, who are permanent entities. The function of nouns is hypostatic; whatever is designated by a noun becomes a thing, a substance with properties; and for speakers whose vocabularies consist as largely of nouns as ours do, the world consists mainly of physical objects. Next in importance is the category of property words, adjectives, and verbs which assign the named properties to named entities; especially the form of the verb "to be" known as the "copula" in Aristotelian logic, and read "is a." The pure structural business of a verb is to serve as a kind of "logical glue," literally a "copula," joining words into propositions.

But verbs are very interesting elements in our essentially static conceptual frame of entities and properties, because they have the further function of referring the propositional complexes to the actual world of events, and therewith creating the entirely new dimension of truth and falsehood. Truth and its negative, falsehood, are not logical concepts, but basically metaphysical. The fact that they can be treated like properties of propositions has led to the most far-reaching, systematic confusions logicians have ever encountered, probably in any age and any advanced culture. The classical statement of these difficulties as a whole, made at the time when they were becoming apparent, is in the introduction to the second edition of the great *Principia Mathematica* of A. N. Whitehead and Bertrand Russell, Volume I. It was the shift from the logic of language to that of mathematics which suddenly showed how many problems of meaning—logical, semantical problems—lie buried in the Indo-European linguistic forms we take for granted.

No society known from observation or historical records is primitive in the sense of showing us man in transition from a prehuman phylogenetic phase to full humanity. Often the most complicated ideas and institutions of savages, if they differ from ours, are called "primitive," merely on the assumption that anything such people think and do must be relatively childish, cruder and simpler than our ways, and exhibiting a stage of culture we have already passed through. Similarly, any language built on different principles from ours is often deemed "primitive" and even supposed to be inadequate for communication, but no language that has ever been studied by linguists has borne out this assumption. It seems rather that—as true scholars, from Wilhelm von Humboldt (1884, p. 42) to some of our own contemporaries, have realized and declared—a spoken language grows with the intellectual needs it has to meet and is always adequate to the thinking of the public that uses it, though not always to the most advanced individual thought. In this way language exhibits a principle of mind which has been remarked by psychologists and pathologists, namely, that the mind tends always to work as a unit, and after localized or specialized impairment restores the balance of functions as a whole even though it has to operate on a lower level generally, developing potentialities in structures which possess them but do not usually realize them in action, so many nervous mechanisms do wholly or largely substitute work. As the late Lord Brain has written: "Where the left cerebral hemisphere is damaged early in life, the right hemisphere usually takes over the speech functions of the left. Hence infantile right hemiplegia is not as a rule associated with aphasia" (1945, p. 839). Where such a complete changeover is not possible, the constituent elements of the lost function may be divided among several agencies according to their respective potential abilities, so that no one mechanism stands in for the lost one, but the system as a whole still performs without it. Sir Henry Head, more than half a century ago, remarked the unity of mental life in spite of losses in sensation, powers of speech, reasoning, envisagement and other capacities by organic lesions, saying: "Each such local disturbance is associated with some specific psychical loss of function. But . . . the field of consciousness remains continuous as before; it closes over the gap as the sea leaves no trace of a rock that has crumbled away" (1923/24, p. 141).

All the products of human minds show this holistic tendency. In another article Lord Brain noted its functioning in severe disorders of the "body image" (which is not so much an image as a total sense of one's own body)—in his example, a loss of awareness of the whole left half of the body—and he noted that his patient had lost not only the perception of that large part, but all memory of ever having experienced it. "The remaining half of the body image," he said, "seems to constitute itself a new Gestalt, and consciousness, having lost the memory of the left half of the body, is unaware of the incompleteness of what remains" (1950, p. 478). Similarly, a damaged sculpture, a temple ruin, a partly obliterated drawing can maintain its appearance of organic form, letting physical insults go to astounding lengths before it loses its implicit unity. It seems to reorganize its appearance after every mutilation, as a living creature reorganizes its functional pattern on a smaller or simpler scale. Hans Thorner, who found that a truncated ringsnake (*Tropidonotus natrix*) moved in the same curves as an intact snake of the same length instead of the curves it had described before operation, called this tendency, "neoplastic" (1932, p. 13). Walter Börnstein, who made investigations on traumatized auditory mechanisms and their subsequent functioning, set up what he called the "law of concentric reduction," which is "that in case of destruction of any part of an auditory cortex, the remainder of that cortex takes over the function of the whole, but suffering a reduction in total strength, according to a fixed principle: the range in which hearing is normally keenest and most important—that wherein speech has been developed—suffers the least; the ranges increasingly far from this center are pre-eminently affected" (1930, p. 120). And apropos of this "law" he remarks that it seems to him to rest on the same principle of organic action as the development of a mutilated sea urchin egg into a normal-shaped but subnormal-sized sea urchin.

Nothing could indicate more clearly that language is not a code invented as a signaling device or, indeed, for any other purpose, but is a biological trait of mankind, than its constant adequacy to the mental needs and capacities of the society in which it prevails. Another sign pointing the same way is the relative autonomy with which separate languages diverge from a common root and undergo series of alterations such as vowel changes, typical changes of word endings (as Latin "*universitas*" becomes "*università*" in Italian and "*universidad*" in Spanish, quite predictably for anyone who knows the respective language patterns), nasalization, suppression of some phonemic combinations, etc., independently of the ways in which other languages change or continue. A further aspect which makes an essentially pragmatic motivation of this paramount human activity implausible is that language draws so many other mental functions into its orbit—very deep and phylogenetically ancient processes of emotive and instinctive character—and lifts them from their animalian state to a new, peculiarly human level. It also engages all sorts of higher, largely cortical mechanisms, producing distinct forms of memory, sequences of recall, logical contradiction, logical entailment, the propositional structure of ideas that is inherent in the conception of fact, and the correlative, largely emotional disposition of the whole mind, belief. The depth to which the influence of language goes in the organization of our perception and apperception becomes more impressive the further one pursues it; communication, no matter how great its role in human society, is only one of the functions of language, and probably one which became more and more important as speech developed.

Whenever an ability develops beyond the current needs of its possessors it is apt to be used for the realization of some other impulse or impulses, sometimes quite unrelated to its original use. So the noises emitted as parts of strenuous acts, incidental to the sympathetic contractions of the chest and throat muscles as an act grows and takes over the whole body, make it audible, as well as inwardly felt and perhaps outwardly visible. The sounds come back as part of it and expand the act itself in a sensory way. Every act tends to expand, and the ability to enlarge a pleasant act by prolongation or obvious effectiveness (whether good or bad for the agent) is an animal value which is often pursued for its own sake. So, if the ancient animal stock that eventuated in human generations had an unusual repertoire of vocal elements, these might have been put to wide and habitual use to accompany all sorts of acts.

We have no hominid brains from ancient times, before speech could have existed, but today it is correlated with a structural peculiarity of the human brain, which may be a specialization evolved by a speaking stock, or an older oddity which underlies the development of the linguistic functions: a noticeable asymmetry in the right and left temperolateral cortices, where one hemisphere, usually the left, normally develops the so-called speech center. This structure is visible to the naked eye in adult brains, and recent researches have revealed the asymmetrical anlage even in newborn infants' brains.

An interesting parallel to these findings is that a similar specialization, apparently peculiar to man, determines his preference of one hand, more commonly the right, over the other. The great, species-specific superiority of the hand lies less in its prehensile uses than in its epicritical sensibility and its expressive power, both of which are said to have some sporadic occurrences in subhuman life, but a real development only in man. These higher functions belong to his intellectual heritage. Lord Brain pointed out the perfectly comprehensible, though indirect, relationship between handedness and the complex language functions. Linguistic and manual development usually both occur in the dominant hemisphere. It is hemisphere dominance that seems to be uniquely human, and although there is at present no explanation of this tendency, Lord Brain did remark that, for speech,

> motor integration seems to require that the motor cortex of both cerebral hemispheres should be under the control of a higher "centre," the motor speech "centre," and that such a "centre" must be single. Speech, in other words, necessitates Broca's area. . . .
>
> Why should Broca's area be associated with handedness? . . . Is it not . . . probable that it was the appearance of a motor speech "centre" in the left hemisphere in man that made that the dominant hemisphere, and the right hand the dominant hand, in contrast to the ape, in which right- and left-handedness develop with equal frequency? (1945, p. 840)

If such a physiological condition underlies the psychical specialization of man, particularly the use of speech in every human population, it is no wonder that the influence of language pervades his entire mentality, even shaping his percepts as he imposes his worded ideas on them. By means of words, any events and objects, no matter how incompatible, may be brought together in thought; they may be connected by the linguistic particle "and," which expresses this most general of all relations. It is this same limitless, potential togetherness in thought that makes a human being's ambient a world. The power of language not only to designate things and communicate facts, but to formulate and establish what is a thing or a fact and define what perception henceforth is to illustrate, gives the human world entirely different dimensions from those of any animal's ambient.

The word, or whatever phonetic usage preceded it, traditional or novel, public or individual and ephemeral, is what holds a concept, while percepts change and leave nothing but a conceptual trail of successive phases of an over-all event, symbolized by the "word." By being expressed in one symbol the phases belong together, as the many moves involved in an act belong together in the realization of a single impulse. And like the subacts in a complex act, many of the perceptual impressions composing a witnessed event occur in a strict, continuous order. Others do not; when an object is given to our vision, our eyes pass in unfixed, saccadic movements over its presented surfaces (though within these passages there is a continuum of effects from point to point). The elements of a visual impression are simultaneous in what William James called a "specious present"—that is, they are psychically co-present, because the perceptual subacts overlap in their cerebral completions if not their retinal inceptions. In the case of auditory percepts, however, this integration is less assured. The tempo of sound reception and impression is much slower than that of light; speech sounds pass away as fast as new ones occur. So, as soon as articulate patterns of sound are to have symbolic value, they have to be held conceptually as units in a greatly extended "specious present"; and this extension is not in space, but in time.

Time is the new dimension which verbalizing and its mental consequence, symbolic thinking, have imposed on the human ambient, making it a world, with a homogeneous spatial frame and a history. The influence on man's mentality has been as great as that on his environment. The two are, of course, correlative. Since the spectacularly and uniquely evolved human organism is more amenable to study than its counterpart, the vastly enlarged ambient in which it lives, we had better deal directly with the former, and with the latter by implication. The part played by time in the human world, for instance, escapes our analysis. The temporal aspect of that world is a completely integrated, essential element in historical thinking, and the historical world of any period is seen through modern eyes, for history, as an aspect of the world, i.e., as an objective datum, is a late discovery—so late that the development of the general concepts of world history or even national history, reaching beyond local chronicles and traditional legends, belongs to ages of literacy, and in European learning is recent even in that epoch (in China it goes back farther, but not in all older literate cultures). In the evolution of mind, however, the influence of symbolic presentation, whereby a behavioral act is projected as a passage from its inception to an external effect, may be logically analyzed and evaluated though we do not know just when each element in the process emerged and what developmental changes it has undergone.

The first radical effect of the symbolizing functions was to initiate the whole complex faculty of memory, which seems to have pre-empted a number of brain structures for its diverse operations. The physiology of memory is practically unknown as yet; pathological losses, so far, have revealed the existence of several relatively independent mnemonic processes, and also some brain areas where they may be selectively interrupted by lesions, but on the whole we know next to nothing of the mechanisms implementing these all-important mental activities. Although the distinction between "short-term" and "long-term" memories has been known for some time, the possibility of their resting on different cerebral activities is a notion of recent date; in today's increasing literature short-term memory already goes by several names: "immediate memory," "primary memory," "current memory," "recent memory" are often used in place of it. Yet some of these variants are not synonymous; for instance, "current" and "recent" memory are not; though both are of short term, there are cases of pathological loss of one without the other.

Current memory seems to come nearest to the animalian pattern of hysteretic retention, the fact that each successive move in a total act changes the motivating conditions in the matrix just enough to induce the next advance, so the organism is influenced by its own past in the enactment of a complex impulse at least to consummation, or—failing in that—to preparing a new internal situation with subsequent potentialities. The difference between such cumulative effects of action, and "short-term memory" of an act in its development, that is to say, step for step, is that in the latter case the act as a whole has been realized as a conception before, during or immediately upon its passage. If that conception cannot be held there is failure of "current memory."

Such cumulative retention, though perhaps the simplest of all our mnemonic talents, already exhibits the radical departure of *Homo* from the rest of the primate order; for it constitutes the primitive conceptual activity that is the substructure of mind, as the matrix of vital acts is the substructure of the organism. It is a subjective version of the unity of the act. Such memory of what has just been said and done, what has been happening and is still going on, and especially of the agent's own intentions and how far they have been realized is the background of human behavioral action, the basic pattern of what is usually meant by "consciousness"; where the pattern is impaired, "consciousness" falls apart. There still is feeling, even simple, familiar response to questions and instructions, but the specious present shrinks to a minimum, the only extension of acts is by repetition, intentions are forgotten before any act requiring several steps is completed, and habit largely replaces the normal adaptation to circumstance, so the agent may continue in a task when its purpose has long been fulfilled. Superficially this condition may resemble animal mentality, but not truly; for the hereditary, pre-formed source of impulses which supports the animalian life of instinct has no systematic counterpart in us, so the impaired human being cannot fall back on the watchfulness and elaborate direct responses of a fully competent animal.

The most primitive sort of conceptual memory is enough to give the human world something which the ambients of other creatures do not have—a time dimension, which extends backward into the past as well as forward to a future. Animal acts are all forward-directed; the influence of the past upon them is physiological, and though it enters constantly and systematically into subsequent motivations of reflex movements and fears, desires and expectations, it is those immediacies that are felt, not any image or idea of the bygone events which "conditioned" them. Just as animal life is lived "here," "there" and en route from one place to the other, but not in a geometric space, so its "time" is a present always heading into a future, but not a homogeneous temporal dimension in which earlier and later events are ranged. Dimensions are conceptual principles, which require symbolic presentation to let them emerge as spontaneous elementary abstractions. This is probably one of the greatest steps dividing man from the rest of the animal kingdom, although it is also one of the earliest.

"Short-term" or "current" memory was apparently the phenomenon which suggested the theory of "circulating messages" in the brain as the neurological explanation of remembering (Wiener 1948), and is still the best empirical support of that hypothesis. But it seems, also, to be the simplest mnemonic process; there are other kinds of memory which cannot be regarded as reverberations of an activity starting from a main, comprehensive impulse to an act with several successive stages. They are sometimes lumped together as "long-term memory," but the first attempts to find a neurological hypothesis to account for such a general category soon revealed that it subsumes several fairly unrelated forms.

Normal long-term memories can often be pieced together to vouch for the actual historicity of stories largely "filled in" with circumstantial evidence, probability, hypothesis and other constructive elements. That is the sort of memory one is asked to produce on the witness stand. Its dangers are well known, yet it is indispensable in human life, because it is what carried the time dimension beyond the single act that is its limit in even the most advanced animal mentality. We have really at least five kinds of memory which seem, offhand, to be distinct and possibly of different derivation. (1) Old childhood memories, usually very circumscribed, a single act or scene such as a person entering through a door, a caught fish jumping, the dusk and smell in a firelit room, or sitting in a deep, motherly lap in a rocking chair that made the room dip and rise. Such memories usually come as intense, very brief flash-backs, and may be classed with later flash-backs. (2) Biographical memory, recollection of what one has heard and seen, which is apt to be somewhat incomplete, but to have enough elements strongly tinged with the psychical quality of "pastness" to admit no doubt as to their actual occurrence in one's own history. (3) Factual memory, or acquired knowledge that something is the case, where the occasion of learning and the source of information may be vaguely known or quite forgotten; this is the memory tested in examinations. (4) Inductive memory, the power of memorizing, generally regarded as a somewhat special endowment, very unevenly distributed among people and apparently with little relation to general intelligence; it seems to be largely limited to words or tunes, and certainly to involve the peculiar mechanism whereby each new unit—word or tonal element—is like a step in a pre-formed progression, being induced by its predecessor in the framework of a phrase, statement or poem (which may have no real linguistic sense), or, in music, a melody. This sort of memory may extend to (or stem from?) concatenated steps, building up ritual movements, and at a much higher level of evolution, but still on the same principle, the use of hands and fingers in the deft playing of keyed or plucked instruments. And finally, (5) there is the primitive sort of memory based on something that is probably common to all the higher animals, though it takes its own subjective form in hominid cerebral evolution: object memory, the basis of recognition. In animals this may be felt more as familiarity versus strangeness than as identity of an object in disconnected situations; in human mentation it holds such diverse situations together and, so to speak, ranges them on a temporal string, making each recognized object an orientation mark to organize its situation.

Yet I think it most likely that several, if not all, the distinct kinds of memory arise from different mental functions, and consequently involve different mechanisms. The fact is that the human specialty, the cortical activity of conception, starting in an early phylogenetic stage, has been invading every cerebral function that progressed to a psychical phase, and in the course of that progress somehow imprints it with an image that symbolizes it and revives it. It is the symbol—whatever it may be—that can be envisaged, thought, and thought again. So perhaps the best way to understand the great variety of mnemonic forms is to trace each one to the felt aspects of the sensory or impulsive action which the imaginative, conceptual procedure has seized upon for its own implementation. By this rather crudely practical method, one is led to the highly diverse sources of the fabric of memorable events which constitute each human individual's own past.

The most elementary sort of memory, giving rise to what Bertrand Russell called "knowledge by acquaintance" (1910) is formed on a cerebral function which has been little understood, so far, in physiological terms, but has recently received a suggestive sidelight from an experimental study in animal neurology, which reveals something of the mechanism whereby an act of perception, when stimulated by one object or motion, automatically isolates its stimulus from rival impingements. Such concentration of vision, hearing, smell or any senses together on one stimulus may be supposed, then, to occur without any added voluntary act of "paying attention"; it is the act of attention itself, and takes place in some way at least wherever there is a forebrain to guide animal behavior. In man, however, it incidentally provides a "servomechanism" for another evolving function, for it abstracts a percept from the whole sensuous array, and this percept promptly takes on the character of an image, without requiring much spontaneous imagination. Very soon, however, the percept is a hybrid of sense impression and dreamlike image; and it is probably in this state that it is remembered and recognized, at least for short times, in infancy. Whenever this departure from animal memory began, that was the mental beginning of our humanization.

Evolutionary advances, as several scientists and scholars have pointed out, do not keep close step with each other; and apparently the species-specific function of imagination at some early period outruns the other mental powers of man. Certainly in our history, presumably for long ages, the human world has been filled more with creatures of fantasy than of flesh and blood. Every perceived object, scene, and especially every expectation is imbued with fantasy elements, and those phantasms really have a stronger tendency to form systematic patterns, largely of a dramatic character, than factual impressions. The result is that human experience is a constant dialectic of sensory and imaginative activity—a making of scenes, acts, beings, intentions and realizations such as I believe animals do not encounter. In fact, it is only in human life that I think one can really speak of "experience." And it is experiences that make up human memory, a psychical background of each normal person's current consciousness and future envisagement. It is this structure that constitutes what we mean by the "life of the mind."

The dialectic which makes up that life is a real and constant cerebral process, the interplay between the two fundamental types of feeling, peripheral impact and autonomous action, or objective and subjective feeling. As fast as objective impingements strike our senses they become emotionally tinged and subjectified; and in a symbol-making brain like ours, every internal feeling tends to issue in a symbol which gives it an objective status, even if only transiently. This is the hominid specialty that makes the gulf between man and beast, without any unbiological addition.

In the early stages of human or prehuman existence, with all the crucial hominid traits already present in some degree, the excess of imagery over sober sense perception may have been really dangerously great. It must have been in such phases that the hordes of ghosts, monsters, spirits and the primitive divinities were produced as tribal symbols and fearsome mysteries simply by being imagined. Once their images had been dreamed or invented they were easy enough to impose on actual constellations of visual data or on the voices in water and wind.

To the average civilized person today, the uncontrolled welter of nightmarish conceptions belongs to childhood, and to a period of intense emotional feeling. It is largely from such early phases of mental life, when the subjectification of all sensory material tended to hold sway over the dialectic of inner and outer feeling, that "flash-back memories" arise later in life. But different temperaments, different religious and intellectual standards prevail all over the world, so the balance between emotional, subjective, creative impulses and analytic perception and symbolic objectification, which constitutes actual personal experience, can vary between very wide extremes. With maturity, the vividness that marked early impressions and still tends to make their memories eidetic, like immediate reality, gives way to a new characteristic of biographical recollection, which has been referred to by several authors as a "sense of pastness."

That designation, of course, does nothing but give the phenomenon a name; I have never seen any analysis or even theoretical suggestion to account for its subjective aspect, despite the fact that objectively all personal responsibility, all factual records, and even all that we have of history rest somewhere on biographical memory. The "sense of pastness" distinguishes such memory from two related mental actions, (1) the eidetic type of sudden, effortless, perfectly convincing "reliving," and (2) sheer imagination, invention, *poesis*, which may also be recalled and rehearsed, but does not normally seem like something that has happened to the subject in his actual, external world. The fact is that a quality, like a "sense of pastness," gives us no clue to understanding anything in even the most tentative, speculative terms; only events, processes, can be factually or hypothetically construed. A quality is a phenomenon to be understood in terms of what is going on in the organism.

The problem of biographical memory, then, is the problem of how current experiences are relegated to memory in a more or less constant, automatic way, lose their feeling of present impact and emergence, and acquire the "sense of pastness" in a normal and steady flow that is the subjective passage of time. Unfortunately, at present, we know too little of the neurological processes involved in memories of any type to hope for a physiological theory to emerge from the existing literature. Empirical description of psychological observations is the best we can expect to construct; and biographical memory is about the most complex mental function of ordinary human life, running like a spine through each individual history, and concatenating the human agent's mental acts into a life of the mind.

There are several phenomena involved in the process of relegating an experience to memory; one is, of course, the "presentational immediacy" of the momentary experience itself, which is the felt dialectic of sensory impact and conceptual interpretation. This dialectic is a transient act at any moment of life, but it involves something more than its own passage; for the interaction of peripheral and central felt processes begets the sense of reality, which holds over from the experience itself to the elements of memory that stem from its actual occurrence. Our conceptual formulation of sensory impacts is generally so smooth and prompt and rhythmic that we are not aware of taking any active part in it at all; yet impacts are remembered with a "sense of reality" that anchors biographical memory to experience, and makes the great difference between such recall and the recall of fantasies entertained before, stories read or heard and other non-actual elements in the background of our mental life.

But our knowledge of our own past experiences is by no means an unbroken flow of memory. The relatively certain recollections are items, held together by conceptual assumptions of what must lie between them to account for their sequences and their deployment in clock-and-calendar time. History is a fabric of memories, convergent circumstantial evidence (i.e., records, chronicles) and rational construction.

The formative element of biographical memory is verbal conception. I doubt that any creature without some sort of speech has a sequential memory of its own life, or the possibility of constructing its own past. Language, propositional thinking and everything that goes with speech is such a special development in the hominid brain that it is not surprising to find verbal memory exhibiting quite different forms and procedures from any other type of recollection. Its chief characteristic is that if a series of words is recollected, the main elements are rhythm, sound combinations, flow and length of phrases, stops and emphatic starts (such as vocative forms and their accents—"O Captain, my Captain!"), with the so-called message often serving as a secondary or even dispensable support. Many people can learn verbal formulae, long poems, even orations in languages they do not understand. Each phrase induces the next; this sort of recollection might be called "inductive memory," and is what we generally mean by "committing something to memory" or "learning by heart." Another distinguishing feature of verbal memory is that its products usually carry no sense of pastness. Very similar processes seem to be involved in memorizing music and possibly ritual movements, elaborate gestures as in dance and other essentially rhythmic actions.

The whole mental shift of the Hominidae away from the rest of the primates is epitomized in the evolution of symbolic activity; and this, in turn, reaches its highest development in the uniquely human function of language. There is so much mentation involved in language that to think of it as a "signaling system" or a social habit encouraged by survival value is worse than superficial, it is simplistic, not to say silly. Language, despite the fact that its development requires the influence of a speaking society during the early years of each individual life, is not only acquired for communal purposes, but even as it is learned penetrates the entire system of cerebral activities, so that perception and fantasy and memory, intuition and even dreaming take their special human forms under its continual and increasing influence. Its complexity is shown quite spectacularly in the pathology of language. There are cases on record of focal cerebral lesions causing inability to name and apparently to recognize animate beings, while maintaining recognition of inanimate objects, and contrariwise, lesions which make such ordinary things as a bottle of milk or a glass, or an automobile, nameless and strange, while the patient calls persons by name correctly. Since in some cases a doll may be recognized as an "animate object" and in another case recognized (or unrecognized) as something inanimate, and the same ambiguous status may be given to false teeth, it appears that some process of classification goes on before any conscious conceptual identification of objects. The basic perceptual distinctions and imposition of categories on experience seem to pervade and modify the elementary functions on which they have grown up. This is, in fact, typical of superposed activities: instead of remaining distinct, separable, advanced forms which might be lost again or destroyed without seriously affecting their older substructures, they so deeply alter their own very roots that their destruction jeopardizes the whole organic system. There is, as far as I know, at present no trustworthy theory to explain this influence of every new advance on the entire forebrain, but there is a suggestion of V. B. Mountcastle that the functional patterns of cortical action are vertical rather than—as generally supposed—topologically "layered" like the cortex (1966, p. 89), and some other casual discoveries of interactions among superimposed structures and their more primitive supports.

The elements of language which may be separately impaired or even completely lost certainly suggest that this apparently simple and single, universal human ability has actually been built up from a great number of mental traits, entrained in the course of a long cerebral evolution by the basic process of finishing excessive neural impulses in the brain itself as symbolic images and utterances.

Another extraordinary fact is that when language is used covertly, i.e., as an instrument of thought, words do not seem to be simple, "assigned" elements of a code, but to mark the center of a wider range of related ideas; so that in case the exact word for a concept is somehow blocked, and another word presents itself in its place, that other word is not a completely arbitrary substitution, but usually denotes something in the same conceptual range. This shows that the cerebral mechanism is much more complex, the process more deeply started and built up, than its usual case and largely automatic progression would lead one to believe.

Another anomalous character of speech which is revealed in many cases of aphasia is the fact that both naming and reading of numbers often remain unaffected where other words, spoken or written, can no longer be produced at will. Numbers seem to have a special status; their symbolic expression by numerals, which every reader verbalizes according to his own language, shows that number concepts are not ordinary elements of vocabulary, but may long have been conceived and conveyed by non-linguistic symbols, and perhaps had a history of their own in our cerebral evolution.

From all these oddities of speech and literacy and especially their pathology we may gather an idea of the complexity and spread of the origins from which man's ability to talk has arisen. Its sources are really as broad as the whole range of conception, personal or communal. Very probably the practice of verbal communication goes back to the beginnings of any group acceptance of articulate utterance; and as it served for intellectual contact it penetrated and formed the mind of every user. Listening to sounds with meanings is not simply hearing and remembering a collection of distinguishable noises and associating them with acts or objects. Listening is an activity involving more than auditory reception. It is a play of impulses which reach the speech apparatus without coming to overt expression, but which fuse with the cochlear stimuli that served in their motivation, to be inseparably consummated as symbolic elements in the conceptual work of the cortex.

The depth to which the influence of language goes in the formation of human perception, thought and mental processes generally is as amazing as its evolution from human feeling, peripheral and central, in all corners and reaches of man's overtaxed psyche. The formation of separate languages does not stem from the variability of semantical codes and deliberate choices of terms and rules of combination, but bears all the marks of organic process: the unplanned growth of grammatical inflections to a stage of high elaboration, often followed by periods of gradual simplification, popular misuse and loss of forms, and in the course of such decline a tendency to generate entirely new languages, much as hereditary taxonomic lines produce intricate forms up to a turning point where these begin to degenerate again, and the stock, temporarily "defeated," tends to speciate, i.e., to initiate various phylogenetically new departures. In its totality, its sound and rhythm and especially its figurative expressions, a language reflects the tempo and emotional base line of the population that speaks and thinks in it; and thought which rises far above that level is apt to employ unusual words and metaphors. Many religious institutions use an archaic or even foreign language in their observances, prayers, chants and recitations. The archaic diction does more than moralists and modernizers realize to remove religious thought from the realm of commonplace interest, exalt the sense of holiness of the worshippers, and hold it at a sustained high tension throughout the celebration.

Many of the deeper effects of language on mental life are revealed only by the subjective experience of polyglot persons. Normally, persons who command more than one language find that they think in one or the other according to what they are doing or thinking about. A language fully possessed is a system of conception; its figures of speech are figures of thought. The mind is so largely formed and its higher functions sustained by words and ways of wording ideas that the linguistic influence is not limited to cortical, rational and semi-rational processes, but reaches far into the emotional sphere, coloring fantasies and wishes and even perceptions; some moods dispose a polyglot individual to favor his earliest, babyhood language, some a later-acquired one if, for instance, it seems more adult and public.

Perhaps the most powerful and also most surprising fact revealed by the use of two or more languages is the entirely unconscious part played by language in the formation of dreams. I happen to be bilingual myself; I did not learn English until I went to school. Then, of course, it became my conversational and intellectual language, and finally my poetic one, too. So it is from personal experience that I say, every dream is dreamt in a language, even if not a word is spoken in the dream; indeed, speeches in a dream may be in another language than the one in which the dream is constructed, which operates at the level of what Freud designated as the dream work. That is the same level at which images are formed, and often stand proxy for words. It is usually by tracing images to their verbal meanings that the language of the dream work is revealed; yet without any such analysis I usually know in which language I dreamt a perfectly wordless dream. It seems that whatever the dream work is, it begins with emotional processes, probably deeply subcortical, and passes through many parts of the brain, entraining recent memories here and very old, buried ones there, before it reaches the visualizing areas of the cortex; and that somewhere along its course all dream material passes through the speech apparatus, where the "dream thought" is sub-verbally formed; which means that those illustrated narratives, our dreams, are something thought.

The life of the mind is so complex and so many-faceted that practically no categorizing or systematizing principle holds without qualification. Even the elementary distinction between impulses to action felt as impacts, usually starting peripherally, and those felt as autogenic acts arising within the organism, and taking shape more slowly before they are overtly consummated, has some exceptions. A thought, a recollection of some forgotten fact or intention, though centrally produced, may break in on the rest of one's thinking with a suddenness and force that can only be classed as impact. As peripheral feeling keeps us generally and quietly aware of what we call "external reality," except when it is intensified and stirred up by special events, so our autogenic mental acts usually run their normal courses, unless suddenly a thought from an entirely different line of thinking breaks in on them with a shock much like that of a real, external blow delivered to the organism. Such a thought is a "realization," which clashes with the rest of the brain's work and is felt as impact. The human brain is so elaborate, and functionally so departmentalized, that one act may impinge on a whole system of other processes; and one word may be the symbol that triggers such a mental and even physical emergency.

In this chapter I have dwelled especially upon the intraorganic influences of man's unique trait, symbolic conception and expression, because their importance and depth have been misjudged by a great number of psychologists and anthropologists who deem the communicative function of speech not only its paramount value, but its entire *raison d'être*, and consequently class it, on the one hand, with technological signal codes, and on the other with animal signs of intention and disposition. But animal values are only incidental to human life, and the techniques of intercourse a constant by-product of conceptual contact among men. Communication is, indeed, the driving force in language-making; but it is communication of ideas, beyond the realm of a present situation, that builds up the human world. The first cerebral finish of a mental act, the first discovery of the unreality of figments created in dream, beget the concept of reality. When the sense of reality embraces events and dangers, the world of time and space becomes the theater of natural powers, all seen in imaginary forms, felt to be actual but incomprehensible denizens of that world. The enormous potency of speech lies in the fact that it can transmit such intangible conceptions to all members of a human group, familial or congregated, and make it a society. Language can grow up only in communicative use, which for human beings is the typical process of contact with one another; Révész was surely right when he pointed out that interindividual contact is the principle which holds every group of gregarious beings together, and that in mankind communication—mental contact—has replaced the physical contact needed by other sociable creatures (1946, pp. 165–70).

It is in society, and more particularly in the verbal intercourse called conversation, that men have acquired what the most intelligent other animals have never developed—intellect. Animal mentation and human intellect rest on different principles. The most organized animal community is not comparable to human society, for only the latter is based on intellectual and moral values—personal responsibility, standards of justice, honor and loyalty to a social order. Society, like the spatiotemporal world itself, is a creation of man's specialized modes of feeling—perception, imagination, conceptual thought and the understanding of language. The rise of his typical way of life as a member of a continuous, recognized society, built up on the ancient and gradual separation of the evolving Hominidae from all other, differentially evolving primate lines, in its advance constantly epitomizes the great shift from beast to man.

V / *The Moral Structure*

19 / *The Spirit-World*

The survival value of man's mental achievements is undeniable, but it may have been a long time in coming to the fore. Speech was certainly a huge advantage from the beginning of its communicative use; before that, its protoforms of spontaneous, semi-articulate utterance may have had many other important functions—the formation of auditory rhythms which, in turn, rhythmicized motions and shaped terminating postures, the sense of communion in the mingling of voices, and (perhaps above all) the concentration of subjective feeling in formalized self-expression, which each individual found in choric chant, yell, or articulate utterance without verbal value. Yet few, if any, of these effects were practical assets that could give direct aid in the struggle for life of the stock; and furthermore, not all human specialties which arose, like the gift of language, from the symbolic substitute consummations of impulses in the overtaxed hominid cortex show even such indirect, ultimate values. The world built up by primitive minds was not what fully humanized minds would build; and present-day people, savage or civilized, have inherited that world of their remotest forebears with varying degrees of modern improvement.

The differences in those degrees are great enough to make the world views of persons in widely separated cultural ambients incomprehensible each to the other's holders. They do grade into one another, yet it is in comparing the present-day extremes—the view of civilized "common sense" with the "common-sense view" of tribal societies in mainly unmodified natural surroundings—that one may see the traces of early forms of thought, still freely mixed with dream elements and instinctual impulses, as they shaped the primitive world.

The first true human beings recognizable as such were not necessarily the cleverest primates (though, in view of their active forebrains, they may have been), but the first symbol-mongers. The erect bipedal South African "man-apes," with their human legs and simian skulls, may or may not have been among those earliest men and women, isolating visual forms by their physiognomic appearances more than by contours, textures, or colors, seeing unreal shapes, eyes, and potential movement everywhere in the bush. Whoever the "dawn men" were, the world their minds created was apparently not modeled on crudely conceived laws of matter and motion, nor on any forerunner of a primitive physics; quite the contrary to the widely accepted theory that they must have been pure materialists, they seem to have had no idea of inert matter and what could be done with it. Although they handled it and even did some remarkable things with it, their use of material was still largely instinctive, their knowledge of it implicit, their thinking concentrated on what was coming of their manipulations; a "thing" was a product of an act, not the stuff that had gone into the new entity.

It is this emphasis on making, giving form, giving life, and initiating growth and change that today marks spontaneous, untutored thinking. And untutored, spontaneous, the primitive modes of thought must have been. Perception of external happenings falls into the mold of the percipient's imagination; we perceive as we are able to conceive. The natural way to imagine an event is in the form of an act; not really as a true act, perhaps, but in that most familiar form of subjectively known progression from one situation to another, the act form of impulse, rise, consummation, and cadence, with the likelihood of entrainment, deflection, or blocking anywhere along the way. There may be no idea at all of an agent behind the passage of an external change; only the passage itself resembles a doing. Several anthropological field workers remarked that the people they were observing had no notion of ordinary causality. The undisturbed savage mind, uninfluenced by any contact with civilized thought and expression, probably never assumes the "scientific attitude." Practical as well as imaginative activity can be carried on in the natural frame, i.e., in terms of motivation, and the two sorts of context require no switch from sacred to secular; that switch, which seems to occur in many cultures, though not in all, can be made within the typical primitive mode so smoothly that a slight emotional lift or drop may be its only sign, ordinarily not even noticed. The anthropologist who remarked the true difference between savage and civilized thought was one who recognized the possible alternative to the "scientific attitude" even for practical conception: that was Dorothea Demetracopoulou Lee. In one of her later writings, she spoke for others as well as herself when she declared: "Anthropologists have realized in recent years that people of other cultures than our own not only act differently, but they have a different basis for their behavior. They act upon different premises; they perceive reality differently, and codify it differently" (1949, p. 501).

Writing specifically of the Trobriand Islanders, Lee realized that savage perception sees any dynamic action only in reference to pattern, which pattern is known as a whole, not as a temporal process. It is fairly obvious that the "pattern," which is self-contained yet dynamic, is the act form. An act is a special sort of natural event arising from a matrix of similarly patterned events, and so organically involved in that matrix that all influences which can affect a particular act must do so by affecting the matrix, or organism, as a whole. That complex relation—causal, but so deeply rooted as to be highly indirect—is the phenomenon I have designated as "motivation." If the "pattern" is the form of the act in question, then it is comprehensible that "realized or not, the pattern is always there." We do not usually think, in our terms, of a causal sequence, such as a cloudburst followed by a local flood, as a "realization"; but in the vital contexts of motivational thinking, the self-contained pattern of any object, event, undertaking, or what not is known as a whole rather than as a temporal process. Once made evident through the dynamic pattern, the total must be realized. Those modern scientists who have recently studied neurological activity in animals have attested the significance of this conception, as they find the minimal act to be prefigured in the complex pattern of its impulse before it leaves the initiating neuron and is passed along the axon.

As the present-day person of European culture ordinarily conceives causality, it is a relation between two terms, known as "the cause" and "the effect," both equally objective and impersonal and typically mechanical. The ambition of the scientific thinker is to break down his materials into inanimate units with known physical properties, and into no others that might be ultimately irreducible to cause-and-effect statement. That such scientific statements may be of staggering complexity is evident; yet by rigorous operational principles and far-sighted logical imagination in the choice of elementary terms and functions, one can build highly abstract mathematical systems which promise to express all occurrences in our known universe as causally related changes, thereby making them not only comprehensible but predictable to astounding degrees. To the laity, such scientific achievements have to be presented in a simpler language as concatenated imaginable events; and that is the language and imagery in which we are habituated to think, perceive, and believe.

The world picture created by the "scientific attitude" is, thus, radically different from the "natural" view of events based on the feeling of organic processes, i.e., in the pattern of impulse, effort, and realization. Impingements and behavioral effects are objective aspects of acts, while impulse and effort and many other elements, gross or subtle, are subjective. The two aspects intersect, alternate, or fuse in experience; one cannot truly say that seeing ambient events in act-like form is "personification" of lifeless objects, though in a somewhat special sense one might call it "animation." Living and non-living things are not conceptually distinguished. People whose thought still runs freely and naturally in the mythic mode do not change to the scientific mode when they employ practical techniques. Even as they cook, build, plant, or shape their hunting gear, they handle the material as something active, not passive.

The constant ritual actions attending the everyday, sober practices of people living in the wild, generally viewed by the civilized spectator as religious or magical and said by the performers themselves (if a white visitor raises such an outlandish question) to insure success in the work or future luck with the product, have a more direct, unavowed purpose of making the procedure comprehensible as it is carried on. An American farmer, similarly, might say to himself, "If this rain-wet hay be put in the loft it might ferment, and the fermentation might produce enough heat to cause spontaneous combustion which might cause a fire and burn down the barn," as he spreads the hay to dry more thoroughly. He thus takes stock of the situation in causal terms; the tribesman does the same thing in motivational terms as he enlists the material, the tool, even the hand, calling them into action.

The motivational conception of events expresses, by its formulation of them, the act of conceiving them; the product of thinking reflects the basic pattern of the thinking process itself, much as the living body, the product of growth, expresses the dynamics of the physiological acts of growing. That is why the act form is the natural form for primitive conception of events to take, and as such it governs the immediate perceptions as well as the imagination of people who have not originated or received the causal perspective. It is, in fact, the development of that causal perspective, and with it the "scientific attitude," that really presents an anthropological problem, and accordingly will be discussed when it arises.

The act-form of experience is so fundamental a condition that it creates a different universe from that which civilized, scientific-minded societies exist (and it is in them that people alternate between the causal pattern of their common sense and the motivational pattern of their religious thought). To understand the mythical beliefs of savage tribesmen—their ritual defenses against hosts of supernatural beings, their magic practices, comprising witchcraft, sorcery, divination, exorcism, and mysterious personal powers such as flying or climbing a rope that stands on end—one has to realize, above all, that a fundamental attitude of mind entrains and encourages particular mental acts which are in harmony with it. At the time when conceptual thought began and language arose, imagination, even if fragmentary and brief, was still free from all rational constraints, and perception presented material for its work rather than revealing the limits of its excursions. The basic elements of all supernatural beliefs, from the earliest we know to the ones we hold seriously today, were probably created in that pristine, hyperactive phase of untrammeled fantasy, when wholly subjective consummation of mental acts was new. A new ability, even a newly discovered voluntary muscle, invites a creature to exercise it for pure enjoyment. First dream, asleep or awake, then intentional envisionment and its objectification in speech made the teeming spirit-world into which our earliest human ancestors were born. When one looks at the assortment of spooks held in honor by people living today, some in remote corners of our world, some in the midst of advanced societies, it seems very likely that many of those phantasms go back to what one French psychologist, Émile Cailliet (1936), called the "vegetative" period of symbol-making, when any unusual sounds, shapes, or lights and all distinct phenomena of nature received some exciting interpretation.

However and whenever this great rise of imagination took place—slowly or explosively, repeatedly or only once—it added a whole new dimension to man's world, the supernatural dimension. With that evolutionary breakthrough transcending the confines of animal realism came the host of imagined beings that fill his world: deities and demons, ghosts, ghouls, and goblins, mythical heroes and legendary ancestors. Where every event appears in the guise of an act instead of an instance of simpler, non-biological mechanics, some agency seems to be implicated even where none is apparent. It has created a spirit multitude, so great that the earth could not contain it but was expanded to possess higher and lower realms holding a limitless number of beings—gods and goddesses, demiurges, sometimes living a dim life under the earth or suffering there in a fiery furnace for their sins. The belief of most Christians, Moslems, and Jews in heaven above and hell below, making a three-story edifice of the world—perfect, imperfect, and utterly horrible—is a restrained version of the widely held notion that there are many levels, many *Lebensräume*, piled one above another. These are not necessarily distinguished by relative values, and even if they are, those values are not always what we would consider moral values.

Stranger than the many heavens, hells, dreamlands, and limbos of ancient creative fantasy are their supernatural possessors. There seems to be really no limit to the macabre forms that these will take, especially for people living in the wild. Our own conception of ghosts as diaphanous white human figures embodying spirits of dead or absent persons, and generally doing nothing more violent than to warn, accuse, or prophesy, is a very tame sort of bugaboo beside the uncanny spooks that are popularly known to savages and may be encountered by them at any time in darkness or daylight, in jungle or veldt, while hunting, working, lovemaking, or by night in dreams.

One may well wonder how human beings who are intelligent enough to carry on the practical affairs of life can possibly imagine such absurdities and assert them as facts, and even more how anyone besides their inventors can give credence to them. The answers to those two questions prove to be indicative of a whole psychological dimension involved in the motivational view of the external world. The primitive outlook raises its own problems of psychology and even epistemology, i.e., not only of the sources of belief, but of its grounds, the standards of reality and knowledge. They are different from the scientific or at least factual standards of our own common sense. The gap between the savage mind and the civilized is greater than the European-based administrators of uncivilized conquered peoples realize, so great that the rulers and their subjects view each other as inane, if not insane. One consequence of this basic mutual repellence is the abuse, often unintended, of persons or whole populations in the colonial holdings of European powers, which will come under discussion in a later chapter; another is the fantastic character attributed by many tribal societies to the white invaders, who are said to walk on their heads at home in their own domains, to be able to disappear in the earth and move under its surface with tremendous speed, and to be cannibals. Several quite unrelated peoples believe that individuals of other races are only half-human.

The difference between the two modes of interpretation, which I have called the motivational and the causal, respectively, rather than the religious and the scientific (since either may, ideally, cover the whole realm of thought), is not enough to meet all the problems which the beliefs and practices of wilderness dwellers pose for the anthropologist. Each of these ideas or actions has its own etiology in the general context of act-oriented thought and language, and has to be traced to its own evolutionary conditions. In the course of such speculation and reflection (for that is really all our theorizing on prehistoric human mentality amounts to) some interesting psychological principles come into play. Most of these have been discovered by psychologists, anthropologists, or other scholars in special connections, but in the biological frame of the present study they come together from all quarters to form the rational basis of thought even in its most primitive stages. For, although it is fairly certain that no human stock on earth is older than another and none living today is truly "aboriginal," those people who have not developed the causal view of nature still reveal connections between cerebral activities and more general patterns of vital function which scientific civilization has obscured. Some of their mental productions may be very old indeed, for they strongly suggest processes that are likely to have played a vital role in the formation of mind itself, drawing on all the brain's potentialities, laying the foundations for the later specializations—the arts and sciences, moral and legislative controls—as we know them in historic times. Once we recognize a truly primitive trait of human experience in a naive form, we usually end up by finding it still operative in our own subjective experience.

So we may question, first of all, how perfectly sober people with pressing social and economic interests could ever invent such nonsense as the mating of a sword handle with a spindle, reported from Borneo, and regard it as the historic source of themselves and of their gods. One important step toward the answer, I think, may have been given by Daniel Essertier, who pointed out that assertion is one of the primary acts of mind, both in phylogeny and in ontogeny. Of its phylogenetic role he said:

> This is not a simple matter of linking concepts, but of a double and indivisible affirmation: in affirming anything, the mind affirms itself. And even further: it is for the sake of thus affirming itself that it makes any affirmation at all. Similarly, when the hand of a little child closes as tightly as it does on an object it grasps, that is less from the fear of losing the object than in order to feel its own strength.
>
> Thus the horror of doubt is natural to consciousness. Doubt is its supreme menace, for it threatens the keystone of the whole mental structure: the affirmation of the self. Dogmatism and lazy-mindedness are usually, above all, primitive means whereby somewhat weak and vacillating personalities parry that threat.
>
> Consequently the assertions of primitive minds are first and foremost immediate, arbitrary, and unconcerned about their objective content. (1927, pp. 57–58)

In the asserter's own thinking there was probably never any question of the truth or falsity of his allegations; anything he could imagine served for a statement. Essertier's text goes on to say just that. The double function of assertion—affirmation of an idea and of the mind itself—may have been what carried the human activity of propositional thought from its earliest, sporadic beginnings a long way toward easy and complete articulation, before any question of plausibility ever arose.

But what would lead other people than the author of a fantasy to believe his words? Another facet of the same condition; in the earliest stages of human mental evolution, when thinking and verbalizing were new and therefore exceedingly active functions, not yet reduced to the servosystem attending on practical life that they are, for the most part, today, people may have been ready to accept not only their own but also any other notion born of any flash of imagination, any suggestion no matter how it was made, much as some gregarious animals like geese or schooling fish fall in with a suggested act at the first move of the first companion to give overt expression to an impulse befitting the momentary situation. Similarly, in the irresponsible thinking of truly primitive human beings, the production or reception of a thought may have involved no judgment whatever of truth-value; it probably was more like a direct sparking-over from the impulse generating the subjective act of ideation to the feeling of reality pervading the figment even as it took shape; that is to say: the character of reality, which for us today requires some credentials such as objective perception or trusted information, may originally have belonged to all ideas and may only have acquired a distinctive value with experiences of disillusionment and the gradual discovery of fictitiousness.

It is a curious fact, often undiscovered and unappreciated, that the most primitive humanizing requirements seldom—if ever—are entirely transcended. They may be met in such new ways that they do not seem the same demands as before. I think this is true of the need to make assertions in order to assure ourselves of our own mental power. We are no longer in the world-building stage of rampant imagination, when every person could indulge in the most extravagant fantasies and every invention passed for a reality; most civilized people today limit their categorical religious assertions to the affirmation of formally stated tenets shared by a number of other persons. The number may be small—the membership of a deviant sect or even a secret cult—or immense, like that of the Roman Catholic Church, Islam, or Hinduism, each uniting millions. The passionate feeling with which we tend to profess our faith shows that even in modern society the average person has a deep need of asserting the nature of his world, in order that he may constantly realize and confirm his own being. The content of such assertions is, of course, no longer individual in the framework of a great religion. With the passing of the pre-rational, boundlessly creative ages of symbolic thinking, other growing functions such as logical judgment, evaluation, and negation made the plethora of rival ideas a battle scene that discouraged and frustrated the average thinker's personal production of assertible beliefs. Then there had to be tenets the unimaginative, intimidated, or confused could borrow; and as such conceptions had not emerged spontaneously from the mind that employed them, there had to be supports to its self-affirmation. This may explain the emotional value of conservatism and dogmatism, which is often expressed in a defensive, merciless intolerance.

The degrees to which the loss of spontaneous fantasy and personal assertion has extended in various populations differ widely. Anthropologists who base general conclusions about "the savage mind" on their observations of extreme conservatism in two or three tribal societies, or on the opposite attitude found in one or more, may not have noted the exact circumstances that determine the degree of freedom or conformism in the cultural pattern of those tribes. For example: the Yạnomamö in the jungle of the Amazon sources, described in detail by Napoleon Chagnon (1968, p. 44), seem to have great liberty to exercise their own poetic talents and to elaborate religious ideas. Their springs of imagination have certainly not run dry. The reason is that they have not let them.

Most people, "primitive" or sophisticated, today concentrate their religious fervor on a received dogma. Their spirit world is not built on original experiences, but on tradition; and because they do not feel as if their own creative genius could replace any lost deity, ancestry, or mythic history, yet have still the psychological need of testifying to the structure of their world for the sake of self-affirmation, the content of their traditional belief tends to be conservative, even to a point of fanatical defense against the smallest threat of heresy. But if the contents of assertions which were made first of all for the sake of self-affirmation are, as Essertier maintained, unimportant and arbitrary, why do those contents not consist of trivial, everyday items concerning familiar objects and routine affairs? Why do they deal with cosmic events, the origins of the world and of man? The double function which Essertier attributed to mythological assertions—to say something about the world, and to affirm the power of the mind to say it—runs through all our assertions to this day, though certainly without awareness, let alone intention. But trivial statements make no affirmation of their maker's whole mind; they give implicit assurance of detailed mental functions, of this or that potentiality of discrimination, concatenation, response, recollection, the covert, subjective counterpart of the overt expression, to which the motives controlling the latter are irrelevant. Recognition of this action lends some support to John Locke's "axiomatic" belief that the mind is intuitively aware of its own activities. But intuition is a conscious, cognitive act, and the self-asserting process of which Essertier spoke takes place far below the conscious level of thought. The function of self-affirmation in such current, chiefly communicative acts is, after all, only one element in their motivation, so ubiquitous and familiar that only the affront of contradiction brings it to our notice in a surge of emotional feeling, which may be of any degree from scarcely discernible to uncontrollable.

It is in making assertions about the world as a whole that the mind affirms itself as a whole; hence the sacredness and inviolability of the cosmic myths that are incorporated in religions. These are the tenets to which Essertier's remarks about the "horror of doubt" fully apply. Yet this horror is probably a fairly late cultural phenomenon; as long as all allegations about unknown realms, the distant past or the future (that is, anything beyond personal experience), were uncritically received as true, there could be no concept of untruth except with respect to empirical, still current facts, no acknowledged fictions except lies. Myths of world creation, human origins, destiny, and life after death (whether as a ghost in familiar haunts or as a denizen of some other world) are products of unhampered imagination, and the wildest tales often prove to be acceptable. Such myths tend to disappear as the higher divinities are developed and exalted in religious conception; but the more universal themes—the origins of the world and of man—however fantastic, are more tenacious and prone to accommodate new symbolic imagery which arises with expansions, reverses, or other changes befalling the community; new visions and rites may push out decadent ones, but if the sacred tradition is to live the new sacra must be as mystical as those which they displaced.

Myths of creation and long-past events, of impending dangers or conquests, and of life continued in other realms after death have been as important to man's orientation in his mind-made world as his belief in the snake or stony rim that encircled the ocean to hold it in place, the heavens above his head and hells beneath his feet, for as such fabled geography first gave the world spatial dimensions, so the myths of origins and superhuman adventure have given it the character of duration, or time.

In the context of motivational thinking, however, time is not the one-dimensional structure that it is in civilized thought, arbitrarily divisible into temporal segments—years and days, hours, minutes, seconds, and for scientific purposes milliseconds—into which historical fact and observable events are fitted to present the causal order of nature. For intuitive perception, time is a stream of acts; and acts, like mixing and branching currents in a river, and unlike metrical units, have forms, proportions, interrelations, so the time they define has a complicated flow: it eats into the future and builds up a past, and those two components meet in an ever-changing, yet ever-present "Now." From that center they both appear in perspective, but each in its own, for acts record themselves primarily in feeling, nameable or nameless and not necessarily emotional, and the respective appearances of past and future are made, if not out of very different conceptual elements, at least by radically different involvements with the "specious present" "Now," giving the two orders quite distinct qualities. The past is a structure in the mode of memory; not composed of memories, though a person's own past may embody a great many, but composed of events (for motivational thinking, of acts) which have entered ineradicably into the subsequent world situation. They may never come to awareness, or, if they do, may be quickly forgotten, but their traces are left upon the progressive "Now." This is as true of imaginary historical elements as of realistic ones. It is the basic, unsystematic "time past" which naive as well as ingenious minds may embroider as they will, covering few or many ages (usually reckoned by lifetimes) and weaving great or small figments to fill in that universal background.

The "sense of pastness" that belongs to normal recollection is produced by several psychological effects, chiefly upon our attitudes, of acts that appear finished but are still providing motivations of present overt and, particularly, covert acts. The most striking characteristic of such acts (which need not be one's own) is that no matter what behavior or thought they motivate, their own occurrence can no longer be eluded. They contain no potentialities, offer no choices; nothing can block or deflect them. A. N. Whitehead once remarked that it takes a strong spirit to contemplate history because of its unalterable reality. Events which have occurred are given in the situation of every individual matrix of activities forever after; that is "the Past."

The Future is built up of cumulative conceptions containing many of the same elements as the Past, but these play a different role: they constitute the situation of emergent acts which are all, as yet, at least partly potential, though many (for some people, most) are rooted in the near past and are, in fact, in process of realization. So-called "projects" may be entirely unrealized, their only connection with the Past being the continuity of their motivating mental acts of imagination, perhaps felt as desire, possibly even as intention; if they have reached the stage of impulse and orientation toward a goal, they also involve expectancy. But if they are purely acts of imagination, they have a present rather than a future character.

In any case, precisely those attributes which past events possess—finality, definiteness of the smallest details, permanent existence, however infinitesimal, as elements in the world for all subsequent acts—are lacking in the natural conception of future time, which is filled with options, potentialities, rational and irrational hopes, well-founded fears, and nightmarish dreads. Hopes and fears are directly related to human wishes, and wishes are strong motivating conditions which may lead to overt action or, in case such action is obviously unfeasible, to alternative, intracerebral consummation, i.e., dream or daydream or other symbolic substitute. The Past, being in the mode of memory, is closed, inalienable, and irreparable; if its "data" undergo any change, that is a change in our knowledge, and the present subjective act of correction adds itself to the judging individual's history as a complication of his Past from that moment onward. The Future, on the other hand, is an open-ended progression, and our most amazing, precise predictions are a play of emergent realizations with intellectually engendered expectancies. The whole structure of time apprehended in motivational terms is an immensely complex web, with a large "specious present" dividing two very different extensions of that central "Now," which changes as they change in a direction marked by progressive realization ever making the Past, and newly emerging situations creating the vista of potentialities, the Future.

In such a framework events can have no specific dates. One may be known to have come before another because it enters into the motivating situation of the latter, but apart from such interrelationships the Past is a perspective of lifetimes, ranged in grades of vividness from actual memory contents, through historical tradition, to utterly unrealistic, supernatural myth where time has no measure any more, not even by generations. Mythical beings and acts are contemplated with a "sense of pastness," i.e., are conceived in the literary mode of memory, but their occurrence was "in the beginning," "very long ago," before mankind as it is known today existed.

That remote prehistory is the principal domain of free, irresponsible assertion of the most arbitrary fantasies, which seems to inspire belief simply upon suggestion. The visibly approaching future contains too many real expectations, anxieties, intentions, hopes, and prognostications to permit sheer imagination to possess it. If it is to harbor dream images, these must be removed from actuality by being projected beyond the dreamer's life, into his "hereafter." Even at that distance, they and their setting still resemble earthly life far more than the miracles of origin.

In filling the vanished ages before anyone's memory with fantastic acts of gods and goddesses, demons, animals, supermen, and beings compounded of any or all of these, what motivates such irrational inventions? And as countless minds contribute to the multitude of "supernaturals" and their stories, what is the basis of choice among them, so that at least they shall not contradict each other when a firm mythic tradition is finally created?

The motivation is essentially the same as that of dreams: the spontaneous production of "natural symbols" for ideas that are intellectually too advanced, too great with implications, or emotionally too disturbing for conscious formulation and expression in words. The production of such symbols, and their conglomeration due to the dense fusion of their meanings below the level of rational conception, is what Freud, in the bold, speculative sixth chapter of his first revolutionary book, *The Interpretation of Dreams*, called the "dream work." But dreams are not its only products, nor are they, in the evolution of mind, its most important. Dreams are, perhaps, all-important safety valves in personal lives, taking care of emotional strains which frustrate normal thoughts and actions and threaten the mental balance of the individual; in the long run, however, in the life of the human race, the paramount contribution of the dream work is myth.

Mental products, like all organic specialties, tend to take on further functions as soon as the ones they originally grew up with do not preempt them completely. Freud himself discovered that the meanings of "natural symbols" may be multifarious, and called such a plethora of simultaneous meanings "overdetermination" of the symbolic figments. What he did not consider—because it was not relevant to his research—was that those figments might have still other possible functions in a different, concomitant system of significance. With the beginning of speech, symbolism entered a new era, the fully human era of hominid life; the primitive need in that evolutionary stage was to make assertions, trivial ones or sweeping cosmic ones, for the sake of self-affirmation and orientation in the world. That instinctive activity, which automatically created time, universe, and society, required material to fashion assertible propositions; and dream ideas were the readiest contents for eager, perhaps vehement assertions, particularly as dream images and events usually carry a somewhat disproportionate cargo of emotional feeling.

The favored fantasies are likely to have been richly overdetermined ones, which, while they gave many people some emotional catharsis, gave a few of them a mythical formulation of precocious insights which were not remotely ready, as yet, for literal statement: conceptions of life, with little distinction between human and animal or even plant life, and all the circumambient forces of nature, winds, waters, earthquake, and fire; beginnings, growth and its metamorphoses; and the intolerable, unbelievable breakdown of every personal life in death. Gradually, by dint of much repetition, connection with the fixed features of place and tribal activity, and the intrinsic emotional value of dream symbols, the tales that expressed an apprehension of such realities became traditional; and tradition, the greatest phyletic product of communication and assertion, is essentially sacred. At the same time those venerable stories were acted out in dance, while their personages were acknowledged in sacrificial rites; and as human mentality developed, even the thoughtless average person felt (rather than perceived) their import, so the myths were established without any decree, and became the basis of life and religion.

But what of the inconsistencies and even flat contradictions that would surely result from such a casual composition of ghost stories and animal fables into a body of serious beliefs, the basic beliefs of the tribe? The answer is that in tribal societies there frequently is no real body of myth, no coherent dogma at all, and contradiction does not trouble people. They seem to think of a single narrative at a time, as one does with a fictitious story, but while they tell it or contemplate it thus in isolation they believe it. Perhaps it were better to say they "believe in" it; for they are excited by its meaning, which is not literally expressed, and affirm the ostensible facts without any "scientific attitude," i.e., without conceiving them factually and fitting them into a larger historical frame. Because the "culture heroes," deities, and spooks of primitive imagination are natural symbols, they are generally overdetermined, and the development of their implicit (and profoundly unconscious) interpretations in several directions makes different cycles of myth which are related only by being centered in one personage, not through story elements cohering with each other. Consequently, on the face of it, they look irrational, yet the contradictions do not trouble the believers.

The deep, unconscious, evolutionary motivation of myth, the early but driving effort to conceive world and man in terms of symbolic imagery and dreamlike action, is even more apparent in ritual than in story. Ritual is almost certainly older than narrative, because its materials are given in an entirely prehuman state of animal existence, with the rise of emotional, self-expressive movement. Such movement is unintentional, instinctive, perhaps even unconsciously performed. But it has two biological properties which destine it to become the stuff of symbolic rather than directly symptomatic expression: the tendency of habitual animal acts to become formalized, which supplies strict repetitious patterns of movement apart from immediate, close-fitted stimulations, and the fact that the expressive acts are visible to the performer and his fellows so that they, and he himself, experience the influence of a powerful suggestion. Add to this the proneness of any specialized element of behavior, such as a purely self-expressive act without practical aim, to take on new functions, and the invitation is given to develop symbolic gestures.

Such gestures, furthermore, may be overtly and also mentally addressed by their agent to another being, human or superhuman, real or visionary. Because the rite is an actual performance, the sacred objective, even if invisible, is given a convincing reality by the enactment of the attitude people bear toward it. This in turn fixes the attitude and articulates more detailed symbolic elements in the ritual, exploiting the expressive possibilities of gesture, posture, utterance, and sometimes the look and feeling of manipulated objects, in which some mysterious import is seen as an inherent quality, "holiness," until the addressed being takes shape for contemplation as deity, ancestral spirit, or totem. The various beliefs in supernatural agents, enchanted places, staggered planes of existence, and the mythic past where everything began are not formed in succession, but grow up all together to produce the spirit-world.

It is natural for a person reared in the atmosphere of European common sense to assume that the use of ritual in connection with ordinary, daily chores—gardening, hunting, fishing, handiwork—must have a practical aim, and to ask a native of forest or veldt how his work would be affected if the sacred forms were omitted. The native informant can only attempt to answer the question, which is meaningless to him, by saying that something would surely go wrong, the effort would not succeed. Perhaps he would be stimulated to improvise on the theme, and invent thinkable disasters, and tell them all as if they were generally expected results of such breaches, when in fact he had never thought of the proposed impiety in terms of an effect on the particular work in hand. The natural consequence that might occur to him would be "ghost sickness"—sent by angry dead progenitors—that might befall him or the whole society, for the omission would not be a technical error or folly, but a sacrilegious act, incurring personal punishment or general retaliation according to the feelings of the offended spirits.

The true need of weaving ritual actions into such quotidian occupations as planting, fishing, harvesting, and household chores is to give them a stamp of ancestral sanction, submitting them for approval to the assumed watchers and constant critics of the tribal life as it continues in its wonted way. There is no formal code for social customs except the round of rites that makes the patterns of sentiment on which anthropologists have often commented. But such statements are supported by the belief, held in most tribal societies, that some "first beings" or one divine progenitor set the example for the daily, seasonal, or yearly activities of men, and the ancestors of the present generation continued them, so that the current ritual enactments express a sacred tradition.

In Europe, the advance of civilization, led more and more unmistakably by scientific thought, has steadily tended to break such traditions and relegate their expressions to private, elected styles of life or to religious institutions rarely binding, at the present day, on entire populations. The ascendancy of causal thinking has transformed the spirit-world into a mechanical world of impersonal progressive events, requiring other principles of explanation and expectation than concepts of impulse and agency. So it is a common belief among us that public ritual belongs to primitive cultures where, on a basis of false notions of cause, it is used as a means of controlling nature, but that of course it is out of place in the business of modern life. Yet there have been high civilizations which never abandoned their motivational conception of the world and never gave up their ritualized behavior in its frame. The civilization of ancient China rose to great heights, even to the creation of a recognized single empire, internally organized by feudal states or, at other times, by districts each with its hierarchy of crown officials that constituted a graded aristocracy. What made the formation of an empire possible at all under these early conditions was a ritual practice that was natural and acceptable to very lowly village communities and to the godlike emperor himself: the worship of one's own progenitors. This practice needed no studied organization, it fell of itself into a pattern of successive generations, a family seen in retrospect with the line of the worshipper's "fathers" running clearly through the web of agnatic parallels and affinic entrances. Ancestor worship is a familiar phenomenon to anthropologists the world over. It is known in Africa, in Australia, to some of the most naive savages, and to the sophisticated literati of

China and Japan. It can take various forms, from real worship of totemic ancestral animal gods to the veneration of progenitors whose spirits, instead of being deified, are treated as continuing members of the living society. The same essential rites can serve superstitious peasants to express their beliefs, and sages to attest their sense of social obligation and their loyalty to the emperor. The basic idea was understood everywhere. The work of the great philosophers rested on the principle of self-education for public leadership by moral example and precept. Confucius had set up the idea of *jen*, or "humanity," i.e., human as against animal existence, dignified by both humanistic and humanitarian values, which is the nearest an individual can come to the *tao*, or "perfect virtue"; Mencius expounded the idea of *yi*, the way to *jen*; it was Hsün-tsu who saw that the method which implemented that approach was the regular enactment of rites, known as *li*, expressing emotional feeling, and by constant formal expression holding such feeling steady throughout life. *Li* is the dominant theme of his book, which teaches that the aim of a *chün-tsu*'s (cultivated man's) education is the refinement of feeling, from which superior behavior naturally follows (Chai and Chai 1965, p. 253).

A society largely regulated by traditional rites—"no one knows whence they came"—seeping down through its illiterate populace from the highest seats of culture, is inevitably conservative. To our age and outlook it seems that such an ideal must spell hopeless stagnation for the society that abides by it. Just because the rituals concerned universal human relations and expressed the attitudes appropriate to them, their basic meanings could be conceived on many levels. So it was possible to make them binding on the whole population as a unifying form of behavior and belief.

The classical Chinese ideal of morality was the cultivation of feeling, giving it form, rather than repressing it or letting it break loose in an uncontrolled flood. Hsün-tsu, especially, treated the rites or "proprieties" imposed on emotional behavior as receptacles to hold and convey and thereby articulate and modify one's feelings. How completely free this ancient philosopher was from savage superstition is evident from his attesting the symbolic nature of the mourning ritual and clearly rejecting any notion of bodily presence or participation in it by the dead.

This cultivation of feeling is pure ritual, "adorning" expressive acts and formulating them to fit into the system of motives, impulses, and realizations that "natural symbols" present. The great Chinese moralists have developed that system as a basis for personal and public life, quite beyond what any modern Western philosopher has been able to construct in his own accepted terms of material causality. This fact corroborates the observation of the French philosopher Ignace Meyerson (1948) that the Asian civilizations, built on conceptions of impulse and act, motivation and realization, were not likely to yield a science of physics but might well produce advanced ethical theories; whereas the Western system of thought leads readily to scientific concepts and their amazing applications but not to any great understanding of human values.

Yet, however far beyond popular mentality the thought of Chinese and Indian sages might go, it is certainly true that the vast majority of men all over the earth did and do meet their surrounding world of spirits—celestial, infernal, or intimately mundane—with magic, and that, in all but the most civilized societies or even small parts of these, ritual is used mainly for magical purposes. Psychologists have evinced surprisingly little theoretical interest in this universal human foible, apart from attempts by those who share various popular superstitions to "prove" their hypotheses concerning such processes, known as "mental telepathy," "extra-sensory perception," and "thought control," by statistical demonstrations that the phenomena they would thus interpret do occur. The names given to the alleged abnormal events, of course, attach the theoretical interpretation to the very mention of them, so any skewed-looking table of statistics "proves" the fancied spiritual, electrical, magnetic, or frankly magical nature of mysterious happenings. Anthropologists, too, have been content to record the practices of magicians and the effects on their clients, apparently without seeing any significance for the theoretical aspect of their science in the intriguing problem of such a fundamental tendency to unrealism in the most intelligent animal.

The fact is that the answer, which I think is not unattainable, is none the less rather difficult and elusive because it involves many coincident conditions, some of them reaching back to animal mentality, others of purely human character impinging on them to produce peculiar developments of imaginative expectancy and dreamlike, often nightmarish belief. The paramount importance of magic in savage life is certainly not easily accounted for along Darwinian lines of reasoning, though retrospectively it may fit into them well enough. But it is so central to man's life in a spirit-world that the serious discussion of it must be deferred to the next chapter.

20 / *The Dream of Power*

To say that psychologists and other investigators have spent relatively little theoretical thought on the etiology of the world-wide, persistent belief in magic is, of course, not to say that no one has attempted to construct a theory to account for that seemingly un-zoological behavior pattern. But the psychological explanations which so far have been proposed are frail scaffoldings for so ubiquitous and central a phenomenon, which is really the most perplexing practice in precivilized life, where all serious undertakings are accompanied, if not dominated, by supposedly efficacious ritual: curing sickness, or, on the contrary, inflicting sickness, killing people; making rain (in many regions of earth, the prime concern of the "medicine man" or "medicine woman"); controlling the movements of game, fish, and fowl; calling plants up out of the soil to bear fruit. These are only the ordinary uses of magic. More extravagant examples are the alleged achievements of magicians flying through the air, often to remote places and back in the twinkling of an eye, perhaps to heaven. The hypotheses which anthropologists and psychologists have proposed to account for so unlikely a method to attain practical results as the recitation of words, especially names, in long formulas and the manipulation of "medicines"—leaves, bits of clay, or less aesthetic substances, birds' down, human blood, plus all the potent ingredients that went into the cauldron of Macbeth's weird sisters—have been mainly in terms of emotion, need, intense desire, and "wishful thinking."

Psychologically, the gestures which usually constitute a magical performance might well be regarded as substitute acts where no physically effective action is possible. Yet in view of the popularity of magic despite its causally inappropriate techniques, its unfailing, ubiquitous presence and especially its long persistence make such an explanation seem inadequate; they point to some deeper roots. I find it hard to believe that an accepted type of conduct which pervades all but a small fraction of human social life and forms a basis, in large measure, of individual status and even tribal power should be essentially a by-product of despair or fury. In our own society a person in utter desperation or driven by hate might resort to occult practices, but it is unlikely that his fellow men, young and old, would expect to see a miracle take place in response to his behavior.

The reason why the emotive theory found such ready acceptance was probably the recent impact, at the time when it was proposed, of Freud's psychoanalytic doctrine, with its powerful concepts of symbolic substitutes for repressed or frustrated action and of the unconscious and irrational origin of symbols, which had thrown a veritable bombshell into the psychological field.

Deep, unconscious desires and fantasies are undoubtedly expressed in the symbolic gestures and words of magicians. So are they in the fabrication of myth, where they probably have furnished the dreamlike stuff of the assertions that have come casually and uncritically together to make some strange articles of belief. But magic, even more than superstition, legend, or cosmogony, is only incidentally a vehicle for symbolic expression of desires. It may be used where the magician has no personal concern. It may be produced by amateurs or professionals. It is always mystical and fascinating, but does not seem unnatural.

To understand the ubiquitous, everyday acceptance of magic one has to realize what it means to live in a spirit-world: far more than to live in the ambient which to modern men—especially those with a European heritage—is "reality," only with a large cargo of spooks and fanciful beliefs thrown in. It means to live not among things, which may be used, ignored, or destroyed, and which may have been produced by skillful handling of materials according to physical laws, but to live among hosts of agents largely non-human, whose ways of action are inscrutable, their means often invisible, their wills autonomous. Things, however produced or originated, need not be anthropomorphized to seem capable of hearing, responding, or refusing their part in human actions. Clouds need not be thought of as persons in order to be called to assemble and bring their gifts of water. No one sees how they carry it or how they pour it out in drops; and it is perfectly natural for such beings then to make themselves invisible again.

The making of the spirit-world probably goes back as far as the rise of language, and like that greatest of man's assets rests on deeply buried, species-specific organic conditions. One of these came to light, in the teen-years of the present century, through a surprising observation made by Wolfgang Köhler (1931) on the chimpanzees in his ape colony, which showed a striking difference between simian and human perceptual acts. It impressed everybody with the curious shortcoming of the ape's mentality, but no one seems to have seen its implication for the human departure, the overdevelopment and progressive specialization of the brain that has set the track of our evolution inestimably far apart from that of any other primate.

The talent in question is so familiar, so common to all people on earth that we are simply unconscious of it as a special possession: our ability to project our own bodily feelings of balance or imbalance into other physical objects, real or even apparent, that is given to us solely through vision. To a human being every laterally symmetrical, upright form expresses the feeling of balance he maintains in his own body when he stands erect; every asymmetry suggests falling, being pushed out of the vertical. It is perfectly possible for us to "see" a center of gravity, sometimes in a purely visual presentation such as a picture, where no mechanical supports and no fulcral points actually exist. We know by sight how far the foot of a ladder must be from a wall against which the top of it leans to keep the ladder from falling away from the wall. This is not an instinctive judgment; young babies cannot make it. But the ability to learn it is one of our special powers. In a very short time after a child begins to build with blocks it recognizes the gravitational relationships between uprights and lintels, leaning blocks and their supports. Its eye replaces the experimenting hand, and projects the feelings of balance or imbalance into its visual image of the little structures. In viewing objects much too large for a weighing hand—rocks, buildings, statues—a human being, even a child beyond babyhood, can "see" poise and counterpoise, weight distribution, security or "top-heaviness." Köhler aptly referred to this insight as our system of "naive statics."

Other primates, monkeys and even the great apes, seem incapable of projecting bodily feeling into forms presented to the eye. Apes are extremely visual-minded, at least as much so as men; their bodily experience of balance is highly developed; yet they seem to make no spontaneous transfer of situational response from one sensory mode to another, i.e., from their body sense to their visual sense. The same lack of mechanical insight appears with regard to objects too long and thin, such as sticks, planks, or ladders, to stand up on end. They will place a ladder in any unstable or stable position which places it optically in closer contact to its objective than if it were supported at four points in human fashion. Visually, the ladder looks neither firm nor infirm to the animal's eyes; and that is the interesting point. Any object an animal uses instrumentally is an extension of its body, more like a prosthesis than a tool. Another of Köhler's observations supports the idea that external objects enter an animal's awareness only as elements in its own acts, and in doing so are assimilated to its behavior and treated as parts of itself.

Evidently the ape's static sensations are in no way "projected" into the visual aspect of objects in his surroundings. They are kept strictly at home in his kinesthetic and equilibrant mechanisms, which may be the reason why his bodily balance, unconfused by suggestive virtual presentations, is generally superior to man's. We have sacrificed some of our athletic ability in developing our peculiar talent for seeing, as well as physically feeling, gravitational relationships. But the new talent, small though it may seem as a step in evolution, was far from small, and indeed was well worth the sacrifice; for the mental act of "projecting" a subjective element into a percept given to a distance receptor such as the eye is an act of objectification. It lets the subjective element come back as an impingement and be perceived as an external datum, i.e., as a quality belonging to an independently existing object; and that object, which thus presents our own sensory feeling to us, is a primitive symbol, conveying the first retainable idea of an all-important sensation and, at first perhaps solely, the possibility of its loss. Body feelings may be the first thing man projected and thus, all unwittingly, imputed to everything he objectified as material bodies in his world. The very existence of "things" is modeled on his own inward expectation of strains, directions, and limitations of his felt actions; the wholeness and simplicity of molar objects is that of his own soma. To this day we speak of "heavenly bodies," meaning inorganic masses of minerals and gases, and near the other end of the magnitude scale we term the tiniest mote in a person's eye a "foreign body." We refer to the parts of our earthly environment as the "foot" of a mountain, an "arm" of the sea, etc., and, in a humbler context, the "neck" of a bottle and the "legs" of a chair. This kind of analogizing has been remarked so often that it requires no further comment; but its origin in the projection of subjective feeling into the external world is not generally recognized, nor is the biological novelty of that process appreciated as the crucial evolutionary event it seems to have been.

The reflection of our own bodily sensations in outward things, animate and inanimate, gives those things a symbolic function, but on so low a level that one can hardly call them symbols; their conceptual value is entirely embedded in the presenting form; there is no hint of an abstract thought inspired by their appearance of balance or imbalance, danger or security. Even today those elements impinge most directly on our faculties as qualities of the things perceived, and in the case of primitive men could at best have appeared in that way. Yet they are the basis of that conceptual seeing which S. T. Coleridge called "primary imagination" (1834, chap. 13), and which appears to be a hominid specialty. It is for this reason that mind is a purely human phenomenon, evolved from a unique mental proclivity, and that a treatise on mind is an essay on human feeling.

The objectification of the subjective sense of balance—and, perhaps, of physical tensions generally—has a natural counterpart, the subjectification of the protosymbolic object as an image. The feeling projected into the well- or badly balanced external object comes back to its producer as an image of equilibrium, secure or precarious as it may be; the object looks centered or off-center. On the same principle all other kinesthetic, thermal, tactual, in short corporeal feelings are "seen" in the shapes that meet our eyes, and give such shapes the meaning of spatial entities, potential opportunities for action if not actual ones at the moment; they confront us as possible implements, obstacles, more or less permanent carriers of their own qualities. The recognition of characteristics like form, relation, and every sort of meaning is the lowest denominator of intellect, the function of intuition.

The development of that faculty must be very ancient in man, and may have gone through many apparently useless steps before the dawn of voluntary imagination and of symbolic thought beyond the production of dream. Today, when that first dawn is fairly far behind us, man's entire way of perceiving is shot through and through with intuition. In all our seeing there is the dialectical interchange of objectification and subjectification, external dictate and autogenic creation—"*La recréation du réel*," Philippe Fauré-Fremiet (1940) called it. This dialectic, so highly developed in contemporary man, savage or civilized, that it functions automatically below the level of consciousness, is "experience" in the distinctively human sense. Our sole contact with the world around us is through our sense organs, yet they are also the gatekeepers, the electors and composers of what the mind accepts; they formulate, even in the swiftest transmission, the images it retains, the sensory impingements it will imbue with feeling and find significant; that constant dialectic of projection and symbolically transformed "feedback" is the dynamism of experience.

To see our ambient as a homogeneous and permanent space furnished with other bodies besides our own is the modulus of intuitive perception; as we project our muscular and gravitational sense into those external things we also, just as involuntarily, see our other feelings reflected in their shapes, which consequently seem to present attitudes—threatening or peaceable, tense or free or somnolent. And with expressive attitudes they objectify emotional feelings, which seem to be in them, even when they do not happen to be ours at the moment.

Weeping willows drop no tears and heave no sobs, yet look mournful; swift little brooks laugh, robins sound happy, the wood thrush's note has a yearning quality that belongs to the tone rather than the pattern of its call. Above all, the skies may look benign or angry, breakers may howl and tower, trees loom and shake their branches, and all the individuated forms of nature appear as so many potential agents which "have" the attitudes and impulses they display symbolically. Heinz Werner (1945) gave this stage of symbolic intuition the name "physiognomic seeing," a perception of expressiveness which may not only accompany, but, in naive minds, even precede any clear comprehension of the physical shape and properties of a confronting object. Before the full development of language people's conception of "things" may frequently have gone no further than that.

These earliest forms of symbolic response probably did not arise in due succession, one upon the other, but in confusion, each unfolding aspect furthering some related or quite unrelated advance, gathering force in the intellectual dimension (here, the imaginative), while cutting off forever some of the pristine potentialities of the lineage. In this way the growing functions of the overstimulated, differentiating human brain carved out the channels that were to carry the flood of myths and dream figments. At the same time there must have been a beginning of realistic concern for the future, a dawning awareness of the constant threat of disasters, attacks by disease or violence, starvation, the scourge of fire, flood, or lightning. But such possibilities could hardly be conceived apart from any actual occurrence, without a symbol in the prevailing mode of spontaneous, concrete envisagement, which is the dream mode; so whatever sounds in nature were heard as voices and whatever objects, shadows, or creatures showed a fearful aspect became nightmare figures to embody the menacing powers. Only then could names be given to them, which served equally as common and proper nouns, i.e., designated both the idea and its mythical incarnation.

By this process the human race has surrounded itself with countless superhuman wills and powers, all the forces of nature converging on it with intent to devour or extinguish its members upon the slightest occasion or even without any motivation except to exercise their caprice. There is no defense against such agents in fisticuffs or showers of arrows. But, as those enemies were creations of the over-excitable, over-growing hominid brain, the only opposition they could encounter was a contrary action of that same great mental organ, which strove to control them even while it constantly and profusely engendered them. The creative function, of course, is always far below the psychical limen; the defensive activity is equally spontaneous, but consciously directed against the symbols already formed, which in dream are the manifest content and in waking life the gods, ghosts, and demons of the spirit-world.

The mainspring of magical thinking is as deeply buried as that of symbol-making. The edifice of mind is so complex that the evolution of magic is as polyphyletic as that first un-animalian function, symbolization. All of the chance conditions and concomitant developments that have entered into magical practices—ardent desire, frustration, concentration of thought to the point of self-hypnotism—have been looked upon as its source; but its phylogenetic origin lies below them all, on the physiological level where even the highest cerebral impulses work and are felt before they take any distinct psychical form. It is the feeling of mental activity—of an invisible doing—that underlies the notion of exerting a non-mechanical influence on the course of events, without physical contact, without push or pull on the external objects and persons involved.

The magic-monger's apparent ignorance of causal relations, which has been the most puzzling aspect of savage mentality to anthropologists and missionaries alike (traders seldom worried their heads about it), is not simply ignorance at all, but a matter of evaluation. Causal relations are known well enough, but they are taken for granted; the primary purpose of techniques is to implement magical processes. Those processes are essentially symbolic and their important functions conceptual; that is why imaginary results are so easily satisfactory. The counter-force to the spirit-world is the human mind at its center.

The conception of an activity, such as thought, without any physical phenomenon to show for it was surely quite impossible for the earliest thinking beings, as it is for some people, not only savages, even now. But the symbolific tendency in those dawning intellects took care of that. Every stirring conception would activate some fantasy to illustrate it, and every illustration become at once the symbol and embodiment of the thought it conveyed; and somewhere among all the shapes in surrounding nature this imagined form would be suggested and emerge as a reality, the product of the clearly felt act of thinking, the invisible work of the conjurer. A monstrous figure seen in the trunk of a twisted tree would make that concrete object as convincingly a ghost tiger or a bush devil as the tree which it also was.

The basis of such creations is a very common trait of human beings (perhaps not strictly limited to them) which certainly has long been known, though not seriously studied until about a century ago: the principle of perceptual interpretation, or "gestalt." Percepts, as everyone recognizes today, are not the pure sense data that naive empiricism assumed; they are, quite literally, what we make out of the sensations that impinge on our receptors. Especially visual gestalten are heavily dependent on the organization given to them by the percipient's way of looking at things: the focus of his eyes and of his attention, his choice (usually unconscious) of perspective, and the spontaneous action of the visual organ that causes any strong line closing on itself to become, as with a jump, the contour of an area. Most people have had the experience of looking at a honeycomb pattern, for instance in a spread of hexagonal tiles, and seeing the hexagons organized in different groupings according to whichever tile is chosen as the center. Such patterns generally convey no meaning except for the organization of space which they help to effect. Yet there is a modicum of interest, even for sober, civilized adults, in playing at changing their arrangement simply by a shift of attention from one central form, briefly held steady, to another that brings a different pattern into prominence. All the designs are there all the time; but when one is selected the others disappear. They cannot be combined, only alternated. At the same time the display itself of perfectly similar forms is difficult to see as such because it falls so readily into figurations on a precarious, tentative background that threatens at every moment to swamp the virtual array and alter the focus-created image.

A similar phenomenon may be produced in a more complex visual experience, where a further potentiality of the form-perceptive primate eye comes into play, i.e., the rapid diminution of object size with distance, and with it another interpretational factor, the judgment of given forms in three dimensions. The principle of perspective adds a new element of ambiguity which is not based on a simple displacement of focus; it takes a subjective reorientation of vision to change one's perspective judgment of three-dimensional form. Such reorientation may occur by chance or may be induced by tricks of viewing. A picture of a pile of blocks or of a flight of steps will suddenly and quite irresistibly reverse its perspective values if it is held upside down, as Figure 20–1 shows.

As any line that meets itself is normally seen as the contour of an area (the honeycomb pattern, really marking, in nature, the openings of empty cells seen end-on, in a diagram suggest flat surfaces like tiles), a three-dimensional form is seen as a solid. A line drawing will do the same thing if it is sufficiently analogous to the outline of a familiar or readily imaginable object.

The examples here adduced are all artificial constructions, but the same challenge to imaginative selection of contours met the eyes of men in primitive stages of mental evolution. Forms seen in clouds furnish one of the commonest illusions; flying human shapes, huge birds, angels, witches riding the winds have all been seen in the sky. The shapes seen in clouds, usually shifting to other shapes that invite interpretation, are obvious forms for supernatural beings in control of the earth. Meanwhile, earth itself provides its virtual images in the trunks of distorted trees and serpentine branches, or more elusive ones in their wrinkled bark and in rock surfaces and jutting profiles. A person stealing through lonely jungle tracks can see his spooks almost anywhere.

A pure succession of different apparitions, even in one fixed place,

Figure 20–1. Reversal of Perspective Values with Change in Angle of View.

might not be enough to beget the idea of transformation in a very simple and naive mind; but the fact that the illusory forms seen in natural conformations may change back and forth, and that while the beholder lets them alternate there is always a convincingly physical object held in abeyance but vouching for their reality and, despite the incompatibility of their appearances, for their identity, helps to negotiate that somewhat precocious conception. The change in itself seems, of course, to be objectively given rather than brought about by the subject; but with it there is always a deeply felt sense of his own mental activity as he himself shifts his centered attention and therewith changes the thing that meets his eyes. Perhaps the momentary resistance of the previous form to the radical transformation, as he alternates his fixations, makes him feel the impulse as his own; the thing before him obeys him; and there we have the magical act. Once that experience is his, the idea expands, and magic is man's mental power, not only to transmute the characters of external things but, by dint of his imagination thus excited, to influence their doings and destinies. The power of magic has no known limits. A person knows, in a fair way, his own physical capacities; but the reaches of his mind are indefinite and, to his feeling, infinite.

The subjective sense of power, however, has some sobering consequences that tend to balance the odds of man against nature again: the process of transformation is quickly abstracted from the circumstance that probably engendered the idea—the ambiguity of sensory impressions—and conceived apart from his action, as a capability of all living things; all sorts of beings, then, may make their own magic changes and transform themselves into animals, monsters, clouds, persons, or whatnot. They may even ensorcel him. As the magician gains new potentialities, so does the spirit-world he faces. This is, of course, a purely hypothetical reconstruction, which I would be ready to abandon at once for a more illuminating theory. We do not—and perhaps shall never—know how the notion of magical transformation arose.

The result of this spread of imputed magic to the whole living world—which, for primitive men, may take in not only animals and plants but stones, stars, rainbows, and man-made things like tools and traps—is that the earth is peopled with a host of uncertain characters which may be anything or anyone other than themselves, by temporary self-transformation.

Magic is intense, awesome, but not an emotional outburst. It is in essence an expression of ideas, and as such is symbolic. Its ubiquity in the life of man stems from his specialization, the overactivity of his forebrain, which he feels as an exertion, and he looks to the external world for its effects because outward effects have been the result of all his felt impulses from the infancy of his life and of his race, and are his only criteria of consummated action. Instinctive behavior normally leads to physical achievement; and in unchanging savage existence practical activity, even with highly developed manual and technical skills, is still largely instinctual, though not purely instinctive, being helped or hindered at every turn by ideas. That incursion of ideas, envisagements, suggestions, and whims is constant in human life, yet in simple societies the basic patterns of self-maintenance are uncritically received and followed. Instinct is perseverative, conservative; the force of tradition is its modified version in mankind.

On this habitual round of behavior the dreaming, inventing, apprehensive mind imposes itself, giving all the familiar recurrent acts—shooting, fishing, planting, and above all the daily occasions of eating—a heavy cargo of symbolic functions. Being repetitious, their various detailed subacts have attained a natural economy and order; it is this fixed design of concatenated subacts, rather than the purposive act as a whole, that offers models for expressive gestures and manipulations. The emotional attitudes of people toward the plants and animals that provide their food, or toward the spirits that are thought to control them, are the contents of their hunting, gardening, and other protective or persuasive rituals; and the rites themselves usually involve some representation of the acts they celebrate. In our anthropological literature this is known as "sympathetic magic."

A better term, perhaps, would be "empathetic magic"; for the rationale of the practice appears to rest on a conceptual assumption which is probably unconscious today even in the lowest savage mentality, though its vestiges are still alive as the principle of such magic-making:

the assumption that an act may be initiated by one being and picked up in its course by another. If this feeling (to use the least committal word) really underlies the mimetic performances which are expected to evoke responses of such agents as clouds, trees, rivers, or the yams in a garden, then the elements, at least, of enchantment by mimesis would seem to stem from the earliest phases of our existence as true human beings, when instinct still held the main rule not only over behavior but over subjective reactions as well. At that time the bonds among fellow men were animal-like, and as the Hominidae are a gregarious genus, moments of empathetic feeling may have been frequent and familiar. An impulse starting up in one person would be naturally picked up from the smallest bodily sign, as it appears to be among many subhuman beings from bees to birds, and even wolves and dogs, so the impulse seems to run through an intimate unity of beings; and the experience of empathy may have seemed as natural in that close-knit human society as it appears to be in a beehive or a school of herring today.

Empathetical magical action is not imitation; it is an incentive move to start the desired action of the natural and supernatural beings that have its completion in their power. The relation between the intention and the realization of the act is supposed to be helped by imparting motivation to those divine or ghostly agents as some animals seem to pass an impulse from one ready agent to another. In this way human beings hope to participate in the natural event, the work of clouds, winds, etc., before its overt phase has begun. But if the ceremonial is, as here proposed, a mental push to get the impulse started and support it on its course, it is really the opposite of imitation; it is the priming and starting of an act, and the initiators naturally look for its continuance in the external world. They have handed over the initiated action, and the rest of it is expected to run on from agent to agent in the spirit-world, by its own impetus. The jumping of a spatiotemporal gap by the causal influence of the magician's performance is generally considered the essential mark of "sympathetic magic." The same criterion applies to the empathetic character of a spectator's spontaneous gestures in watching an athletic feat, and also the use of such movements formalized in ritual.

In the war dance of many savages it is the offensive autogenic acts that are dramatized in the mounting fury of the dance and perhaps in a final triumph scene, with the expectation that the warriors will be given extra strength by their totemic or other patron spirits who may be invisibly participating in the act, and that the spears and clubs carried by the dancers will cooperate in the actual battle.

In the context of motivational thinking there is nothing irrational about that expectation. When every eventuality, in nature as in society, is conceived in the act form, it is imagined as beginning in an intention, which gives shape and direction to a venture. The aim of a mimetic rite is to formulate and, indeed, to perform that stage of the desired act, with instinctive confidence that any visible or invisible agent in close proximity will fall in with it and realize the whole thing. Nothing "crosses" an empty space or time; but the driving impulse, and the act already coming to realization in its initial, in its mental phase, are expected to be taken up and to hold over in the consciousness of the spirits just as the concentrated excitement the warriors have whipped up in themselves is expected to carry their undertaking from the preparatory dance to the victorious consummation.

Here, I think, we have an interpretation of the primitive practice of sympathetic magic as a supposed occult event, thought to take its course without any gap in the universal rhythm which pervades the interpenetrating spheres of divinity and humanity. Magic, from this angle, is seen not only as a mystical relation between an earthly and an otherworldly activity, both its terms taken *in toto*, but a transference of each successive human behavioral impulse to the spirit or spirits hopefully adjured to consummate it. Perhaps this explains why the detailed subacts of vitally important actions, such as planting, gathering, sharing, and eating, are the substance of the formalized elements from which mimetic ritual is elaborately built.

The radical difference between the savage's and the European's thinking is never more apparent than when a pragmatically minded field worker argues with a native doctor about the efficacy of magic as a method to induce physical events. The tribesman does not see it the visitor's way, but cannot explain how he does conceive the magical process; neither his abstract thinking nor his language can encompass the problem, which has never been raised before. The inquirer, for his part, is prone to interpret the answer in his own terms, making the "doctor" either a knowing psychologist or a swindler exploiting the credulity of his fellows, but in any case a sophisticate, thinking like the white man and manipulating the ignorant savages.

Mimetic ritual is a drama, and all its elements belong to the stage; but its stage is the world. Its elements are gestures, its acts produced as they would be in the theater: semblances, whose import is reality. They are presentational symbols; and as almost invariably is the case with such symbolism, there is no clear distinction between symbol and meaning. The image is the thing itself in the drama. The doctor's hidden objects—well known to most lay members of the tribe, at least the older men—are theatrical "props," symbolizing actual evils or remedies. Their symbolic nature, together with their actual existence, fills them with a magic which amounts to holiness, both wonderful and dangerous. But their sacredness and potency depend, to varying degrees, on the occasion of their use.

White visitors have sometimes been shocked at the ribald way people of highly religious cultures may indulge in mock seances and horseplay apparently "debunking" magic action. It seems to be, for these people, like using words in second intension, that is, as items, not vehicles of thought; taking the ritual act as a theme and playing with it. In our society that would be deemed sacrilegious by most people, and by others at least bad taste; the action itself is considered holy and not to be played with. But for some cultures moral valuation evidently permits it; the holiness of the religious form stems from the ancient context, the address to the spirits, who enter into the serious communication and understand the human crisis just as, in happier moments, the spirits really understand a joke. Without the mysterious, invisible action of a commanding will the rite would have no force. The magician, far from thinking in terms of any such physiological and psychological facts, is the most firmly convinced of his own magic powers, because he feels the activity in himself as concentrated effort and strained attention.

Not all magic is as obviously pantomimic as dance, but its overt acts are nevertheless techniques of the theater, symbolic representations which mean real events and are identified as such. When a "clever fellow," or Australian medicine-man, extracts a bone that has been "sung" or "pointed" into his patient, he does not excite himself to an overt heroic attack like a fighter going into battle; yet he starts the act that is to be taken up by the illness he is exorcising and symbolically presenting in the theatrically produced bone. The initiation of that act is the mental concentration of his desire for the convalescence of the sick person. He may be a hired magician with little or no emotional feeling for the sufferer, but his concern for his professional competence makes every test a crisis; what he is building up is his own sense of spiritual power, the power of his wish, his command to the spirit-bone that he imagines in the stricken body, coming out and passing into the tangible image he holds ready for it. The emergence of the phantom and its entrance into the physical proxy is an invisible process, and has to be effected in secrecy; his sleight of hand, which literal-minded European observers judge as a mean deception, is to him and his native audience a mystical moment.

The shaman is an actor in a sacred drama which is still entirely in the realm of actual belief, and his involvement in the histrionic creation is so profound that the dramatic idea supervenes over any factual condition. A German commentator on the theater, Peter Richard Rohden, analyzing the German compound word *Schauspiel* ("stage play") into *Schau* ("sight") and *Spiel* ("play"), remarked that the "sight" was given not only to the spectators, as the external presentation, but also to the actor, as insight into the character whose part he is playing. The true comedian inclines to the "play" element; he enjoys changing roles and quite literally "playing" with transformations of his social self into other personages. The typical tragedian is apt to enter so deeply into the being he is incarnating that, as Rohden puts it, "whoever is personally acquainted with actors of this type has probably noticed that sometimes they keep the expression, particularly in their eyes, of a character they have represented, for hours after the performance" (1926, p. 39).

A shaman, priest, or magician usually plays no other role than his own, but in that role he is always acting, with full conviction of its seriousness and reality. There is no cleavage between the domain of fantasy in which he acts and the worlds of affairs wherein his mystic acts are efficacious. The demands of practical necessity give the continuous spiritual interpretation its adaptive twists and turns, as the guiding and constraining banks of a stream to the pressing waters, but they are the limiting framework in which daily life is lived, and their governing forces are ritually unadmitted.

It is the relation of magical, theatrical ritual to the round of practical life that bewilders the civilized observer, rather than this or that particular piece of inexplicable behavior in an exotic culture. Underneath every such exhibit lies the whole structure of that ancient human mentality from which our own conceptual scheme of causality and "natural law" is a special offshoot. One gets glimpses of the older pattern, which is fully functional in societies where its typical traits have been cultivated instead of repressed and overborne, from incidental remarks in the writings of anthropologists reporting from the field. There one reads of the amazing ability of some savages—even children at play—to withstand pain, yet of intense fear—in adults as well as children—of magical influences, especially "spirit abstraction"; their great openness to suggestion; their credulity and belief in the power of persons in the magic profession. The most important and striking of those findings seems to me to be the ease with which savages generally, and some people of high culture, especially in Asia, enter into states of altered consciousness that comprise all stages from dreaminess to genuine hallucination. Apparently, the autonomous work of the mind in those persons is less constantly triggered and guided by the impingement of sensory "data" than that of the European, who upholds his empirical standard of reality at every turn by his experimental methods and logical thinking. The untrammeled imagination of savages and confirmed by mystics is highly active, creative, and preemptive; that is why its activity is felt, so the thinker, dreamer, or fabulist naturally looks for some effect of his mental exertion on the tangible world.

It has often been said that some magical exhibits can only be achieved by a process of mass hypnosis and suggestion. Such a claim may well be sound. The physiology of hypnosis is still very little known, as it is not readily amenable to neurological study, and other investigations tend all too much to slip into the shaky theoretical framework of "psychical research" with its assumption of "parapsychological" forces and talents. The alleged displays certainly admit of very little other factual explanation; yet they have too many witnesses to be brushed aside as meriting no explanation at all.

Since any hypnotist in our own society who conjured such phantasmagoria as, for example, the cutting-up and restoring of a human being would certainly be aware of his own trickery, white people who receive the medicine-man's tale judge him to be a charlatan feathering his own nest in society by shameless means. Yet it is not necessary to think of him as an unscrupulous impostor, hypnotizing his fellows to show them magical acts he does not really believe himself to be performing; he probably believes in them implicitly, being himself the first and most deeply hypnotized, speaking aloud out of his own dream to his receptive hearers.

Hypnosis practiced under conditions of savage life is not comparable to any that we know from our own experimental or therapeutic work. We have our techniques for inducing the trance condition; it takes no shaman or especially gifted person to hypnotize a subject, though not everyone is susceptible to the treatment as we practice it. In savage society entrancement seems to be universally feasible, which is not surprising where trance states are cultivated and part of the intellectual life—medicine, religion, myth, knowledge of the world. The most radical difference between a medical or academic session and a seance is that in the civilized session the suggestions for post-hypnotic behavior are not exciting, the inculcated beliefs not marvelous, so that after emerging from the trance the believer would naturally let his own fantasy continue the experience. If our aims are medical, the hypnotist's statements are practical—"It doesn't hurt," "You don't like candy and cake," "You can breathe freely again," etc. If they are experimental or didactic, the suggestions are usually trivial—small, silly acts, to be carried out with apparently insufficient motive, such as taking a plant from a windowsill and setting it on the floor. Sometimes a minor dishonest action has been proposed to see whether the agent could be influenced to commit it (which usually he cannot). But there is no thrill of wonder or mystery, no revelation of superhuman powers, though subjects who reach the state of so-called "somnambulistic trance" do have visions and hear unreal voices or other sounds. In a brief article, "Hypnosis as a Healing Art" (1975), Dr. Manoochehr Khatami summed up the effects which even our methods, used under our usual conditions, have been known to elicit: "Subjectively, some patients report change or distortions in body image and perception of reality. Some subjects report feelings of floating, sinking, or moving outside of one's self." Subsequently, on the same page, listing the stages from light trance to somnambulistic, or deepest trance, he mentions "kinesthetic delusions" even at a medium depth and, at the greatest depth, both visual and auditory hallucinations.

A genuine fakir employing hypnotism operates in a circle of tribesmen who are all involved in the marvels they have witnessed up to the moment; the natural surroundings in moonlight and firelight, or even in broad desert daylight on cliffs and vast expanses, demand very little to be shut out by conscious concentration on a fixed focusing point. The magician provides that point, his chant repeats the suggestive words, and the hypnotic trance begins not in his fellows but in him.

His displays are extremes of ritual dramatization, made possible by the constellation of subjective and objective circumstances: the participants' openness to suggestion, their persisting susceptibility to empathetic transference of feeling, the whole motivational pattern of their conceptions, their typical lack of individual judgment, and the apparently limitless flow of every person's imagination, together with the natural environment full of voices and rustlings, human forms and ghostly motions and muttering drums. Add to these conditions the well-established fact that the process of hypnotization is greatly accelerated by repetition, taking less time and effort on each successive occasion, and it is not hard to believe that people who have been subjected periodically to hypnotic influences since puberty might require scarcely more than a "sign stimulus" to enter the trance state. Moreover, they might well have no need of a consciously operating hypnotist. In the mystical, expectant mood created by the seance, the presence of the awe-inspiring shaman and surrounding crowd ready for a miracle, each person could easily learn his own technique of almost instant self-hypnotization, and the words of the magician weave the visionary scene for all alike. The hypnotic effect, familiar and prepared as the climax of a magic performance, spreads through the circle of watchers and listeners and draws them all into the one inescapable experience. So the shaman may work in perfectly good faith and impart his fantasy to his fellows, who meet it with their own self-hypnotic technique, embracing his suggestion as he sings his miraculous adventure.

Now, what is the point and purpose of all these unrealistic claims and illusory performances? The answer is implicit in the primitive human scene. The world of nature is a theater of superhuman physical powers, against which the strength of every living species and, indeed, of every tiny separate life is pitted. Perhaps it is man's misfortune to know this; but since he does know it his primary desire is for power to hold his own amid the hosts of antagonists that surround him. Even their conflicts with each other, quite regardless of him, may crush him between them. In every case he must seek protection by one against another and, of course, try to take his stand under the wing of the strongest. In a cosmic arena where even the most impersonal events appear as acts he cannot but suppose that behind every thunderbolt, cloudburst, fire, or flood there is an angry agent willing it, as there is a benevolent spirit behind every good harvest, happy landing, or big drove of game animals. To counter the dangers of his haunted world and of particular foes—hostile tribes, witches, ghosts, offended ancestors, or whatnot—every person and every united group of persons seeks to build up its defensive and maintaining power.

The worship of power is not peculiar to primitive cultures, even if some conceptions of the origins and embodiments of power are. Civilized modern men are as prone to that worship as the crudest savages. It is built into our popular turns of speech: we speak of "the powers that be," "Money is power," "Knowledge is power." Our sovereign countries are called "Powers," and their dealings with each other "power politics." But intellectually we consider all "powers" to be reducible, by one analysis or another, to physical forces; most psychologists hold as a basic belief that psychological dynamisms as well as somatic ones are physiological, and involve no metaphysically distinct "mental energy" or spiritual substance, though we have certainly not mastered any but the crudest cerebral mechanisms. We work on the assumption that acts are causal phenomena which some day will be comprehensible in physicochemical terms.

Not so the uncivilized thinker, to whom his own mental power is still the most thrilling mystery, holding possibilities beyond any of the tangible things in nature. People generally have a fair idea of their own physical strength and its limits compared to that of most animals of their size, and know it is inferior; but their mental capacity has no definite bounds. They can imagine it as infinite, measured only by their subjective sense of potentiality. So it is mental power they seek and hope to exercise in their spirit-world. All the techniques of conceiving it—that is, finding or creating symbols whereby to imagine and represent it—make up their repertoire of magic: verbal formulas, sometimes long poems, manipulations, animal voices and masks, miming and sundry less common means of dramatization. With these the magic-maker shapes his intentions which are designed to start off an act that is more than his own, as other beings are expected to take it up and carry it to completion.

Magic power is the highest possession a person can boast in societies that believe in its existence. Everyone has at least a small amount of it, usually enough to make his curse on a personal enemy effective. Some people, however, are endowed congenitally with the power to harm others simply by projecting an evil wish from their minds to someone else; such persons are born witches. Witchcraft may be an unintended function, and where it is regarded as such it is morally distinguished from sorcery, which is always deliberate, as it requires accessories: plants, bones, or parts of the victim—hair, nail-parings, blood, excrement, etc.—to implement its work. Anyone can perform sorcery, or "black magic," insofar as he knows a charm and can acquire the necessary objects to manipulate in support of it. In some societies the accusation of sorcery is a dreaded possibility, since every non-violent death is attributed to magic influence, and in each case part of the shaman's business is to find the culprit.

There are degrees of magic power, ranging from the normal ability to use love charms bought from a magician who has them for sale, to the wildest exploits of shamans who kill persons at a distance by visitations of horrible diseases and tortures. Between these extremes there may be, in some cultures, ordinary men or women who own special "tabus," meaning in this case the ability to induce particular illnesses and the exclusive power to remove them. Spells are passed on from one generation to another by inheritance; that is to say, they are family possessions. A person who has inherited a considerable store of such secrets is a rich member of the tribe.

But the holders of the highest magical powers have amassed their wealth in more strenuous ways. Medicine-men may be born to their calling, but in most societies they have also to be made, either by their prospective peers or by ghosts, human or animal ancestors, or deities. They may be ritually operated on, having viscera and bones removed and exchanged for new ones and having magic objects or creatures put into them at the same time; or crystals, lizards, and magic cords may be "sung into" them as they lie entranced.

The young shaman certainly believes in the experience he has had, apparently in a deep hypnotic dream induced by his initiators, or even self-induced in a long, solitary fast—a dream that may have taken him to heaven, where the ordeal was conducted by spirits. When he returns he feels the invisible activity of his mind (which he may be locating in his stomach) as a vast power to meet the numberless occult powers that surround him and his people. His newly liberated talents come close to giving him a life-and-death control over many other people, for he may be hired either to cure or kill; he can interpret dreams and other signs of the future and provide magic defenses against its imminent threats.

Naturally, such a personage holds an exalted position and is constantly concerned to keep and augment it. The tribe relies on him to control rain and sunshine, avert disaster, and above all to cure disease. His status, in turn, depends on his success, which has to be sustained not only by sufficient happy outcomes but also by convincing explanations of the cases where nature does not do its part. The system of thought in which he lives and works fortunately allows for such exigencies, just as in our causal system some further reflection usually lets us explain events that disappointed our expectations. The medicine-man's interpretations are not lame excuses, as white observers too commonly rate them. They are reasonable modifications of common-sense judgment in motivational terms.

The possession of magic, however, is not an entirely comfortable asset. Pure superhuman power in itself is neither good nor bad; but as soon as it is put to a particular use it enters the realm of good and evil, which is the moral realm. The danger inherent in its possession is a known risk, and the shaman who seeks to increase his magic repertoire expects to pay for each new acquisition. Since he has entered the occult realm of supernatural forces, he finds himself challenged by an inestimable host of willful, often invisible agents, and no amount of power that he can wield seems to be enough.

The conception of magic as a reification of meaning and consequent wielding of symbols as effectual instruments of will (one's own will or some other which they already embody) readily explains the extraordinary power attributed to words, and especially to proper names. Words are the paradigms of symbolic expression, for they have no other *raison d'être*. There is a whole great department in the world's religious literature dealing with the magical use of words and the mystical potential stored in verbal formulas, above all in divine names, which may embody powers to kill or to save, in some high cultures even to beatify, and are sometimes held secret, like buried stores of "overkill" materials.

The feeling that words embody some efficacious force is not peculiar to primitive thinking, at least as the average civilized person would judge what is "primitive"—not his own thinking, of course. The belief in their efficacy is natural enough, since we all use words to command, beg, suggest, and generally direct each other's thought and action, and their influence in such intercourse is obvious. Where all happening seems like action, all nature may be expected to respond to our verbal utterances. "The Word"—the utterance of a god, of the civilized man's God—is the mightiest symbol today's religious thinkers can conceive: "In the beginning was the Word"; in Greek, "Logos" means "reason," "order," or "mind," as well as "word," but the English translators' choice, "the Word," names the symbolic embodiment of them all; the power of speech can stand proxy for everything mental, conceptual, or in any way non-physical, of the spirit and the spirit-world.

Speech is the essence of symbolism; for the motivational thinking of savages it holds the essence of magical potential. It can be marvelously and elaborately manipulated, composed into poetic forms that are self-identical yet immaterial, and when uttered, felt to spring from subjective action, carrying the speaker's wish, the real mental force, through the air (though the sound may vanish for ordinary ears) to its target. Verbal spells are prized possessions among magicians, whether shamans, priestly diviners, witches, or laymen. They usually have to be recited word-perfect, but accompanied by conscious wish; any formal error in their utterance breaks the spell.

Yet the employment of formulas which are pure abracadabra to their users seems to be rare. I suspect that where we encounter such practices we are dealing with a deteriorated culture. Among such people—detribalized savages, or ignorant and superstitious persons in the backwaters of our own civilized populations—one is likely to find completely ungrounded, disconnected beliefs in good or bad forces inherent in charms which are meaningless strings of syllables to be repeated a stipulated number of times. That is a mental reversion to what John Murphy called "the Primitive Horizon" of man's religious thought, and described as "a simple belief in *power* in all things mysterious to him" (1943, p. 2).

It seems that almost from the beginning of social life, on the lowest levels of culture, men tried to bolster their bodily strength with the additional energies they could feel but could not understand, their mental energies, given to their intuitive perception only symbolically as magic power inherent in all sorts of things, perhaps physiognomically suggested, perhaps derived from dreams and frights. But in the course of mental evolution on its broad, general front—however various its many separate advances and regressions may be—the symbolic forms which serve as the instruments of magic tend to become more and more vital and even psychical, until the magician himself becomes the chief symbol, possessing a wealth of specific powers to control nature and oppose spirit attacks on his life. Often these powers are thought to be quite literally in him. A man may, in fact, become loaded with powers; at that point he resorts to the ancient principle, never quite abandoned, of crediting inanimate objects with mystical attributes, and sings or wishes his overload of magic into weapons, fire-sticks, pointing-bones, and *churingas*, which thereupon are charged with his spiritual potential. This points up the problem of the grave dangers contained in all magic, which become imminent threats when the wielder of occult forces acquires too much of such a dynamic cargo.

A similar relation of magic power to danger, even death, is not so much the danger of being overwhelmed by the greatness of one's own potential as the price of its acquisition. Men can become "drunk with the sight of power." Where the notion of magical control over other men and magical propitiation of "supernaturals" prevails, they vie with one another for possession of such assets and feel themselves ever pitted against each other and against invisible presences, spirits of evil, in self-defense. There are always greater forces threatening, so their desire for more magic potency may become obsessive, like the pathological avarice of a person craving more money no matter how much he has, or of an Alexander, a Napoleon, or a Hitler for conquest far beyond anything he could hold and rule.

Now, what is the basic reason for this magic-madness that is apt to develop in savage societies, this extreme and constant fear and defense? The cause, I think, lies deep in a tenet which many anthropologists have recognized and recorded, but which does not betray its pervasive influence at once: the belief that death is always an infringement and violation of a life, no matter what may be the sufferer's age or general condition when it occurs. It is always brought upon one by a hostile act of a human or superhuman agent. Death is not something natural.

The image of life is that of a stream, which gathers up all trickles and rills that enter it and carries them along, mingled but present; the individual is imagined—perhaps one can hardly call it "thought"—in the same way, with a distinct beginning in the rather spectacular act of birth but no distinct end. It may be true that each person is defeated sooner or later; but without defeat by human or superhuman force nothing would bring about his death, however long he might have lived already. This is, indeed, the phylogenetic form of life, the vital pattern of the stock, going back to times when organisms ceased to be generated from chemicals in the earth's surface and envelope, and survived only if they were already procreative enough to continue in endless lines. Perhaps it is quite natural for unreflective minds to impose the same image on the living individual as on the presumptively deathless tribe.

Nothing, perhaps, is more comprehensible than that people—savage or civilized—would rather reject than accept the idea of death as an inevitable close of their brief earthly careers. If they can maintain a confident hope of going along with an endless stream of life, their way of feeling their own vitality can really take the form of the phylogenetic continuum, a completely open-ended progress, punctuated by brushes with death but always expecting to triumph or escape, without end. In many of the world's hinterlands such an attitude really seems to prevail; contacts with civilization bring in new ideas, missionaries set up new gods, but ideas and powers are assimilated at once to the basic feeling of life itself, and take its primitive form.

Yet gradually, reluctantly, humanity comes to recognize the closed form and the brevity of each personal life. It is a complex, problematic insight, as even an elementary study of comparative religion and eschatology evinces. It meets with resistance and "ritual ignorance" where it has certainly dawned. The interesting fact is that it does dawn, inevitably, on people who do not discuss it and do not seem to think about it; and that wherever and whenever they come to realize that death is not, in essence, an extraneous force pitted against the vital impulse but is inherent in the form of human life itself, there is a momentous change in their experience that marks no less than a phylogenetic step in the history of Mind.

21 / Dream's Ending: The Tragic Vision

> Ach, wie dunkel ist es in des Todes Kammer!
> Wie traurig tönt es wenn er sich bewegt,
> Und nun aufhebt seinen schweren Hammer,
> Und die Stunde schlägt.
>
> **Matthias Claudius**

At first thought it seems strange, even fanciful, to regard a conceptual insight like the realization of natural mortality as a milestone on the road of man's evolutionary advance. On longer consideration, however, one can see many reasons to class it as such, both because of the conditions which its attainment has required and the influence it has had on the subjective and objective course of human life wherever it has taken root as a genuine conviction. It marks no direct physical change, though indirectly and subtly it may produce many; its historical significance and its crucial function belong to the advance of mind, not of physique.

Yet that mental advance is of one piece with the rest of human evolution. Despite the vastness of time and change that must have prepared what we call "the Mind" today, I hold that the elements of that marvelous structure may all be found in nature, and the principles of its formation are those of organic chemistry, electrochemical action, or whatever substitutes for such current concepts the progress of scientific thought may dictate in future. If this is an audacious assumption, I can only plead that it seems to me the most promising to open, and keep open, a way to a rational concept of human mentality.

The making of mind has been such a weaving of coincidences,

asynchronous changes and readjustments, and especially chance opportunities for new realizations of potential acts that it is only after the whole foregoing survey of animal life that this strangest of vital phenomena—Mind—can appear in its biological setting; and even when we see it in that context, its own, unparalleled history has only begun to emerge for us. We have to follow its course a long way before we come upon the origins of its characteristic products: society, religion, conceptual thought, and personal intent and action.

It is in a fairly recent phase of that evolutionary course that the realization of death as the inevitable finale of every life has overtaken mankind; in fact, it is not entirely complete in some of the remotest corners of the earth. In most of the present world population it has been met and dealt with in various ways—religiously, philosophically, and sometimes (though not widely) by simple admission. Its long preparation, however, has been as natural as the wholly unplanned developments which culminate in the peacock's ornamental tail or the beaver's landscape architecture; for it is an implicit consequence of a basic evolutionary process, individuation.

The persistent tendency of acts to nucleate and form matrices of mutually involved, integrating, and ever-augmenting acts gives rise to individuals, long-lasting or transient, partial or self-sufficient, to all degrees. The avenues of physiological development, progressively opening up new options, lead to the tremendous proliferation of organic activities that have recorded themselves, since the beginning of life, in the complexities of even the simplest vital mechanism, simpler than a cell. Roughly in parallel, sometimes in dialectical progression with that "complexification" (to borrow Teilhard de Chardin's apt neologism), runs a tendency of strong impulses to gather up smaller or weaker ones, and for acts in the accelerating phase to assimilate lesser acts in progress or seem to commandeer incipient ones to serve them as elaborations of their own development. That is the principle of entrainment, which simplifies the tangle of separately directed impulses by massing their expressions into a few organizing acts.

Entrainment is the fundamental process of individuation, as it is of nucleation and inward coherence. How an act arising from one impulse can exert a force on other acts from equally original impulses so as to pace and plot their courses is a puzzling question; yet there can be little doubt that there are autonomous physiological rhythms which not only mesh in very intricate ways with others from different sources but also seem to control a creature's larger, facultative acts, its behavioral cycles adapted to ambient conditions, and even unique responses. The difficulty of explaining them lies, I think, in a tacit common-sense assumption that the energy mobilizing an act must be supplied from outside the organ (or organelle) which performs it, and ceases when—and because—"the need of the organism" is served. But if every living structure does all it can at any time, the nature of entrainment may not be the effect of a force *a tergo* at all, but rather the opening of a way for small impulses to find expression in the wake of a great and vigorous one, whose progression from moment to moment proffers and limits the opportunities of many lesser impulses in the agent's vital advance, which would otherwise be smothered, but can adapt to those opportunities to fit into the larger unit as elaborations of its passage.

As the entrainment of small spontaneous impulses by greater ones, especially by such as are already launched on their realization, organizes a center of cyclic biochemical rhythms, the matrix, so it also makes the division between the vital organism and the world in which it exists. The activity of the matter involved in a life is hard to conceive; it holds its environment at bay by living, somewhat as an eddy in water keeps its distinct shape, perhaps even while traveling downstream, by the centripetal motion that feeds surface water into it and the centrifugal phase that keeps its funnel expanded. The vortex is a very simple dynamic form which dissolves again, leaving the water unchanged; but the organism, being built of acts—in themselves highly complicated events—makes permanent changes in the material it exploits. The elements it retains are metabolites which enter into the biochemical round and create the distinct protoplasmic structure which is functionally centralized and thereby divided from its environment. That is the process of individuation, the counter-aspect of the integration that establishes the matrix.

In the course of this process the variations of living form appear which distinguish taxonomic groups, for there are crowding and competing started lines of development within a living system, each seeking its own chances of growth and expansion and maximum activity. It is the same dynamic pattern as individuation, wherefore some earlier biologists, notably Charles Manning Child and N. S. Shaler, called every limb, tentacle, or even transient pseudopodium an individual. I think it better to call them articulations, since the impulses of their outgrowth and formation spring quite directly from the central organic complex. But the phenomenon of bodily articulation into distinct limbs, organs, and other special parts is a result of the unit character of acts, the inherent push of each impulse to its own expression, and the consequent general imbalance of tensions in an organism. This ever-changing yet ever-renewed condition drives forward the process of individuation whereby a being is formed, a process which has stages and directions, and very different rates in its various reaches. Individuation may go far in some plant or animal species and remain incomplete in others; and in the ontogeny of specimens the same principle governs the formation of their features.

Any internal strain or external impact on living tissues seems to be a trophic or functionally activating stimulus; the autonomic function of an organ, usually a lifelong workload, is enough to promote its continued development and potency, so it tends to increase and variegate unless its career is checked by other developing processes, and if it happens to find an uncommonly long free course it may eventuate in some very uncommon species-specific feature, which may have a radical influence on the life of the specialized stock. Consider what the elephant's trunk means to the possessor of that fantastic nose! Grubbing animals have long noses which are also refined tactual organs. But a prehensile nose—one that can seize and uproot a tree, draw water by a precisely started and stopped breath and squirt the water over its manipulator's back or into his mouth, and double for the vocal apparatus by serving as a trumpet—is really a far-reaching overgrowth and endowment of the oldest and lowliest special organ! The elephant's life is as different from that of other long-snouted mammals as his nose is from theirs; that versatile and powerful appendage gives him almost the benefit of a hand. In any case, the elephant carries around a spectacular exhibit of what can happen when circumstances favor one organ very much above the others in the evolutionary rise of a stock, and thus produce a specialization, particularly one that creates many new potentialities.

But the example of such uneven development that concerns us here is the most far-reaching in natural history: the overgrowth and hyperactivity of the opercular lobes of the human brain. How this might have resulted from the combination of general primate traits with the peculiarity of man's upright stance and bipedal gait has already been discussed at some length, as have the most fundamental psychological changes which evidently followed from the overabundance of cerebral acts; but the most radical product of his symbolific mentality, his cultural life—in embryo, perhaps as old as his existence—has been meeting a crisis piecemeal, partly in prehistoric and partly in historic times, so it is not utterly impossible to trace it even to an evolutionary source.

That source is a particular phase in the process of individuation which seems to overtake every human society sooner or later, paced by the rate at which the activity of the cerebral cortex outruns the needs of the animal organism, as it typically does. For no matter how adequately those needs are met, the great neural complex does not come to rest; it goes on producing its figments, dreams and thoughts, wishes and emotions, apparently below as well as above the fluctuating limen of feeling. The possibilities of varying, combining, and deriving further images and conceptions from prior intracerebral acts are practically endless, and lead the brain on to more and more symbolic play. But every act also leaves its trace in the action-built matrix, the physical organism; every metabolic rhythm in its somatic structure, and especially every behavioral act, from a whole performance down to each muscular movement or tension, inscribes itself on the cumulative formation of the historic individual. And so does every act of mentation. Since countless mental acts are started and finished in the brain, their main effects are likely to be on that organ. The material involved in their passage seems to have very little bulk; after a few childhood years, growth of the brain stops and leaves a free field for elaboration of structures and functional patterns. Since the cerebral cortex seems to be the most intensely active center in the normal human makeup, its self-contained activity tends to build a matrix of its own, wrought mainly of memory traces and consequently composed in large measure of residual feeling, thought, dream elements, emotional and intellectual experience. The brain, in other words, tends to individuate, and to establish a dependent yet distinct pattern of mental life within the physical life of the organism, even while it serves that organism as a vital part. It achieves a partial individuation, a functional matrix, which appears subjectively as a sort of homunculus or autonomous "inner man," the Mind.

There are some indications of this semi-independence of the brain, or rather of its readiness to form a relatively closed and isolated system, which, with abnormal evolutionary advancement, might produce something close to an autonomous matrix. It seems that the brain, even in rather low animals, amphibians, is more complex than their behavior betrays, and has reserves of very plastic and reactive tissue only half-committed to special functions, but ready to take them on. The tendency to develop somewhat apart from the needs of the organism seems to be an ancient trait of central nervous systems, which may be found where it is of no apparent importance to the survival of the stock. Another sign of the brain's readiness for an independent course of development, seen in more than one class of vertebrates, was pointed out by Tilly Edinger on the basis of her paleontological studies of fossil crania and their evolutionary changes in comparison with the concurrent changes in the skeletons to which they belonged (1949, p. 19). From these studies it is quite evident that the growth and general form of brains advance at rates which may differ, sometimes even extremely, from the rates of progress of other parts shown in the fossil record.

The anlage to separateness, then, lies in the physical mechanisms of vertebrate nervous systems, ready to come into play when unusual opportunities invite the human brain to outgrow its original cybernetic functions and develop something like interests of its own, accommodating the tremendous excess of its burgeoning impulses to each other by building whole systems of ideas and emotional attitudes centered on them, units of motivational power. That such systems comprise more than felt acts has been long established as a result of psychoanalysis; a mind is something more solid than any "content of consciousness," or, on the other hand, any pattern of "behaviors." It is a physiologically based, intraorganic functional entity, a relatively independent complex of vital rhythms supporting facultative mental acts.

The tendency of that complex to nucleate into something like a subordinate matrix of activities is at the same time a tendency to become an individual being, to emancipate itself from the organism in which it developed. That, of course, would be a fatal achievement; the service of the brain to the rest of the body is of its own essence. Yet the partial individuation which can take place only in the confines of a complete animal economy is the same biological process as the individuation of the whole.

To think of individuation as an intraorganic process makes for a somewhat different concept of individuality. The most natural way to define that term is, of course, through the criteria whereby we judge its exemplifications; so the concept of individuality is usually based on the traits which distinguish a given organism from most others of its kind, and the particular assemblage of unusual features or actions provides a unique characterization. Such distinctive attributes are undoubtedly our main indices of what we call an individual. But in the human context, of course, the word "individual" means more than a physically separate entity. It even means more than a being endowed with traits deviating from the ordinary pattern exemplified by most members of a population. The word has an aura of superior strength, in our society, moral superiority.

The fact is that to define a phenomenon in terms of the criteria whereby we recognize it as such may be conceptually crippling. There are some clear and highly important concepts which have application to reality, such as "Truth," yet have no sure criteria for cases of their applicability—for instance, where the decisive signs are not directly observable, as in this case, where they are (for our present ignorance) covert events. We can only construe them from what we do observe. But if we accept deviation from an accepted standard as the measure of individuality, then that all-important property becomes the same as oddity, and a person extolled as a "great individual" appears to be honored essentially for his abnormalities, which cannot go very far without putting the "great individual"'s life in jeopardy. Also, deviations may be acquired in many circumstances, through ambient conditions or organic disturbances, and lead to alienation, which usually seems to impair rather than increase the subject's individuality, such as it is, great or small.

A better criterion of individuality seems to me to be the origin of all a being's acts in a highly organized matrix of impulses. It is the organic unity that makes its acts strong, by linking them all on the level of their embryonic impulses, so that the organism is ready to go into action at once with a complex response to a fairly high challenge, because the deep linkages prepare minor impulses to follow greater ones in large expressions. In that way the forms of the agent's acts are characteristically and peculiarly its own.

Individuality, in this sense, belongs to every living being, and may be present in great numbers of organisms that are as like each other as Tweedledum and Tweedledee. If they are alike in their genic makeup their normal appearance and actions should be similar by being true to the pattern of their respective natures. Of course, no two genomes in different beings are really identical, not even in uniovular twins, nor their separate products impervious to external forces, especially early in life. As somatic activities become more numerous and devious in a living system, their record in its tissues becomes highly intricate and the fabric of its life increasingly dense, until it is tightly woven into a distinct and central agent, a coherent individual.

If, now, the activity of the human brain so far outstrips that of the rest of the body that its symbolic renderings form an internal situation which motivates more and more mental impulses, the pseudo-matrix which the covert consummations of those impulses tend to establish will be composed largely of symbolic elements, traces of such cerebral acts. The psychical phases they are apt to attain differ rather radically from those of somatic, muscular, or even perceptual acts, where these last are purely alertive and directive, built into behavior as in animals. Consequently the partial individuation of the mind produces a peculiarly non-physical appearance of what seems to each person the essential agency within his own body.

Among people of very communally organized cultures, that agency is but vaguely conceived; their interest is in acts, and the most interesting acts of their daily lives as well as special occasions are tribal affairs. Every actor in such a horde feels the effort he is putting into the current undertaking more as the power of the working, fighting, or dancing group than of his separate body; through him the power of the whole is flowing. A man's (and even more, perhaps, a woman's) private routine of chores does not evoke enough feeling to make the person so engaged aware of any particular achievement. But in communal work, hunting or fishing, and even agriculture which is ritually performed so it creates at least a modicum of emotional tension most persons experience a lift of a general vital feeling which some German writers have called *Lebensgefühl*, "sense of life." In the most primitive societies this sense seems to be somewhat diffuse and impersonal, like the acts which inspire it; the agent is not really "I," but "we." The homunculus is not strongly felt as a single being, but at best as a great, continuous power, the Mind of a human tribe, set in the midst of natural forces it seeks to control by thought and magic mastery; the "doctor" or priest speaks for the tribe, and when he dies (by influence of a hostile magic) he joins the great company of ancestors who are still involved in tribal affairs, and someone else of the lineage steps into his place to continue his acts. It is the human society whose life is felt by each member as a power streaming through his limbs.

In such a stream, an individual death is an episode, not a finish. The *Lebensgefühl* may rise and ebb with war, expeditions, disasters, or the seasons, but it has no real form of its own. What it does seem to bring with it, however, is the intuitive conviction that every creature "has" its life, as we "have" our mind (and may lose it). A person may change form, become a spirit or a were-tiger or what not, but his life—his identity—continues. The distinction between the mental homunculus and its incarnate appearance has already begun in the most backward hordes we know; long before it is conceived as an indwelling agent that leaves the body at death or even, perhaps, in sleep, it is quite unconsciously expressed in the notion of metamorphosis.

Human *Lebensgefühl* is a sense of continuous activity, because it comprises something more than body-feeling, something added to it by the cerebral function of "primary imagination": the vague but constant adumbration of potential action, from which arise intentions, wishes, or simply fleeting half-conscious ideas with various cathexes to keep them close to the limen of feeling, often playing across it. Those merely conceived possible acts are a large part of the mental matrix, i.e., of that integrated *substantia* of inner stirrings and outer impingements we call "consciousness"; and so are the acts we have forgone in performing the ones we did, for every realized option entails the rejection of an alternative, which thereupon is no longer potential, but negated. The existence of conceptual alternatives in the mind makes the behavioral options in human lives choices, not automatically decided on physiological and purely sensory grounds, as animal reactions are.

With the development of the mental quasi-matrix by the constant activity of a brain that far outruns the needs of the somatic system for cybernetic control, the basic feeling of life becomes centered in that organ, too, and attains a distinct holistic form. As a German "existentialist" psychiatrist, Kurt Schneider, noted in an early article, the *Lebensgefühl* gradually becomes a unitary phenomenon in which various phases can be distinguished, all of a dynamic character, such as rise and decline, vigor or weakness, health, illness, etc.; and also autonomous, influential activities, because the feelings of which a subject is capable anticipate the effects of stimulations by predetermining their possible values, the experiences they could elicit if they should occur: the special qualities of the fear, desire, thoughts, and other tensions they might evoke in that particular human being (1920, pp. 282–83).

In the context of the present theory of mind built on the act-concept, it is unfortunate that Schneider, like most, if not all, other disciples or followers of Max Scheler (1921), regards an act as "timeless" and "not a process." If such it were there could, of course, be no further research into its etiology or physical functioning. But Schneider's observations of the nature of vital feeling point even a sober naturalist to the source of man's inescapable recognition of his own mortality. The articulation of the *Lebensgefühl* with the progressive individuation of the Mind lets each person feel the rise and expansion of his life, its gathering impetus and the establishment of his world with maturing interests and commitments—but also the decline, past the zenith, when he finds that the life-long continuum of choices and the renunciations they automatically entail are slowly infringing on his sense of boundless potentiality, and many major options no longer exist. This emergence of biological form into feeling comes with the progressive elaboration of mental acts, as they have to adjust to their own increase by more and more integration and mutual concession; so, with evolutionary advance, the fabric of cerebral acts becomes so close-woven that it makes the individuated mental life seem like a single, all-embracing act.

Where this point is reached, the *Lebensgefühl* of the subject takes shape as a sense of personal agency, not tribal power flowing through an instrument of human action, but the mental power of one human individual activating an obedient body of inexactly known ability and readiness. That inexact knowledge of one's own capacity is enough to stake out a rough general limit for the act of living, which now is felt to emanate from the quasi-matrix of mental activity, as every act expands from its impulse to its consummation and cadence (which may be obscured by entrainment, dispersion, etc., in other acts). The sense of life becomes concentrated and reduced to a feeling of selfhood—the *Lebensgefühl* to *Ichgefühl*, as the German phenomenologists would say. And with the rise and gradual conception of the "self" as the source of personal autonomy comes, of course, the knowledge of its limit—the ultimate prospect of death.

The effect of this intellectual advance is momentous. Each person's deepest emotional concern henceforth shifts to his own life, which he knows cannot be indefinitely preserved. Instead of the typical savage carelessness of death as an episode in the course of communal acts, personally only a change of status, one finds a new seriousness meeting "the blight man was born for"—the impending relinquishment of all power, the end of the Self.

As a naked fact, that realization is unacceptable; there are few societies, savage or civilized, that admit it today. Consequently, where it has been met or its recognition is in progress, it is often possible to follow the ways people are dealing or have dealt with it, from their earliest evasions and simple rejections of the unwelcome knowledge to the most fully developed religious eschatologies. All stages of the defensive counter-action are still to be found in living populations.

However deep the repressions go and however high the bulwarks against the threatening truth, the process of individuation goes forward with the overgrowth of the cerebral organ, and gradually the defenses break down. In one society after another—and within each, over the centuries, for one mind after another—the central *Lebensgefühl* takes on an articulated form, the act form, until it presents as one act of living that spans all other acts which arise from the mental quasi-matrix, the Mind; and the rest of the organism, requiring only a part of the Mind's activity, seems to belong to it rather than to possess it as an organ. With that development, a human individual feels his own agency no longer as the stream of tribal life flowing through his limbs but as his unique, autonomous Self living its unique, inviolable life.

With the idea of such a personal, single act of living comes the understanding of the place of death in nature. Death is inherent in human life itself, and as life is power, so death is defeat of man's power. The defeat may come soon or late, but come it will for every individual.

If that insight were to break in suddenly on the old dream of limitless power, it would be shattering. But the mind has its filters and screens as the body has its skin. It takes centuries, if not millennia, for such a diffuse and nameless feeling to become common in a society, so people are quietly taking it for granted, and even then its admission may be stayed through ages by ritual ignorance or taboo. Nevertheless, of course, one intelligent person after another would know when his life was waning, and either fight hysterically against some unconvincing, alleged hostile influence or—more and more frequently—lose faith and interest in magic at that juncture, and resign himself to death. Then people would accept such mythical explanation as priest or medicine-man provided so they could dispense with the inquest and vengeance expedition.

Finally, the small scope of any possible individual life-act has become a terrible, inescapable fact. When that realization is accepted, no one is aware of the crisis that has occurred because evolutionary crises are longer than oral memory which covers a half-dozen generations. But the change in feeling and outlook is radical. No longer is the joint tribal act, whatever it may be at any hour, the prime interest of each participant, but his own life-act, his one and only life. Instead of undergoing a metamorphosis into a spirit, handing over any act in process to other persons, each person must expect to leave his unfinished works or parts undone, his grievances unavenged, and, above all, his potentialities cut off, his world and his self dissolved. Most societies today have been through it, as the truly naive ones who have not faced it yet are dwindling in our world. But none, perhaps, have remained in that state of conviction very long; there is too much emotional necessity to deal with it conceptually and somehow give it a tolerable semblance.

One of the great basic rhythms of the life process, which is felt only in a fairly advanced stage of mentality, certainly not below the human plane and not universally even above it, is the inward rhythm of each individual life. Each life is a rhythmic structure, as its every smallest act is drawn into its passage and enters the next situation, which motivates subsequent acts to meet the new condition. The inward rhythms of different individuals vary widely and provide the groundworks of their separate personalities. Yet despite their uniqueness they all exemplify one deeply felt rhythm which goes beyond the familiar *Lebensgefühl*: the rising impulse of the single life-act, its great spanning tensions from youth to age, and the cadence, the decline to death.

This sense of wholeness is a new feeling of a dynamic pattern which is not itself new, but has newly risen as a whole to psychical phase; and our bitter experience of it is the price of our advanced individuation. We have, indeed, two ways of feeling the passage of life itself, one the old continuum of acts which may be dimly felt by all biological forms, being simply the rhythm of action that belongs to the undying stock, and the other the highly articulated rhythm of the death-bound life of man.

The recognition and expression of these two contrasting dynamic forms is certainly not within the range of tribal cultures, however vitalistic their rituals and their thinking may be; it is today outside the scope of most scientifically oriented civilized people. Its only sure grasp has been by creative artists, namely, poets, and not early in the development of their art, but first, I think, in the great "golden age" of Greece—certainly not a primitive phase; it makes its appearance with the conception of tragedy and the consequent distinction of that dramatic form from the much older one of comedy.

Greek tragedy is, I believe, the first conscious presentation of the tragic rhythm of life, the movement of the greatest act whereof a human individual is capable, his single life-act. Its form is one overarching parabolic curve from youth to death—symbolically, of course, from birth or even conception, through the prime of life, to its close. The classical "fatal error" committed by the protagonist is not a realistic story element but a dramatic device to signify the turning-point from the expanding, upward course to the downward, the cadence, literally the "descent." The hero's or heroine's death in the drama is not necessary; it is only the usual finale. In Ibsen's *Ghosts*, the tragedy is completed in the last scene with the breaking of Oswald's mind, when he says: "Mother, give me the sun.—The sun.—The sun." The death of the mind is the end of a human career.

The rhythm of comedy creates a different frame; it is the rhythm of society, more anciently felt and apprehended than the passage of an individuated life. In the realm of literature it figures as the "comic" rhythm in contrast to the "tragic," but in life, and as a fundamental form of life, it were better called the "social" rhythm, for it belongs to the indefinitely self-rejuvenating life of the stock. The word "comic" is derived from a Greco-Roman god, Comus, whose festival was a processional celebration of life; "comic" does not originally mean laughable, but denotes the feeling of that joyous rite, which moved from rise to rise with a lilting progress, every rise tending to break into laughter as waves break into whitecaps. But the laughter may be of very different kinds; for there is not only merry comedy, but also heroic, like the dramatic art of India, in which the high moments are exalted, not trivial and humorous as in our popular comic theater. The term applies to the vital rhythm, not essentially to the subject matter of the drama.

The stage is a mirror of human feeling, and gives us an abstractive, concentrated, and intensified image. The first recognition of the tragic rhythm—the first clear tragic vision—was expressed in its starkest and simplest outline. Nothing could be more pared down to essentials than *Oedipus Rex*: two actors—Man, and the Seer of his fate; the chorus—the magnification of that fate as something universal, embracing every individual, but each one alone.

The natural reaction to the growing and widening insight that no magic can overcome or indefinitely stem death is despair of human power. But mankind does not easily succumb to despair. As every creature and even every living tissue responds to stress with heightened activity, so the mind meets the challenge its own evolution has created by a radical deepening of religious feeling and dawning of religious ideas. If a man's own power seems minuscule beside the dreamed omnipotence he no longer sees in possible reach, where is real power to be sought? From the Supernaturals, of course. They have always possessed more of it than mortals and dispensed it as they pleased, so the human hope is to borrow strength and luck from them.

With the progress of individual feeling to the point of personal self-awareness, the relation of men to their gods becomes more subjective, too, so they no longer perform the old efficacious rites only in a tribal fashion, to ward off illness and public disasters, but each person also tends to pray in his private interest. That leads him to think of the being he is imploring in a more intimate way as his particular guardian ancestor, ghost, or herm, and his chief concern, therefore, is to find his protector equal to the task and always willing to perform it. So he imagines his deity more and more powerful, and at the same time tries to win his or her grace by praises and by protestations of his own dependence and trust. But as long as there are other spirits hearing other people's prayers, perhaps with incompatible requests, the special patron cannot have full sway; and the best solution men find is to assume a still higher power and finally a ruler of the world, and to delegate all human power and all forces of nature to that supreme being, giving men an infinite reservoir of power on which they can draw by prayer.

This development of religious ideas has often taken place, notably, of course, in the great monotheistic religions—Judaism, Christianity, and Islam—but also in some smaller spheres. It is easier to achieve in societies which conceived of a highest god even before they lost confidence in their own infinite magical potency than for people whose spirit-world has no central godhead but is a conglomerate of unrelated beings with no Jove-like image to dominate the assemblage. With the acceptance of an all-cherishing highest god, the obvious works of the old, demoted dispensers of wrath and punishment—the gods who had to be placated—have to be somehow accounted for, too; this has sometimes been done by giving the god an opponent, Ahriman, Satan, or any other embodiment of all evil, whom he is supposed to conquer at some future end of the devil-ridden world; while his present tolerance of man's terrible ills is accredited to him as his justice, and the responsibility for them assigned to the sufferers, whose sins incurred whatever pains and terrors he permits. Or, again, both good and evil may be attributed to one great power whose existence has both aspects, like the supreme god of the Lugbara, Adroa, whose evil aspect is immanent in nature while his perfection resides in heaven. In the oldest well-known religion of our historic civilizations, Brahmanism, it is the material world itself, the world of illusion and deception, that militates against the life of the mind.

The reason why a highest god, where such a being is postulated, is so often regarded as a remote power not in direct touch with humanity is that most people, civilized or savage, cannot imagine it as a presence in their daily lives. The creator is an abstraction, not a personage; they cannot make a guardian and helper out of it. So they continue to address their prayers to the old, trusted ancestors or to some traditional local spirits, who become intermediaries between them and the cosmic life-giver and death-dealer. In a great world-wide religion like Christianity, these tribal Supernaturals are replaced by canonized saints who assume the role of intercessors. The characteristic conservatism of ritual (especially in speech formulas, which above all uphold articles of belief) helps to tide people over the dangerous changes of thought, for under its "cultural lag" new meanings can grow up and permeate the old symbols, to which the most modern thinkers in any age can resort to shield them from their own fear of change.

There is, however, another problem that arises with the conception of each individual life as an act, the single life-act of the personal agent at its center: that is the fact that the definite form thus given to his life also defines the form of its negative, the time before and after his existence. Before him was the long chain of lives in which his own was implicit—represented by the ancestors, going back to the origin of humanity in the dreamtime or in some mythical act of creation; but after? Logically, of course, nothing more in the way of individual experience or action, if the soul is now thought to join the ancestors. But once the feeling of life has become personal, the impersonal existence of those ancestral spirits offers no substitute for its lost embodiment; it is hard to conceive the non-being of a person once known, and for most people it is quite impossible to imagine their own annihilation. At that point and thereafter, an individual existence beyond the grave is spontaneously and quite unquestioningly assumed; and the shift of feeling from general act-consciousness to self-consciousness makes each soul want its own happiness and fear its own frustration. This leads to all kinds of anxious speculations about the future state.

As often happens in nature, the same condition that creates an impasse for a living stock also produces the means of its solution. This biological principle extends to the evolution of the mind, and is involved in the imagined greater situation to be met by the surviving soul after death. In life, a pious person wins the favor of his deity by acts which please that holder of all power: prayer, praise, and sacrifice. The god is the judge of the worthiness of such devotional acts, and rewards them if he finds them good. With the progressive forming of a whole life as one act, that life attains a unity which allows it to be judged as a single act, and to be found holy or unholy, clean or unclean, good or bad; and at death or at some juncture in the hereafter, that whole life can be thought to be presented to the god (or gods) as a sacrifice. Such a ritual gift can surely be deemed great enough to meet the needs of the whole future state.

What constitutes "the good life" is highly variable within the compass of human society; but in keeping with the progress of cultures to civilization it tends to take in more and more non-ritual elements and gradually become a pattern of moral actions, with the religious performances as its framework. This life can be presented to the god, with or without priestly or mystical mediation, to win his favor and be rewarded by a happy existence in the hereafter. Then the conceptions of man's afterlife become clearly defined by the priesthoods, which use them to bind their laities to a system of moral dictates by hopes of heaven and especially by fears of hell. So there is, indeed, something that mortals can do to shape their expected future, by conforming in all their behavior to the will of their godhead.

Here is the link of mortality with religion. In naive religious thinking there is generally only an incidental connection between these two elements of social life, in that certain trespasses such as a break of tabu or any neglect of a deity or ancestor require ritual atonement; the condition awaiting the dead, however, is the same for good and bad people. But once the shift is accomplished from the easily offended spirits (with or without the distant, unconcerned high god) to a supreme god who ultimately judges the quick and the dead, a really momentous change has also occurred in every individual's feeling of responsibility; for the incubus of guilt, which in savage society is carried only from an episodic sin to the expiatory sacrifice that cancels it, now is laid to account as a part of the whole moral life, even if modified by penance and pardon.

The price of our individuation is a heavy one in many ways, but heaviest, perhaps, in this deepened consciousness of personal continuity and, therewith, of cumulative responsibility. It is a product of phyletic maturation which repeats itself in ontogeny with every passage from infancy through adolescence to adulthood. A young child, forgiven a misdeed, is wholly forgiven, without carrying any stigma; in later youth he can still achieve such a reversal of mind that he "lives down" many wrongs, though really serious past delicts will sear his conscience and cloud his image in the public eye; as an adult he has to carry his transgressions. He may atone for them, even reform his ways, be religiously absolved and socially reinstated, but the stain on his inner life is there.

The awakening of one people after another from the old dream of magic power to the gradual dawn of the tragic vision of human life is a long, sobering experience, especially in its side effects such as the concept of death as inevitable, the god (or gods) as omnipotent, and the work of meeting the divine demands as a lifelong task. It has many elements of a defeat of human mental power. Yet it is a forward step in the very development of that power. As biologists have found in their studies of evolutionary changes, the most radical advances seem to take place in epochs when the evolving species is "defeated"—small in size and numbers, poor in territory. So it seems to be with the evolution of mind too. The reduction of human feeling from the expansive sense of tribal action filling each individual agent's consciousness to the small, centralized awareness of his own being has been (and in some cases, still is) at once the cadential close of one phase—a great imaginative phase—of man's mentality and the upswing of that eternal pendulum, history, to the next, a phase of elaboration and realization of his teeming brood of ideas.

22 / *The Ethnic Balance*

Ethos is the fundamental quality of acts in human conception. It is wider than their evaluation as right or wrong or even as good or bad; it includes the spontaneous perception of acts as important or trivial, holy or profane, instrumental, obstructive, intentional or not, dangerous or not, noble or base—all elements that modify our estimate of their ethos, by virtue of which they enter into the human scene. An act may be good without being noble, as ordinary peaceable behavior usually is, or terrible, like many religious sacrifices, without being base, and even without being received as evil. The finer gradations of value are made with increasing intellectuality in the course of mental life; the two primary reactions, approval and disapproval, may rest on moral or various other grounds. These grounds—often tacit, unformulated assumptions and beliefs—and the traditional pattern of accepted action against which specific acts are seen and evaluated by any given community constitute its ethos.

Approval and disapproval, primitive as they are in social life, do not exist for animals. For them there are only reactions of tolerance, conflict, or (especially in gregarious species) falling in with the action, which are limited to directly given situations and such as concern the agents themselves at the time. There is no impersonal critique of what other creatures do or fail to do; there is no ethos. The phenomenon of ethos marks the departure of man from the common animal estate of the other high vertebrates. Its beginning probably goes back to the very origins of that departure when symbolic communication—speech—first opened the vast realm of ideas which could be shared by a whole population. Then acts could be conceived and talked about before and after they had been performed or even without any instance, and in contemplation they could appear as good or bad, to be approved or disapproved as something that should or should not be done. Ethos arose with the feeling of mental potentiality that makes our *Lebensgefühl* seem to reside in the mind rather than in the body.

The perception of quality, as that of form and relations, is an intuitive perception, a datum for human sensibility. It seems to be directly given, like the famous "pure sense data." And so, perhaps, it is, on the empirical level of knowledge, though it may take a highly elaborated nervous system to create such an apparently direct presentation. Also, like sense data, it can change with ambient changes, so a later intuition does not necessarily match the first. Evaluation of acts is a constant process that normally goes on near the border of consciousness, springing from deep activities and rising above the limen of feeling, sometimes barely, sometimes acutely to culminate in a judgment.

The perception of values alone would not beget an ethnic society, were it not met and entrained—that is, used and thus promoted—by another advance, the growing sense of agency, both actual and potential, in each individual mind. Even in communities in which the mental individuation of their separate members is still somewhat incomplete, so they tend to act and think in concert rather than singly, the inward consciousness of action exists in each one; and although any larger intentions and impulses are generally directed to some joint undertaking, each agent is realizing the whole venture and, in case it miscarries, suffers the whole failure.

This meeting of two evolutionary trends has led to a new attainment, the really crucial step in humanization: the sense of responsibility. In the dangerous course of the mind's individuating out of the physical organism, this common concern for the acts of other persons as a context and continuance of one's own, felt subjectively as such, is the deepest bond holding each independent self to the generative stock as its society. It is not a tie between particular persons but an indirect and unbreakable union, comparable to the internal bonding of an organism by the repetition of its genome in every cell. Yet a society, though organic, is not an organism; it is a community of minds, activated by symbolic thought and symbolic communication. Its whole integral being is a product of the novel elements engendered by the new functions of human forebrains which have advanced to the stage of pseudo-matrices in mental interaction with each other. In the course of each life, the physical intimate unity of mother and child does not simply melt away as it does with the maturing of young animals, but is transmuted very gradually, one tie after another, into a conceptual understanding of the maternal-filial relation, which is a permanent, socially recognized element of family structure. The comprehension of a relationship which lasts whether the instinctual attachment does so or not requires words, such as forms of address and terms of reference; and such comprehension, no matter how it is learned (i.e., how it is triggered), is intuitive. Its acquisition makes the shift from instinct to intuition.

The same is true, of course, for other human relations; their recognition and abstract conception gives them the permanence of a formal framework, in which the persons as personages find their orientation toward one another first of all as members of the natural family, but soon—as a result of the statuses realized by each actual union or birth—capable of wide elaboration and is the basic form of tribal organizations, which exist (or have existed) in many varieties.

The original quality of ethos is the fitting of acts into the frame of statuses based on the interwoven lines of descent and cross-relationships in a familial community, the elementary ethnic unit, or society. The distinction between a society and an animal colony is immediately apparent by the fact that the human, conceptual order includes not only all of each person's living relatives but the dead as well. The dead, in fact, are apt to be the real holders of power; in many traditional cultures the ancestors inflict all punishment for serious wrongs, which are mainly of a ritual nature—neglect of sacrifices whereby the ordinary sins of social living are wont to be expiated. The punishments for omissions of these constant symbolic penances are not purely symbolic at all, but quite physical and visited on the family, the village, and the tribe or tribal segment as a whole: sickness, drought or flood, no game, no fish, no harvest. Extensive sickness is the most usual chastisement.

The hazards and difficulties of life are, of course, world-wide; but why their interpretation as supernatural punishments should be so common that it is really a normal phase of human conception, somewhat higher than the primitive notion of magical powers in people or things accounting for personal bad luck but essentially an extension of that same idea to the realm of the Supernaturals once these are imagined, is a philosophical challenge; for it involves the much-mooted but little-understood basic concept of punishment itself.

The function of punishment is a very complicated topic, for in the course of its evolution it has gathered many secondary aims deriving from different sources, and consequently has received at least as many interpretations. Yet its central and universal motive has rarely been recognized because it lies too deep in emotional feeling—far below the level of rational thinking—to be easily apparent. Some great thinkers have even rejected the corrective value of punishment altogether; Spinoza, for instance, held that regret and repentance, which punishment is supposed to engender, only compound the evil of wrong already done. Others have seen it as a regulated form of vengeance, saving society from violence which might spread and turn into wholesale internecine blood-feuding. The most widely accepted purposes today certainly are correction of the offender's behavior and prevention of similar acts in other people by threats of the same consequences, two aims usually entertained together. The preventive power of punishment is small, the corrective even smaller, at least as it is practiced through our courts; prison only brings felons together to abet each other in their antisocial intents. Yet in our society any major offense that is allowed to pass without the infliction of punishment on the culprit or culprits fills a normal, law-abiding public with deep misgiving.

Even these obvious uses, however, are accessory; the idea of punishment is older, and prevails in cultures where its personal corrective effect serves only for childhood training and is hardly distinct from simple adult intolerance, or sometimes is not used at all. Its primary conception has a historical origin in the very shift to human life, and a growth concomitant with that long physiological process. The tendency to individuate and develop a paramatrix, the mind, with interests of its own, always threatens to lure the mental organ from its primitive function of steering its possessor through the hazards of physical existence. The danger in every aberration from the instinctive round of hereditary behavior is that it is an act of self-assertion, and self-assertion is an overt sign of the agent's growing individuation. It is that basic, unconscious gesture of selfhood that has to be balanced by some display of the biological claims of the stock upon each living generation.

The true intent of punishment, therefore, is symbolic, not "conditioning." Its practical effect only underscores the element of disapproval so it cannot be ignored or defied. That is why, under relatively primitive conditions, the penalizing power belongs to the Supernaturals and is exercised against the community, which is "Man," and why vicarious punishment may redeem the actual offender; why young princes sometimes were not punished for naughtiness, yet punishment had to be dealt, so it fell on a hired "whipping boy"; and why, to this day, one person may pay another's fine for a civil offense, such as a breach of traffic rules, and why fines are the same for rich and poor, though the penal burden is not. No educational principle could be more dangerous to morality than the teaching that "crime doesn't pay"; for it shifts the basis of right and wrong from the recognition of the moral structure to the problem of successful personal operation within that structure.

Since, as aforesaid, most wrongs which tribal gods or ancestors are wont to punish are ritual faults—insufficient sacrifices, errors in recitations, the utterance of tabooed names or eating of tabooed food, etc.—they are themselves concerned with symbolic gestures, which have the same basic motivation as the supernatural penalties for their neglect or distortion, namely, the expression of every individual's commitment to his human responsibility, not only in his transgressions but in his normal independent acts. It is the advance of mentality that has to be held in check so it shall not outstrip the support of its soma. A brain which produces such fantasies that it drags its bodily self into a fictitious world and gives its whole allegiance to the postulated beings of that world and to their demands soon loses its realities and is alone, literally "alienated" from the greater human life that engendered and still carries it. This danger exists not only for individuals but even for whole societies. In all evolving species, there is always some function ready to take the lead in growth and elaboration and, in so doing, to throw the cycles of instinctive life of the mutant strain out of balance. Then a rival impulse or some limiting condition has to retard the excessive advance until the rest of the evolutionary process can catch up with the needs which the radical change is creating, or the stock becomes unviable. The great shift from animal mentality to human, conceptual mentality is no exception to that law of life. Since the beginning of our cerebral overgrowth—whenever that was—the odd human specialty has led and largely constituted our natural history. A new potentiality launched on the course of its realization tends to flourish at the expense of other functions, not only in other organs but even in the organ in which it is itself originating; and for the human brain so many new potentialities opened with the rise of symbolic imagery and expression that it must often have been in grave danger of becoming possessed by its own creations, to the loss of its life-preserving essential work.

But with the beginning of the imbalance between the overactive cerebral cortex and the less progressive, sometimes even regressive limbic parts, there arose—from the very same developments which led to the dangerous tension—the conceptual talents that gave a symbolic function to the products of imagination and intuition, and made the complexes of communally held ideas that imposed themselves on mankind, everywhere on earth, as patterns of culture. There is no speech-gifted horde, however crude and backward, that does not have some cultural rule to live by; and the acceptance of the rule is undiscussed, unquestionable, simply manifest in sacred custom. The sacredness of custom derives from the punishments that descend on the community in the case of a breach. Since imperfections can be found in every ritual performance, and bad luck is always present in some degree, these two evils could easily be linked so displeasure at the former was generally imputed to the Supernaturals, whose overt response was seen in the latter. What prompted this world-wide interpretation was the growing sense of agency together with the naive conception of all events as acts, which led almost ineluctably to the assumption that natural occurrences, especially disasters, were motivated acts of conscious, willful agents. The need of doing something in defense against such misfortunes could usually be met only symbolically; hence the ritualistic form of service and appeal to the controlling deities, ancestors, or local spirits, and even in societies that could hardly be called religious, the symbolic character of their magical practices to counter the inimical mysteries of nature.

The bare possibility of linking two events would not be enough to establish an explanatory connection between them if such connections were really found by empirical methods, but they are not. They are parts of an imaginary scheme, which is imposed on the world by seeking and finding exemplifications of its formal elements in actual experience; and quite trivial experiential items will do to verify the scheme. The explanation in terms of motivation thus provided for natural events is only an incidental achievement in the course of such thinking. Its real aim is to maintain the equilibrium between the drives of mental individuation and the integrity of the biological continuum, the rhythmically self-perpetuating stock. That equilibrium is the ethnic balance.

The principle of balance runs pervasively through all human life. The significance of punishment as a symbol of censure and recall to the social sphere is only one—albeit a primary one—of the many expressions of that basic principle. The whole advance of mind proceeds by piecemeal, dialectical movements, for every fully competent human brain strives, even without conscious intent, for emancipation from its somatic and reciprocal organic duties and for freedom to shape and follow a purely mental life of its own. Yet the physical organism in which that mental life is rooted has to be functionally represented and guided by the same organ that creates the mind. The higher the cultural expression of a society rises, the more tenuous becomes the balance between the physical security and strength of the stock and the autonomy of its members. Every behavioral act carries the possibility of upsetting the equilibrium of the social order in which successive generations are born, mature, and age, think, command, negotiate their conflicts and develop their separate minds, each unique, unlike any that ever was before. The primal and perennial work of social organization is not to fix the bounds of behavior as permanent lines, which would make all evolutionary process impossible, but to retrieve the vital balance every time some act, public or private, has upset it.

Meanwhile, the traditional rituals practiced in most societies—"rites of passage"—are expressions of the claims of society on the individual (often its first acknowledgment of his individuality), symbolizing his inherited responsibility for the welfare and continuation of the interwoven lineages, his people, that represent humanity to him.

There is a very ancient rite—how old we cannot tell, for its existence goes back further than our earliest historical records—so widespread in the world that it must have a primitive symbolic function: the rite of circumcision. Like punishment, it is rarely, if ever, seen in the light of its basic meaning but has been given various interpretations in the different cultures where it is practiced. It has been interpreted as a sign of membership in this or that particular society or religious cult; but Jews and Moslems carry the same mark, which is also borne by many Australian, African, and even American tribesmen and is said to have been known in Egypt before the infiltration by the Israelites in Joseph's day.

It bespeaks, I think, a darkly apprehended intuition of the danger that lurks in an excessive spiritualization of man, the tendency to develop a mental life in defiance of the biological mainstream and let the physical stock degenerate or even cease. Circumcision is the branding of the organ of procreation as a possession of society. Wherever this rite obtains, it symbolizes the necessary balance between the development of individual minds and the continuously creative matrix of social life, the slower, broader advance of mankind. Like many vital safeguards, it anticipates by long ages—probably millennia—the occurrence of any conceptual insight into its basic significance. Yet that unrecognized, purely felt function imbues the rite with sanctity, no matter how inadequate its conscious rationalization may be.

If the interpretation here proposed is accepted, a fair range of other practices may be viewed in the same light, namely, as branding the individual with the mark of his tribal or national involvement. The symbol may not be placed on the sex organ but in the face, such as a quill or other decor worn in the pierced nasal septum, like the ring in a bull's or boar's nose; as the animal's freedom is thus effectively curtailed, the human being's subjugation is symbolically attested. The essential process is to effect some visible symbol of the young person's socialization, the limitation of his selfhood, to be borne on his body for life.

The growth of the mind, however, goes on even in the confines of its natural duties, which it gradually comes to feel and conceive as moral impositions; and as the vague feeling becomes more and more conceptualized, the permanent physical symbol may no longer be required (provided it has not, meanwhile, taken on a supplementary patriotic or religious meaning), so a person's identification with a purely mental kindred may be ritually established without a bodily sign—by a promise, an oath, a spoken commitment. The accompanying rite may be a sacrifice or a manipulation of sacred objects, a transient ordeal, or a presentation with or without priestly or choric dance and prayer.

A familiar example of such entirely symbolic attestation of a moral status is baptism. The fact that in its most common form today it is given to very young infants who cannot even take an active part in the commitment which is made for them by their elders shows with peculiar clarity that it expresses a social claim, even though it is consciously thought to bestow personal salvation. That putative efficacious power keeps it in the mystical realm, so it is not felt to be a conceptual symbol but a religious event.

Every rite that has traditionally marked the progression of a person's life from one phase to another gives expression to his inescapable involvement in the greater life of his lineage and the still greater life of humanity. But that does not mean that this inherence is the most important meaning of every rite of passage, as it is of birth and puberty ceremonies. In most cultures the usual next sacrament is marriage; and in all tribally organized societies marriage is more than a commitment to an established pattern: it is the making and upholding of the pattern itself, which is the skeleton of the social order. The fact is, I think, that the most primitive human tribes recognize quite abstract symbolic contents where a natural form is presented and anciently familiar, perpetually repeated or sustained; then words are gradually coined for all its aspects and drawn together by the process of association that builds language in the first place, until a very elaborate relational system grows up through centuries, and is directly, intuitively, perceived as a pattern. Yet its originators cannot freely invent a systematic symbolism, so the complexity of their social structure seems utterly out of keeping with their crude cultural life. The expanded family is a fairly fixed, slow-changing image which each individual learns to use as his symbol of society. If, however, the rules of marriage are suddenly abrogated or changed by a conqueror's fiat, not only domestic security but even political authority lose their footing in tribal tradition and find no other principle of allocation and support.

Finally, there are the rites that confirm the end of each individual life on earth; and these mark the point that is really the growing tip of the "Golden Bough," the point where religious ideas take shape, using whatever ritual practices there are to suggest meanings, and sometimes elaborating these into mythical eschatologies—fragmentary and inconsistent, yet offering a general background for any particular speculation a thoughtfully inclined person might pursue. In some societies more than in others such imaginative flights are pursued, and a general scheme of divine powers gradually finds acceptance.

There are today very few societies which have not produced some such scheme and carried it to the extent of conceiving the powers as personal wills. The mental gestation that leads from the first awareness of outside forces to the notion of such forces as living agents is not achieved in one step but is synthetic, like all important vital processes, and its contributing elements may look strange if one sees them in isolation. The first objectification of external power may be not by its attribution to a living being (real or imaginary) at all, but to a concrete ritual object that is thought to influence events which are beyond human control. Such an object is a fetish, and from the atavistic remnants of fetishism that still exist one may gather that it was once a phase in the origination of abstract thought.

The fetish represents human mental power and, characteristically, is supposed to contain and exercise the efficient "principle" it embodies for its user. This visible representation of the conceptual function of mind may not merit the name of religion, but it is the first stage of mystical, non-physical thinking, the forerunner of all conceptions of supernatural forces on which religion is built. From these most rudimentary beginnings still extant in our world to the highest theological doctrines, just about every possible stage and variant of religious belief is to be found in some society today. Even as the power of symbolic thought creates the danger of letting the mind run wild, it also furnishes the saving counterbalance of cultural restraint, the orienting dictates of religion.

The typical expression of religious feeling is sacrifice. This in itself is a highly suggestive fact. Literally, "sacrifice" means "making sacred," "hallowing"; it has no connotation of destroying the dedicated object, but only of sanctifying it, as by giving it to a holy being or power whose acceptance of it lends it holiness. Yet wherever the word is used in its religious context it carries the idea of renunciation, yielding something, giving over, depriving oneself. In secular use it has lost all other meaning. Commercial advertisements announce that such-and-such goods are to be "sold at a sacrifice." No one thinks they are to be made sacred, but only that the seller will take a loss of his potential profit to sell them at all. Obviously the idea of forgoing, yielding, is essential to the meaning of the word, even though its Latin form lays stress exclusively on the element of sanctification.

Popular usage, which commonly confuses and degrades the real sense of words, in this case seems to have preserved a primitive content which points to the fundamental nature of that basic rite, perhaps the most ancient in the world, and provides a cue to its biological source and function, its wide dissemination and variability, and its apparent deathless persistence.

The original motivation of sacrifice was, I believe, a sense of danger in the performance of an autonomous overt act that changed the agent's situation. Any such act, initiated by a single or multiple agent, is an exercise of mental power, and as such demonstrates the individuating activity of mind. It made the performer (and his witnessing fellows) feel a shift in the balance of power between him and the tribe or, if the tribe was the doer, between it and the powers of nature, at whatever stage of mystical representation or deification the latter might be. Something had been autonomously done; to restore the biological balance something would have to be yielded; and the readiest symbol of submission to the claim of the greater, ancestral life force is to give up some precious thing to it, i.e., to make a sacrifice. That sacred transaction expresses the continued responsibility of the individual to his kind, represented for him by his lineage, his society, or, in higher cultures, his deities. Sacrifice is *par excellence* the means of restoring the ethnic balance; and in this capacity it is never without a basic sense of loss and surrender.

Since the ultimate, intuitive aim of sacrifice is to symbolize the retrieval of a balance, its magnitude is determined for each occasion by that of the committed self-assertion. An act of self-assertion is not the same as an act of aggression; it need not be directed against any other creature, although aggression is, of course, always self-assertive, and therefore most obviously requires ritual compensation. Any bold thought is at the same time a gesture of independence; so are all our decisions, choices, voluntary acts. It is in these normal ways that the mind takes its own course, and develops the self-feeling that has to be balanced *in toto* by an equally generalized ritual of maintained communion.

In the early days of Yahweh worship, the demands of the Lord were not so much moral as ritual, and unintended sins were sins nevertheless. This aspect of the ancient ethos has often puzzled modern moralists but is found throughout the uncivilized tribes of man and well into some high civilizations; and if one regards sacrifice as a symbolic restoration of balance between individual freedom and hereditary responsibility, it is reasonable. Blunder as well as wickedness can upset the equilibrium of life.

An evolutionary history of sacrifice if carried out in sufficient detail might be a revealing contribution to the history of mind; for the unfolding of mind in all corners of the earth—in the heart of Africa and the remote headwaters of the Amazon as well as in India, China, the Mediterranean, the white man's Europe, and its global reaches—has recorded itself in a mosaic (or better, perhaps, a pointillist picture) of locally evolved tribal rites which, for all their differences, have a common element, a central act of sacrifice. This continuity of the historical record of sacrifice makes the biblical account an invaluable display of religious expression, change by change, age by age, where each impinging exotic influence has inscribed itself; for the rise of Christianity as well as the unbroken life of Judaism has carried it on to the present day, when it has become an entirely symbolic action, as it did a thousand years earlier in the minds of Chinese sages.

Culture, however crude, is an essential safeguard to regulate the advance of mind in its present state of functional elaboration. The first phase of that evolutionary step was the terrifying growth of imagination, which provided a flood of emotional stimuli, probably more than the organism could deal with, and also kept itself activated by the envisagement of more and more unrealities. This may have driven the human species to articulate utterance and laid one of the foundations of speech; but speech, in turn, allowed fantasies to be shared, and in that way augmented the load on each brain, until the tendency to form a pseudo-matrix, the mind, and let it individuate beyond its physical supports became a lethal threat to the race. At that point, however, the widening possibilities of symbolic expression offered a saving device, probably well ahead of any intellectual use, the ritual demonstration of each individual's yielding and subjugation to society, however that greater felt life presented itself—as the tribe, the tribal ancestors, a family of divinities like the Greek and Roman gods, or a single divine ruler, Yahweh. In every case the intuitive sense of the balance between man's mental activity and the claims of his physical nature has been upheld by the offering of sacrifice in one form or another.

Religion, even the most primitive and superstitious, is inevitably a beginning of culture. It is not possible without some kind of symbolic expression, at least on the non-discursive level; and evidently it does not long remain on that level, but breaks over into communicative speech and begets dramatic gesture, dance, and chant, feelings of heightened power, and ideas of surrounding invisible beings. Under the protective restraints of religious actions, especially dance and the many forms of sacrifice, the shift from herd life to social life could take its jerky, piecemeal course through all the rocky rapids of fantastic thinking. It was fortunate for our kind that one of the first intuitions was the projected and metaphorized sense of imbalance, which held back the mushroom growth of imagination and let other functions—memory, reasoning, judgment—catch up with it; for in the evolution of mind imagination is as dangerous as it is essential.

So great a phenomenon as religion has, of course, more than one part to play where it prevails. Its original function may have been to keep men's minds in balance with the rest of nature, but what has led to its own elaboration is a purpose it soon acquired: the denial or masking of death. This task has provided a challenge to reason as well as to imagination and served as a disciplinary guide in the development of thought, using the floods of spontaneous fantasy as materials instead of final products of mind.

But a much deeper change came with the realization of mortality, too—unperceived, biological, a new orientation that overtook one people after another until almost all but the most unenlightened savages have experienced it: the gradual shift from the ideal of boundless personal power to a demand for the highest degree of vital action in the small possible span of earthly life. No matter how firmly we may hold to the interpretations which would make death trivial or unreal, its actual constant approach has its unconscious psychological effect—so completely unconscious that it might better be called neurological, cerebral. The desire for maximal experience is easy enough to understand, but it is not the whole story; the part that one might not expect is that with the wish for fullness of life there comes a higher potentiality for action, a great new mental potentiality.

A little reflection on the rhythms of growth and change, however, makes this accelerated gain not really surprising. Every change of internal as well as external conditions tends to activate an evolving stock subjected to it, and elicits intensified, even new, reactions. The fact that the crucial stimulus in this case is not physical but conceptual, yet reaches to the very matrix of each organism shows that by this time the intellectual functions of the brain are well in the lead in directing and shaping the conative and emotional life of humanity, even though actual lures and threats play over its surface in an everyday pattern.

The present races of *Homo*, self-styled "*sapiens*," live in the long consummation of the evolutionary "great shift." The radical change from animal life to human is still in progress and, I suspect, far from the limit to which it may ultimately go. Meanwhile, each major loss and replacement takes its separate course, and usually the loss of the old, animalian function outruns the development of the new, symbolically negotiated one. We have lost many valuable instincts. The "righting reflex" of animals in falling, most obvious in cats but present in most mammals, is almost completely lost in man, since his natural posture is not pronograde. And the "moro reflex" of newborn infants has been interpreted as a trace of an old clinging response.

Even the universally accepted "sex instinct" in man has suffered some deviation from the general pattern of the higher vertebrates, in being no longer seasonal except for a trivial rise of libido in spring that is only statistically demonstrable. There are good reasons for the frequent claim of biologically oriented psychologists that the sexual rhythm is the real pacemaker of animal emotions, wherefore the general temperamental responses of beasts and birds depend to some extent on the time of year. In man the vernal rise and culmination of this basic excitability is all but lost; he is ready for sexual activity at every season. The result is that his sex experiences are distributed and transformed into a wave pattern instead of a cycle, and as the effects of the endocrine stimulation very commonly outlast their stimuli, his erotic tensions fuse into a fluctuating but unbroken continuum supporting a more or less coherent emotional life. This short pulse of intensified vital feeling, and perhaps of all feeling, by the organic pacemaker may have been an important factor in sustaining the stimulation of felt cerebral acts to the point of making many of them terminate in symbolic expression.

The most radical change, however, which must have started with the very beginning of humanization and is generally effective today, is the loss of the relationship among animals that is properly called "empathy," the intense degree of suggestion that transmits the feeling of one creature directly to another so it appears to the latter as its own. We experience it ourselves upon occasion, but the physiological way it seems to work in animals, at the impulse level, is rare with us. Our usual response to indications of another person's sensory or emotive feeling is to imagine his experience and have a reaction of our own to the imagined feeling we attribute to him. That indirect reaction is not empathy, but sympathy, which has become the normal replacement for empathy in human life.

The word "sympathy" immediately suggests pity, understanding, and well-wishing; but in fact the worst instances of sadistic behavior—deliberate cruelty, torture—which are practiced only by human beings, depend on a constitutional element of sympathy in ordinary social awareness. If the tormentor could not imagine his victim's pain, he would find no satisfaction in inflicting it. In animals, and unusually in men, a sudden empathetic seizure can stop an aggressive impulse, but there is nothing whereby the agent can purposely evoke it or hold it, nor can he evade it when it spontaneously occurs. Sympathy may be both evoked and by-passed; it normally varies directly with imagination, though it can, in emotionally responsive persons, overwhelm and block the act of imagining beyond a point. At that point it may possibly be touching off an atavistic moment of empathy.

The shift from the direct, physiological contagion of feeling to the conceptual form, sympathy, is slow and irregular, like most evolutionary advances, and the varying rates at which its elements progress set up some extreme tensions in human life. Every society rests on at least a minimum of fellow-feeling; but in the course of our mental evolution the growth of sympathy has not kept pace with the loss of the animal reaction, empathy. So, although the exchange is clearly an essential step in the process of humanization, it also opened the way to mankind's most shockingly "inhuman" but apparently natural practice, cannibalism. Among the higher animals few, if any, of the carnivores—bears and wolves, lions and other great cats—habitually prey on their own kind. What restrains them? Hardly an accepted tradition of respecting signals of surrender. Very likely it is a ready empathetic response, so common and effective that it takes no principle, moral or other, to safeguard the members of a species against each other's appetites under ordinary conditions. Cannibalism, such as is widely known in savage societies where civilized conquerors have not suppressed it, is more natural to mankind than to most wild beasts. The reason, I think, is that men have lost their prompt empathetic reactions, while their more complex cerebral functions are slow to engender new sensibilities to replace the former instinctive inhibition. The incidence of cannibalism may thus be seen as a perfectly logical transitional stage in the evolution of man. What appears to the eye of a moralist like a terrible reversion to bestiality is really part and parcel of an elementary, exceedingly slow, advance.

Even the lowest savages, however, seem to feel the need of some balancing restraint upon the potential overgrowth of the cerebral organ when it reaches the stage of envisagement, fantasy, and speech, as it has done in every human stock. That need is met by ritual, especially sacrifice, apparently with a basic intuition that to keep the organic balance of mankind amid the vast opportunities for mental action requires some concession to the natural forces surrounding and upholding it. The ritualization of common activities such as eating, hunting or fishing, and gardening or gathering is probably a spontaneous reaction to the earliest conception of non-human powers as elements in the circumambient world, to be met with recognition, bids for favor, or defense—mental, magic defense—against their threats. Ritual is older than religion; it is the scaffolding in which all religious thought has taken shape. In its practice the symbols of power are created. So without plan or deliberate intent society becomes culturally organized in a sacred round, its recurrent cycles punctuated by seasonal public rites, while on a smaller scale each individual life goes through its own "rites of passage," from its admission to the social order (usually with name-giving) to the closing ceremonial acts which each person's fellows perform for him. It is those last rites that undergo a grave change of meaning when people are inescapably faced with the enigma of the final "passage" from the familiar scene of daily life to the inconceivable state of being dead.

The effect on mankind as a whole, however, has been not only a pervasive deepening of thought and subjective feeling, but also a quite unrecognized change of fundamental values; for instead of seeking indefinite length of life, we tend to seek a maximum of activity and experience in the short span which, we know, is all we can hope for, even if we reach a relatively ripe age. The brevity of that greatest human act, the passage from birth to death, makes any personal agent seem incomparably small within the stream of the ancestral stock, constantly proliferating into new death-bound individuals, in its immediate temporal dimension; and when the source of that stream is conceived as a godhead to which all power of animate and inanimate nature has been delegated, the contrast between human and superhuman potency becomes overwhelming. There no longer seems any danger of man's rivaling God's supremacy. The balance between mental individuation and vital dependence has, in fact, shifted in the direction of the latter, so the strongest minds feel quite safe and free to put out their utmost ability in defiance of death and fill a precarious lifetime with all the personal experience they can crowd into it. Gradually, quite unconsciously, the weaker souls follow the pioneers, until the daily anxiety to make sacrificial atonement for human arrogance is assimilated to the general religious background and given into the care of the priesthood.

A trauma to a special organ, however, while it may briefly confuse or even interrupt its operation, typically produces a concentration of energy in it which presently leads to abnormal growth, elaboration, or—most immediately—a burst of its functional activity. The mental organ naturally responds to an abnormal strain with acts of imagination and emotion and, at a level where ideas can disturb it, with cogitation. So the understanding of mortality, which comes as a blow to the mind in its phyletic progress, starts an epoch of heightened mental action and drives it to more intellectual advance and more individuation than ever. That has happened in most societies where the realization of personal mortality has dawned; and, reflecting the nature of its motivation, the new preoccupation is with a vision of life not as an indefinite length of days in the world of the living or in a similar world of the ancestral spirits (with spirit-bones and beards and tempers), but as a brief phase in an ascent of the mind to a higher sort of life without death. What aids the conception of such a life is the relatively huge impetus the forebrain has received, the furious activity beyond that of the somatic functions whereby the mind is so abetted and encouraged that it is apt to be still unexhausted when the rest of the life is finished; consequently most people feel the tension between their love of life and their loss of strength to live. The body threatens to be through before the spirit is through. Then the relations of death and life become urgent and central. The greatest thinkers, founding their speculations on the mythic premises of the religious traditions current in their day, elaborated theological and eschatological doctrines until fantasy and logic together wrought the conception of earthly life as an episodic ordeal (somewhat like an initiation) to prepare the human soul for a projected endless existence after death.

There are many ways of restoring the balance between the mind's individuation and the earthbound hold of its roots in animal nature, the enormous potential of mental life and its tiny allowance of time for realization. The great religions are our present promises of a more proportionate future. In the centuries and millennia during which those promises were given and reiterated until they built a bulwark against death, a change overtook humanity's symbols of its highest value: the old symbols of power yielded their paramount place to life symbols. Even before abstract thought reached the stage of contemplation where people could envisage either an eternal life after death or a sovereign god, their life symbols acquired the status of supreme significance. Ian Oswald's experimental work, reported in *Sleeping and Waking. Physiology and Psychology*, corroborates the verity of preconscious evaluation. Speaking of what stimuli will or will not arouse a sleeper, he makes quite clear, by implication, that the evaluation of signs occurs at the impulse level of physical acts, below the limen of conscious judgment (1962, p. 160). The same condition appears to hold for symbolic values of objects, rites, and even imagery; their import is felt as sacredness to a distinct degree before it is intellectually understood. The great importance and formal role of gifts in most precivilized societies rests on this preconscious evaluation. Especially a gift of food is received as a gift of life.

One ritual act which might be regarded as transitional between the worship of power and of life is contained in the Jewish blood rite. When the blood of the sacrificed animal was poured out before the altar, the priest was enjoined by the scripture to take some of it on his finger and daub it on the horns of the altar, which were the symbols of God's power. Here the two values, power and life, are almost equal; but it was the blood rite that went on to make cultural history, for the concept of atonement by blood sacrifice underlay the subsequent Graeco-Judaic development of the Christian myth.

Wherever the balance between man and the greater powers that surround him has been established by some fundamental religious expression, as it has largely been today, it fills the background rather than the foreground of conscious thought. But no balance holds itself passively for very long in the course of evolution. A state of equilibrium in nature generally indicates a fulcrum between two antagonistic forces. Even though we may be in the midst of an eon of cerebral elaboration rather than radical mutation, intellectual drives and cultural checks are always shifting the ethnic balance, and its present direction seems to be toward internalization, i.e., toward a centering of the fulcrum of social equilibrium not between men and Supernaturals, but in society itself. We may be at the very bottom of a new ladder of mental and moral ascent, in a human world stunned by civilization, and in a moment of pause in its otherworldly concerns, meeting the challenge of its own technical and economic construction of a world-wide civilized society.

23 / The Breaking

As the development of religious and moral codes records the evolution of subjective new experience, the overt expression of that same process is a long, spectacular achievement: the rise of civilization. That aspect of man's mental advance has inscribed itself objectively on the face of the earth, in spite of the obliterating forces of time which have caused many of its effects to return to the dust again. There is still enough cumulative progress to mark its course, even to spelling out some of the acts, prehistoric, ancient, or recent in history, which turned forested mountainsides into barren rock or won fertile lands from the sea that used to cover them, separated continents by cutting canals through the isthmuses that joined them, built lakes and harnessed the dammed-up power of their waters. All these grand scars on the earth, however, tell only indirectly the newest chapter in the story of man, the emergence and persistent growth of civilization; for the story itself is the life history of the mind, and the new chapter began only a few thousand years ago.

The most spectacular aspect of the new age is the rise of cities in several far-separated parts of the world, at shortening intervals and, once started, in rapidly increasing numbers; and the surest sign that this phenomenon marks an evolutionary step in human history is that various apparently independent occurrences have different motivations, yet converge in their consummations. Cities arise under widely varying conditions. The oldest sites so far found by present-day archeologists are still the ruins, sometimes deeply buried, in Mesopotamia, or even further east, in central Asia. No one knows what caused the ferment in one people after another, who had apparently lived for thousands if not hundreds of thousands of years in family groups formed by the occurrence of births and deaths in natural lines of descent, which automatically expanded into village settlements as overlapping generations built up groups of related families. Uncounted millennia seem to have witnessed only increasing complexities of tribal organization, developing rules of exogamy or endogamy, formal agnatic and affinic relations, taboos a-plenty and peculiar liberties, totemic divisions and sometimes a separation into moieties that were not totemic. But there came definite times—though very different times in different parts of the world—when there was, apparently, a growing tendency for persons of unusual courage and energy to arise out of each habit-bound general population, and go venturing beyond the familiar foraging grounds, perhaps ostensibly in search of food, but really from a deeper impulse in search of excitement, discovery, adventure—in short, of greater potentiality for action than their known world offered. Such people are "born leaders"; and where a leader appeared, it was easy enough to find followers in a society that was still prone to act in concert if anyone suggested and led the move. Perhaps just a modicum of the restlessness that possessed the leader stirred in the average man, too; in any event, there arose a wish and readiness among men to go afield on expeditions.

That common readiness and the rise of forceful personalities prepared the first break in the tribal pattern of human society, though it must have gone quite unnoticed by the people who enacted it. There had surely been leaders in village affairs before—men who spontaneously organized and led the occasional or perhaps frequent migrations of the hordes when hunger, land desiccation, enemies, fire or flood, or even regular seasonal changes of conditions that closed one wild habitat and opened another drove them from their homes. Migration in itself need not break up the familial pattern of primitive society; the villagers simply move their households, taking babies, dogs, and even their home fires with them. That does not disturb the social order.

Expeditions, however, are a different matter; for instead of being decided and directed by the elders of a community, they are conceived and led by young pioneers. An expedition party makes its own arrangements around a charismatic leader whose directives are voluntarily followed. Sometimes his authority becomes vested in his leadership, and chieftaincy is born in his society without regard to age. That new function may be temporary, tied to the occasion, or reach beyond it as a permanent status.

The latter tendency became paramount when men began to move on the waters. Many historians and prehistorians have recognized the crucial impact of seafaring on tribal society, notably Gustave Glotz, as early as 1904. Glotz made a fair reconstruction of the archaic conditions which sent active young men out on the sea, when the restraints of low birth, being late in a sequence of many brothers, lack of land and means, or sometimes even exile because of a blood feud deprived them of a normal chance and sphere of action.

At a time when land and cattle were collectively owned by families, bands of merchant-pirates were formed outside and at the expense of the regularly constituted families. In time, these marauders set up permanent colonies on land, around harbors where they were wont to cast anchor. This soon changed their attitude toward piracy. They tried, naturally enough, to organize their communities on the model of the villages they had left, but that organization could not be achieved under the new conditions. Their new settlements were cut out of whole cloth, so to speak, not grown from any family cores; they were founded as cities, not villages. The seafarers had picked up companions from many places who had the same motives as the original members for leaving their homes, so the colonists had no common ancestors or clan allegiances. The obvious design for their social structure was that which had developed at sea, where it was the only possible one—the captain with his crew: one commander, and his men bound to absolute obedience. This, in turn, led naturally to the rise of royalty and the founding of kingdoms, each centering in a city and extending as far as the terrain was controllable and defensible. Here the new pattern of life was at least temporarily free to develop.

We know little about that early phase of human settlements around the Mediterranean because it reaches so far back in history that the beginnings of Greek, Italian, and more westerly cultures, as they must have been under savage conditions before invasion or infiltration by peoples from the east, are hard to establish on any better grounds than anthropologically plausible surmise. The Viking age in northern Europe, however, illustrates step by step (with occasional backward and sideways as well as forward ones), the course of the change from tribal society to civilization; and there we can see most plainly the forceful influence of maritime organization on the companies that landed on foreign shores and built their settlements according to their own simple societal framework. Bertha Phillpotts's (1913) well-authenticated account of this early adaptation of shipboard relationships to the new city on land shows the natural development of monarchy from the position of the captain among his men. The great break with the kinship pattern of society which came with the increasing desire of men to rove, discover, win, and possess was made in principle and practice by the change from the ancient authority of elders to leadership by young and adventurous men.

In Byzantium the Nordic warriors and traders found a new and fabulous sort of city, ancient in comparison to their oldest wicks and emporia, and of dazzling splendor: an imperial city on its steep hills above the Golden Horn such as they had never seen. Byzantium, for all its westward trade through Venice and the Sicilian kingdom, belonged to another culture. It represented the closing phase of the oldest civilization we know from archeological researches, that which began in Mesopotamia some time before the dynastic period of Egypt. Those Near Eastern cities had a different history from the urban centers of medieval Europe, which were walled towns, sometimes of Roman colonial origin but dominated, after the loss of that linkage, by feudal lords, ecclesiastic or lay, and animated by trade and industry. The ancient cities of Mesopotamia were not originally designed as trade centers, but were founded with a grander motivation, as seats of power raised by royal conquerors for their own glorification.

The wealth of their kings was derived originally from conquest and tribute more than from trade, for war and plunder were the basis of their ascendancy. Each city was served by its surrounding villages and so constituted a city-state; and its resources came from conquered princes and the slave labor of their captured rural populations. How did these kings rise to their royal estate? The cities they founded were chiefly in the great river valleys of the Nile, the Euphrates and the Tigris, yet none of them were built by seafarers. The time of their origin antedates by many centuries the age of ships and maritime adventure, such as seems to have made kings and henchmen out of the Norse captains and crews. Yet somehow the old tribal pattern had broken long ago in the Near East and given rise to an organization of rulers and subjects, which became progressively intensified in Mesopotamia to a much higher degree of despotism and thralldom than western Europe ever knew.

In Asia, perhaps, some of the tribes in the south-western part of that great continent fell under a natural influence not unlike that of the sea, a terrain which has some of the vastness and emptiness of the open sea—the desert. Like the ocean, it could be braved only by organized expeditions, which gave rise to kingly leadership much as the life of mariners did. Perhaps it was the deeply, unconsciously accepted influence of the yellow sand as much as the potentialities of the green river valleys that made Mesopotamia and Egypt, the two horns of the "fertile crescent," the first keepers of civilization.

In Egypt, the self-exaltation of a single line of individuals, the Pharaohs, reached an apotheosis quite beyond the superficial emperor-worship which later was demanded by the Roman Caesars. It seems to have arisen gradually from the tribal stage rather than to have been imposed by a superior power. The peculiar nature of that country caused human life not only to be fixed in a definite zone by the conformation of the Nile Valley, the waterless wastes hedging it in and the broad, shifting delta, but also held it to a time schedule and rhythm of activities by the annual flood. This inescapable round seems to have molded the native population in a highly uniform pattern and slowed the phylogenetic process of individuation, so that most people had not felt the drive to self-assertion against their ancient tribal stock when the first dynasty was founded, or it could never have reached such divine proportions.

The Egyptians either went through a different process of individuation from that of other people or else, perhaps, the uniformity of their lives imposed by their environment held that process back and elaborated an early stage which never developed as fully anywhere else, the "god-man" that personally lived what he was set up to express, the awesome representative Individual. A sign of this significance of the Pharaoh for his people is the special law for his family permitting brother-and-sister marriage, which in almost all tribes and nations is under one of the most elementary taboos; the motivation of the moral protest usually evoked by sibling incest is the fear of the concentration of family power, family interest, and increased talents, especially magical, which would be abetted in such an inbred single line to the degree of making an organism within the social organism a state within the state. In the case of a pharaonic dynasty this danger did not threaten; the more pure and authentic the origin of that divine Being, the more potent was his presence.

The Egyptians, in their three thousand years of continuous though shifting prosperity, and despite occasional major crises, had reached the stage of city-building. Their cities, however, were of neither the eastern nor the European kind. Two kinds of urban settlement were, indeed, unique Egyptian foundations: the pure temple city, of which Karnak was a grandiose example, and the "pyramid cities" that arose with the building of those huge monuments. They were sacred cities of the dead, erected round the sites of pyramids in process of their building, and afterwards maintained to house the thousands of people engaged in their upkeep, safeguarding, and the constant religious services of homage to the gods and to the deified Pharaohs.

Between the spectacular cultures of Mesopotamia and Egypt which had sprung up separately at the two ends of the "fertile crescent" lay the deserts of the Levant and northern Arabia, traversed by treasure-laden caravans; and, naturally, cities grew up at the oases which punctuated the long journey and made the Bedouin commerce possible. Thus Palmyra became one of the world's greatest caravansaries.

That the Near East had an ancient high culture is well known, but it is hard to realize what a full-fledged civilization—literate, urban, economic—had risen on that indigenous culture some five thousand years ago. With conditions of trade and genuine high finance, mobility and competition, the rise of civilization was spectacular, especially in the cities; besides material wealth, knowledge and invention and tales of wonder traveled with the caravans from one royal capital to another. So did great complexes of thought, mythological ideas, and a cumulative medley of rites—in other words, religions—that gathered like storms and clashed. Then city after marvelous city collapsed in flames. But not only militant Moslems and Christians destroyed the products of civilization; war was an endemic scourge throughout the civilized world. Kings and adventurers did their share of destroying what their predecessors—often recent ones—had created.

Such wanton destructiveness was much more common in Asia than in Europe, and historians have raised the question of a reason for the difference. The source of the difference is, I think, the earlier difference in the motivations whereby Western and Eastern cities, respectively, were established. In Europe they were chiefly of Roman origin and administrative function, and as long as they implemented political control of the countryside they could change hands, from emperors to popes, to princes and kings, and more locally from governors to bishops, to feudal lords, to burgomasters and aldermen. Under the Pax Romana the cities of early western Europe did not have to fight each other. Their fortifications were against Vikings and Mediterranean pirates, hordes of Huns, Goths, and other unconquered migrant tribes, not rival Roman provincial towns. Even when the disasters of war swept through them, the breaches in their walls were mended, their temples cleansed of fire damage and ashes, houses gradually rebuilt, and the life of the town continued; for the constant aim of Rome was to rule orderly people and to be the center of a balanced economic system, a single civilized world.

The splendid cities of the East were differently conceived; since they were the individual works and personal possessions of absolute monarchs asserting their supposedly unlimited power, symbols of self-exaltation, to overcome a rival for majesty and honor in the worldly contest meant, above all, to destroy his capital; and such destruction, having as much symbolic as political purpose, went beyond the needs of military victory. The city had to be totally annihilated, because that represented its founder's annihilation, the demolition of his name and fame.

Not only in the Near East but throughout the Caucasus, Baktria, the great land of Persia, and all across India cities rose and fell in this same way. Here or there in India, where war was especially likely to sweep over them, they might be fortified or otherwise protected, but for the most part they relied on the power of their princes, who dictated their laws and safeguarded their lives. That power was exhibited and asserted in the splendor of their palaces, which defiantly challenged destruction and usually received it.

Finally, in China, the archeologist excavating ancient sites that speak of long occupation meets with a peculiar frustration: there seem to be no foundations, no urban ruins where a civilized traditional culture would lead him to expect them. Even an archaic sort of dynastic rule could hardly have arisen without a seat of authority, the equivalent of a capital from which the ruler issued his decrees; and he would certainly be surrounded by his own descent-group, i.e., the royal clan, as well as by an army, or earlier a horde, of defenders; also there must have been servants (hirelings or slaves) and a food-producing peasantry. Here are all the makings of a city; the exalted position of the king is enough to make a classification of the society he rules into noble and common people; among the former, degrees of nearness to him determine degrees of privilege, while the latter, the commonality, fall into social strata according to the functions assigned to them.

Yet the modern diggers for palace foundations, floors and steps, vaults and pilasters, find no signs of any royal establishment, nor of temples, nor of ancestral halls such as all Chinese families have owned since time immemorial and very probably had at the very beginning of kingly power, statehood and urbanism.

From another source, however, we may gain a picture of the Chinese city, which shows it not as an edifice or collection of such, nor even as a place; in his book *Early Chinese Civilization: Anthropological Perspectives* K. C. Chang has reconstructed the earliest urban establishments to reveal not only a new type but, to most Western people (and today to his own compatriots, too), a new conception of "city," namely, as a group of people organized by fixed relations to each other apart from common descent or marital connections—functional relations, over and above familial ties or age groups, i.e., apart from clan structure; though the latter may persist with regard to marriage regulations, mourning ceremonies, ancestor veneration, and other close-linking substructures of social life. The physical frame of the city seems to have been no more than clay-and-wattle, chiefly one-storey, houses, with roofs of thatch and floors of pounded earth. The most extraordinary aspect of those ancient royal cities, however, is that they were not anchored in their locations on the earth. They could be moved, at the king's behest, from one place to another. These most radical ventures in urban renewal may account for the absence of monumental architecture. In Chinese terms, Dr. Chang writes, "The city was the institution, not the site" (1976, p. 51).

No wonder it is hard to define the word "city," in view of the many forms its designatum may take. Urbanization is essentially a sign, a product, and at the same time an implement of cultural advance to civilized life. But it is not the only crucial influence effecting the basic phenomenon, the change of social structure which has begotten the modern world. The breaking of the old order had many beginnings, some rising with or upon the rise of the city, some starting from elsewhere to meet it. So, for instance, what in each actual case was the character of the fighting force a city-state could send into the field depended largely on the type and degree of its organization; for with the growing power of kings there was a concomitant shift in military control and strategy as the combatants changed from warriors to soldiers. The formation of armies under a single command was a radical departure from the fighting of independent warriors who met their adversaries man to man by their own decision. The solid ranks of Assyrian heavily armed men, the Greek phalanx, the Roman legion mounted or afoot were soldiers, components of a war machine manipulated by the commanding generals.

This innovation, wherever it occurs, makes a revolution in the social significance of war. Organized warfare is part and parcel of civilized life, though it begins early on the road to that gradual attainment. In savage societies fighting is apt to be brief and relatively harmless to the tribe as a whole; indeed, the further one descends the cultural ladder, the briefer and less important become the armed encounters. Among true savages most fights are bursts of temper in people whose acts normally draw everybody else into any fray.

Even organized conflicts, staged at higher levels of precivilized life, may threaten no serious destruction to either of the parties involved, as, for instance, the custom of raiding neighboring villages for wives or, in more established societies, for cattle. The raid is a typically tribal phenomenon which may, under extenuating circumstances, even be viewed as pardonable, not only by uninvolved people but by those who, in self-defense, have to repulse it. The raid among tribesmen may incur retaliation, but not legal judgment and sentence, because there is no vested judiciary above the antagonists. Punishment is at the will of the injured party, namely, vengeance. Raiding, in tribal society, belongs with war, not crime; and war is deemed an honorable action.

But with the rise of powerful commanders and their men, raids became more serious acts of war; not cattle pens but cities and towns were besieged and plundered. The advance of ship-building raised a particular problem for island and coastal settlements, the problem of piracy. In the Mediterranean there have repeatedly been long historic periods when the beautiful Aegean islands—the Cyclades, the Dodecanese—were rendered uninhabitable by the depredations of such seaborne marauders. The pirate ships appeared suddenly, made land in a precalculated favorable spot and moment, and could get away to unknowable distant spaces with the loot of a day or an hour.

In the northern European seas a simpler vessel, for hardier men, opened the same opportunities, which always found heroes to take them. Though the Vikings were explorers and city-builders, they were above all fighters, plunderers, daredevils; there was always a large element to whom the pirate's life was the ideal life. These people, too, made raiding their regular practice, not a rare act of desperation but their means of existence, and as such, of course, it could not endure indefinitely amid the cultural developments of Europe, which were on a rapid rise.

So, with the advance of European cultures, the typical civilization of today arose, as the older civilization of the Near East had risen a thousand years before from the Mesopotamian and Mediterranean cultural heritages. But no one in Europe or Asia suspected what was going on in another part of the earth, an unknown and even unsuspected part—the Americas.

In that great Western world, an extraordinary thing occurred: an impressive civilization took shape without, apparently, any true humane culture underlying it. The most striking exhibit of that historical process is the Inca supremacy which arose in Peru; the most terrible, the Aztec war culture which, at its height, held Mesoamerica in thrall and terror.

What does not seem natural is the almost universal practice of cannibalism among people who have built cities with temples and palaces, military roads, aqueducts, baths, walled plazas, and great flights of rock-hewn or rock-built stairs. These edifices were not the megalithic monuments which usually belong to a prehistoric phase of culture, but planned and directed works. To find thriving cities like Cuzco in Peru or, in Mexico, Tenochtitlan with its markets, boat traffic, causeways, and temple-crowned pyramids, inhabited by savages who were evidently their builders but who went naked except for belts and feather ornaments, sacrificed human beings on their altars and indulged in cannibalistic feasts is ethnologically bewildering, to say the least. Something unusual must have happened to their societies to engender such paradoxes.

It seems, on the face of it, that the earliest Americans, when they finally reached the countries in which they developed their astounding civilizations, had found ideal conditions to make their swift advance from the primitive hunting and foraging stage of savagedom to urban life and rule. They found fertile valleys where important vegetable species—corn, peppers, tomatoes, and potatoes—grew wild and responded to cultivation, where there were guinea pigs and larger game, vines and fibers that yielded cordage, and rivers which lent themselves to irrigation projects. Above all, the human newcomers found freedom to develop their natural talents, which in some departments were remarkable.

This very freedom, however, may have been a dangerous advantage; for it let any dominant hereditary trait of the forming population run to its full expansion without being limited and modified in normal cultural competition with peoples of other stock and mentality. Consequently an outstanding talent could—and did—throw their cultural advance out of balance, letting the exercise of that special gift become a prime value which entrained or else smothered all other interests.

The Amerindians possessed a veritable genius for military organization and political mastery. Most of them must have reached the New World at a very early date in their history, for they were evidently completely savage, being at the stage of evolution which seems to be universally marked by successive forms of cannibalism, from simple manslaughter for meat to solemn religious ritual. Cannibalism is an early step in humanization; not the very first, which probably occurred with the beginning of speech, but perhaps the next, for it belongs to the breaking up of the empathetic bonds which unite wolves in packs and once united prehuman primates and held them safe against each other in a horde. The amazing thing is how long an evolutionary transition can take, how late it may have set in, and what atavisms can persist even for millennia, protected by religious dread and cherished as mysteries while a new imaginative activity, still deeply unconscious, is preparing a new feeling of human beings toward each other: sympathy.

The transition, in the case of the long-established primitive life of American humanity, was very irregularly achieved due to the immigrants' peculiar phyletic history, which seems to go back to a time when successive droves of the Asiatic population, still in the semi-social condition known to anthropologists as the "band" state (i.e., before tribal organization), were pushed out of their homelands by changing natural conditions or possibly demographic pressure. That does not mean that all the earliest migrants were at the same cultural stage (or pre-cultural, if that is possible for genuine hominids) whenever and wherever they entered the New World. But after their entry their further history was extraordinary.

One of its notable characteristics was certainly its headlong progress, another, however, its instability. Since, at the time of the Spanish invasion, the ruling power in South America—the Inca or Peru with their great conscript armies—numbered hundreds of thousands, the weakness of their proud, fortified, and sternly governed cities is as surprising as their indigenous rise in the isolation of the Andes plateau. And there had been civilizations in South America before the Inca Empire, along the northwestern coast and its populous river valleys, centering in cities with public squares and buildings, gates, markets, and defensive walls running from the shore up the hillsides; and not only on the coast, but also in the high sierra, from Quito in the north to Tiahuanaco south of Lake Titicaca, and on the shores and islands of the lake. Yet somehow those civilizations had broken down again; their great installations belonged to vanished ages.

The Inca were not ideologically superior to the tribes they conquered. Their ethos always had a peculiar frangibility, extremes of royal pomp mingling with equally great extremes of wildness and backwardness. This is most evident in the contrast between their systematic urban administration, their bureaucracies and concepts of order and authority, and the very low level of their religious thinking, almost too low to be classed as thinking at all.

None of the politically important South American tribes had progressed even as far as a belief in anthropomorphic gods at the time when the military alliance was formed which later became the Inca state. The recipients of their worship and sacrifices were so-called "huacas," chiefly natural objects—fantastic rocks or lava formations, strange trees, even posts or columns, caverns, pools and hot springs. These were genuine fetishes, of magical rather than divine character. Such a wide gap between the different intellectual achievements of a generally homogeneous society makes one wonder what held back its religious development while its worldly advances progressed without obstacles by their own push and growth.

The trouble seems to have been deeply hidden (even from themselves) and subjective, and to have stemmed from that very freedom which permitted their phenomenal rise to power and dominion—a fatal by-product of their millennia of isolation. Apparently, in this human stock so long separated from the rest of mankind, there were tensions between the different rates of mental development which had become too great to be taken in stride much longer. The separation had been long enough to permit even some evolutionary processes to depart from the normal pattern and run their courses as an exaggerated pace while others were unhurried or actually dragged in their advance. This happens to some extent in all complex organic developments, but as a rule the pressions of the given human situation obviate any extreme discrepancy before it can endanger the ethnic balance on a wide cross-section of hereditary lines. The history of the American savages is probably unparalleled in its lack of cultural influences or foreign models to call customs and traditional values in question. No one knows when they entered the phase of cannibalism. It seems, in fact, that every human stock in the course of its humanization goes through that phase as the empathetic animal reactions of its members to each other weaken and the rudimentary intellectual function of sympathy for human beings as such, rooted in a subjectifying imagination, has not evolved far enough to replace them.

There is a phase in the evolution of mind, while the realization of mortality is gradually asserting itself, overcoming rejection, denial, and protest, but has not really won the day, when people try by every means, from magical defense to offers of ransom, to stave off the never-admitted, ineluctable end. In this phase of realization the most progressive natives of South and Central America seem to have bogged down, instead of transcending it by accepting and hallowing death. At the time of the Spanish conquest they were still buying their emperors' lives and their own, from day to day, with bloody sacrifice.

This interpretation is, of course, hypothetical, but there are other phenomena that strongly corroborate it; one of these is the peculiar practice known as the emperor's *panaca*, said to have been introduced by Inca Roca; it was a *post mortem* fictitious upkeep of each late Inca's court, wherein ever-new, living persons played the roles of his former entourage.

A fairly clear symptom of the Incas' recoil from thinking about death is the pathetic state of their eschatological ideas. Their pantheon contained no *Thanatos* and their cosmos no heaven or hell; their priesthood served its huacas to avert evil and influence the community's earthly luck, and especially its continuity. A sense of mystery and holiness surrounds every huaca, but it is all centered on the creative power of the fetish or of the god whom the fetish may ultimately come to represent. Their mythology is concerned almost entirely with origins—emergence of "first beings" from caves or a body of water, or from the hands of a divine potter. Such poverty of ideas points to the unwillingness of their theological thinkers to follow out any long thoughts on the subject of death, the ghost, and its final fate.

Nothing is so directly opposed to cultural advance as fear to develop a line of thought or face one's own knowledge. The most dangerous effect of the South Americans' intellectual timidity, which held them for generations to a long-outgrown mythology, was the ever-widening gap between their military and political achievements and the low level of their religious conception, which evidently strained to the limit the unity and coherence of their minds. By the time the Spaniards came upon them, the Incas' administration of conquered lands and cities rivaled that of the Caesars in Rome, while their philosophical reflection was on a level with that of Andaman Islanders and Tasmanians except where it was invented with purely political motives to deify the emperor. The great Inca civilization, for all its wonderful achievements and constant religious rites, was spiritually hollow.

Actually, however, most of the South Americans were well past the mental state of denying the ineluctability of death even for their emperors. The rejected knowledge could no longer be quite successfully masked by pretense. The Incas' unadmitted realization grew more and more defiant and desperate, and that dreadful insecurity was reflected in their treatment of all their subjects, nobles and underlings alike, above all, of course, their newly conquered cities and most recently vanquished tribes. Their rule was increasingly based on terrorism, cruelty, threat and ferocity, and boundless self-elevation and alienation from the populace, so that just before the Spanish invasion took the Western world by utter surprise, their armies and subjugated peoples were already in revolt. All that the Spaniards had to do was to finish the collapse.

Much the same kind of ethnic distortion as in South America occurred in Mesoamerica, where several impressive civilizations have flourished only to break up on internal, deep-lying weaknesses at the first rude shock of a truly foreign contact, if not before, under their own inward strains. The Mayan tribes whose chief concentration was in Yucatan, and the widely influential Toltecs to the north and west of them laid many foundation stones for the brief but meteoric history of the last purely Indian power, the Aztecs. These latest wild invaders developed a spectacular civilization in no more than a hundred years.

The secret of their rapid advance was an extraordinary receptivity for ideas, techniques, and opportune suggestions, however daring. They probably did not make as many true inventions as their Toltec and Mayan predecessors, but translated everything they found into tangible or usable realities. At the time of the Spanish invasion the Aztec capital, Tenochtitlan, built on an island in Lake Texcoco and connected with towns on the mainland by long causeways and busy canoe traffic, was one of the finest cities in the world.

In this unmistakably civilized area of the Aztec realm there was a small royal clique of cultivated intellectuals often recognized by modern historians as "poet-kings" or "philosopher-kings." Most noteworthy was the emperor Topiltzin, who took the epithetical name "Quetzalcoatl." Topiltzin Quetzalcoatl, like Akhenaton in Egypt before him, made premature efforts to introduce a humane religion based on worship of the sun as a symbol of life and a ritual of equally symbolic, largely bloodless sacrifices of tamales, snakes, butterflies, and flowers. But if the Egyptians were not ready for such high thinking, much less so were the Amerindians. Their ethos always had a peculiar frangibility, so that with the destruction of a capital city their whole civilized life broke down again. Cities rose and fell in Europe and especially in Asia, too, but their scattered and often enslaved denizens did not generally turn back to nudism and cannibalism; affluence and starvation are the extremes of fortune on any level of cultured life, but even desperate hunger does not usually abolish all standards of human society in a population which, after all, manages to survive. And at the time of the Spanish invasion the Inca were certainly not a defeated people.

Neither were the Aztecs. By all material evidence they were triumphant in their wealth and power. No outside dangers were threatening them. It takes close looking to see the signs of weakness at the core of both civilizations. The signs were different in the two cultures, each of which extended over and beyond the political hegemony of the master tribe at its center, but both bespoke the same condition of unbalanced mentality, probably due to the immigrants' excessive freedom from both social stimulation and social restraint. In Peru the Inca capitalized for a while on the degeneracy which afflicted the oldest past societies first and worst and left them unresisting, while their conquerors fought and destroyed the still warlike braves around them. But along the coast the symptoms of decay were obvious. They showed up as a widespread tendency to drunkenness, drug addiction and sexual aberrations of all sorts. The varieties of psychedelic drugs these people without any systematic knowledge of chemistry managed to derive from plants and even animals around them indicates their interest in possible sources of alterations of consciousness.

Sometimes the final failure of a progressive action will reveal what unsuspected conditions are really required to let it succeed. The Aztecs, like the Inca, suffered from their lack of intellectual conflict and competition. Though they were a bellicose people, their enmities were not based on conflicts of ideas. Their mental development could fall as far apart as it did because, in spite of an occasional "philosopher-king," there was no challenging source of radically new conceptions such as people met, especially in wanderings or migrations, in the Old World. If the Amerindian felt disinclined to think about death he could insist on offering blood in return for life until his whole religion became an emotional bulwark around the specter of death.

It seems, indeed, that an evolving mind requires limitations of opportunity to achieve a unified phyletic career; it needs the pression of complex and crowding humanity to hold its form and balance in the ecological stream. Usually a biological function contains its own antagonist in a suppressed but still potential form striving for active expansion; the function of the brain in human beings to produce concepts which rule the flow of ever-changing actual expectations is normally hedged by the felt, even though unavowed, awareness of possible contrary assumptions. This remaining presence of the negative in every choice is what gives life and thought its dialectical form. But in a multi-millennial isolation such an essentially logical awareness is not enough to straiten the diffuse welter of otherwise unopposed ideas. The dialectic of thought alone, without a social need to evade or resolve inconsistencies arising from different basic concepts, does not generate enough "drive" to maintain a progressive mental life. And the lack which thus becomes apparent only with a relaxation instead of an increase of hardship reaches far down to the roots of human intellect.

In the speciation of the human race through its several crises of speech, fantasy, ritual, and the tribal feeling which finally has to break to make way for the cultural move to civilization, the phase of family organization has been so long extended that one may well wonder what has been going forward in all that enormous length of time during which the thousands of internally structured, blood-related units of society were naturally ordered by generations, each unit ruled by the eldest living generation within it. A tradition or even a tendency that has no function in the further development of the stock does not usually persist as the rule of elders has done in tribal groups from the beginning of human society to historic times.

Perhaps we owe it our longevity beyond the age of procreation, which has puzzled many evolutionists, especially those of a neo-Darwinian turn, who assume—rightly, I think—that a useless element such as the survival for decades of uncontributive members should be bred out of a species. The explanation that there is simply "no selection against it" is unconvincing, at best. The aged survivors eat, require space and even charitable attention to live, and in only a few very primitive cultures are denied their necessities so they may "starve in the midst of plenty" or be abandoned on the road. As long as the clan or settlement is traditionally ruled by elders, these have a function; and a brain with a function provides its own stimulus to survive and enlist the services of the rest of the organism, as procreation used to do.

But civilized countries are not organized by staggered generations, nor ruled by the most venerable of them. What happens, then, to the aged when they are no longer serving the community? That depends on how little or much that community honors the individual as an end in itself, not as a thing of relative value, however high, but as the ultimate measure of all value. According to our present social feeling it is the duty of the community to serve them in return for their past discharges of their human responsibilities; and this duty toward the old and, perhaps, decrepit is directed to them as a class, though in most cases it falls upon individuals by virtue of a legal code or, in better and rare cases, of personal charity.

Charity, nobility, honor, and even pity are never in very generous supply among average people. Sometimes the inherent viciousness of human beings breaks out in "crime waves"; sometimes it appears more generally in long, slow periods of degeneration, when cynicism desecrates and corrupts even the most basic ethical commitments. Sometimes great individuals without fame live by their ideals from birth to death with purest candor in the "worst of possible worlds." As far back as we can trace or reconstruct the social history of man, such differences in personal worthiness and responsibility seem to have made the average distance between him and his avowed standards roughly the same at all ages in the long run. So what do we mean by the "moral advance" of society?

Perhaps, even though practice may never come much closer to its precepts than in any past ages, the advance has been on a different level of value; on the conceptual level of the moral structure itself. It is the standard that changes, and carries all idealistic effort, casual conformity, and ardent condemnation with it to a higher plane, usually without most people's conscious feeling of the change. And what holds true for the moral character of Mind does so as well for its intellectual quality. A new great age is long prepared, and finally is born with the rise and expansion of a new idea which automatically transforms the outlook and reach of human mentality, in our present evolving age, even to effect the evaluation and re-evaluation of the criteria of thought itself. That is the office of philosophy.

It is this progression by qualitative shifts—the current one some three thousand years old, if not more, in its preparation—that requires human culture as a whole to keep a certain balance between its highest and lowest degrees of change. A leading achievement can only lead by entraining the countless psychical activities that make up a mental life and an individual's or society's *Weltanschauung*. That seems to be why a culture capable of supporting a great civilization requires a single, complex yet balanced advancing front of many crowding evolutionary stocks and battling faiths to uphold the drive of incompatibilities.

In Europe, in our own passing era, a growing civilization has built itself up under intensely demanding pressures, from roots of inestimable depth enmeshed with tributaries from every possible source—Asia, Africa, Oceania, perhaps lost continents with earlier prehuman primates than we have found. Egypt, Babylon, Greece, Rome, Phoenicia, and Jewry poured their cultural achievements into that little promontory of the vast Eurasian land mass Europe; in Europe the process has continued and is still increasing, being still supported by a many-sided mental development, religious, artistic, and, above all, intellectual. First one salient line of growth would lead, then another would overtake and all but strangle it, but the front was always moving, until Europe became the tiny heartland of the world's most powerful systematic thought, driven by success and steadied by its own reciprocal checks, spreading today over the whole small planet Earth.

VI / *Mathematics and the Reign of Science*

Foreword

This study of mind should culminate, of course, in a well-constructed epistemological and possibly even metaphysical theory, at least as firmly founded on other people's knowledge and hypotheses as any earlier parts of this essay which have been written in preparation for such a reflective conclusion. But the hindrances of age—especially increasing blindness—make it necessary to curtail the work at what should be its height, and contract the end into no more than a sketch of its presumptive final section. Further research is impossible when footnote print, photostat, or typewriting are unreadable, and normal fonts not much easier. So even the epistemological heading of the intended sixth part, with its promise of a theory of knowledge and truth, which was projected in the beginning of the book, has to give place to a more modest finale, dealing with the new intellectual standard, the concept of fact, and its impact on a human age which has but lately opened with the brilliant rise of mathematics—the age of mathematical physics, physico-chemistry, electro-physico-chemistry, electro-biochemistry, and whatever still may follow.

But even in its curtailed form, I hope my little concluding essay to end an Essay may serve what I consider the true purpose of the whole book: to suggest some ideas which other people may be able to use for their own work, anywhere and everywhere in the great domain of philosophical thought. Whatever may be wrong with it, all the dross that needs elimination notwithstanding, my fondest wish for it is that what is true or new in it may eventuate in a parade of projects for young thinkers with long ways to go.

24 / *The Open Ambient*

In what today we deem the modern world, the evolution of man has come to be primarily the evolution of his brain, known by its incredible functional complex, the mind. The transition henceforth is not so much to new somatic forms and functions as to new elaborations and powers of the brain. These changes, physically unobservable as they have always been and still are, nevertheless have radical overt effects which produce stage after stage of our intellectual advance. The first step in the shift was almost certainly the rise and growth of speech, which I think has been sufficiently mooted, not only in this book but in a steady flow of writings since the first appearance of Ludwig Wittgenstein's *Tractatus Logico-philosophicus* in 1922. Of course there had been other philosophers, sometimes not professionally of that narrow stripe—mathematicians, grammarians, translators, and Bible scholars—who had been aware of the part which linguistic forms play in conceptualizing experience, establishing memory, and recording the fictions of dream and free fantasy, expectation and fear; but the modern movement that found its philosophical spokesman in Wittgenstein had another broad intellectual base in what seems, at first sight, a distant, parallel advance of mental achievement. That great new phenomenon is physical science.

Civilization was well established in several parts of the world, and had even come and gone in some of them, yielding to new barbarian conquests and devastations, when a great, fresh, and immensely fertile concept emerged in the Greek cultural tradition: the concept of causality as a direct dyadic relation between two events, without any third term, such as an agent, to negotiate between the first event—the cause—and the second, the effect. The idea that anything could occur without an agent to will and start the movement was difficult for people everywhere who had always thought in terms of acts with immediate aims and covert intentional phases preceding their overt performances. Historically we meet the concept of causality scarcely before Aristotle, who lumped purposes, forms, materials, and motions together as so many kinds of "cause," and subscribed to the confusion of causality with agency to the extent of postulating a "prime mover" for every automatically continuous sequence of transmitted motion.

With the concept of causality as an impersonal relation between two events—Aristotle's "efficient cause"—came an equally innocent but all-important acceptance of such events as two simply given, knowable, impersonal "facts." It has taken learned, scientific thinkers extraordinarily long to realize that a fact of nature or of history is not a direct sensory datum, but a highly interesting cognitive construct. That emerging idea has been a harbinger of a new core of knowledge, setting up an explicit logical standard and stringent methodology, great with a radical change of attitude, intellectual ambition, and its own frustrating mistakes.

The concept of fact is the foundation of our natural science; and science is the wonder of our current evolutionary age. The meaning of "fact" is, therefore, a basic philosophical question, and as such has been mooted for the past half-century with varying results. That facts are conceived under the influence of language is generally recognized; that they determine the truth and falsity, respectively, of some kinds of proposition is also usually conceded. But when it comes to analyzing even quite ordinary and apparently clear statements to see what concepts have gone into their construction, what relations those concepts have to each other and to the facts which we see in their images, and especially what assumptions they imply or tacitly require, what conditions make a proposition as a whole true or false—there we are in the midst of the present-day labyrinth "logico-philosophicus."

Alfred Tarski has shown, I think, in "The Concept of Truth in Formalized Languages" (1956) that in any unformalized (i.e., "natural" or "ordinary") language no analysis is likely to reveal a set of unambiguous propositions which could be directly matched with a known set of facts constituting the actual world, so that the phrase "true proposition" could be defined as meaning an element in a logical, coherent system of verbal statements which could be correlated with a systematic array of facts composing the world or a determinable part of it.

Despite this discouraging prognosis, with its very real ring of truth, semanticists today are still hoping and trying to narrow down the principles of ordinary discourse to scientific precision and fixity. They are evidently convinced that conceptual clarity and especially permanence of word meanings are inherent in correctly used language and that the logic of empirical science must underlie such correct usage; that consequently it is possible to describe the actual world systematically in scientific terms culled from ordinary language. Yet all attempts to do so founder in the depths of more and more sophisticated linguistics. Whole books (largely, today, collections of articles) and the most serious philosophical journals are filled with theories that end in a despairing resort to behaviorism (as Wittgenstein himself did) or metaphysical questions which do not find metaphysical or scientific solutions but only more and more elaborate linguistic sidetracks.

To formalize any observed relationship, especially in biology, one has to start from natural phenomena that show a distinct tendency to exhibit the hypothetical functional pattern and, upon more precise statement, to reveal further and further instances of that pattern in the empirical realm which yields their factual material. Growth, metabolism, procreation, in plants some highly special developments, as, for instance, for seed dispersal, in higher animals voluntary movement, are such phenomena. But upon closer acquaintance with language, which is a biological function, though peculiar to the single primate genus *Homo*, one finds no tendency of words in "ordinary" use to approach single, exact meanings; technical uses are consciously established and as soon as they are assimilated to colloquial speech they lose their precision and may even change their literal meaning, as non-technical words do. "Edify" no longer means to erect an edifice, nor does "lady" today mean "giver." Yet words do organize our thinking around centered conceptual symbols, however vague those central images or other carriers of meaning may be, and define a context in which that core of meaning is embedded; it is the contexts which are not at all a logician's ideal. Each word, according to its grammatical form and syntactical position, immediately determines its own transitory context. But the many implicitly assumed conditions that give sense to our conversational exchanges do not necessarily fit together to form a single and coherent background of verbal rules or verbally established facts, which might be expected to verify our true contingent propositions. They tend rather to make large and small islands of interrelated notions, each one a limited but logically organized context for a phrase or grammatical variant of a key word. Our thinking is adapted to this constant shift of ambient ideas. It is one of the essential powers of language to negotiate the turns of that mental kaleidoscope, though we are not aware of it. Language has so many functions in the shaping of mind out of the most intense, felt processes of lower animal brains that it goes no further in the perfection of any activity than the impulse reaches before most of its potential elaborations have been eclipsed, their energies entrained by other, overtaking impulses and distributed, perhaps to many parts of the brain, perhaps to restricted but complicated areas.

Where, then, do we get the abstract ideas on which we have modeled our standard of abstractness? There seems to be no particular cerebral locus for such thought-processing. But suppose areas, centers, regions, are not the whole or even most important seats of our concentrated mental activities; suppose some phenomena take shape between the stations where we have found them most ready to be elicited or, if they are in action, to be interrupted. It is possible (I would propose no more) that the abstraction of pure concepts occurs in the shifts from one island of orientation to another, from one mental focus to another, from the nimbus of one part of speech to another. Such a transitional consummation is not altogether unknown in physiological acts; consider some of the observations cited in Chapter 16 on birds and beasts with eyes placed far apart and quite laterally on the head, so that even with a large field of vision in each eye they always have two views of their surroundings at once, which they seem to unite into one image by looking at an arresting object with alternately lifted and lowered, perhaps slightly rolled head, or with one eye after the other. Somewhat similarly, the play of conceptions instigated and kept going by words with rapid, shimmering changes of peripheral relations may precipitate a central concept common to all the grammatical variants of a verb or other highly inflected part of speech and make it stand more and more *in abstracto.*

Yet "ordinary language" shows no steady tendency to impose a coherent pattern on the world of facts which it constantly creates for us. Even hundreds of definitions cannot satisfy a strict thinker if the definitions themselves bring him back to the ordinary language again. It takes something else than the transient agreements of our spontaneous discourse to work out ideas that are ready to be built into the great intellectual systems of present-day physics, which has enabled men to fly in their machines to the moon, disembark on its lifeless, waterless, airless surface, and return to earth.

The spectacular success of the physical sciences has made them the models of exact thought. But the most searching linguistic studies give us no elements comparable to the things scientists talk about—atoms, molecules, or measures of energy in other forms. Words are incorrigible weasels; meanings of words cannot be held to paper with the ink. The abstraction of pure concepts may occur under stringent controls of technical terms, but the inveterate tendency of even such terms to become assimilated to common parlance and share the ways of "ordinary language" leads one to wonder whether the great frame of science can possibly be made of word-borne thought.

The formulation of "fact" may stem from language, but "science" in the modern sense does not. Its foundation is a younger achievement, though its beginnings may go back into the earliest ages of man—go back through eons of existence without realizing their potential. The instrument of scientific thought is mathematics, and the evolution of such thought had to wait for the development of concepts of number at least far enough to reach two essential functions: enumerating and calculating. Enumerating—counting—probably came first, but even that has been very late compared to the humanizing work of language.

Mathematics, though generally treated as part of the gift of speech, on closer examination appears to have had a separate origin and prehistory; numbers and words have different primitive characteristics. In the first place, while words have always tended to broaden the use of language by their penchant for metaphorical extensions of meaning, numbers have no such tendency. They may have mystical associations—numerology, astrology, and all sorts of superstitious uses—but with the exception of the prime mystery that One may be Three, numbers generally keep their literal meanings. Instances of "three," "four," "seven," and the fearful "thirteen" express the same numerosity in arithmetic as in tea-leaf reading, in counting as in magic-mongering.

Yet counting, which seems simple to us, has really been one of the difficult problems of abstraction and presentation, for it has required a shift from essentially physical consummations to symbolic ones in the human brain. Its elements—similar conceptual units following each other in a series—are almost certainly first presented by the visual and kinesthetic perception of our own bipedal steps, under control of old cerebral mechanisms. Their expression belongs to the legs and feet, whose functions are among the least intellectual of our voluntary behavioral acts.

Those same physical units, however, created bodily rhythms that entrained the whole musculature of a person's trunk and limbs, and broke up spontaneously into divisions within the steps even while, as wholes, they formed passages of movement often culminating in leaps or violent gestures. That created the Dance. The effect of this communal art was certainly enhanced by another motive, perhaps older (there is no telling), that was emphasized by the formed bodily movement: the corresponding mobility of the visual ambient. The Dance, above all else, animated the dancer's world at the command of his own voluntary movements, and must have been a magical activity from its beginning. All this seems, on the face of it, to have had nothing to do with mathematics, but it established the reality of the whole realm of distinct, self-identical units on which that recently emergent technique is based.

The emotions of uncivilized people are stormier and harder to bear than those found in more sophisticated society. From earliest times they must have required the forceful imposition of formal expression which dancing provides in all situations of tribal excitement. The elaborations of steps went on to high degrees before anyone thought about the exactitude of their divisions; fractions were danced for thousands of years without awareness of their relations to single (or, more often, dual) steps. As pure dance elements they might never have led even to the art of counting.

Fertile ideas of relations among numbers seem to have arisen only where people counted on the fingers of both hands. Perhaps the natural advantage in finger-counting, which is not directly visible, is that it involved the most trainable and responsive appendages of the body, the hands; one might even say the most educated, for their skill is based on a highly developed sensitivity to feel their own positions and contacts and to judge, without words, of the extraneous surfaces they touch. Such articulate feeling bespeaks a high specialization of cerebral acts somewhere in hand-controlling "centers" or "areas," and makes those locations good candidates for an intellectual function, which might arise and grow to quite a high form without drawing in the other main source of intellect, the original humanizing apparatus of speech.

A really crucial advance in evolution is apt to be complex, and therefore long-prepared before several lines of successive changes meet at an apparently casual, incidental juncture and start a major development. Some traits of future value may have entered a gathering mainstream and been mingled with its swelling progression early in its formation, without showing themselves for biological eons. Gradually, in the differentiating brain, points of high activity find expression in specialized overt acts which influence the bodily parts employed in their performance, from large movements to smallest details of independent muscular reactions, involuntary or semi-voluntary reflexes like those of the eyelid, protective overgrowths like our fingernails.

This aspect of protoplasmic response to stimuli is a well-known source of articulation, to which D'Arcy Thompson called attention early in the present century (1917); but its influence on the forms of organisms goes further than even that great functionally oriented anatomist saw. It is probably the cause of the apparent tendency to duality in the vertebrate frame and of the various forms of symmetry in lower organisms. The relation of shape to the increase of vital functions is a matter of conditions offered for the upkeep of growth in a total being while the differentiating influences are acting on and in it. Its need of a constant stabilizing process is met first of all by the persistent metabolic changes carrying on its life; but the specialized forms of organs or appendages may need more than the self-propagating activity of the matrix *per se*.

This consideration throws some light on the obviously differential survival of organisms with and without bilateral symmetry, and on the evolutionary strength of the former to develop the most complex specializations. Paired anatomical forms immediately present a new potential source of energy, for they grow from their embryonic *Anlagen* under competitive conditions. Each cerebral hemisphere harbors its own neural mechanisms, usually for control of the contralateral side; this brings about a functional duality which tends to be unevenly developed, so its own inherent potentialities drive each member to assert itself against its counterpart until their progressively heightened trophic responses lead to a more and more articulate structure, through their need of perpetually retrieving their formal balance. Perhaps Aristotle's "formal cause" had a causal function after all.

Obviously, the parts of a symmetrically structured creature which are most affected by such mutual stimulation are the limbs; and in a biped the hands and feet are developed from time immemorial under the influences of different functions. The brain centers closest to the ones which are directly involved in speech, and therewith in conceptual acts, are those activating and controlling the hands (the tendency of many people to gesticulate when they talk supports that widely held hypothesis); the feet, represented furthest away, seem to be less connected with the symbolic powers of mind.

Yet it is the step—that specialty of our two-footed stance and gait—that becomes all-important in some very elementary acts, walking and dancing. The equal pace of the human walk and its elaboration in festive dance provide some elements of pronounced bodily rhythm which have their own ways of breaking up internally, without losing their unity as whole elements. Only, because dance rhythms are too spontaneous, too quickly and fully consummated in action, they are not likely to enter into non-physical complexes and support any intellectual functions. If such basic patterns as the step—walking or dancing—were to be entrained by higher cerebral processes, something would have to effect a shift from footwork to a more versatile neuromuscular system which could entrain the precise, elaborate rhythms of the dance in a new activity.

Now, there is just such a versatile system in our physiological makeup; it culminates in the expressive powers of the human hand, and the instrument which brought it into the center of communal life was the Drum. The drum abstracts the form of the dance and holds it when otherwise it might become frenzied; beats assert their character as a framework more forcefully than movements or voices. Above all, the early and apparently universal use of the drum drew the human hand into the techniques of its expression.

When a favored part such as the human hand reaches a high degree of competence for its normal employment its cybernetic system may acquire new potentialities, which invite shifts of action from other brain centers to its refined and ready ones with their superior distribution of energy. This is likely to have happened wherever a dawning intellect felt the impulse to use the fingers as counters, and soon discovered the many ways they could be used to advantage over other means. In such progressive societies the fingers of men and women were skilled and sensitive, so their innervation, clear back to its origin in the brain, must have been ahead of most of the physical organism and made the whole hand complex a dominant structure. The walking step may have furnished the first sense of equally spaced similar units, and the dance imposed its elaborations on them, but it was very probably the drum, activated by the hands, that clinched the evolutionary shift, already prepared in several ways—the decimal systems born of finger-counting, which, despite their varying details (lifting or flexing the fingers, starting with thumb or little finger, left or right, etc.), embody the same algorithmic principle of naming ten numerals (i.e., 0 through 9) and composing all higher numerosities out of these in a simple order of positions, rendered in oral communication by a few verbal devices, e.g., suffixes like -teen, -ty, or prefixes made of large figures which had long acquired names—"one hundred," "two thousand"—with the simple connective "and": "four thousand, one hundred and twenty-three," for example.

The invention of a method of designating large and small numbers with equal ease marks the confluence of two great streams of mental evolution, language and number sense. It is hard to realize how long a non-linguistic talent which is really not at all rare can lie fallow in human beings, only to spring into meteoric career in a few centuries when the right forms of expression are found. The basic operations (excepting for a long time the most difficult, division) emerged as of themselves from the practical uses of number concepts once they were drawn into the frame of a formal language. It has always remained a formal language, but of inestimable power for its purposes.

We feel that power today as an overwhelming force—physical science. It has risen on the foundation built up tier on tier by the outpourings of mathematical thought, like ever-recurrent lava flows from fires in the earth. The changes wrought in practical life have affected the average person remarkably little, because past conditions are quickly forgotten in struggles to estimate and exploit what is new; but the head-on clashes of old faiths and new scientific and (especially) pseudoscientific persuasions are more often fateful encounters. Some mathematicians themselves have tried to reject the knowledge that most physical observations present us with ineluctable facts, mundane and cosmic, and that these facts are expressible in equations from which other presumptive facts, with exact future dates and pinpointed locations, are calculable. They have based their objections on ideal grounds, such as that a material interpretation debased the noblest and purest product of human thought, which should have no application to practical aims; but most of the great creative logico-mathematical thinkers today even try to justify their life work by claiming its scientific uses and empirical results.

So great a stride in the evolution of man cannot fail to throw his whole ambient, social and physical, into convulsion and cause worldwide waves of emotional conflict to build up in every society, savage, barbaric or civilized. We live in a precipitous, heady transitional age, the Age of Science. Transitional—from a past whose image itself is changing under the influence of that very transformation which is triggering the new mentality, to a future (if our use of Science does not abrogate the further life of man on earth) as unpredictable today as were the towers and tunnels of New York when the first self-propelled organisms crawled out of the ocean for little sojourns on its brineless edges.

It will surely take long and different ages to retrieve the moral and mental balance mankind itself has blasted in the last three or four centuries (to start only with the time of terrifying acceleration), and there is no way of guessing whether or how we shall retrieve it, because that newest of natural phenomena—Mind—still faces the mystery of all things young, the secret of vital potentiality.

References

Ardrey, Robert. 1966. *The territorial imperative: a personal inquiry into the animal origins of property and nations*. New York: Atheneum.
Armstrong, E. A. 1955. *The wren*. London: Collins.
Barbour, Thomas. 1926. *Reptiles and amphibians*. Boston: Houghton Mifflin.
Barfield, Owen. 1928. *Poetic diction, a study in meaning*. London: Faber and Gwyer.
Bills, A. G. 1931. Blocking: a new principle of mental fatigue. *American Journal of Psychology* 43:230–45.
Blum, H. F. 1957. On the origin of self-replicating systems. In *Rhythmic and synthetic processes in growth,* edited by D. Rudnick, 155–72. Princeton: Princeton University Press.
Bogert, Charles M. 1949. Thermoregulation in reptiles, a factor in evolution. *Evolution* 3:195–211.
Bonner, J. T. 1952. *Morphogenesis: an essay on development*. Princeton: Princeton University Press.
Börnstein, Walter. 1930. Der Aufbau der Funktionen in der Hörsphäre. *Abhandlungen aus der Neurologie, Psychiatrie, Psychologie und ihren Grenzgebieten* 53:1–126.
Bosanquet, Bernard. 1915. *Three lectures on aesthetic*. London: Macmillan.
Bowie, Henry P. 1951. *On the laws of Japanese painting*. New York: Dover.
Brain, W. R. 1945. Speech and handedness. *Lancet* 2:837–41.
———. 1950. The cerebral basis of consciousness. *Brain* 73:465–79.

Bullock, T. H. 1961. The origins of patterned nervous discharge. *Behaviour* 17:48–59.

Cailliet, Émile. 1936. *Symbolisme et âmes primitives.* Paris: Boivin.

Caldwell, D. K. 1955. Notes on the spotted dolphin, *Stenella plagiodon*, and the first record of the common dolphin, *Delphinus delphis*, in the Gulf of Mexico. *Journal of Mammalogy* 56:467–70.

Carpenter, C. R. 1934. *A field study of the behavior and social relations of howling monkeys.* Comparative Psychology Monographs, no. 10. Baltimore: Johns Hopkins Press.

Chagnon, Napoleon. 1968. *Yąnomamö: the fierce people.* New York: Holt, Rinehart and Winston.

Chai, C., and W. Chai, eds. and trans. 1965. *The sacred books of Confucius and other Confucian classics.* New Hyde Park, N.Y.: University Books.

Chang, K. C. 1976. *Early Chinese civilization: anthropological perspectives.* Cambridge, Mass.: Harvard University Press.

Coleridge, Samuel Taylor. 1834. *Biographia literaria.* Orig. pub., 1817. London: Leavitt, Lord.

Conrad, Klaus. 1954. New problems of aphasia. *Brain* 77:491–509.

Craig, W. 1918. Appetites and aversions as constituents of instinct. *Biological Bulletin* 34:91–107.

Crawford, M. P. 1937. *The cooperative solving of problems by young chimpanzees.* Comparative Psychology Monographs, no. 14. Baltimore: Johns Hopkins Press.

Danielson, R. N. 1941. The melanophore responses of fishes in relation to contrast in the visual field. *Physiological Zoology* 14:96–102.

Da Vinci, Leonardo. 1882. *Das Buch von der Malerei.* Vols. 15–16 of *Quellenschriften für Kunstgeschichte und Kunsttechnik des Mittelalters u. der Renaissance.* Translated by H. Ludwig. Contains Italian text of *Libro di pittura*, Codex Vaticanus, no. 1270.

Donovan, J. 1891. The festal origin of human speech. *Mind* 16:498–506.

———. 1892. The festal origin of human speech. *Mind* 17:325–39.

Du Brul, E. L., and D. M. Laskin. 1961. Preadaptive potentialities of the mammalian skull: an experiment in growth and form. *American Journal of Anatomy* 109:117–32.

Dye, J. A., and F. S. Kinder. 1934. A prepotent factor in the determination of skull shape. *American Journal of Anatomy* 54:333–46.

Edinger, Tilly. 1949. Paleoneurology versus comparative brain anatomy. *Confinia Neurologia* 9:5–24.

Eibl-Eibesfeldt, I. 1950. Beiträge zur Biologie der Haus- und Ährenmaus nebst einigen Beobachtungen an anderen Nagern. *Zeitschrift für Tierpsychologie* 7:558–87.

Eliot, T. S. 1920. Tradition and the individual talent. In *The sacred wood: essays on criticism and poetry.* London: Methuen.

———. 1932. "Hamlet and his problem." In *Selected essays, 1917–1932.* New York: Harcourt, Brace.

Essertier, Daniel. 1927. *Les formes inférieures de l'explication.* Paris: Alcan.

Evans, W. F. 1968. *Communication in the animal world.* New York: Thomas Y. Crowell.

Evans, William E., and Jarvis Bastian. 1969. Marine mammal communication:

social and ecological factors. In *The biology of marine mammals,* edited by H. Andersen, 425–75. New York: Academic Press.

Fauré-Fremiet, Philippe. 1940. *La re-création du réel et l'équivoque.* Paris: Alcan.

Fergusson, Francis. 1949. *The idea of a theater.* Princeton: Princeton University Press.

Fontaine, Maurice. 1956. Analyse expérimentale de l'instinct migrateur des poissons. In *L'instinct dans le comportement des animaux et de l'homme,* edited by P. P. Grassé, 151–75. Paris: Masson.

Francastel, Pierre. 1948. Espace génétique et espace plastique. *Revue d'esthétique* 1:349–80.

———. 1951. Naissance d'un espace: mythes et géometrie au Quattrocento. *Revue d'esthétique* 4:1–45.

———. 1952. *Peinture et société; naissance et destruction d'un espace plastique de la Renaissance au cubisme.* Lyon: Audin.

Gardner, R. A., and B. T. Gardner. 1969. Teaching sign language to a chimpanzee. *Science* 165:664–72.

Garstang, Walter. 1962. *Larval forms, with other zoological verses.* Introduction by Sir Alister Hardy. Oxford: Basil Blackwell.

Gehlen, Arnold. 1950. *Der Mensch: Seine Natur und seine Stellung in der Welt.* 4th ed.; 1st ed., 1940. Bonn: Athenäum.

Gibson, J. J. 1950. *The perception of the visual world.* Boston: Houghton Mifflin.

———. 1962. Observations on active touch. *Psychological Review* 69:477–91.

Head, Henry. 1923/24. The conception of nervous and mental energy. *British Journal of Psychology (Section, General)* 14:126–47.

Hebb, D. O. 1949. *The organization of behavior: a neuropsychological theory.* New York and London: John Wiley and Chapman and Hall.

Held, R., and A. Hein. 1963. Movement-produced stimulation of visually guided behavior. *Journal of Comparative and Physiological Psychology* 56:872–76.

Holst, Erich von, and Ursula Saint Paul. 1960. Vom Wirkungsgefüge der Triebe. *Naturwissenschaften* 18:409–22.

Horel, J. A., F. R. Treichler, and D. R. Meyer. 1963. Coercive behavior in the rhesus monkey. *Journal of Comparative and Physiological Psychology* 56:208–10.

Horowitz, N. H. 1955. On the evolution of biochemical syntheses. *Proceedings of the National Academy of Sciences* (1945), 153–57. Reprinted in *Great Experiments in Biology,* edited by Mordecai L. Gabriel and Seymour Fogel, 297–300. Englewood Cliffs, N.J.: Prentice-Hall.

———. 1959. On defining life. *Proceedings of the International Symposium on the Origin of Life on the Earth, Moscow, 1957.* Edited for the Academy of Sciences of the U.S.S.R. by A. I. Oparin et al., 106–7. New York: Pergamon.

Humboldt, Wilhelm von. 1884. *Sprachphilosophische Werke.* Berlin: F. Dimmler.

Kandinsky, Wassily. 1947. *Point and line to plane.* 1st ed. (German), 1926. New York: Museum of Non-Objective Painting.

Katz, David. 1925. Der Aufbau der Tastwelt. *Zeitschrift für Psychologie und Physiologie der Sinnesorgane,* Suppl. Vol. 11:xii-270.

Kavanau, J. L. 1963. Compulsory regime and control of environment in animal behaviour. I. Wheel-running. *Behaviour* 20:251–81.

Khatami, Manoochehr. 1975. Hypnosis as a healing art. In *The human influence in medicine*. Philadelphia: Merck, Sharp and Dohme and the University of Pennsylvania Hospital.

Klein, Marc. 1956. Aspects biologiques de l'instinct reproducteur dans le comportement des mammifères. In *L'instinct dans le comportement des animaux et de l'homme*, edited by P. P. Grassé, 287–344. Paris: Masson.

Koenig, Otto. 1962. *Kif-Kif. Menschliches und Tierisches zwischen Sahara und Wilhelminenberg*. Vienna: Wollzeilenverlag.

Köhler, Wolfgang. 1931. *The mentality of apes*. Orig. pub., 1917. Translated by Ella Winter from the 2d German ed. New York and London: Harcourt, Brace and Kegan Paul, Trench, Trubner.

La Barre, W. 1954. *The human animal*. Chicago: University of Chicago Press.

Lazarus, R. S., and R. A. McCleary. 1951. Autonomic discrimination without awareness. *Psychological Review* 58:113–22.

Lee, Dorothea Demetracopoulou. 1949. Being and value in a primitive culture. *Journal of Philosophy* 46:501–15.

Leyhausen, Paul. 1965. Über die Funktion der relativen Stimmungshierarchie dargestellt am Beispiel der phylogenetischen und ontogenetischen Entwicklung des Beutefangs von Raubtieren. *Zeitschrift für Tierpsychologie* 22:412–94.

Locke, John. 1690. *An essay concerning human understanding*. London: Th. Basset.

London, I. D. 1944. Psychologists' misuse of auxiliary concepts of physics and mathematics. *Psychological Review* 51:266–303.

Lorenz, Konrad Z. 1957. *King Solomon's ring*. Translated by M. K. Wilson from the German, *Er redete mit dem Vieh, den Vögeln, und den Fischen*, ca. 1952. London: Pan Books.

Meng, Mathilde. 1958. Untersuchungen zum Farben- und Formensehen der Erdkröte (*Bufo bufo* L.). *Zoologische Beiträge*, n.s., 3:313–63.

Meyerson, Ignace. 1948. Discontinuités et cheminements autonomes dans l'histoire de l'esprit. *Journal de psychologie normale et pathologique* 41:273–89.

Morley, Derek W. 1953. *The ant world*. Baltimore: Penguin Books.

Mountcastle, V. B. 1966. The neural replication of sensory events in the somatic afferent system. In *Brain and conscious experience*, edited by J. J. Eccles, 85–115. New York: Springer.

Murphy, John. 1943. *Lamps of anthropology*. Manchester: Manchester University Press.

Nachmanson, David, ed. 1954. *Nerve impulse. Transactions of the Fourth Conference, March 4, 5 and 6, 1953, Princeton, N.J.* New York: Josiah Macy, Jr., Foundation.

Noble, G. K., and H. T. Bradley. 1933. The mating behavior of lizards; its bearing on the theory of sexual selection. *Annals of the New York Academy of Sciences* 35:25–100.

Norris, K. S., and J. H. Prescott. 1961. Observations on Pacific cetaceans of Californian and Mexican waters. *University of California Publications in Zoology* 63:291–402.

Oparin, A. P. 1938. *Origin of life*. 1st ed. (Russian), 1936. Translated by S. Morgulis. New York: Macmillan.

Oswald, Ian. 1962. *Sleeping and waking. Physiology and psychology*. New York: Elsevier.

Phillpotts, Bertha. 1913. *Kindred and clan in the Middle Ages and after: a study of the Teutonic races.* Cambridge, Mass.: Harvard University Press.

Pieron, Henri. 1956. L'évolution du comportement dans ses rapports avec l'instinct. In *L'instinct dans le comportement des animaux et de l'homme,* edited by P. P. Grassé, 677–704. Paris: Masson.

Platt, John R. 1961. Properties of large molecules that go beyond the properties of their chemical sub-groups. *Journal of Theoretical Biology* 1:342–58.

Pötzl, Otto. 1917. Experimentell erregte Traumbilder in ihren Beziehungen zum indirekten Sehen. *Zeitschrift für die gesamte Neurologie und Psychiatrie* 37:278–349.

Read, Herbert. 1955. *Icon and idea: the function of art in the development of human consciousness.* Cambridge, Mass.: Harvard University Press.

Renshaw, Samuel. 1945. The visual perception and reproduction of forms by tachistoscopic methods. *Journal of Psychology* 20:217–32.

Révész, Géza. 1944. *Die Menschliche Hand: Eine Psychologische Studie.* Translated from the Dutch, *De menschelijke Hand,* 1941. New York: Karger.

———. 1946. *Ursprung und Vorgeschichte der Sprache.* Bern: A. Francke.

Roffwarg, H. P., J. N. Muzio, and W. C. Dement. 1966. Ontogenetic development of the human sleep-dream cycle. *Science* 152:604–19.

Rohden, Peter Richard. 1926. Das schauspielerische Erlebnis. In *Der Schauspieler,* edited by E. Geissler, 36–40. Berlin: Bühnenvolksbundverlag.

Russell, Bertrand. 1910/11. Knowledge by acquaintance and knowledge by description. *Proceedings of the Aristotelian Society,* n.s., 11:108–28. Reprinted in *The problems of philosophy* (New York, 1912) and in *Mysticism and logic, and other essays* (New York, 1918).

Russell, W. M. S., A. P. Mead, and J. S. Hayes. 1954. A basis for the quantitative structure of behaviour. *Behaviour* 6:153–206.

Sachs, Curt. 1937. *World history of the dance.* Translated by B. Schönberg from *Eine Weltgeschichte des Tanzes.* New York: W. W. Norton.

Schaefer, Karl Ernst. 1968. Physiologische anpassung bei Meeressäugetieren. In *Ueberleben auf See, 2. Marinemedizinisches Symposium in Kiel,* 183–91. Kiel: Schiffahrtmedizinisches Institut der Marine.

Schaller, G. B. 1965. The behavior of the mountain gorilla. In *Introduction to primate behavior: field studies of monkeys and apes,* edited by I. DeVore, 324–67. New York: Holt, Rinehart and Winston.

Scheler, Max. 1921. *Der Formalismus in der Ethik und die materiale Wertethik.* Halle: M. Niemeyer.

Schiller, Paul H. 1957. Innate motor action as a basis of learning. Manipulative patterns in the chimpanzee. In *Instinctive behavior: the development of a modern concept,* edited by Claire H. Schiller, 264–87. New York: International Universities Press.

Schneider, Kurt. 1920. Die Schichtung des emotionalen Lebens und der Aufbau der Depressionszustände. *Zeitschrift für die gesamte Neurologie und Psychiatrie* 59:281–86.

Shapiro, Arthur. 1967. Dreaming and the physiology of sleep. A critical review of some empirical data and a proposal for a theoretical model of sleep and dreaming. *Experimental Neurology,* Suppl. Vol., 4:56–81.

Simpson, George Gaylord. 1949. *The meaning of evolution.* New Haven: Yale University Press.

Sommerfelt, Alf. 1938. *La langue et la société; caractères sociaux d'une langue de type archaïque.* Oslo: Aschenhoug (W. Nygaard).

Sondhi, K. C. 1963. The biological foundations of animal patterns. *Quarterly Review of Biology* 38:289–327.

Tarski, Alfred. 1956. The concept of truth in formalized languages. *Logic, semantics, metamathematics.* Oxford: Clarendon Press.

Thompson, D'Arcy. 1942. *On growth and form.* 2d ed.; 2 vols. 1st ed., 1917. Cambridge: The University Press.

———. 1951. *On growth and form.* Vol. I. Orig. pub., 1917. Cambridge: The University Press.

Thorndike, E. L. 1911. *Animal intelligence.* New York: Macmillan. Orig. pub., 1898.

Thorner, Hans. 1932. Die harmonische Anpassungsfähigkeit des verkürzten Nervensystems, untersucht an Schlangen. *Pflügers Archiv für die gesamte Physiologie des Menschen und der Tiere* 230:1–15.

Tinbergen, Nikolaas. 1953. *The herring gull's world: a study of the social behaviour of birds.* London: Collins.

Titchener, E. B. 1911. *A textbook of psychology.* New York: Macmillan.

Tumarkin, A. 1955. On the evolution of the auditory conducting apparatus: A new theory based on functional considerations. *Evolution* 9:221–43.

Uexküll, Jakob von. 1909. *Umwelt und Innenwelt der Tiere.* Berlin.

Volkelt, Hans. 1912. *Über die Vorstellungen der Tiere: Ein Beiträge z. Entwicklungspsychologie.* Leipzig: Engelmann.

Washburn, S. L. 1950. The analysis of primate evolution with particular reference to the origin of man. *Cold Spring Harbor Symposia on Quantitative Biology* 15:67–78.

Watterson, R. L., ed. 1959. *Endocrines in development.* Report on the Shelter Island Symposium of 1956. Chicago: University of Chicago Press.

Webster's New World Dictionary of the American Language. 1960. Cleveland and New York: World.

Werner, Heinz. 1945. Motion and motion perception: a study in vicarious functioning. *Journal of Psychology* 19:317–27.

———. 1956. Microgenesis and aphasia. *Journal of Abnormal and Social Psychology* 52:347–53.

White, R. W. 1959. Motivation reconsidered: the concept of competence. *Psychological Review* 66:297–333.

Wiener, Norbert. 1948. *Cybernetics: or control and communication in the animal and the machine.* New York and Paris: John Wiley and Hermann.

Zotterman, Yngve. 1959. The nervous mechanism of taste. *Annals of the New York Academy of Sciences* 81:358–66.

———. 1961. Studies in the neural mechanism of taste. In *Sensory communication,* edited by W. A. Rosenblith. Cambridge, Mass., and New York: M.I.T. Press and John Wiley.

Zuckerkandl, Victor. 1956. *Sound and symbol.* New York: Pantheon.

Index

Abstraction, 40, 86, 87, 95, 269–70, 321, 394; in art, 68–79; generalizing, 68–70; "isolating," 73, 74; presentational, 70, 89
Act concept, 103–17, 139–40
Act form, 126
Action: defined, 116–17; formalization of, 271–72; newly developed, 273; somatic to voluntary, 177
Activities, 117, 142, 143; neonate, 179; symbolic, 17; vital, 117
Act-like events, 108–9, 120, 123
Acts, 80–81, 87, 120, 149; assertion as primary act of mind (affirmation of self), 307, 309; autonomic, 179; behavioral, 106, 112–13, 114, 151, 152, 155, 159, 165; and the brain, 342–43; and causality, 391–92; consummatory, 174, 189; cycles, 142, 143, 160–61; and development of selfhood, 346–47; "display," 208; and entrainment principle, 340–41; ethics as evaluation of, 354–55; evolution of, 134–53; and feeling, 103–17, 118–33, 134–53, 154–66; the future and emergent, 311; growth of, 154–66; and human life as an act, 347, 351–52; impulsive, 191–92; individuation and involvement of, 118–33; instinctive, 176, 178–79, 189, 190, 209–10; integration of, 132; intended, 105; intensity of, 178; intention and realization of, 328; internal, 179; intraorganic, 140, 157, 159; life of devotional, 352; magic and recurrent, 327; organic, 256; outward-directed, 179; the past and mental, 311; perseveration of, 176; and potential, 114–15, 116; and primitive man, 301; proto-acts, 108–9; protracted instinctive, 209–10; purposive, 190; reactive, 169–70; reduction of, 141–42, 143; REM and behavioral, 259; ritual and animal and expressive, 313–14; sensory, 156–57; social equilibrium and behavioral, 359; specialized be-

407

Acts (cont.)
havioral, 244; species-specific, 174, 175–76; subacts, 120, 145, 151, 152, 154, 188, 232; superacts, 120, 152; "telescoping" of behavioral, 191–92; true, 120; unity of, 141; vital, 106–7, 125–26; wholeness of, 169. See also Act concept; Acts, animal; Behavior; Behavior, animal; Subacts

Acts, animal: behavioral, 171; conjoint, 232–33; cooperative, 225–27; of "dismissal," 215; intentionality of, 219, 222; interpretations of, 202–3, 204, 219–22; joint, 225–26, 230; motivation of, 220; "organized," 198; reactive, 169–70

Actualization, 115, 129, 139

Adaptability, 160

Adaptation, 137–38, 139, 160; to ambient, 238–39, 241; physical, and lack of specialization in man, 238

Adaptedness, 138, 160

Aesthetic attitude, 49

Aesthetic values, tactual, 252

After-images, 254–55

Afterworlds: analysis of spirit, 305; concept of (analysis), 351–52; earthly life as episode to, 368; and the future, 311–12

Aged individuals, treatment of, 384

Agents, 117, 118, 120, 125, 139, 142–43; and causality, 392; supernatural, 314; and symbolic gestures and ritual, 314

Aggression, animal: inhibition of, 215–16, 217; and vocalization, 208

Aid-rendering, in animals, 227, 230

"Allo-grooming," in animals, 223–24

Ambients, 110–11, 128–29, 130, 141–43, 156–57, 163, 165; adaptation to, 238–39, 241; animal, 193; human, 287, 288, 289–90; response to, 175–76

Ancestors, 314; and hereafter concept, 351; punishment by, 356, 357; and ritual action, 315–16

Animals: and approval and disapproval, 354; art of, 60–62; behavior of, 155; bodily balance of, 320–21; cannibalism of, 366; and empathy, 365, 366; high structure of brain in behaviorally simple, 343; inorganic inclusions in, 130; instinctive reflexes in, 365; mentality of, 93, 158; repertoire of, 152, 163; species-specific features, 342; tools used by, 321

Anthropomorphism, in animal studies, 202, 207, 216, 230, 231, 232, 233. See also Behavior, animal: general

Ants, 234

Apes: and bodily balance, 320–21; use of tools by, 321

Aphasia, 295

Appetitive behavior, 174, 198

Arboreal phase, prehuman, 247

Ardrey, Robert, 215

Aristotle, 43, 83, 283, 392, 397

Arm, human, 247

Armies, organization of, 377

Armstrong, E. A., 191, 244

Art: abstraction in, 68–79; animal, 60–62; and artist's idea, 49–67; balance in, 56; depth in, 83; design in, 55–56; and feeling, 29–31, 35–48, 49–67, 68–79, 80–99; formalization in, 55; function of, 51; gradients in, 85, 86, 87; Greek, 73; growth in, 85–86, 92, 165; imitation in, 73; import of, 35–99; individuality in, 84, 91; individuation in, 91–93; inevitability in, 91; living form in, 66–67, 80–99; livingness in, 66, 67, 74, 92; logic of, 40; magic in, 58, 96, 98; movement in, 94–95; necessity in, 91; non-representational, 40; objectification in, 49, 51, 72; Oriental, 74, 85; paleolithic, 55, 58–59, 73; primitive, 61; projection in, 35–48, 80, 84, 86–87; realization in, 42, 77; relationships in, 80–83; Renaissance, 73; representation in, 40, 42–43, 72; strangeness in, 96, 97; tension in, 47, 71–72, 74, 81, 83, 89; transcendence in, 98; uniqueness in, 84, 91, 92; unity in, 82, 83; works of, 91–93

Art symbol, 29, 40, 43, 44, 47–48, 80, 81, 83, 94

Articulation of human speech, 274, 277, 280

Artist, and his work, 28–29, 49–67

Artistic conception, 39

Artistic expression, 28, 38–39, 41, 46, 55, 59–60

Artistic idea, 38, 54, 66, 69, 84, 93, 98

Artistic quality, 48, 54, 55

Asia, ethical thought in, 316–17

Assertion: as affirmation of mind, 307–

10; punishment and self-assertion, 357
Atlantic murre, 240
Attention, 257–58, 291
Auditory perception, animal, 208–9
Australopithecus, 245–46
Autistic acts, animal, 209
Autogenic action, 9–13, 41, 175, 209
Autotrophism, in molds, 180
Awareness, 158; in dreams, 265
Aztec civilization: analysis of, 382–83; lack of humane thinking, 378

Babble, and human speech, 273
Baboon, 225
Balance (the state of equilibrium), 369; and change, 358; man's mental activities and physical nature, 364; as principle in continuity of human stocks, 359; religion and ethnic, 367; sacrifice and ethnic, 362–63. See also Art: balance in; Bodily balance; Ethnic balance
Baptism, 360
Barbour, Thomas, 250
Barfield, Owen, 96
Bastian, Jarvis, 231
Bat, 184
Beauty, 55, 56, 89; "phase beauty," 85–86, 87
Beaver, 243
Beethoven, Ludwig van, 119
Behavior, 111, 114, 139, 152, 155, 158, 161, 164; adaptive, 192; changes after elimination of REM, 259; dialectics of, 173; and feeling, 260; innate, 172; instinctive, 158, 163, 190–91; organic, 173; pre- and postnatal, 172; reactive, 169–70; repertoire of, 179; as response to external conditions, 172; species-specific, 174, 193; verbal, 16. See also Acts; Acts, animal; Behavior, animal
Behavior, animal. See also Acts, animal; Behavior; Subacts
—general: basic concepts of, 169; circularity of, 197; experimental studies of, 177; facilitation of, 199; interpretation of, 181, 203–5; and neural center control, 189; and physiology, 176; stereotypic, 173
—specific: aid-giving, 227–30; brooding, 176; coercing, 234–35; collaborating, 226; command-giving, 234–35; cooperating, 226–27; courting, 191–92, 208–9, 223; deceiving, 223; defecating, 218 (see also "marking"); feigning, 222–23; fighting, 215, 217–18; "filial," 195; following, 195; grooming, 223–24; homing, 196; hunting, 225; killing, 229; "marking," 218, 221–22; maternal, 228; mating, 192, 209; obeying, 234–35; planning, 198, 225; playing, 229, 272; rescuing, 230; retrieving, 207; "submissive," 215–17; territory-staking, 221–22, 224; throwing of missiles, 218, 220–21; "training the young," 224; urinating (see "marking")
Behavioral acts, 106, 112–13, 114, 151, 152, 155, 159, 165. See also Acts
Behavioral sciences, 6, 19, 21
Bertalanffy, Ludwig von, 30, 122, 134
Bethe, Albrecht, 186
Bills, A. G., 258
Binocular focus, in human eyes, 253
Biogenesis, 121–23
Biographical memory, 290, 293–94
Biographical view, in psychology, 178
Biology: and the foundations of mind, 340; modified concepts in, 107
Bipedalism, human, 246, 249–53
Birds: memory of, 194; migration, theory of, 184–85, 196; practice flights of, 198
Blum, H. F., 122
Bodily balance, 320–21, 322. See also Balance
"Body image," in man, 285
Bogert, C. M., 171
Bolk, Louis, 238
Bonner, John Tyler, 136
Boole, George, 64
Börnstein, Walter, 285
Bosanquet, Bernard, 51, 55
Bowie, Henry P., 74
Boxfish, 249
Boyd, Rutherford, 7
Bradley, H. T., 192
Brahmanism, 351
Brain, 12, 162, 174, 227, 250; animal, 174, 227, 250, 261; asymmetry of, 286–87; Broca's area in, 287; and conceptual mentality, 358; evolutionary advance of, 343; function, 262;

Brain (cont.)
    and hands and feet, 397; hemisphere dominance, 287; high structural development of (in behaviorally simple creatures), 343; and imagination, speech, and fantasies, 363–64; and images, 254–55; and measures of individuality, 343–44; and memory, 288–89; partial individuation of, 342–43; receptiveness, 253; as specialized organ, 239; and spinal cord, 253; structure, 250; weight, 250
Brain stem, 174, 248, 250
Brain, W. R., 284–85, 287
Brains, mechanical, 116, 135
Broca's area, 287
Bullock, T. H., 115
Byzantium, 373

Cadence, 86, 95
Cailliet, Émile, 305
Caldwell, D. K., 244
Cannibalism: of Amerindians, 379, 380; and sympathy and empathy, 366
Carpenter, C. R., 219, 220, 225–26
Cartilage, basal, 249
Cassirer, Ernst, 4, 39
Cat, 184, 186–87, 229
Categories: Aristotelian, 283; conceptual, 295
Causality, 111, 112, 316; concept of, 392; lack of development of, 306–7; and magic, 324; savage tribesmen and external facts of, 301–5; and transformation of spirit-world into mechanical world, 314–15
Causation, 109–10, 111
Cause-and-effect theories, 175
Cells, 128–29
Central nervous systems, 11, 162, 163, 250, 254
Cerebral: acts, 256; cortex, 342–43, 358; lesions 295
"Ceremony," animal, 204, 271
Chagnon, Napoleon, 309
Chai, C., 316
Chai, W., 316
Chameleon, 242
Chang, K. C., 376
Chick, imprinting of, 195
Child, Charles Manning, 341
Chimpanzee: bodily balance, 320, 321; foot, 246; intuition, 270; learning, 226; perceptual acts, 320
China: architecture of cities in, 376; development of high culture and cities in, 376; ritual practice and empire of, 315; ritual reflecting moral order in, 316–17
Chomsky, Noam, 277
Christianity, 351, 363
Chromosomes, 241
Churchill, Winston S., 119
Circadian rhythms, 160
Circularity, in animal locomotion, 198
"Circulating messages," in brain, 290
Circumcision, interpretations of, 360
Cities: in America, 378, 381, 382; Chinese high culture and development of, 376; destruction of Near Eastern, 375, 376; in Egypt, 374; in the Levant, 374–75; in the Near East, 373–74; as personal royal monuments, 373, 375; rise of, 370–71; stability of European, 375; Vikings as builders of, 372
Climate changes, and animal migration, 198
Coazervation, 119, 122
Coelenterates, 129
Coleridge, Samuel Taylor, 58, 322
Colonial insects, 226
Color: in dream, 269; vision, 183
Comedy, concept of, 349–50
Commands, animal, 234–35
Commensalism, 131
Common sense, 26–27, 137, 302; ritual and European, 314
Communal conception of life, 345–46
Communication: animal, 203, 208–9, 223, 225, 231–32, 235–36, 279; defined, 231; human, 103, 231–32, 280, 298; and language, 272–73, 277–78, 283, 285
Communion, 228, 231–32, 274, 278–79
Competence, 109
"Complex-quality," 188
Comprehension, 280
Computers, electronic, 116, 135
Comte, Auguste, 15
Concept formation and use, human, 268, 270–71, 275, 282–83, 287–88, 295–96
Conception, artistic, 39

Conceptual mentality, 358, 391
Conceptual reality, 112
Conceptualization, 110
Confucius, 316
Conrad, Klaus, 75, 76
Consciousness, 4, 12, 93, 203, 259, 289, 346; state of altered, 331
Consummation, 174, 190, 206–7, 229, 253, 261
Contact: physical, 228, 232, 233–34, 252, 274; symbolic, 278, 298
Continuity, of life, 204
Convergence, in forms of life, 240, 242–43
Contours, and visual perception, 325
Counting: appearance of, 395; by body part, 392; and Dance and numbers, 395–96; and Dance and walking, 397–98; by fingers, 396; and hand and drum, 397–98; and words, 395
Conversation and speech, 277, 298
Cooperation, 224–26, 228, 232–33
Coral, 241
Cortex, 250, 286–87, 291, 295
Cowering posture, animal, 222
Craig, W., 190
Cranial bones, hominid, 247–48
Cranium, human, 245, 248
Crawford, M. P., 226
Cruelty, 366; of the Inca, 381
Cultural competition, 379, 383
Cyclicity, animal, 198

Dance, 133, 364; and counting, 395–96, 397; empathetic character of magic and war dance, 328; expressive, 273–74, 279; of honeybee, 233; magic as pantomimic rite of, 330; primitive, 275; and song, 275; stories acted out through, 313
Danielson, R. N., 231
Darwin, Charles, 137, 138–39
Da Vinci, Leonardo, 73
Dead, the: of the Inca, 381; and punishment, 356. See also Death
Death: and afterworlds, 352; and Chinese funeral rites, 316; development of the mind and analysis of, 347–49; and the Inca, 381; as inevitable, 340; as inherent part of life, 338; and magic power, 337–38, 350; and mythical insight, 313; and religion, 367–68; religion serving for denial of, 364; and ritual, 361; and tribal concept of "we," 345; and understanding of mortality, 368
Declarative function of language, 278
Deer mouse. See Mouse
Degree, concepts of, 87
De Jong, B., 122
Deprivation, sensory, 258
Depth, in art, 83
Descartes, René, 108
Design: in art, 55–56; in repeated images, 267
Detail, perception of, 263–64
Determination stream, 127
Dewey, John, 19
Dialectic, principle of, 81
Dialectic process, in behavior, 173
Dialectical rhythms, 124–25
Dialectical structure, 81–83, 87
Diet, hominid, 247
Diffusion rhythms, 127
Digital perception. See Touch, sense of
Discrimination, sensory, 206
Discursive thinking, 69
"Displacement activity," 254
"Distraction display," 222, 223
Dog, 184, 217–19, 221, 226, 249, 252
Dolphin, behavior, 227–29, 230, 244
Dominance, hemisphere, in human brain, 287
Donovan, J., 275, 276–77
Drama, 96; and conception of tragedy, 349–50; healing as, 329–30
Dream: after-images, 254–55; analysis of (in evolution of mind), 312–13; in animals, 261; childhood memories in, 266; distortion in memory, 263–64; and hallucination, 261, 268; image, 254, 262–63, 264, 265–67, 268–69; interpretation, 264; and language, 297; mode, 323; recollection of, 262–63; and symbol, 268–69
Dreaming, human, 253–54, 259, 261, 263
"Dream thought," 263
"Dream work," 268, 270, 297
Drives, 112
Drums, and counting, 397–98
Du Brul, E. L., 248–49
Dye, J. A., 249

Echolocation, 184
Ecological niche, 139, 142
Ecosystems, 182
Edinger, Tilly, 343
Egocentrism, animal, 209, 216–17
Egypt, and the Pharaoh, 373–74
Eibl-Eibesfeldt, I., 222
Eidetic memory. *See* Memory: eidetic
Élan vital, 272
Elephant, 244, 251, 342
Eliot, T. S., 50–53
Emotion, 9, 38, 41, 252, 262, 266
Empathy: animal, 209, 216, 217, 221, 228, 234; in art, 72; and cannibalism, 379, 380; defined, 211; human, 278; loss of (with development of sympathy), 365–66; and magic, 327–29; and ritual dramatization, 333
Empiricism, 5, 25
Endgestalt, 76, 77
Endocrine system, 210
Endothermy, 171–72
Energy, 106, 111, 113–14
Engram, 72. *See also* Memory: "traces"
Entities, discrete psychophysical, 5
Entrainment, 125, 139, 144–45, 150; principle of, and acts and the mind, 340–41
Environment, 9–10, 110–11, 139, 142; adaptation to and control of, 220, 238–39, 241; change in, 170, 182, 198, 220; and instinctive impulse, 192–93; and motivation in animals, 177
Environmental situation, 110–11
Eobionts, 123
Equivalents, technical, 88–89
Essertier, Daniel, 307, 309
Ethics: and cultivation of feeling, 316–17; as evaluation of acts, 354–55; and group action, 355–56
Ethnic balance, 369; and religion, 367; and sacrifice, 362–63. *See also* Balance
Ethology, terms used in, 203, 214, 231
Europeans, misconception by colonial, 306, 329–30
Evans, W. F., 215
Evans, William E. 231
Events: act-like, 108–9, 120, 123; external, 110–11; natural, 118
Evolution, 129, 136, 146, 160–61, 180, 239, 245–46; of acts, 134–53; and brain development, 343; and conceptual activity, 358; and dreams and the mind, 312–13; and "great shift," 365; and the mind, 339–40; "oriented," 182; and selection, 384; of speech, 272–73; and survival, 180
Experience, 253, 292, 293–94, 322
Expression: artistic, 28, 38–39, 41, 46, 55, 59–60; emotive, 38; mathematical, 38; self-expression, 41, 60
Expressiveness, "intrinsic," 74–75
Extensions, organic, 130–31
External events, 110–11. *See also* Stimulus
External form, 40
Eye. *See also* Vision
—animal, 240
—human: binocular focus, 253; in neonates, 259; saccadic movements of, 258–59, 261; scanning, 259

Facilitation, process of, 143
Fact, 392, 394
"Falsehood," in logic, 284
Family, 361; and gaining of magic power, 335; group action and structure of, 356; prehistory of, 371; and survival of aged individuals, 384
Fantasy, 280, 292, 294
Fauré-Fremiet, Philippe, 30, 44–45, 62, 322
Feeling, 3–14; and acts, 103–17, 118–33, 134–53, 154–66; and art, 29–31, 35–48, 49–67, 68–79, 80–99; corporeal, 322; of mental activity (magic and), 323–24; objective, 292; of passage, 206–7, 349; and prescientific knowledge, 23–31; projecting into visual objects, 321
Feeling and Form, 35–36, 44, 50
Feigning behavior, animal, 222–23
Fergusson, Francis, 96
"Festal" theory of speech, 277, 278. *See also* Speech
Fetal organisms, 150
"Fetalization" of man, 249
Fetishism, and symbolic projection, 362
Field theory, 18
"Filial response" of animals, 195
Fingers: counting on, 396; and the use of drums and numbers, 397–98
Fish: migration, 197–98; vision in, 231
Fixed action patterns, 115

"Flash-back" memory, 290, 293
Flocks, "intention movement" of, 212
Focusing, visual, 240
Following behavior, animal, 195–96
Fontaine, Maurice, 197
"Food-carrying" hypothesis, 246
Food: and emotional attitude, 327; as symbol, 369
Foot: animal, 246, 247; human, 246–47
Force, concept of, 112
Forebrain, animal, 291
Form: act, 126; external and internal, 40; living, 80–99, 124, 126; organic, 159; spatial, 43
Form perception, 264–65, 267, 269–70
Formalization: in art, 55; of behavior, 271–72; of images, 267–68
Francastel, Pierre, 41
Freedom, 91
Freud, Sigmund, 8, 262–63, 264, 266, 268, 270, 297, 312–13, 319
Frog, 176, 184, 190–91, 250
Functional shifts, 150, 164–65
Functions, 134–35, 155–56; organic, 149–50
Future, the (structure of), 311–12

Gardner, R. A., 235
Gardner, B. T., 235
Garstang, Walter, 238–39
Gehlen, Arnold, 238, 239, 253
Gemmation of sponges, 171
Generalization, 20
Generalizing abstraction, 68–70
Genes, 128, 138, 151, 241, 249
Genetic code, 142
Genetic inheritance, 128
Gestalt principle, 72, 74
Gestalten, 26, 73, 74, 75, 76–77, 82–84, 88
Gestures, 327, 357–58; magician's symbolic, 319; ritual and symbolic, 314; and theory of magic, 319
Ghosts: breach of ritual and sickness from, 315; dreamed, 305–6
Gibbon, 248
Gibson, J. J., 200, 251
Gifts, importance of in precivilized societies, 369
Glotz, Gustave, 372
Goal orientation, animal, 207, 218
God, delegation of power to, 350–52
Gods: and punishment, 357; supremacy of, 367
Goethe, J. W., 236
Goldschmidt, Richard B., 127, 367
Gorilla, 246, 248
Gradients: in art, 85–86, 87; in nature, 126–27, 132
Graham, Martha, 71
Grammar, forms of, 281
Grasping reflex, in toes, 245
Greek thought, and concept of tragedy, 349–50
Grooming, animal, 223–24
Group action, 355–56
Group feeling, in dance, 273–74
Growth: of acts, 154–56; in art, 85–86, 92, 165; in nature, 126–27
Gull, 207

Habitat: imprinting, 195; "place," 198
Hallucination, 253–54, 268–69
Hamlet, 52–53
Hand, 247, 250–51, 287; development of, 397; and the drum and counting, 397–98; intellectual potential of, 396
Handedness and speech, 287
Hardy, A. C., 239
Harmonic space, phenomenon of, 94–95
Hartline, H. K., 159
Hayes, J. S., 114
Head, 249–50
Head, Sir Henry, 285
Healing, theatrical aspects of, 329–31
Hearing, 184, 208–9, 271, 285, 296
Heat-sensitivity, animal, 171–72
Heaven, 305. See also Afterworlds
Hebb, D. O., 125, 257–58
Hedinger, H., 192
Hein, A., 187, 194
Held, R., 187, 194
Hell, 305. See also Afterworlds
Hemisphere dominance, in human brain, 287
Herd, behavior of, 212
Heredity, 128, 138–39, 209–10
Historical thinking, 288
Hive, 233
"Holiness," primitive sense of, 271
Holistic tendency of human mind, 285
Holst, Erich von, 174
Homeostasis in organic behavior, 173
Homer, 48

Homing, animal. *See* Migration, animal; Navigation, animal; Orientation: animal
Hominidae, 237, 247
Homoiothermy, animal, 172
Honeybee, 233–34
Horel, J. A., 235
Hormones, 193, 198, 210
Horowitz, N. H., 122, 180, 191
Howling monkey, 219, 220–21, 225–26
Humboldt, Wilhelm von, 284
Husserl, Edmund, 30
Hypnagogic images, 266–67
Hypnotism: mass, 331–33; of self, 324
Hysteric retention, animal, 289

Idea, artistic, 38, 54, 66, 69, 84, 93, 98
Ideas, transmission of, 231
Ideation, 269–70, 279
Ideational series, 257
Illusions: primary, 70, 71, 82, 94, 96; secondary, 82, 94–98
Illusory forms, perception of, 324–26
Illusory performances: and attitude of mind, 304–5; and hypnosis and suggestion, 331–33
Images, 25–26, 28, 29–31, 42, 43–44, 45, 46, 48, 65, 67, 83, 98; and brain, 261–62; and conception, 276; in dream, 261–63; fictitious, 254–55; and perception, 205, 264–65, 269–70, 291–92; remembered, 269; retinal, 254–55, 266–67; as symbol, 268–69, 275–76; visual, 253
Imagination, 42–44, 46–47, 265, 267–68, 280, 283, 292–93, 307, 364, 368; the past and mental acts of, 311; primary, 322; primitive, 304–5, 313; and speech and fantasies, 363–64; and sympathy, 366; voluntary, 322
Imitation, 212, 272; in art, 73; of events, 328
"Immaturity" of man, 238
"Immediate memory," 289
Impact, 9, 10–11, 13, 163
Implementation, 140–41, 149
Import, of art, 33–99
Imprinting, 194–95
Impulse: and behavior, 181–82; and communion, 231–32; consummation, 190, 205, 229–31, 264; and hormones, 198, 210; and instinct, 192–93; migratory, 196, 197–98; potential, 142; primary, 141; remembrance of, 206–7; repetition of, 257; rival, 181; theory, 254; vicarious completion of, 254
Impulses, 113–16, 141–45, 149–51, 158, 162–63, 164
Inca civilization: analysis of, 380–82; and degeneracy, 383; growth of, 379; isolation of, 383; lack of humane thinking, 378; and sacrifice, 380, 381
India, cities in, 375
"Indirect perception," in dreams, 263
Individual, 119
Individuality, 119; in art, 84, 91
Individuation: in art, 91–93; biological aspects of, 341–42; concept of, 344–45; and involvement, 118–33, 364, 368; lack of, 374; and the mind and punishment, 357; personal responsibility as price of, 353; and primitive societies, 345–46; and selfhood concept, 346–47; and subjective activity, 279
Induction, 110, 125, 140
Inductive memory, 290–91, 294
Inertia and migration, 184
Inevitability, in art, 91
Information transmission, 231
Inheritance, genetic, 128
Inhibition, 125, 181, 216–17
"Inhibitors," 181, 202, 203, 216
"Injury-feigning," animal, 222
"Innate releasing mechanism (IRM)," 203
Inorganic inclusions, in animal bodies, 129–30
Insects, 183, 232–33
Instinct: theories of, 189, 236; and shift to intuition, 358
Instinctive: action, 232–33; acts, 175, 176, 178–79, 185–86, 190, 191, 192–94, 230; behavior, 158, 163, 175, 178–79, 209, 233, 365–66; impulses, 192–93; life, 213; and magic, 327, 328
Integration: of acts, 132; biological process of, 131–32
Intellect, human, 298
Intelligence, 158, 176
Intended act, 105
"Intention movement," animal, 212
Intentionality, animal, 221, 223, 231
Interaction, 224, 231

Internal form, 40
Internal selection, 147
Interrogation, 278
Intervening variables, 112
Intraorganic acts, 140, 157, 159
Intuition, 41, 56–57, 62–63, 89, 269, 270, 277–78; and mind's awareness of own activities, 309; and perception, 322, 323, 337, 355–56; and sacrifice, 363; semantic, 69; shift from instinct and, 358; and symbols, 322–23
Invention, 293
Involvement, 92; and individuation 118–33
Inward situation, 110
"Isolating abstraction," 73, 74
Isomorphy, 37

James, William, 228, 288
Japanese painting, 74
Jargon, 16
Jen, 316
Joint acts, animal, 225–27, 230
Judaism: blood rite in, 369; and circumcision, 360; and sacrifices, 363. *See also* Yahweh worship

Kandinsky, Wassily, 96
Kant, Immanuel, 89
Katz, David, 251–52
Kavanau, J. L., 219–20
Khatami, Manoochehr, 332
Kinder, F. S., 249
Kings: and Chinese capital city, 376; cities as personal monuments to, 373, 375; development of, 372; and loss of authority of elders, 373; Pharaohs as, 373–74
Klein, Marc, 192
"Knowledge by acquaintance," 24, 291
Knowledge, prescientific, 23–31, 106–7
Köhler, Wolfgang, 30, 320–21
Koenig, Otto, 215
Kroh, Oswald, 75

La Barre, W., 137
Language, 7, 45–46, 301; and animal communication, 231, 235; and concepts, 287, 296; declarative function of, 278; and fact and logic, 392–95; as human trait, 285–86; logical, 4–5; and numbers, 395, 398; origins, 273–75, 280, 286; pathology of, 295–96; and perception, 283–84, 285, 287; and polyglotism, 296–97; second, 296–97; and semantic intuition, 268; shifts in, 77–79; and speech, 272; syntactical, 281; technical, 16–17, 135–36; and thinking, 282–84; uses of, 280–81, 287, 295. *See also* Concept formation and use, human; Nouns and naming; Speech; Utterance; Vocalization; Words
Languages: Asiatic, 282; ASL, 235–36; Australian, 282; Indo-European, 284
Langur monkey, 245
Lashley, K. S., 186, 188
Laskin, D. M., 248–49
"Law of concentric reduction," 285
Lazarus, R. S., 206
Leaders: and the desert, 373; and organized command of seafaring, 371–73; rise of, 371
Learning: animal, 186–88, 219–20, 226–27, 235; human, 283, 294
Lebensgefühl ("sense of life"): the act form of, 348; and sense of selfhood, 345–47; in tribal communities, 345–46
Lee, Dorothea Demetracopoulou, 303
Levant, cities in, 374–75
Lewin, Kurt, 18
Leyhausen, Paul, 188, 244
Li (Chinese rite), 316
Liberalization, of concepts, 20
Life: as an act, 347–48, 351; conception of, 313; defined, 104; religion and idea of, 367; origin of, 120–23, 128; and the self, 348; and selfhood concept, 346–47; shift from power worship to worship of, 369; tragic rhythm of, 349; tribal conception of, 345–46; without death, 368
Life processes, matrix of, 126, 140
Line drawings, and visual perception, 325
Linguistics, comparative, 277
Listening, 296
Living form: in art, 66–67, 80–99, 124; in nature, 124, 126
Livingness, in art, 66–67, 74, 91–92
Lizards, 192
Locke, John, 5, 57, 309
Locomotion, animal, 170, 195, 198
Logic, 284, 392–93; of art, 40; and thinking, 64–65

Logical conviction, 63–64
Logical languages, 4, 5
Logical symbolism, 38
London, I. D., 18
Long-term memory, 288–89, 290
Lorenz, Konrad, 181, 189, 190, 202, 215–18

McCleary, R. A., 206
Magic, 270–71, 279; accumulating or bestowing power of, 337; in art, 58, 96, 98; and death, 337–38, 350; and healing as drama, 329–30; importance of (in savage life), 317; as inherent in human life, 337–38; and instinctive behavior, 327; persistent belief in, 318, 319; power (seeking of), 334–36; and ritual, 317; savage tribesmen's view of, 302–3; shaman as actor in sacred drama, 330–31; sympathetic being empathetic, 327–28, 329; theory of, 318–19; and transformation, 326–27; and words and names, 336
Magicians, 317, 319, 330–37
Magnanimity, animal, 215, 217
Magnetism and migration, 184
Malleability of man, 238
Man: reflexes and evolution of, 365; traces of (on earth), 370. *See also* Primitive man
Manipulation, 250. *See also* Hand; Paw
"Marking," animal, 218, 221–22
Marriage, 361
Maternal behavior, 228
Mathematical expression, 38
Mathematics: and bilateral symmetry, 396–97; and counting on fingers, 395–96; and Dance and numbers, 395–96; and hand and drum, 397–98; and intellectual potential of hands, 396; and language and number sense, 395, 398; and walking and dancing, 397–98
Mating, 192, 209
Matrix, of life processes, 126
Mayas, 382
Mead, A. P., 114
Mechanical brains, 116, 135
Mechanisms, 106–9, 134–36, 141, 146–47, 149–50, 159, 204
Medicine-men. *See* Shaman

Memory: animal, 186, 188, 194, 206–7; biographical, 293–94; childhood, 290; cumulative, 289; current, 289, 290; and dream, 265, 267–68; eidetic, 293; factual, 290; and forgetting, 263; images, 269; inductive, 290–91, 294; kinds of, 290–91; and "knowledge by acquaintance," 291; long-term, 288–89, 290; for numbers, 295–96; object, 291; and poesis, 293; primary, 289; recent, 289; reliving in, 293; and ritual, 276; short-term, 288–89, 290; and symbols, 288; "traces" ("engrams"), 203. *See also* Recognition; Recollection
Mencius, 316
Mendel, Gregor Johann, 152
Meng, Mathilde, 189
Mental activity, and magic, 323–24
Mental life, human, 284–85
Mentality, 93, 202–3, 237. *See also* Mind
"Mercy," animal, 217
Metabolic synthesis, 180
Metaphor, 271, 296; sensuous, 77–78, 84, 94
Methodology, prescriptive, 16–17
Meyer, D. R., 235
Meyerson, Ignace, 316–17
Migration, animal, 184, 196–99; and man, 371
Mimesis, 73; and magic, 328–29
Mind, 5, 6, 21–22, 23, 25, 38, 63, 80, 82, 118–20; and the brain, 342–45; and concept of punishment, 357; and death, 347–49; and development of selfhood concept, 346–47; and devotional acts, 352; and hereafter concept, 352; and human evolution, 339; and individuation, 341–47; and personal responsibility, 352; and power delegated to God, 350–51; and primitive societies, 345–46; and principle of entrainment, 340–41; symbolic powers of and limbs, 397; and tragic rhythm of life, 348–50; and tribal "we" and individual "I," 345
Missile throwing, by animals, 218, 220
Mob behavior, 211
Models, 25–26, 28, 29–31, 43, 132, 135, 191
Molds, 180
Mole, 243

Monkey, 242, 246
Morality, and Chinese ritual, 316–17
Morley, Derek W., 234
"Moro reflex" in infants, 365
Morphogenesis, 131
Motif, 90
Motility, 170
Motivation, 90, 109–12, 120, 139, 140, 154; animal, 177, 188, 204, 214, 216–17, 218, 224–25
Motivational conception of events, 304; and ritual, 315–16
Motives, 90, 109–10
Motor cortex, human, 28
Mountcastle, V. B., 295
Mouse, 219–20, 222
Movement, in art, 94–95
Movements, 106, 109
Murphy, John, 337
Muscular: acts, 179; feeling, 195
Music, 71, 88, 94–95
Musical space, 94–95
Mutations, 138, 145–47, 180
Mutilation, 171, 285
Muzio, J. N., 259
Myth: and attitudes of mind, 304–5; as natural symbols, 312–13; origin of, 312–14; and the past, 311; sacredness and inviolability of cosmic, 309–10

Nachmanson, David, 159
Names: and magical invocations, 318; as nouns, menacing powers of, 323; power embodied in, 336
Natural events, 118
Natural law, 42, 137
Natural selection, 122, 135, 137–39, 140, 142, 146, 182, 276
Nature: and evolution, 136; gradients in, 126–27, 132; growth in, 126–27; living form in, 124, 126; myths and forces of, 313; pattern in, 115, 126–27, 129; ritual and control of, 315; tension in, 106, 115–16, 124, 146–47
Navigation, animal, 198–99
Near East: cities in, 373–74, 375; civilization of, 374–75
Necessity, 91
Neo-Darwinism, 145–46
Neoteny: and evolution, 239; human, 238–39
Nervous system: central, 11, 162, 163; control, 210; impulse, 279; tension, in animals, 204. *See also* Reciprocal innervation
Neural "centers," 181, 189
Newton, Sir Isaac, 19
Nietzsche, Friedrich Wilhelm, 55
Noble, G. K., 192
Norris, K. S., 244
Nouns and naming, 276, 280, 283–84, 295
Numbers, as symbols, 295–96; and Dance, 395–96, 397–98; drums and development of, 397–98; and words, 395

Object, 13
Objectification, in art, 49, 51, 72
Objective, defined, 13
"Objective correlative," 51–53
Objectivity, 17, 64
Objects: animal awareness of external, 321; projecting feelings into visual, 321; protosymbolic, 322; tangible, 83; transfer of power of shaman to, 337; viewing of, 320
Object-subject relationship, 13, 92
Ontogenesis, 148–49, 162–63, 164
Oparin, A. P., 121–22
"Optical melody," and animal orientation, 199–200
Organic extensions, 130–31
Organisms, 9–11, 80, 111, 118–19, 120, 125, 126–33, 134, 154–66; activity of, 169
"Organized" acts, animal, 198
Orientation: animal, 196–97, 200; human, 196
"Oriented evolution," 182
Orthogenesis, 143, 144
Oswald, Ian, 254, 368–69

Pacemaker, 144–45, 161
Pain, savages and endurance of, 331
Painting, 40–41, 74
Palmyra (biblical Tadmor), 374
Pantomime, 272–73
Parallels, sensory, 77–79
Parasites, 10, 131
Past, the (structure of), 310–11
Path-finding, animal, 184–85, 193–94, 198–99. *See also* Migration, animal; Navigation, animal; Orientation

Pattern: fixed action, 115; and illusion, 325; in nature, 115, 126–27, 129; prepatterns, 127, 159
Paw, 251, 252
Pedomorphy, 238–39
Perception: animal, 185–86, 188, 194, 205, 206, 210, 212, 234, 251, 320; "Complex-quality," 188; and dream, 263–64; incomplete, 264–65; integrity of, 257; intraorganic, 253; and intuition, 322, 323, 337, 355–56; and language, 283–84, 285, 287; "phase sequence" in, 257; physiognomic, 59, 74–76; pictorial, 269–70; of "place," 194; primitive modes of, 302; in psychology, 205–6; of relationship, 230; sensory, 183–85, 206, 207, 251–52, 253, 256–57; of shape, 187–88, 257–58; spatial, 185–87, 193–94, 195, 196–97, 203; sustained, 257; tactile, 251–52; visual, 186–87, 210–11, 231, 266–67, 270; and visual experiences, 324–26
Percepts: animal, 185–86; human, 255, 283, 291–92
"Peripheral impressions," 264
Perspective, and visual perception, 325
"Phase beauty," 85–86, 87
"Phase sequence," in perception, 257
Philippe, Jean, 42–44
Phillpotts, Bertha, 372–73
Phylogenesis, 144, 161
Physical science, 15, 17, 391, 394, 398
Physicalism, 5
Physics, and changes in scale, 107
Physiognomic perception, 59, 74–76, 323
Pieron, Henri, 261
Pigeon, 200, 208
Piracy, 372, 377–78
"Place habitat" animal, 198–99
Plankton, 169–70
Planning, 198, 225
Plants: behavior of, 136–38; chemistry of, 161
Plato, 173
Platt, John R., 107
Play, 229, 272
Plover, 245
Poesis and memory, 293
Poetry, 96, 97
Poikilothermy, animal, 172–73
Pollex, 250–51

Polyglotism, 296–97
Pongid physique, 247–48
Portmann, Adolf, 30
Posture: animal, 215, 222; human, 246, 247–48, 253
Potentiality, 82–83; and development, 239–40, 240–41, 245
Pötzl, Otto, 263–64
Power: delegation of, 350–51; magic, 334–36, 337; of magic rite, 330; symbols of (shifting to symbols of life), 369
"Practice" flights, 198
Prehensility, animal, 242, 247, 251; human, 287
Prepatterns, 127, 159
Prescott, J. H., 244
"Presentational immediacy," 293–94
Pression, 140, 142, 144, 146, 229
"Primitive" culture, 274, 284, 292
Primitive man: and assertions of primitive mind, 307; conception of life, 345–46; as first symbol-monger, 302; "magical" and "scientific" attitudes of, 302–5; materialistic nature of, 302; and pain, 331. *See also* Man
Projection, in art, 35–48, 80, 84, 86–87
Proto-acts, 108–9
Psychical phase, 8, 12, 201
Psychoanalysis, 9
Psychology, 3, 5, 6, 9, 15, 23, 25, 29; animal, 216, 223
"Psychopathology of everyday life," 264
Psychophysical entities, 5
Psychophysical organism, 80
Punishment, 356–57, 358, 359
Purposeful acts, 176, 189–90
Pyramidal tract, in brain, 227

Quality, artistic, 48, 54, 55
Quokka, 172

Raids, as tribal phenomenon, 377
Rat, 184, 187–88, 248–49
Rationality, 64, 65; and memory, 294
Rationalization, 64
Reactive behavior, 169–70
Read, Sir Herbert, 54–56
Reality: concepts of, 5; conceptual, 112; and history, 311; phenomenal, 112, 319; and savage tribesmen, 302–3; and thinking of primitive people, 307–8

Realization, in art, 42, 77
Reasoning, 62; and animals, 158
"Recent memory," 289
Receptivity, 210–11, 270. See also Perception
Reciprocal innervation, 181
Recognition, 205, 206, 269, 270, 291. See also Memory
Recollection, 280, 294. See also Memory
"Re-creation," 44
Reflexes, 106, 174, 175, 245, 365
Relationships, in art, 80–83
"Release mechanism," 181
Religion: and assertion, 308; and cosmic myths, 309–10; and death, 367; and delegation of power to high god, 350–51; and denial of death, 364; images in, 292; and primitive people, 302; ritual and thought in, 367
REM (Rapid Eye Movement), 258–61, 265
Remembrance, 206–7, 263, 269
Renshaw, Samuel, 165
Repertoire, of animals, 152, 163
Repetition: in behavior, 230, 272; of perceived forms, 267
Representation, 186; in art, 40, 42–43, 72–73
Repression and memory, 263
Responses, 112, 159, 163
Responsibility, sense of, 355; and individuation, 353
Retina, 255, 266–67
Révész, Géza, 251–52, 278, 298
Rhesus monkey, 184, 234–35
Rhinoceros, 240
Rhythms, 81–82, 86–87, 93, 109, 123, 124, 144–45, 148–49, 160–61, 171, 173, 234, 257, 270; "circadian," 160; dialectical, 124–25; diffusion, 127; simultaneous, 127; spatial, 94–95
Richter, Curt, 261
Rite: animal, 204, 271, 274; human, 271–72, 273, 275–76, 279–80
Ritual: analysis of, 313–16; of death, 361; and dramatization, 333; and magic, 317; mimetic, 328–29; and people living in the wild, 304; as reflection of moral order in China, 316–17; and religious thought, 367; and sacrifice, 362; and savage tribesmen's attitude toward magic, 302; and shaman healing, 329–30; as society's claim on the individual, 360–61; symbolic nature of, 316
Roffwarg, H. P., 259
Rohden, Peter Richard, 330–31
Russell, Bertrand, 4, 24, 284, 291
Russell, W. M. S., 114

Saccadic eye movements, 258
Sachs, Curt, 55, 274
Sacrifice: and the Aztec, 382, 383; and Dance and mythical formation, 313; the essential ritual act of, 362; and the Inca, 380–81; punishment for neglect of, 356; as symbol of submission, 362
Sacrilege, 315
Saint Paul, Ursula, 174
Sander, Friedrich, 75
Scanning, visual, 240
Scent, post, 218–19, 221
Schaefer, Karl E., 277
Schaller, G. B., 232
Scheler, Max, 346
Schiller, Paul H., 226
Schindewolf, Otto H., 238
Schneider, Kurt, 346, 347
"Scientific" attitude: in Europe, 315; and fact, language, and logic, 392–95; of savage tribesmen, 302–4, 313
Sea horse, 242
Seafaring, 372–73, 377
Seasonal impulses, 198, 365
Sea urchin, 285
Segregation, law of, 152
Selection: internal, 147; mechanism of, 146–47; natural, 122, 134–35, 137–39, 140, 142, 146
Self-affirmation, and assertion as primary act of mind, 307, 309
Self-assertion, and punishment, 357
Selfhood concept: and death, 348; development of, 346–47
"Sense of life." See Lebensgefühl
"Sense of pastness," 293
"Sense of reality," 294
Sense organs, 11, 156–57, 164, 322; intellectuality of, 322; and perceptual interpretation of visual experience, 324–26; and species-specific features, 342
Senses. See Orientation; and under name of individual sense
Sensibility, 157

Sensory acts, 156–57
"Sensory deprivation," 258
Sensory parallels, 77–79
Sensory perception: animal, 183–85, 207; human, 251–52, 253
Sexual behavior, animal, 192, 209, 234
Sexual intercourse, evolution of man and instinct concerning, 365
Shaler, N. S., 341
Shaman: as actor in sacred drama, 330–31; and healing as drama, 329–31; and illusory performances, 331–34; magical powers of, 334–36
Shape, 257, 269, 270–71
Shapiro, Arthur, 254
Sherrington, C. S., 181
Shifts, functional, 150, 164–65
"Short-spine" gene, 249
Signals (signs), human, 212
"Signs" (signals), animal, 203
Simpson, G. G., 182
Situation, 110, 114, 119
Situational images, 26
Skull: animal, 248–49; human, 245
Sleep, 258–61
Sloth, 261
Smell, sense of, 183, 218
Social organization: of Chinese cities, 376; and group action, 355; and punishment, 359; and seafaring, 372–73; and tribal "we" and individual "I," 345–47; and verbal abstractions, 361; and warfare, 377
"Social signals," animal, 203, 231–32
Society, human, defined, 298
Sommerfelt, Alf, 283
Sondhi, K. C., 127
Sorcery, 334–35
Sounds: animal, 208; human, 208; as symbols, 270–71. *See also* Speech
Space: harmonic, 94–95; tensions, 71; virtual, 43
Spatial forms, 43
Specialization, 238, 239, 240–41, 242–45
"Specious present," 288. *See also* Time
Speech: development and importance of, 301–2; and early human mental evolution, 307–8; and handedness 287; and imagination, 363–64; impairment, 295; and intellectual advance, 391; and intuition, 63; and language, 272; origins of, 272–73, 275, 276–77, 280; and symbolism, 313, 336. *See also* Language
Spinal cord, human, 253
Spine, 248
Spinoza, Benedictus de, 357
Spirit world: and ancestor worship, 315–16; and assertion as affirmation of mind, 306–10; beings in, 319; and colonial Europeans, 306; and ghosts, 305–6; and magic power, 337; and origin of myth, 309–10, 312; and primitive imagination, 304–5; and primitive man's attitude, 302–5; and primitive man's nature, 301–2; and ritual, 304, 313–17; and stories as real to primitive mind, 313–14; and structure of past and future, 310–12; worlds in, 305
Sponge, 171, 241
Standards, 384
Statistical method, in animal psychology, 177–78
Stimulations, 158
Stimulus, 111, 159, 163, 175, 192, 210
Stock, 128, 129, 133, 141, 154
Strangeness, in art, 96–97
Structure, dialectical, 81–83, 87
Subacts, 120, 145, 151, 152, 154, 188, 232
"Subception," human, 206
Subject, 13
Subjective: activity, 279; defined, 13; feeling, 292
Subject-object relationship, 13, 92
Subject-predicate relationship, 283–84
Submission, animal, 215, 216–17; human, and sacrifice, 362
Substrate, 126, 149
Suggestibility, animal, 212, 232, 234, 274, 279
Suggestion, 308, 314; in animals, 211–12, 218; and magic, 331–33
"Sun-compass" theory of animal pathfinding, 185, 199
Sunfish, 249
Superacts, 120, 152
Supernatural beliefs, 304–5
Supernaturals: and delegation of power, 350–51; nonbiologic events as acts of, 358
"Superstition," animal, 204, 271
Suppression, in dream, 264

"Surrender," animal, 215–17. *See also* Behavior, animal, specific
Survival value, 134, 165
Symbiosis, 131
Symbolic projection, 37, 46–47, 58
Symbolic transformation, 75
Symbolism, 38, 39, 40, 45–46, 57; and conceptual talents, 358; and fetishism, 362; and life-supporting function saved by symbolic activity, 358–59; magic and theory of, 319; and origin of myth, 310; and ritual, 314, 316; speech as essence of, 336
Symbols, 36–37, 38–40, 44, 66, 204, 253, 268–69, 270–71, 296; and animal acts, 216, 271; art, 29, 40, 43, 44, 47–48, 80, 81, 83, 94; and concept, 277, 294; in dance, 274; in dream, 268–70; and empathy, 278; and image, 267–70, 275–76; and intuition, 322–23; and magical thinking, 324; and magic power, 337; natural, 312, 316; presentational, 70, 329; and primitive imagination, 304–5; and primitive man, 302; and rhythm, 270; and speech, 277, 294; in thinking, 268, 287, 288; and utterance, 273
Sympathy, 72, 211, 379, 380; and cannibalism, 366; loss of empathy with development of, 365–66; and magic, 327–28, 329. *See also* Empathy
Synchondrosis, 248–49

Taboos, 335, 357–58
Tactual perception. *See* Touch, sense of
Tail, 242
Tarski, Alfred, 392–93
Taste, sense of, 184
Teamwork, animal. *See* Behavior, animal; Cooperation; Joint acts, animal
Teilhard de Chardin, Pierre, 340
Teleology, 90–91
Temporal lobes. *See* Cortex
Tension: in art, 47, 71–72, 74, 81, 83, 89; and different rates of mental development, 380; in nature, 106, 115–16, 124, 146–47; space, 71
Territoriality, animal, 221–22
Thermoregulation. *See* Heat-sensitivity, animal
Thinking: animal, 268; contemplative (in the West), 317; discursive, 69–70; and early human mental evolution, 307–8; ethical (in Asia), 316–17; human, 258, 279–80, 287, 288, 295, 297; and logic, 64–65; primitive modes of, 302; symbolic, 322; process of and thought, 304
Thompson, D'Arcy, 67, 85–86, 396
Thorndike, E. L., 186
Thorner, Hans, 285
Thumb, 250–51
Thyroid, 249
Time, 280, 288, 289–90, 293. *See also* Memory
Timeless moment, 96
Tinbergen, Nikolaas, 181, 189, 202, 207–8
Titchener, E. B., 250, 259
Tolerance, principle of, 148
Topiltzin Quetzalcoatl, 382
Torture, 366
Touch, sense of, 251–53
Trade: and Byzantium, 373; caravan, 375; and piracy, 372
Tragedy, and rhythm of life, 348–49
Traits, phylogenetic, 242
Transcendence, in art, 98
Transformation, analysis of, 326–27; symbolic, 75
Treichler, F. R., 235
Tribal societies, 301–2; and conception of "we," 345
"Trigger" and instinctive act, 175
Trophallaxis, 234
Trunk, elephant, 244, 251
Trunkfish, 249
"Truth," in logic, 284
Tumarkin, A., 137
Tunicates, 239

Uexküll, Jakob von, 110–11, 186
Umwelten, 110–11, 182
Unconscious, the, 8
Uniqueness, in art, 84, 92
Unity: of acts, 141; in art, 82, 83
"Unrealism," in human mentality, 292–93
Urination, animal, 218, 219, 221–22
Utterance, 208, 273, 276–77, 279–80

Value perception, 185, 205–6, 252
Variables, 16; intervening, 112

Verbs, 283–84
Versatility of man, 237–38
Vertebrate frame, duality of, 396
"Vestiges," 245
Vikings, 372–73, 378
Viruses, 104
Visceral response, 219
Vision, 394; animal, 183, 186–88, 230–31, 239–40; formalization of, 270–71; night, 239; panoramic, 239; and perceptual interpretation of illusory forms, 324–26; retinal, 267. *See also* Eye; Perception: visual
Visual: forms, 270; imagination, 255; impairments, 285; impression, 287–88; orientation, 186–87; percept, 266; system, 255
Vitality, 55, 56, 163
Vocalization: animal, 184, 208–9; human, 272, 275. *See also* Language; Speech
Volkelt, Hans, 186, 188, 200
Vorgestalt, 76–77

"Waggle dance" of honeybee, 233
War dance, and empathetic nature of magic, 328. *See also* Dance
Warfare: organizational nature of, 377
Washburn, S. L., 245

Watson, John B., 186
Watterson, R. L., 125
Weiss, Paul, 125
Weltanschauung, 65
Werner, Heinz, 75, 323
White, R. W., 109
Whitehead, A. N., 4, 11, 174, 284, 311
Wiener, Norbert, 131
Wittgenstein, Ludwig, 4, 391, 393
Wolf, 215–17
Words: and concepts, 287; counting and, 395; magician's symbolic, 319; power embodied in, 336–37; and primitive people, 361; and scientific precision, 393; as symbols, 236; and thinking, 393, 394
"Working concepts," in animal psychology, 174–75, 202. *See also* Ethology, terms used in; Psychology
Wren, 191, 244

Yąnomamö, and inventive poetic imagination, 309
Yahweh worship, 363, 364. *See also* Judaism
Yi, the way to *jen*, 316

Zotterman, Yngve, 184
Zuckerkandl, Victor, 95

ABOUT THE AUTHOR

At the time of her death in 1985 Susanne K. Langer was research scholar and emeritus professor of philosophy at Connecticut College. Her work on the *Essay,* beginning in 1956, extended over nearly three decades. Volume I was published in 1967, Volume II in 1973, and Volume III in 1982. Among her other books, the most widely known are *Philosophy in a New Key* and *Feeling and Form.*